MW01438413

# History Of The United States Of America

George Bancroft

Copyright © BiblioLife, LLC

This book represents a historical reproduction of a work originally published before 1923 that is part of a unique project which provides opportunities for readers, educators and researchers by bringing hard-to-find original publications back into print at reasonable prices. Because this and other works are culturally important, we have made them available as part of our commitment to protecting, preserving and promoting the world's literature. These books are in the "public domain" and were digitized and made available in cooperation with libraries, archives, and open source initiatives around the world dedicated to this important mission.

We believe that when we undertake the difficult task of re-creating these works as attractive, readable and affordable books, we further the goal of sharing these works with a global audience, and preserving a vanishing wealth of human knowledge.

Many historical books were originally published in small fonts, which can make them very difficult to read. Accordingly, in order to improve the reading experience of these books, we have created "enlarged print" versions of our books. Because of font size variation in the original books, some of these may not technically qualify as "large print" books, as that term is generally defined; however, we believe these versions provide an overall improved reading experience for many.

# HISTORY

## OF THE

# UNITED STATES OF AMERICA,

FROM THE DISCOVERY OF THE CONTINENT.

BY
GEORGE BANCROFT.

The Author's Last Revision.

VOLUME III.

NEW YORK:
D. APPLETON AND COMPANY.
1888.

COPYRIGHT,
BY GEORGE BANCROFT,
1876, 1882, 1868.

# CONTENTS OF THE THIRD VOLUME.

## THE AMERICAN REVOLUTION

### IN FIVE EPOCHS.

#### II—BRITAIN ESTRANGES AMERICA

### CHAPTER I.

#### ENGLAND AS IT WAS IN 1763.

#### 1763.

|  | PAGE |
|---|---|
| England | 3 |
| Its limited monarchy. Its church | 4 |
| House of lords | 5 |
| House of commons | 7 |
| Its literature | 9 |
| Its courts of law. Its system of education | 12 |
| Life in towns. Life in the country | 13 |
| Its manufactures | 15 |
| Its nationality | 16 |

### CHAPTER II.

#### ENGLAND AND ITS DEPENDENCIES. IRELAND.

#### 1763.

| | |
|---|---|
| British dominion in the East Indies. In America. Ireland | 18 |
| Its conquest. The Irish parliament | 19 |
| The church. Colonization of the Scotch | 21 |
| Ireland after the restoration. After the revolution of 1688 | 22 |
| Disfranchisement of the Catholics. Their disqualification | 23 |
| Laws prohibiting their education | 23 |
| Their worship | 24 |
| Their possessing lands | 25 |
| Their keeping arms. Restrictions on their industry | 26 |
| Rise of the Irish patriot party | 27 |
| Scotch-Irish Presbyterians | 28 |

## CONTENTS.

### CHAPTER III.

**CHARLES TOWNSHEND PLEDGES THE MINISTRY OF BUTE TO TAX AMERICA BY THE BRITISH PARLIAMENT, AND RESIGNS.**

#### February–May 1763.

|  | PAGE |
|---|---|
| America after the peace of Paris. Townshend in the cabinet. His colleagues. | 30 |
| His policy | 31 |
| Protest of New York | 32 |
| An American standing army and taxes by parliament proposed | 33 |
| Loyalty of America. Grenville enforces the navigation acts | 34 |
| New taxes in England. Townshend resigns | 35 |
| Grenville succeeds Bute at the treasury. His character | 36 |
| Charles Jenkinson | 38 |
| Thomas Whately. Richard Jackson Grenville's protectionist American policy | 39 |
| Shelburne | 40 |

### CHAPTER IV.

**PONTIAC'S WAR. TRIUMVIRATE MINISTRY.**

#### May–September 1763.

| | |
|---|---|
| The West. Origin of Pontiac's war | 41 |
| Pontiac. Detroit | 42 |
| Its siege. Illinois. Loss of Sandusky | 43 |
| Of Fort St. Joseph's. Fort Pitt threatened. Loss of Fort Miami | 44 |
| Of Fort Ouatanon. Of Michilimackinac. Of Le Bœuf and Venango | 45 |
| Of Presque Isle. Indian ravages. Fort Pitt summoned | 46 |
| Detroit relieved. Defeat of Dalyell | 47 |
| Fort Pitt summoned again. Bouquet's march | 48 |
| Battle of Bushy Run. Pittsburg relieved | 49 |
| Amherst puts a price on Pontiac's life. The Senecas | 49 |
| Conduct of the French | 49 |

### CHAPTER V.

**THE MINUTE FOR AN AMERICAN STAMP-TAX. MINISTRY OF GRENVILLE.**

#### May–September 1763.

| | |
|---|---|
| Shelburne at the board of trade | 50 |
| The treasury pursues its plan. The king wishes a stronger ministry | 51 |
| Death of Egremont | 52 |
| The king invites Pitt to enter the ministry. Rejects his advice | 53 |
| Retreat of Bute. Bedford joins the ministry | 53 |
| Affairs in America. Annexation of Vermont to New York advised | 54 |
| Strife in South Carolina. Stamp act ordered to be prepared. Its origin | 55 |
| Why a stamp-tax was preferred | 57 |
| Richard Jackson opposes. Grenville adopts it | 58 |

# CONTENTS.

## CHAPTER VI.

**ENFORCEMENT OF THE ACTS OF NAVIGATION. GRENVILLE'S ADMINISTRATION CONTINUED.**

### October 1763–April 1764.

|  | PAGE |
|---|---|
| Grenville and the acts of navigation | 59 |
| Navy and army assist to enforce them. The sea-guard | 61 |
| Boundaries of the new provinces. Pacification of the West | 62 |
| Extension of settlements | 63 |
| Florida. Grenville meets parliament | 64 |
| He carries large majorities. Strife of Virginia with the clergy | 65 |
| Patrick Henry against the parsons | 66 |
| Grenville opposes an American civil list | 68 |
| Affair of Wilkes. Thomas Pownall contends for the taxation of America | 69 |
| Grenville encounters opposition to the American stamp act | 70 |
| Defers it for a year and seeks the consent of the colonies | 71 |
| Offers the colonies bounties on hemp. A wider trade in rice. The whale fishery | 71 |
| Grenville's first budget | 72 |
| New combinations of American trade and taxes | 73 |
| Grenville's interview with the colony agents | 73 |
| Advises the colonies to consent to the stamp act. His self-satisfaction | 74 |

## CHAPTER VII.

**HOW AMERICA RECEIVED THE PLAN OF A STAMP-TAX. GRENVILLE'S ADMINISTRATION CONTINUED.**

### April–December 1764.

| | |
|---|---|
| France surrenders Louisiana to Spain | 75 |
| America alarmed. Samuel Adams | 76 |
| Boston instructions | 77 |
| Excitement at New York. The legislature of Massachusetts | 78 |
| Committee of intercolonial correspondence | 79 |
| Bernard's counsel to the ministry | 79 |
| Otis on colonies | 80 |
| Lord Mansfield on Otis | 82 |
| Mayhew's resolution | 83 |
| Hutchinson's argument for the immunities of the colonies | 83 |
| Bradstreet's expedition | 85 |
| Canada as a British province | 86 |
| Vermont. Bouquet's expedition | 87 |
| Exchange of prisoners with western tribes | 88 |
| Spirit of New York | 89 |
| Of Connecticut. Massachusetts silent about rights | 90 |
| Of Rhode Island. Of Pennsylvania | 91 |
| Of Carolina and Virginia | 92 |
| Advice of American royalists to the British government | 93 |
| Temper of the ministry | 94 |

## CHAPTER VIII.

### THE TWELFTH PARLIAMENT OF GREAT BRITAIN PASSES THE AMERICAN STAMP-TAX. GRENVILLE'S ADMINISTRATION CONTINUED.

#### January–April 1765.

| | PAGE |
|---|---|
| Hutchinson's history of Massachusetts Opinion of John Adams | 95 |
| Grenville's interview with Franklin. Soame Jenyns on the stamp act | 96 |
| Military power in the colonies. Grenville moves a stamp-tax | 97 |
| Speeches of Beckford, Jackson, Barré, Charles Townshend | 99 |
| Barré's reply to Townshend | 100 |
| Vote in the house of commons | 101 |
| No American petition against the stamp bill received | 102 |
| The bill for a stamp act becomes a law. The American post-office | 104 |
| The mutiny act Bounties. Americans selected for stamp officers | 105 |
| The success of the measure not doubted | 106 |

## CHAPTER IX.

### THE DAY-STAR OF THE AMERICAN UNION.

#### April–July 1765.

| | |
|---|---|
| Power of the oligarchy. Restrictions on American industry | 107 |
| Taxation of America | 108 |
| Opinion of Otis on the stamp-tax. Of Hutchinson | 109 |
| Boston May meeting Action of Virginia Patrick Henry | 110 |
| Meeting of the Massachusetts legislature | 112 |
| Otis proposes a congress. The press of New York | 113 |
| Opinions of the people | 115 |
| Their rights as Englishmen | 116 |
| Restrictions on industry. Retaliation | 117 |
| The Bible for freedom. Independence hinted at | 118 |
| Virtual representation | 119 |
| Wrongs of Vermont Union in danger Colonies proceed with caution | 120 |
| South Carolina decides for union. Christopher Gadsden. Joy of Otis | 121 |

## CHAPTER X

### THE BATTLE BETWEEN THE KING AND THE DUKE OF BEDFORD.

#### April–July 1765.

| | |
|---|---|
| The king proposes a regency bill | 122 |
| Its progress through the house of lords | 123 |
| Pitt incited to form a new administration. Riot of the silk weavers | 124 |
| Bedford's interview with the king | 125 |
| Pitt declines office | 126 |
| The king capitulates with Grenville. The king and his ministers | 127 |
| Pitt at the palace | 128 |
| New ministry | 129 |

# CONTENTS.　　　　　　　　　　　　　　vii

|   | PAGE |
|---|---|
| Rockingham and Burke | 130 |
| Grafton and Conway | 131 |
| Dartmouth | 132 |
| Measures of the new ministry | 133 |

## CHAPTER XI.

**AMERICA REPELS ITS STAMP-TAX. ADMINISTRATION OF ROCKINGHAM.**

### August–September 1765.

| | |
|---|---|
| The Connecticut stamp-master at Boston | 134 |
| The Massachusetts stamp-master forced to resign | 136 |
| Riot at Boston | 137 |
| General resignation of the stamp officers | 138 |
| Pusillanimity of Bernard. Connecticut deals with its stamp officer | 139 |
| Influence of the clergy | 141 |
| The Rockingham ministry prepare to execute the stamp act | 142 |
| Appeal of John Adams | 143 |
| Opinion of Daniel Dulany, of Maryland | 145 |
| Of Washington | 146 |
| The plan of a congress prevails in Georgia. Pennsylvania. Rhode Island | 146 |
| Delaware. Samuel Adams enters the Massachusetts legislature | 147 |
| Events in New York | 148 |

## CHAPTER XII.

**THE STAMP ACT LEADS AMERICA TO UNION. ADMINISTRATION OF ROCKINGHAM.**

### October–December 1765.

| | |
|---|---|
| Opening of the first American congress | 149 |
| The principle of union | 150 |
| The English take possession of Illinois | 151 |
| Colonization of Missouri | 152 |
| Choiseul foresees American independence | 152 |
| The Rockingham ministry show prudence and lenity toward America | 153 |
| Debates in congress on the liberty of America; on freedom of trade | 153 |
| Its memorials and petitions | 154 |
| Excitement on the arrival of the stamps | 155 |
| Union formed. Answer of the Massachusetts legislature to the governor | 156 |
| Character of Samuel Adams | 157 |
| The stamp act in New York; Connecticut, Rhode Island | 158 |
| No stamp officers remain. Non-importation agreement | 159 |
| The first of November. Conduct of the people. The press | 159 |
| The "New London Gazette" | 160 |
| Events in New York | 161 |
| The colonies adhere to the congress | 162 |
| They plan a permanent union. Advance toward a revolution | 163 |
| Unanimity of America | 164 |

## CHAPTER XIII.

HAS PARLIAMENT THE RIGHT TO TAX AMERICA? ADMINISTRATION OF ROCKINGHAM.

### December 1765–January 1766.

|  | PAGE |
|---|---|
| Fluctuating opinion in England | 165 |
| English liberty sustains America. Effect of Cumberland's death | 166 |
| Meeting of parliament. Debate in the house of lords | 167 |
| In the commons | 169 |
| Progress of American resistance | 170 |
| Argument of John Adams on the nullity of the stamp act | 171 |
| Union projected. Spirit of the press | 172 |
| Bernard reports no submission before subjection | 173 |

## CHAPTER XIV.

WILLIAM PITT INTERVENES. ROCKINGHAM'S ADMINISTRATION CONTINUED.

### January 1766.

| The ministry undecided. Meeting of parliament | 174 |
|---|---|
| Elaborate speech of William Pitt | 175 |
| Of Conway. Of Grenville | 178 |
| Pitt's rejoinder | 180 |
| Grafton desires Pitt as chief minister | 184 |
| Want of agreement between Pitt and Rockingham | 185 |
| The petition of the American congress not received by the house of commons | 186 |
| It becomes the law that parliament may bind the colonies in all cases whatever | 187 |

## CHAPTER XV.

PARLIAMENT AFFIRMS ITS RIGHT TO TAX AMERICA. ROCKINGHAM'S ADMINISTRATION CONTINUED.

### The Third of February 1766.

| Debate of the lords on the right to tax America. Speech of Camden | 188 |
|---|---|
| Of Northington | 189 |
| Of Mansfield | 190 |
| The division. Debate in the commons | 194 |
| The modern tory party | 196 |
| The certainty of reform | 197 |

## CHAPTER XVI.

THE REPEAL OF THE STAMP ACT. ADMINISTRATION OF ROCKINGHAM.

### February–May 1766.

| Confirmed resistance of America | 198 |
|---|---|
| A defeat of the ministry in the house of lords | 199 |
| Reversed in the house of commons. A further difference | 200 |
| Bedford and Grenville ask aid of Bute. Franklin before the commons | 201 |

## CONTENTS.

|  | PAGE |
|---|---|
| The repeal resolved upon | 204 |
| The question debated in the house of commons | 205 |
| The division | 206 |
| Opinions of Smith, Reid, Robertson. Warren demands freedom and equality | 207 |
| The declaratory bill and the repeal of the stamp act | 208 |
| The declaratory bill in the house of lords. Speech of Camden. Of Mansfield | 209 |
| Debate on the repeal. The repeal is carried. The Bedford protest | 210 |
| The Grenville protest | 211 |
| Rejoicing in England at the repeal. Further measures relating to America | 212 |
| Joy of America at the repeal | 213 |
| Gratitude to Pitt | 214 |

## CHAPTER XVII.

### THE CHARTER OF MASSACHUSETTS IN PERIL. THE FALL OF THE ROCKINGHAM WHIGS. THE EARL OF CHATHAM.

### May–October 1766.

|  |  |
|---|---|
| Reaction against the stamp act | 215 |
| Views of the Americans | 216 |
| Events in Massachusetts | 217 |
| Charles Townshend threatens a new system | 218 |
| Altercation with Bernard | 219 |
| Mayhew and union | 220 |
| Connecticut. South Carolina. New York | 221 |
| Bernard advises coercion | 222 |
| Plans of the Rockingham ministry | 223 |
| Pitt forms an administration | 224 |
| Character of his administration. Displeasure of Rockingham | 225 |
| Pitt becomes earl of Chatham | 226 |
| Choiseul receives a report from his agent | 227 |
| Effect of Chatham's ill health | 228 |
| Progress of liberty | 229 |

## CHAPTER XVIII.

### CHARLES TOWNSHEND USURPS THE LEAD IN GOVERNMENT. ADMINISTRATION OF CHATHAM.

### October 1766–March 1767.

|  |  |
|---|---|
| Disputes in the colonies | 230 |
| Paxton sails for England. Plan for Illinois. The West | 231 |
| North Carolina and its regulators | 232 |
| Progress of the dispute in Massachusetts. Joseph Hawley | 233 |
| Shelburne's candor | 234 |
| The legislature of Massachusetts compensates the sufferers by riots | 235 |
| Gadsden and South Carolina. New York. Chatham and the aristocracy | 236 |
| His last appearance in the house of lords as minister | 237 |
| Townshend proposes an American civil list. He browbeats the cabinet | 238 |

x · CONTENTS.

| | PAGE |
|---|---|
| Hutchinson usurps a seat in council. Dispute on billeting troops | 239 |
| Shelburne's colonial policy | 240 |
| Opposed by the king and by factions | 242 |
| Defeat of the ministry | 243 |
| Earl of Chatham withdraws from the direction of his administration | 244 |

## CHAPTER XIX.

PARLIAMENT WILL HAVE AN AMERICAN ARMY AND AN AMERICAN REVENUE. ADMINISTRATION OF GRAFTON.

### March–July 1767.

| | |
|---|---|
| Character of Townshend. He rules the ministry | 245 |
| Bedford in the house of lords | 246 |
| Choiseul sends Kalb to America. Conciliation still possible | 247 |
| Townshend unfit to conciliate. He opens his system to parliament | 250 |
| Strength of the opposition | 253 |
| Chatham visited by Grafton. Grafton prime minister. Jonathan Trumbull | 255 |
| Townshend carries his measures | 256 |

## CHAPTER XX.

COALITION OF THE KING AND THE ARISTOCRACY.

### July–November 1767.

| | |
|---|---|
| The king governs | 258 |
| Rockingham negotiates with Bedford and Grenville. Failure of the coalition | 259 |
| Policy of Choiseul | 260 |
| Discontent in the colonies | 261 |
| Death of Townshend | 262 |
| Lord North succeeds him. The colonies and the new taxes | 263 |
| Conduct of Boston | 264 |
| The Farmer's Letters | 265 |

## CHAPTER XXI.

MASSACHUSETTS CONSULTS HER SISTER COLONIES. ADMINISTRATION OF GRAFTON. HILLSBOROUGH SECRETARY FOR THE COLONIES

### November 1767–March 1768.

| | |
|---|---|
| The Bedford party join the ministry. Hillsborough colonial secretary | 267 |
| His interview with Johnson, of Connecticut | 268 |
| He pensions Hutchinson | 271 |
| The Massachusetts assembly plan resistance | 272 |
| Their letter of instructions to their agent | 273 |
| Their petition to the king | 274 |
| Their circular to the sister colonies | 275 |
| Memorial from the commissioners of the revenue | 276 |
| Massachusetts discourages importations | 277 |
| Du Châtelet goes to England as ambassador from France | 278 |

## CONTENTS.

|  | PAGE |
|---|---|
| Bernard and the commissioners wish the aid of troops | 279 |
| State of the question | 280 |
| Character of the twelfth parliament. Temper of the colonies | 281 |
| Prophecies of American independence | 282 |
| Of an American constitution | 283 |

### CHAPTER XXII.

WILL MASSACHUSETTS RESCIND? ADMINISTRATION OF GRAFTON. HILLSBOROUGH SECRETARY FOR THE COLONIES.

#### April–July 1768.

|  |  |
|---|---|
| Hillsborough orders Massachusetts to rescind its resolves | 284 |
| Virginia approves the measures of Massachusetts | 285 |
| The thirteenth parliament. Progress of opinion in the colonies | 286 |
| Fresh altercations in Massachusetts | 287 |
| Hutchinson not re-elected to the council | 288 |
| Ships and regiments ordered to Boston. Riot of the tenth of June | 289 |
| The commissioners of the revenue, except Temple, withdraw from Boston | 290 |
| Boston town-meeting and Bernard | 290 |
| Report of the crown officers. Instructions of the town of Boston | 291 |
| The Massachusetts assembly refuses to rescind. Progress of opinion | 293 |
| Choiseul's projects | 294 |
| Duplicity of Bernard and Hillsborough | 295 |

### CHAPTER XXIII.

UNION OF BEDFORD AND THE KING. THE REGULATORS OF NORTH CAROLINA. HILLSBOROUGH SECRETARY FOR THE COLONIES.

#### July–September 1768.

|  |  |
|---|---|
| The ministry incensed | 296 |
| Intrigues with Corsica | 297 |
| Policy of the British cabinet toward America | 298 |
| Boston celebrates the fourteenth of August | 299 |
| Choiseul's inquisitiveness | 300 |
| Advice of Mansfield and Camden | 301 |
| The judicial system of South Carolina. The regulators of North Carolina | 302 |

### CHAPTER XXIV.

THE TOWNS OF MASSACHUSETTS MEET IN CONVENTION. A COMMONWEALTH IN LOUISIANA. HILLSBOROUGH SECRETARY FOR THE COLONIES.

#### September–October 1768.

|  |  |
|---|---|
| Samuel Adams desires independence | 306 |
| Massachusetts without a legislature. A Boston town-meeting | 307 |
| It summons a convention | 308 |
| Bernard asks the council to quarter troops within the town | 309 |
| Meeting of the convention | 310 |

|  | PAGE |
|---|---|
| Firmness of the council. Prudence of the convention | 311 |
| Two regiments land in Boston | 312 |
| Disputes on quartering them | 313 |
| Return of the commissioners of the revenue | 314 |
| Shelburne dismissed. Chatham resigns. Rochford as secretary of state | 315 |
| Grenville advocates reform. Affairs at New Orleans | 316 |
| The people expel the Spanish government | 318 |

## CHAPTER XXV.

### THE KING AND PARLIAMENT AGAINST THE TOWN OF BOSTON. HILLSBOROUGH SECRETARY FOR THE COLONIES.

### October 1768–February 1769.

|  |  |
|---|---|
| The West. Missouri and Illinois. Indiana | 319 |
| Stuart negotiates a boundary with the Cherokees | 320 |
| Treaty with the Six Nations. Botetourt in Virginia | 321 |
| Meeting of parliament | 322 |
| Lord North will have America at his feet | 323 |
| American petitions rejected. South Carolina sides with Massachusetts | 324 |
| Choiseul's watchfulness | 325 |
| The ministry and parliament resolved to enforce authority | 326 |
| Character of Boston | 327 |
| Du Châtelet foretells the new order of things | 329 |
| Hillsborough moves resolves in the house of lords; Bedford an address | 330 |
| Firmness of Boston. New election in New York. Letters of Bernard | 331 |
| Of Hutchinson and Oliver. Effort to take off Samuel Adams | 332 |
| Debate in the house of commons | 333 |
| Speculations of the statesmen of France | 334 |
| Another debate in the commons | 335 |
| Free trade is the liberator of colonies | 336 |
| Spain sides against the colonies | 337 |

## CHAPTER XXVI.

### VIRGINIA COMES TO THE AID OF MASSACHUSETTS. GRAFTON'S ADMINISTRATION. HILLSBOROUGH COLONIAL MINISTER.

### March–August 1769.

|  |  |
|---|---|
| Spain resolves to recover New Orleans | 338 |
| Choiseul and Du Châtelet wish its independence | 339 |
| Contrast of England and Spain | 340 |
| Firmness of the colonies | 341 |
| Choiseul warns England against the ambition of Russia | 342 |
| The colonies form agreements for non-importation | 343 |
| Repeal of the revenue act refused. The affair of Wilkes | 345 |
| The cabinet vote to retain the duty on tea | 346 |
| The resolves and circular of Virginia | 347 |
| Its non-importation covenant | 348 |
| Bernard is recalled. His strife with the Massachusetts legislature | 349 |

It refuses supplies to the troops. Agreement of the merchants not to import. 350
Bernard's character . . . . . . . . . . 351

## CHAPTER XXVII.

GROWTH OF REPUBLICANISM IN LOUISIANA, KENTUCKY, AND MASSACHUSETTS. LORD NORTH FORMS AN ADMINISTRATION.

### May 1769–January 1770.

Affairs at New Orleans . . . . . . . . . . 352
Landing of O'Reilly and his army. Arrests . . . . . . 353
Trials and executions. Census of New Orleans. Pioneers of the West . 354
Daniel Boone in Kentucky . . . . . . . . . 355
Hutchinson as governor . . . . . . . . . . 357
New York and Boston enforce the agreement of non-importation . . 359
Affray between Otis and Robinson. Boston appeals to the world . . 360
Hutchinson a governor and a trader. Inactivity of the troops in Boston . 361
Botetourt in Virginia promises a partial repeal of the revenue act . 362
One and the same strife in America and in England . . . . 363
Great debate in the house of commons . . . . . 364
In the house of lords . . . . . . . . . . 365
Fresh attack on the ministry. Camden dismissed. Death of Yorke . 366
Grafton resigns. Lord North prime minister . . . . . 367

## CHAPTER XXVIII.

THE BOSTON "MASSACRE." LORD NORTH'S ADMINISTRATION.

### January–March 1770.

Hutchinson prorogues the assembly . . . . . . . 368
Troops supplied with ammunition He capitulates with the merchants . 369
Conflict with the troops in New York. Effect on Boston . . . 370
Disputes at Boston between the soldiers and the townsmen . . . 371
The fifth of March . . . . . . . . . . 372
The town-meeting on the sixth . . . . . . . . 375
Samuel Adams overawes Hutchinson . . . . . . . 377
The troops ordered to leave the town . . . . . . . 378

## CHAPTER XXIX.

THE KING VIOLATES THE CHARTER OF MASSACHUSETTS.

### March–October 1770.

Instructions of the town of Boston . . . . . . . 379
Dispute in Massachusetts on prerogative. Chatham on the revenue act . 380
Lord North retains the preamble and the tax on tea . . . . 381
Character of George III . . . . . . . . . . 382
State of parties in England . . . . . . . . . 383
Character of Thurlow . . . . . . . . . . 384
Proceedings in parliament . . . . . . . . . 385

# CONTENTS.

| | PAGE |
|---|---|
| Failure of the non-importation agreements | 386 |
| The king disregards the charter of Massachusetts | 388 |
| The governor surrenders the provincial fortress to the British general | 389 |
| Trial of Preston | 390 |
| And of the British soldiers. Election of Franklin as agent | 391 |

## CHAPTER XXX.

### THE ORIGIN OF TENNESSEE.

### October 1770–June 1771.

| | |
|---|---|
| Virginia and the West | 392 |
| Washington on the Ohio | 393 |
| Robertson on the Watauga | 394 |
| The regulators of North Carolina. Husbands expelled. The riot act | 395 |
| Dunmore in New York. Edmund Burke chosen agent for New York | 396 |
| Some of the Grenville connection join the ministry. Choiseul dismissed | 397 |
| Grievances of the regulators | 398 |
| Tryon marches against them | 400 |
| Battle of the Alamance. Execution of prisoners | 401 |
| The republic on the Watauga | 402 |

## CHAPTER XXXI.

### GREAT BRITAIN CENTRES IN ITSELF POWER OVER ITS COLONIES. HILLSBOROUGH'S RETIREMENT.

### June 1771–August 1772.

| | |
|---|---|
| Samuel Adams stands alone. Continued altercation in Massachusetts | 404 |
| Samuel Adams plans correspondence and union | 406 |
| Conduct of Hutchinson | 407 |
| Jones, of Georgia. Affairs in South Carolina | 408 |
| Discontent in Illinois and Indiana | 409 |
| Protest of Virginia against the slave-trade. How it was received | 409 |
| Jefferson's bill for unrestricted emancipation | 410 |
| Virginia addresses the king against the slave-trade | 410 |
| Mansfield's decision on the slave taken to England | 411 |
| Patrick Henry on slavery | 412 |
| George Mason addresses words on slavery to the Virginia legislature | 413 |
| Burning of the Gaspee | 414 |
| Protest of the Massachusetts assembly against the civil list | 415 |
| Hillsborough retires | 416 |

## CHAPTER XXXII.

### THE TOWNS OF MASSACHUSETTS HOLD CORRESPONDENCE.

### August 1772–January 1773.

| | |
|---|---|
| The cordial understanding between England and France | 417 |
| Contrast with New England | 418 |
| Samuel Adams proposes committees of correspondence | 419 |

|   | PAGE |
|---|---|
| His motion | 420 |
| Committee on the subject appointed. Joseph Warren | 421 |
| The report of the committee | 422 |
| Effects of taxation by parliament on the British revenue | 423 |
| John Temple accuses and is accused | 424 |
| Secret letters of Hutchinson and Oliver sent by Franklin to Massachusetts | 425 |
| Towns of Massachusetts meet and correspond | 426 |
| Thurlow and Wedderburn on the burning of the Gaspee | 428 |
| The spirit of the country people of Massachusetts | 429 |

## CHAPTER XXXIII.

### VIRGINIA CONSOLIDATES UNION.

### January–July 1773.

|   |   |
|---|---|
| The proceedings of Boston considered in England and in Virginia | 430 |
| How Massachusetts came to deny the supreme power of parliament | 430 |
| The towns of Massachusetts continue to meet | 431 |
| Strife in South Carolina. Answer of the Massachusetts council and house | 432 |
| The commissioners on the burning of the Gaspee | 434 |
| Dispute in Massachusetts on the dependence of the judges | 435 |
| Virginia proposes intercolonial committees | 436 |
| Effect of the proposition | 437 |
| The king inexorable. The East India company needs relief | 438 |
| The king rejects the petitions of Massachusetts | 439 |
| The unmasking of Hutchinson | 440 |
| What urgent advice he had given to the ministry | 441 |
| His dejection and meanness. More voices from the towns of Massachusetts | 442 |

## CHAPTER XXXIV.

### THE BOSTON TEA-PARTY.

### August–December 1773.

|   |   |
|---|---|
| The East India company will export tea to America | 443 |
| Samuel Adams prepares resistance | 443 |
| He takes counsel with Hawley | 444 |
| Great influence of Franklin. Secret circular to all the colonies | 445 |
| Spirit of Philadelphia. Of South Carolina | 446 |
| Of the people of Illinois | 447 |
| A public and a town-meeting in Boston. The tea consignees refuse to resign | 448 |
| Boston and the four nearest towns to all other towns in the province | 449 |
| A tea-ship arrives | 450 |
| A great public meeting insist that the tea must be sent back | 451 |
| Two more tea-ships arrive | 452 |
| The Boston committee require the tea-ships to be sent back | 453 |
| Spirit of the country towns | 454 |
| A clearance refused. Great public meeting | 455 |
| The governor refuses the tea-ship a pass. The tea thrown overboard | 456 |

## CONTENTS.

| | PAGE |
|---|---|
| The tea-ship at Charleston. At Philadelphia | 457 |
| The cry for union | 458 |

### CHAPTER XXXV.

#### THE KING IN COUNCIL INSULTS MASSACHUSETTS AND ITS AGENT.

#### December 1773–February 1774.

| | |
|---|---|
| Franklin delivers the address for the removal of Hutchinson | 459 |
| Duel between John Temple and William Whately | 460 |
| Franklin before the privy council | 460 |
| Speech of Dunning. Of Wedderburn | 461 |
| Wedderburn loudly cheered by the lords of council | 463 |
| Franklin and Wedderburn. Franklin and the lords of council | 464 |
| Franklin still takes measures for conciliation. The king implacable | 465 |
| Report of the privy council | 465 |

### CHAPTER XXXVI

#### THE CRISIS.

#### February–May 1774.

| | |
|---|---|
| The ministry decide that there exists in America a rebellion | 466 |
| They soothe the Bourbon powers and drive Charles James Fox into opposition | 466 |
| State of the American colonies | 467 |
| How Massachusetts reasoned | 468 |
| The ultimatum of America | 469 |
| Parliament and the British people agree with the ministry | 470 |
| Penal measures against Boston. Debate on the Boston port bill | 471 |
| Josiah Tucker advises to concede American independence | 472 |
| So does John Cartwright | 474 |
| Lord George Germain takes the lead in support of Lord North | 474 |
| The Boston port bill in the house of lords. Speech of Lord Mansfield | 475 |
| Gage sails for Boston with full civil and military powers | 476 |
| Position of Samuel Adams | 476 |
| The bill for taking away the charter of Massachusetts left America no choice but resistance | 477 |
| Speech of Edmund Burke on a motion to repeal the tax on tea | 478 |
| Relation of Burke to the British aristocracy | 479 |
| Speech of Fox. New York tea-ship. The third penal bill | 480 |
| Bill for quartering troops. The Quebec bill | 481 |
| Decline of liberty in Europe. Freedom to be restored through America | 482 |

# THE
# AMERICAN REVOLUTION

*IN FIVE EPOCHS.*

EPOCH SECOND.

BRITAIN ESTRANGES AMERICA.

FROM 1763 TO 1774.

# BRITAIN ESTRANGES AMERICA.

## CHAPTER I.

### ENGLAND AS IT WAS IN 1763.

#### 1763.

OF the wise and happy people of Great Britain the domestic character was marked by moderation, and, like its temperate clime, would sustain no extremes. The island rose before the philosophers as the asylum of independent thought, and upon the nations as the home of revolution where liberty emanated from discord and sedition. In the atmosphere of England, Voltaire ripened the speculative views which he published as "English Letters;" there Montesquieu sketched a government which should make liberty its end; and from English writings and example Rousseau drew the idea of a social compact. Every Englishman discussed public affairs; busy politicians thronged the coffee-houses; petitions were sent to parliament from popular assemblies; cities, boroughs, and counties framed addresses to the king: and yet such was the stability of the institutions of England amid the factious conflicts of parties, such her loyalty to law even in her change of dynasties, such her self-control while resisting power, such the fixedness of purpose lying beneath the restless enterprise of her intelligence, that the ideas which were preparing radical changes in the social system of other monarchies held their course harmlessly within her borders, as winds playing capriciously round some ancient structure whose massive buttresses tranquilly bear up its roof and towers, and pinnacles, and spires.

The Catholic kingdoms sanctified the kingly·power by connecting it with the church; Prussia was as yet the only great modern instance of a monarchical state resting on an army; England limited her monarchy by law. Her constitution was venerable from its antiquity. Some traced it to Magna Charta, some to the Norman conquest, and some to the forests of Germany, where acts of legislation were debated and assented to by the people and by the nobles; but it was at the revolution of 1688 that the legislature definitively assumed the sovereignty by dismissing a monarch from the kingdom. The prince might no more oppose "his unbounded prerogatives," such are the words of Hume, "to that noble liberty, that sweet equality, and that happy security, by which the English are at present distinguished above all nations in the universe." The new dynasty had consented to wear the crown in conformity to a statute, so that its title was safe only with the constitution. The framework of government had for its direct end not the power of its chief, but personal liberty and the security of property. The restrictions, which were followed by these happy results, had been imposed and maintained under the lead of the aristocracy, to whom the people, in its gratitude for a bulwark against arbitrary power and its sense of inability itself to reform the administration, had likewise capitulated; so that England was become an aristocratic republic, with a king as the emblem of a permanent executive.

In England there was an established church; but its hierarchy had no independent existence; and its connection with the state was purchased by its subordination. None but conformists could hold office; in return, the church, in so far as it was a civil establishment, was the creature of parliament; a statute prescribed the articles of its creed, as well as its book of prayer; it was not even intrusted with a co-ordinate power to reform its own abuses; any attempt to do so would have been crushed as a movement of usurpers. Convocations were infrequent; and, if laymen were not called to them, it was because the assembly was merely formal. Through parliament, the laity amended and regulated the church. The bishops were still elected by a chapter of the clergy, but the privilege existed only in appearance; the crown, which gave leave to elect, named the person to be chosen, and deference to its nomination was enforced by the penalties of a præmunire.

The laity, too, had destroyed the convents and monasteries which, under other social forms, had been the schools, the poorhouses, and the hostleries of the land; and all the way from Netley Abbey to the rocky shores of Northumberland, and even to the remote loneliness of Iona, the country was strewn with the broken arches and ruined towers and tottering columns of buildings, which once rose in such numbers and such beauty of architecture that they seemed like a concert of voices chanting a perpetual hymn of praise. Moreover, the property of the church, which had been enjoyed by the monasteries that undertook the performance of the parochial offices, had fallen into the hands of impropriators; so that funds set apart for charity, instruction, and worship were become the plunder of laymen, who seized the great tithes and left but a pittance to their vicars.

The purity of spiritual influence was tarnished by this strict subordination to the temporal power. The clergy had never slept so soundly over the traditions of their religion; and the dean and chapter, at their cathedral stalls, seemed like strangers lost among the shrines and groined aisles and light columns of stone, which the fervid genius of men of a different age had fashioned.

The clergy were Protestant, and married. Their great dignitaries dwelt in palaces, and no longer used their revenues to renew cathedrals, or beautify chapels, or build new churches, or endow schools. In the house of lords, the church had its representative seats among the barons, and never came in conflict with the aristocracy with which its interests were identified.

The hereditary right of the other members of the house of lords was such a privilege as must, in itself, always be hateful to a free people, and always be in danger; but as yet there was no struggle to be rid of it. The reverence for its antiquity was enhanced by pleasing historical associations. But for the aid of the barons, Magna Charta would not have been attained; and, but for the nobility and gentry, the revolution of 1688 would not have succeeded. A sentiment of gratitude was therefore blended in the popular mind with submission to rank.

Besides, nobility was not a caste, but rather an office, personal and transmissible to but one. "The insolent prerogative of primogeniture" was made most conspicuous in the bosom of the families which it kept up; their younger members placed their pride in upholding a system which left them dependent or destitute. They revered the head of the family, and by their submission taught the people to do so. Even the mother who might survive her husband, after following him to his tomb in the old manorial church, returned no more to the ancestral mansion, but vacated it for the heir.

The daughters of the nobility were left poor, and most of them necessarily remained unmarried, or wedded persons of inferior birth. The younger sons became commoners; and, though they were in some measure objects of jealousy, because they used their relationship to appropriate to themselves the benefits of the public patronage, yet, as they really were commoners, they kept up an intimate sympathy between classes. Besides, the road to the peerage, as all knew, lay open to all. It was a body constantly invigorated by recruits from the bar and the house of commons. Had it been left to itself, it would have perished long before. Once, having the gentle Addison for a supporter of the measure, it voted itself to be a close order, but was saved by the house of commons from consummating its selfish purpose, where success would have prepared its ruin. Thus the hereditary branch of the legislature was doubly connected with the people; the larger part of its sons and daughters descended to the station of commoners, and commoners were at all times making their way to its honors. In no country was rank so privileged or were classes so intermingled.

The peers, too, were, like all others, amenable to the law; and, though the system of finance bore evidence of their controlling influence in legislation, yet their houses, lands, and property were not exempt from taxation. The provisions of law were certainly most unequal, yet, such as they were, they applied indiscriminately to all.

The house of commons represented the land of England,

but not her men. No one but a landholder was qualified to be elected into that body; and most of those who were chosen were scions of the great families. Sons of peers, even the eldest son while his father lived, could sit in the house of commons; and there might be, and usually were, many members of one name.

The elective franchise was itself a privilege, and depended on capricious charters or immemorial custom rather than on reason. Of the five hundred and fifty-eight members of whom the house of commons then consisted, the counties of England, Wales, and Scotland elected one hundred and thirty-one as knights of the shires. These owed their election to the good-will of the owners of great estates in the respective counties; for the tenant used to vote as his landlord directed, and could be compelled to do so, for the vote was given by word of mouth or a show of hands. The representatives of the counties were, as a class, country gentlemen, independent of the court. They were comparatively free from corruption, and some of them fervidly devoted to English liberty.

The remaining four hundred and twenty-seven members, "citizens and burgesses," were arbitrarily distributed among cities, towns, and boroughs, with little regard to wealth or population. Old Sarum, where there was not so much as the ruins of a town and scarce so much housing as a sheep-cot, or more inhabitants than a shepherd, sent as many representatives to the assembly of law-makers as the large, rich, and populous county of York. The lord of the borough of Newport, in the Isle of Wight, named two members, while Bristol elected no more; the populous capital of Scotland, but one; and Manchester, none. Two hundred and fifty-four members had such small constituencies that about five thousand seven hundred and twenty-three votes sufficed to choose them; fifty-six were elected by so few that, had the districts been equally divided, six and a half votes would have sufficed for each member. In an island counting more than seven and a half millions of people and at least a million and a half of mature men, no one could pretend that it required more than ten thousand voters to elect the majority of the house of commons; but, in fact, it required the consent of a far less number.

London, Westminster, and Bristol, and perhaps a few more of the larger places, made independent selections; but the boroughs were nearly all dependent on some great proprietor or on the crown. The burgage tenures belonged to men of fortune; and, as the elective power attached to borough houses, the owner of those houses could compel their occupants to elect whom he pleased. The majority of the members were able to command their own election; sat in parliament for life, as undisturbed as the peers; and bequeathed to their children the property and influence which secured their seats. The same names, from the same places, occur in the rolls of parliament from one generation to another.

The exclusive character of the representative body was completed by the prohibition of the publication of the debates, and by the rule of conducting important business with closed doors. Power was with the few: the people was swallowed up in the lords and commons.

The members of the parliament of those days never indulged in abstract reasoning, and cared little for general ideas. Theories and philosophy from their lips would have been ridiculed or neglected; for them the applause at St. Stephen's weighed more than the approval of posterity, more than the voice of God in the soul. They pleaded before that tribunal, and not in the forum of humanity. How to meet parliament was the minister's chief solicitude, for he hazarded his political fortunes on its vote. He valued its approval more than the affections of mankind, and could boast that this servitude was perfect freedom.

The mode of electing the house of commons might seem to rivet that unmixed aristocracy which is the worst government under the sun; but the English law was so tempered by popular franchises that it was among the very best which the world had thus far seen; and Britons, in their joy at the success of their revolution of 1688 in bounding the prerogatives of the prince, were slow to undertake the reform of the body by which that revolution had been achieved.

Men considered the functions of parliament, and especially of the house of commons. It protected property by establishing in theory the principle that taxes can be levied only with the consent of the people by their representatives. It maintained the supremacy of the civil power by making the grants for the army and navy annual, limiting the number of troops that might be kept up, and leaving the mutiny bill to expire once a year. All appropriations, except the civil list for maintaining the dignity of the crown, it made specific and only for the year. As the great inquest of the nation, it examined how the laws were executed, and was armed with the office of impeachment. By its control of the revenue, it was so interwoven with the administration that it could force the king to accept, as advisers and ministers, even men who had most offended him.

The same character of aristocracy was imprinted on the administration. The king reigned, but, by the theory of the constitution, was not to govern. He appeared in the privy council on occasions of state; but Queen Anne was the last of the English monarchs to attend the debates in the house of lords, or to preside at a meeting of the ministry. In the cabinet, according to the rule of aristocracy, every question was put to vote; and, after the vote, the dissentients must hush their individual opinions, and present the appearance of unanimity. Add to this that the public offices were engrossed by a small group of families, that favor dictated appointments of bishops, of officers in the navy, and still more in the army in which even boys at school held commissions, so that the higher class of England absorbed all the functions of administration, and its cabals were more respected than majesty itself.

Yet, even here, "the great," as they were called, were reined in. Every man claimed a right to sit in judgment on the administration; and the mighty power of public opinion, embodied in a free press, pervaded, checked, and, in the last resort, nearly governed the whole.

Nor must he who will understand the English institutions leave out of view the character of the enduring works which had sprung from the salient energy of the English mind. Literature had been left to develop itself. William of Orange was foreign to it; Anne cared not for it; the first George knew no English; the second, not much. Devotedness to the monarch is not impressed on English literature.

Neither the earlier nor the later literature put itself at war with the country or its classes. The inmost character of the English mind, in the various epochs of its history, was imprinted on its poetry. Chaucer, a man of a most comprehensive nature, living in the days when friars were as thick as motes in the sunbeam, when the land, according to its legends, was "fulfilled of faerie," and the elf-queen with her jolly company danced in many a green mead, recalls the manners and humors, the chivalry and thought that beguiled the pilgrimages, or lent a charm to the hospitality of Catholic England. Spenser clothed in allegory the purity of the reformed religion which the lion of England defended against the false arts of Rome. Shakespeare, "great heir of fame"—rising at the inspiring moment of the victory of English nationality and Protestant liberty, master of every chord that vibrates in the human soul, and knowing all that can become the cottage or the palace, the town or the fields and forests, the camp or the banqueting-hall; ever reverent to the voice of religion in the soul; ever teaching by his true delineations of character a veneration and love for the laws of morality—unfolded the panorama of English history, and embodied in "easy numbers" whatever is wise and lovely and observable in English manners and life. Milton, with heroic greatness of mind, was the sublime representative of English republicanism, eager to quell the oppressor, but sternly detesting libertinism and disorder, and exhorting to "patience" even in the days of the later Stuarts. Dryden, living through the whole era of revolutions, yielded to the social influences of a vicious age, and reproduced in his verse the wayward wavering of the English court between Protestantism and the Roman Catholic worship, between voluptuousness and faith; least read, because least truly national. "Envy must own I live among the great" was the boast of Pope, the cherished poet of English aristocratic life as it existed in the time of Bolingbroke and Walpole; flattering the great with sarcasms against kings; an optimist, proclaiming order as the first law of Heaven. None of all these, not even Milton, provoked to the overthrow of the institutions of England.

Nor had the skepticism of modern philosophy penetrated

the mass of the nation, or raised vague desires of revolution. It kept, rather, what was held to be the best company. It entered the palace during the licentiousness of the two former reigns; and, though the court was now become decorous and devout, the nobility, and those who in that day were called "the great," affected free-thinking, and laughed at the evidence of piety in any one of their order. But the spirit of the people rebelled against materialism; if worship, as conducted in the parish church, had no attractive warmth, they gathered round the preacher in the fields, eager to be assured that they had within themselves a spiritual nature and a warrant for their belief in immortality; yet, under the moderating influence of Wesley, combining a fervid reform in religion with unquestioning deference to authority in the state.

English metaphysical philosophy itself bore a character of moderation analogous to English institutions. In disregard to the traditions of the Catholic church, Locke had denied that thought implies an immaterial substance; and Hartley and Priestley asserted that the soul was but of flesh and blood; but the more genial Berkeley, armed with "every virtue," insisted rather on the certain existence of the intellectual world alone, while, from the bench of English bishops, Butler pressed the analogies of the material creation itself into the service of spiritual life. If Hume embodied the logical consequences of the materialist philosophy in the most skilfully constructed system of idealism which the world had ever known, his own countryman, Reid, in works worthy to teach the youth of a republic, illustrated the active powers of man and the reality of right; Adam Smith found a criterion of duty in the universal sentiment of mankind; and the English dissenter, Price, enforced the eternal, necessary, and unchanging distinctions of morality. So philosophic freedom in Britain rebuked its own excesses, and, self-balanced and self-restrained, never sought to throw down the august fabric which had for so many centuries stood before Europe as the citadel of liberty.

The blended respect for aristocracy and for popular rights was impressed upon the courts of law. They were charged with the protection of every individual without distinction, securing to the accused a trial by sworn men, who were taken from among his peers and held their office for but one short term of service. And especially the judges watched over the personal liberty of every Englishman, with power on the instant to set free any one illegally imprisoned, even though in custody by the king's express command.

At the same time, the judiciary, with a reputation for impartiality in the main well deserved, was by its nature conservative, and by its constitution the associate and the support of the house of lords. Westminster Hall, which had stood through many revolutions and dynasties, and was become venerable from an unchanged existence of five hundred years, sent the first officer in one of its courts, from however humble an origin he might have sprung, to take precedence of the nobility of the realm, and preside in the chamber of peers. That branch of the legislature derived an increase of its dignity from the great lawyers whom the crown, from time to time, was accustomed to ennoble; and, moreover, it formed of itself a part of the judicial system. The house of commons, whose members, from their frequent elections, best knew the temper of the people, possessed exclusively the right to originate votes of supply; but the final judgment on all questions of law respecting property rested with the house of lords.

The same cast of aristocracy, intermingled with popularity, pervaded the systems of education. From climate, compact population, and sober national character, England was capable beyond any other country in the world of a system of popular education. Nevertheless, the mass of its people was left ignorant how to read or write. But the benevolence of earlier and later ages had benefited science by endowments, which in their conception were charity schools, founded by piety for the education of poor men's sons; and the sons of the aristocracy grouped themselves at Eton, or Westminster, or Harrow, or Winchester, round the scholars on the foundation.

The same time-honored constitution marked the universities. As a consequence, the genius of the past claimed a right to linger in their streets, and something of the ancient theory of loyalty long found an asylum in the colleges of Oxford.

The cities were not barred against the influence of the aristocracy. The swelling expenses of the government increased its dependence on the moneyed class, and the leading minister needed the confidence of the city as well as of the country and the court. Besides, it was not uncommon to see a wealthy citizen toiling to amass yet greater wealth, that he might purchase land and found a family; or giving his richly dowered daughter in marriage to a peer. The members of the legislature listened readily to the petitions of the merchants, who, in their turn, rebelled against the necessity of intrusting the protection of their interests to members of the aristocratic organization as little as they did at the employment of barristers in the halls of justice.

But, if aristocracy was not excluded from towns, it pervaded the whole rural life of England. The climate was not only softened by the milder atmosphere that belongs to the western side of masses of land, but was further modified by the proximity of every part of it to the sea. It knew neither long-continuing heat nor cold, and was more friendly to daily employment without doors throughout the whole year, than any in Europe. The island was "a little world" of its own, with a "happy breed of men" for its inhabitants, in whom the hardihood of the Norman was intermixed with the gentler qualities of the Celt and the Saxon, just as nails are rubbed into steel to harden the Damascus blade. They loved country life, of which the mildness of the clime increased the charms, since every grass and flower and tree that had its home between the remote North and the neighborhood of the tropics would live abroad, and except those only which need a hot sun to unfold their bloom, or fix their aroma, or ripen their fruit, would thrive in perfection; so that no region could show such a varied wood. The moisture of the sky favored a soil not naturally rich, and clothed the earth in perpetual verdure. Nature had its attractions even in winter. The ancient trees were stripped indeed of their foliage, so that they showed more clearly their fine proportions and the undisturbed nests of the noisy rooks among their boughs; but the air was so mild that flocks and herds still grazed on the freshly springing herbage, and the deer found shelter enough by crouching among the fern; the smoothly shaven, grassy walk was soft and yielding under the foot; nor was there a month in the year in which the plough was idle. The large landed proprietors dwelt often in houses which had descended to them from the times when England was gemmed all over with delicate and solid structures of Gothic art. Estates were bounded by the same hedges and ditches, counties by the same lanes, as in William the Conqueror's time, and water-wheels revolved to grind corn just where they had been doing so for at least eight hundred years. Hospitality had its traditions, and for untold centuries Christmas had been the most joyous of the seasons.

The aristocratic system was so completely the ruling element in English history and English life, especially in the country, that it seemed the most natural organization of society, and was even endeared to the dependent people. Hence the manners of the aristocracy, without haughtiness or arrogance, implied rather than expressed the consciousness of undisputed rank.

Yet the privileged class carried their watchfulness over their rural pleasures and interests to an extreme. The life of the farmer from generation to generation was but "an equal conflict between industry and want;" and the laboring poor "with all their thrift did not thrive," with all their ingenious parsimony could barely live without extorting alms. The game laws, parcelling out among the large proprietors the exclusive right of hunting, which had been wrested from the king as too grievous a prerogative, were maintained with relentless severity; and to steal or even to hamstring a sheep was as much punished by death as murder or treason. During the reign of George II., sixty-three new capital offences had been added to the criminal laws, and five new ones, on the average, continued to be discovered annually; so that the criminal code of England, formed under the influence of the gentry, was written in blood.

But this cruelty, while it encouraged and hardened offenders, did not revolt the submissiveness of the rural population. The tenantry, holding lands at a moderate rent, for the most part without permanent leases, transmitting the occupation of them from father to son through many generations, clung to the lord of the manor as ivy to massive old walls. They loved to live in his light, to lean on his support, to gather round him with affectionate deference, and, by faithful attachment, to win his sympathy and care, happy when he was such a one as merited their love. They caught refinement of their superiors, so that their cottages were carefully neat, with roses and honeysuckles clambering to their roofs. They cultivated the soil in sight of the towers of the church round which reposed the ashes of their ancestors for almost a thousand years. The island was mapped out into territorial parishes, as well as into counties; and the affairs of local interest, the assessment of rates, the care of the poor and of the roads, were intrusted to elected vestries or magistrates, with little interference from the central government. The resident magistrates were unpaid, being taken from among the landed gentry; and the local affairs of the county and all criminal prosecutions of no uncommon importance were settled by them in a body at quarterly sessions, where a kind-hearted landlord often presided, to appall the convict by the earnestness of his rebuke and then to show him mercy by a lenient sentence. All judgments were controlled by fixed law; and, at the assizes, no sentence could be pronounced against the accused but by the consent of impartial men taken from the body of the people.

The climate, so inviting to rural life, was benign to industry of all sorts. It might seem that the population engaged in manufactures would have constituted a separate element not included within the aristocratic system, but the great manufacture of the material not produced at home was still in its infancy. The weaver toiled in his own cottage, and the thread which he used was with difficulty supplied to him sufficiently by the spinners at the wheel of his own family and among his neighbors. Men had not as yet learned by machinery to produce, continuously and uniformly, from the down of cotton, the porous cords of parallel filaments; to attenuate them by gently drawing them out; to twist and extend the threads; and to wind them regularly on pins of wood as fast as they are spun. In 1763, the inconsiderable cotton manufactures of Great Britain, transported from place to place on pack-horses, did not form one two-hundredth part of the production of ninety years later, and were politically of no importance. Not yet had art done more than begin the construction of channels for still-water navigation; not yet had Wedgwood fully succeeded in changing, annually, tens of thousands of tons of clay and flint into brilliantly glazed and durable ware, capable of sustaining heat, cheap in price, and beautiful and convenient in form; not yet had the mechanics, after using up forests, learned familiarly to smelt iron with pit coal, or to drive machinery by steam.

Let the great artificers of England in iron and clay adopt science as their patron; let the cotton-spinners, deriving their raw material from abroad, perfect their manufacture by inventive plebeian genius, and so prosper as to gather around their mills a crowded population—and there will then exist a powerful and opulent and numerous class, emancipated from aristocratic influence, thriving outside of the old society of England. But at that time the manufacture of wool was cherished as the most valuable of all. It had grown with the growth and wealth of England, and flourished in every part of the island; at Kidderminster and Wilton and Norwich, not less than in the West Riding of York. It had been privileged by King Stephen and regulated by the lion-hearted Richard. Its protection was as much a part of the statute-book as the game laws, and was older than Magna Charta. To foster it was a custom coeval with the English constitution; and the landowner, whose rich lawns produced the fleece, sympathized with the industry that wrought it into beautiful fabrics. Mutual confidence was established between the classes of society; no chasm divided its orders.

Thus, unity of character marked the constitution and the social life of England. The sum of the whole was an intense nationality in its people. They were happy in their form of government, and were proud of it; for they enjoyed more perfect freedom than the world up to that time had known. In spite of the glaring defects of their system, Greece, in the days of Pericles or Phocion, had not been blessed with such liberty. Italy, in the fairest days of her ill-starred republics, had not had such security of property and person, so pure an administration of justice, such unlicensed expression of thought.

These benefits were held by a firm tenure, safe against

revolutions and sudden changes in the state. The laws reigned, and not men; and the laws had been the growth of centuries, yielding to amendment only by the gradual method of nature, as opinions exercising less instant influence slowly infused themselves through the public mind into legislation: so that the constitution of England, though like all things else perpetually changing, changed like the style of architecture along the aisles of its own cathedrals, where the ponderous severity of the Norman age melts in the next almost imperceptibly into a more genial and lighter style.

With all the defects which remained in the form of their constitution, the English felt that they were great not by restraining laws, not by monopoly. Liberty and industry gave them their nationality and greatness. English statesmen, going from the classical schools to the universities, brought up in a narrow circle of classical and mathematical learning, wherever they travelled, were environed by an English atmosphere. They saw the world abroad as if to perceive how inferior it was to the land of their birth. They went young to the house of commons, and were so blinded by love and admiration of their own country that they thought nothing blameworthy which promoted its glory, its power, or its welfare. They looked out upon the surrounding sea as their wall of defence, and the great deep seemed to them their inheritance, inviting them everywhere to enter upon it as their rightful domain. They gazed beyond the Atlantic; and, not content with their own colonies, they counted themselves defrauded of their due as the sole representatives of liberty, so long as Spain should hold exclusively such boundless empires. The house of Bourbon might be struck at wherever it should rear its head. To promote British interests and command the applause of the British senate, they were ready to infringe on the rights of other countries, and even on the essential liberties of the outlying dominions of the crown.

## CHAPTER II.

#### ENGLAND AND ITS DEPENDENCIES. IRELAND.

#### 1763.

So England was one united nation, with its landed aristocracy as the ruling power. The separate character and influence of each of the great component parts of English society may be observed in the British dominions outside of Great Britain.

From the wrecks of the empire of the Great Mogul, a monopolizing company of English merchants had gained dominion in the East, with factories, subject provinces, and territorial revenues on the coast of Malabar, in the Carnatic, and on the Ganges. They looked upon the East India company of France as hopelessly ruined; and, as they pushed forward their victories, they avowed gain to be the sole end of their alliances and their trade, of their warfare and their civil rule.

In America, the middling class, chiefly rural people, with a few from the towns of England, founded colonies in the forms of liberty, and owned and cultivated the soil.

Ireland, whose government was proposed in England as a model for the British colonies, and whose history is from this time intimately blended with the course of events in America, had been seized by the English oligarchy. Half as large as England, it has a still milder climate and a more fertile soil. From its mountains gush numerous rivers, fed by the rains which the sea breeze makes frequent. These, now halting in bogs and morasses, now expanding into beautiful lakes, now rushing with copious volume and swift descent, offered along their courses water-power without limit, and at their outlets deep and safe harbors. The limestone plains under the cloudy sky are matted with grasses whose verdure vies with the emerald.

Centuries before the Christian era the beautiful region had been occupied by men of the same Celtic tribe which colonized the Scottish highlands. The Normans, who in the eighth century planted commercial towns on its coast, were too few to maintain separate municipalities. The old inhabitants had been converted to Christianity by apostles of the purest fame, and the land abounded in churches and cathedrals, in a learned, liberal, and numerous clergy. Their civil government was an aristocratic confederacy of septs, or families with chiefs; and the remote land seemed set apart by nature as the abode of an opulent, united, and happy people.

In the reign of Henry II. of England, and in his name, English barons and adventurers invaded Ireland; and, before the end of the thirteenth century, its soil was parcelled out among ten English families.

As the occupation became confirmed, the English system of laws was continued to the English colonists living within the pale which comprised the four counties of Dublin, Louth, Meath, and Kildare. In the Irish parliament, framed ostensibly after the model of the English constitution, no Irishman could hold a seat: it represented the intruders only, who had come to possess themselves of the lands of the natives, now quarrelling among themselves about the spoils, now rebelling against England, but always united against the Irish.

When Magna Charta was granted at Runnymede, it became the possession and birthright of the Norman inhabitants of Ireland; but to the "mere Irish" its benefits were not extended, except by special charters of enfranchisement or denization, of which the sale furnished a means of exaction.

The oligarchy of conquerors, in the process of time, began to amalgamate with the Irish; they had the same religion; they inclined to adopt their language, dress, and manners, and to speak for the rights of Ireland more warmly than the Irish themselves. To counteract this tendency of "the degenerate English," laws were enacted so that the Anglo-Irish could not intermarry with the Celts, nor permit them to graze their lands, nor present them to benefices, nor receive them into religious houses, nor entertain their bards. The "mere Irish" were considered as out of the king's allegiance; in war, they were accounted rebels; in peace, the statute-book called them Irish enemies; and to kill one of them was adjudged no felony.

During the long civil wars in England, English power declined in Ireland. To recover its subordination, in the year 1495, the tenth after the union of the Roses, the famous statute of Drogheda, known as Poyning's Law, from the name of the lord deputy who obtained its enactment, reserved the initiative in legislation to the crown of England. No parliament could from that time "be holden in Ireland till the king's lieutenant should certify to the king, under the great seal of the land, the causes and considerations and all such acts as it seemed to them ought to be passed thereon, and such be affirmed by the king and his council, and his license to summon a parliament be obtained." This remained the rule of Irish parliaments, and in the middle of the eighteenth century began to be referred to in England as a good precedent for America.

The change in the relations of England to the see of Rome, at the time of the reform, served to amalgamate the Celtic Irish and the Anglo-Norman Irish who adhered to their ancient religion.

The Irish resisted the act of supremacy; and the accession of Queen Elizabeth brought the struggle to a crisis. She established the Anglican Episcopal church by an act of what was called an Irish parliament, in which the Celtic-Irish had no part, and English retainers, chosen from select counties and boroughs and new boroughs made for the occasion, held the ascendant over the Anglo-Norman Irish. The laws of supremacy and uniformity were adopted in the words of the English statutes; the common prayer was appointed instead of mass, and was to be read in the English language, or, where that was not known, in the Latin.

The Anglican prelates and priests, divided from the Irish by the insuperable barrier of language, were quartered upon the land, shepherds without sheep, pastors without people; strangers to the inhabitants, wanting not them, but theirs.

The churches went to ruin; the benefices fell to men who were looked upon as foreigners and heretics, and who had no care for the natives but to compel them to pay tithes. The inferior clergy were men of no parts or erudition, and were as immoral as they were illiterate. No pains were taken to make converts, except by penal laws; and the Norman-Irish and Celtic-Irish were drawn nearer to one another by common sorrows, as well as by a common faith; for "the people of that country's birth, of all degrees, were papists, body and soul."

The Anglican church in Ireland represented the English interest. Wild and incoherent attempts at self-defence against relentless oppression were followed by the desolation of large tracts of country, new confiscations of land, and a new colonial garrison in the train of the English army. Even the use of parliaments was suspended for seven-and-twenty years.

The accession of James I., with the counsels of Bacon, seemed to promise Ireland some alleviation of its woes, for the pale was broken down; and when the king, after the long interval, convened a parliament, it stood for the whole island. But the law tolerated only the Protestant worship; and, when colonies were planted on lands of six counties in Ulster escheated to the crown, the planters were chiefly Presbyterians from Scotland, than whom none more deeply hated the Catholic religion. The war of chicane succeeded to the war of arms and hostile statutes. Ecclesiastical courts wronged conscience; soldiers practiced extortions; the civil courts took away lands. Instead of adventurers despoiling the old inhabitants by the sword, there came up discoverers, who made a scandalous traffic of pleading the king's title against the possessors of estates to force them to grievous compositions, or to effect the total extinction of the interests of the natives in their own soil. This species of subtle ravage, continued with systematic iniquity in the next reign, and, carried to the last excess of perfidy, oppression, and insolence, kindled the rising of 1641.

When this rebellion had assumed the form of organized resistance, large forfeitures of lands were promised to those who should aid in its reduction. The Catholics had successively to encounter the party of the king; the Puritan parliament of England; the Scotch Presbyterians among themselves; the fierce, relentless energy of Cromwell; a unanimity of hatred, quickened by religious bigotry; greediness after confiscated estates; and the pride of power in the Protestant interest. Modern history has no parallel for the sufferings of the Irish nation from 1641 to 1660.

At the restoration of Charles II., a declaration of settlement confirmed even the escheats of land, decreed by the republican party for the loyalty of their owners to the Stuarts. It is the opinion of an English historian that, "upon the whole result, the Irish Catholics, having previously held about two thirds of the kingdom, lost more than one half of their possessions by forfeitures on account of their rebellion."

The favor of James II. wrought the Catholic Irish nothing but evil, for they shared his defeat; and, after their vain attempt to make of Ireland his independent place of refuge, and a gallant resistance of three years, the Irish at Limerick capitulated to the new dynasty, obtaining the royal promise of security of worship to the Roman Catholics, and the continued possession of their estates, free from all outlawries or forfeitures. Of these articles, the first was totally disregarded; the second was evaded. New forfeitures followed to the extent of more than a million of acres; and, at the close of the seventeenth century, the native Irish, with the Anglo-Irish Catholics, possessed not more than a seventh of the island.

The maxims on which the government of Ireland was administered by Protestant England after the revolution of 1688 brought about the relations by which that country and our own reciprocally affected each other's destiny.

The inhabitants of Ireland were four parts in five, all agree more than two parts in three, Roman Catholics. Religion established three separate nationalities: the Anglican churchmen, constituting nearly a tenth of the population; the Presbyterians, chiefly Scotch-Irish; and the Catholic population, which was a mixture of the old Celtic race, the untraceable remains of the few Danish settlers, and the Normans and first colonies of the English.

In settling the government, England intrusted it exclusively to those of "the English colony" who were members of its own church; so that a small minority ruled the island. To facilitate this, new boroughs were created, and wretched tenants, where not disfranchised, were so coerced in their votes at elections that two thirds of the Irish house of commons were the nominees of the large Protestant proprietors of the land.

An act of the English parliament rehearsed the dangers to be apprehended from the presence of popish recusants in the Irish parliament, and required of every member the new oaths of allegiance and supremacy and the declaration against transubstantiation. But not only were Roman Catholics excluded from seats in both branches of the legislature: a series of enactments, the fruit of relentless perseverance, gradually excluded "papists" from having any votes in the election of members to serve in parliament.

The Catholic Irish being disfranchised, one enactment pursued them after another till they suffered under a universal, unmitigated, indispensable, exceptionless disqualification. In the courts of law they could not gain a place on the bench, nor act as a barrister, or attorney, or solicitor, nor be employed even as a hired clerk, nor sit on a grand jury, nor serve as a sheriff or a justice of the peace, nor hold even the lowest civil office of trust and profit, nor have any privilege in a town corporate, nor be a freeman of such corporation, nor vote at a vestry. If papists would trade and work, they must do it even in their native towns as aliens. They were expressly forbidden to take more than two apprentices in any employment except in the linen manufacture. A Catholic might not marry a Protestant, nor be a guardian to any child, nor educate his own child if the mother declared herself a Protestant, or even if his own child, however young, should profess to be a Protestant. The priest who should celebrate a marriage between a Catholic and a Protestant was to be hanged.

None but those who conformed to the established church were admitted to study at the universities, nor could degrees be obtained but by those who had taken all the tests, oaths, and declarations. No Protestant in Ireland might instruct a papist. Papists could not supply their want by academies and schools of their own; for a Catholic to teach, even in a private family or as usher to a Protestant, was a felony, punishable by imprisonment, exile, or death. Thus "papists" were excluded from all opportunity of education at home, except by stealth and in violation of law. It might be thought that schools abroad were open to them; but, by a statute of King William, to be educated in any foreign Catholic school was an "unalterable and perpetual outlawry." The child sent abroad for education, no matter of how tender an age or himself how innocent, could never after sue in law or equity, or be guardian, executor, or administrator, or receive any legacy or deed of gift; he forfeited all his goods and chattels, and forfeited for his life all his lands. Whoever sent him abroad, or maintained him there, or assisted him with money or otherwise, incurred the same liabilities and penalties. The crown divided the forfeiture with the informer, and, when a person was proved to have sent abroad a bill of exchange or money, on him rested the burden of proving that the remittance was innocent; and he must do so before justices without the benefit of a jury.

The Irish Catholics were deprived even of the opportunity of worship, except by connivance. Their clergy, taken from the humbler classes of the people, could not be taught at home, nor be sent for education beyond seas, nor be recruited by learned ecclesiastics from abroad. Such priests as were permitted to reside in Ireland were registered, and were kept like prisoners at large within prescribed limits. All "papists" exercising ecclesiastical jurisdiction, all monks, friars, and regular priests, and all priests not then actually in parishes and registered, were banished from Ireland under pain of transportation, and, on a return, of being hanged, drawn, and quartered. Avarice was stimulated to apprehend them by the promise of a reward; he that should harbor or conceal them was to be stripped of all his property. When the registered priests were dead, the law, which was made perpetual, applied to every popish priest. By the laws of William and of Anne, St. Patrick, in Ireland, in the eighteenth century, would have been a felon. Any two justices of the peace might call before them any Catholic, and make inquisition as to when he heard mass, who were present, and what Catholic schoolmaster or priest he knew of, and the penalty for refusal to answer was a fine or a year's imprisonment. The Catholic priest abjuring his religion received a pension of thirty, and afterward of forty, pounds. In spite of these laws, there were, it is said, four thousand Catholic clergymen in Ireland, and the Catholic worship gained upon the Protestant, so attractive is sincerity when ennobled by persecution, even though "the laws did not presume a papist to exist there, and did not allow one to breathe but by the connivance of the government."

The Catholic Irish had been plundered of six sevenths of the land by iniquitous confiscations; every acre of the remaining seventh was grudged them by the Protestants. No nonconforming Catholic could buy land, or receive it by descent, devise, or settlement; or lend money on it, as the security; or hold an interest in it through a Protestant trustee; or take a lease of ground for more than thirty-one years. If, under such a lease, he brought his farm to produce more than one third beyond the rent, the first Protestant discoverer might sue for the lease before Protestants, making the defendant answer all interrogatories on oath, so that the Catholic farmer dared not drain his fields, nor enclose them, nor build solid houses on them. It was his interest rather to deteriorate the country, lest envy should prompt some Protestant to turn him out of doors. If a Catholic owned a horse worth more than five pounds, any Protestant might take it away. Nor was natural affection or parental authority respected. The son of a Catholic landholder, however dissolute or however young, if he would but join the English church, could turn his father's estate in fee-simple into a tenancy for life, becoming himself the owner, and annulling every agreement made by the father, even before his son's conversion.

The Catholic father could not in any degree disinherit his apostatizing son; but the child, in declaring himself a Protestant, might compel his father to confess upon oath the value of his substance, real and personal, whereupon the Protestant court might out of it award the son immediate maintenance, and, after the father's death, any establishment it pleased. A bill might at any time be brought by one or all of the children for a further discovery. If the parent, by his industry, improved his property, the son might compel an account of the value of the estate, in order to a new disposition. The father had no security against the persecution of his children but by abandoning all acquisition or improvement.

Ireland passed away from the ancient Irish. The proprietors in fee were probably fewer than in any equal area in Western Europe, parts of Spain only excepted. The consequence was an unexampled complication of titles. The landlord in chief was often known only as having dominion over the estate; leases of large tracts had been granted for very long terms of years; these were again subdivided to those who subdivided them once more, and so on indefinitely. Mortgages brought a new and numerous class of claimants. Thus humane connection between the tenant and landlord was not provided for. Leases were in the last resort most frequently given at will, and then what defence had the Irish Catholic against his Protestant superior? Hence the thatched mud cabin, without window or chimney, the cheap fences, the morass undrained, idleness in winter, the tenant's concealment of good returns, and his fear to spend his savings in improving his farm. Hence, too, the incessant recurrence of the deadliest epidemics, which made of Ireland the land of typhus fever, as Egypt was that of the plague.

To the native Irish the English oligarchy appeared not as kind proprietors, whom residence and a common faith, long possession and hereditary affection, united with the tenantry, but as men of a different race and creed, who had acquired the island by arms, rapine, and chicane, and derived revenues from it through extortionate agents.

This state of society, as a whole, was what ought not to be endured; and the English were conscious of it. The common law respects the right of self-defence; yet the Irish Catholics, or popish recusants as they were called, were, by one universal prohibition, forbidden to use or keep any kind of weapons whatsoever, under penalties which the crown could not remit. Any two justices might enter a house and search for arms, or summon any person whomsoever, and tender him an oath, of which the repeated refusal was punishable as treason.

The industry of the Irish within their kingdom was prohibited or repressed by law, and then they were calumniated as naturally idle; their savings could not be invested on equal terms in trade, manufactures, or real property, and they were called improvident; the gates of learning were shut on them, and they were derided as ignorant. In the midst of privations they were cheerful. Suffering for generations under acts which offered bribes to treachery, their integrity was not debauched; no son rose against his father, no friend betrayed his friend. Fidelity to their religion, chastity, and respect for the ties of family, remained characteristics of the down-trodden race.

Ireland and America, in so far as both were oppressed by the commercial monopoly of England, had a common cause; and, while the penal statutes against the Catholics did not affect the Anglo-Irish, they suffered equally with the native Irish from the mercantile system. The restrictions of the acts of trade extended not to America only, but to the sister kingdom. It had harbors, but it could not send a sail across the Atlantic; nor receive sugar, or coffee, or other colonial produce, but from England; nor ship directly to the colonies, even in English vessels, anything but "servants and horses and victuals," and at last linens; and this classing together of "servants and horses" as articles of the export trade gave the sanction of the British parliament to traffic in bond-servants.

Its great staple was wool; its most important natural manufacture was the woollen. "I shall do all that lies in my power to discourage the woollen manufactures of Ireland," promised William of Orange. The exportation of Irish woollens to the colonies and to foreign countries was prohibited; and restrictive laws so interfered with the manufacture that Irishmen would probably not have been allowed to wear coats of their own fabric.

In the course of years the "English colonists" themselves began to be domiciliated in Ireland; and, with the feeling that the country in which they dwelt was their home, there grew up discontent that it continued to be treated as a conquered country. Proceeding by insensible degrees, they at length maintained openly the legislative equality of the two kingdoms. In 1692, the Irish house of commons claimed "the sole and undoubted right to prepare and resolve the means of raising money." In 1698, Molyneux, an Irish Protestant, and member for the university of Dublin, asserted through the press the perfect and reciprocal independence of the Irish and English parliaments; that Ireland was not bound by the acts of a legislative body in which it was not represented. Two replies were written to the tract, which was formally condemned by the English house of commons. When, in 1719, the Irish house of lords denied the judicial power of the house of lords of Great Britain for Ireland, the British parliament, making a precedent for all its outlying dominions, enacted that "the king, with the consent of the parliament of Great Britain, had, hath, and of right ought to have, full power and authority to make laws and statutes of force to bind the people and the kingdom of Ireland."

But the opposite opinion was held with unabated vigor by the Anglo-Irish statesmen. The people set the example of resisting English laws by voluntary agreements to abstain from using English manufactures, and the patriot party acquired strength and skill just at the time when the British parliament provoked the American colonies to deny its power.

But, besides the conforming Protestant population, there was in Ireland another class of Protestants who shared in some degree the disqualifications of the Catholics. To Queen Anne's bill for preventing the further growth of popery a clause was added in England and ratified by the Irish parliament that none should be capable of any public employment, or of being in the magistracy of any city, who did not receive the sacrament according to the English test act, thus disfranchising all Presbyterians. At home, where the Scottish nation enjoyed its own religion, the people were loyal; in Ireland, the disfranchised Scotch Presbyterians, who still drew their ideas of Christian government from the Westminster Confession, began to believe that they were under no religious obligation to render obedience to Britain. They could not enter the Irish parliament to strengthen the hands of the patriot party; nor were they taught by their faith to submit in patience, like the Catholic Irish. Had all Ireland resembled them, it could not have been kept in subjection. But what could be done by unorganized men, constituting only about a tenth of the people, in the land in which they were but sojourners? They were willing to quit a soil which was endeared to them by no traditions; and the American colonies opened their arms to receive them. They began to change their abode as soon as they felt oppression; and every successive period of discontent swelled the tide of emigrants. Just after the peace of Paris, "the Heart of Oak" Protestants of Ulster, weary of strife with their landlords, came over in great numbers; and settlements on the Catawba, in South Carolina, dated from that epoch. At different times in the eighteenth century some few found homes in New England; but they were most numerous south of New York, from New Jersey to Georgia. In Pennsylvania they peopled many counties, till, in public life, they balanced the influence of the Quakers. In Virginia they went up the valley of the Shenandoah; and they extended themselves along the tributaries of the Catawba, in the uplands of North Carolina. Their training in Ireland had kept the spirit of liberty and the readiness to resist unjust government as fresh in their hearts as though they had just been listening to the preachings of Knox or musing over the political creed of the Westminster assembly. They brought to America no loyal love for England; and their experience and their religion bade them meet oppression with resistance.

## CHAPTER III.

CHARLES TOWNSHEND PLEDGES THE MINISTRY OF BUTE TO TAX AMERICA BY THE BRITISH PARLIAMENT, AND RESIGNS.

FEBRUARY–MAY 1763.

AT the peace of 1763, the fame of England was exalted throughout Europe above all other nations. She had triumphed over those whom she called her hereditary enemies, and retained half a continent as the monument of her victories. Her American dominions stretched without dispute from the Atlantic to the Mississippi, from the Gulf of Mexico to Hudson's Bay; and in her older possessions that dominion was rooted in the affections of their people and their possession of as free institutions and as ample powers of local legislation as were enjoyed in the land from which they sprung. British statesmen might well be inflamed with the desire of uniting the mother country and her transatlantic empire by indissoluble bonds of common interest and liberty. But for many years the board of trade had looked forward to the end of the war as the appointed time when the colonies were to feel the superiority of the parent land. In February 1763, thirteen days after the ratification of the peace, the earl of Bute, having the full concurrence of the king, made the change which had long been expected; and Charles Townshend entered upon the office of first lord of trade, with larger powers than had ever been exercised by any of his predecessors except Halifax, and a seat in the cabinet.

In the ministry, there was Bute, its chief, who prided himself on the peace, and shared the belief in the necessity of bringing the colonies into order. As the head of the treasury, he was answerable for every measure connected with the finances; and his feebleness as a man of business left much to his indefatigable private secretary. There was Mansfield, who had boasted publicly of his early determination never to engage in public life "but upon whig principles;" and, in conformity to them, had asserted that an act of parliament in Great Britain could alone prescribe rules for the reduction of refractory colonial assemblies. There was George Grenville, then first lord of the admiralty, bred to the law, and implicitly upholding the supreme and universal authority of the British legislature. There was Bedford, absent from England at the moment, but, through his friends, applauding the new colonial system which he had long ago labored to introduce. There was Halifax, heretofore baffled by the colonies, and held in check by Pitt, willing to give effect to his long-cherished opinions of British omnipotence. There was the self-willed, hot-tempered Egremont, using the patronage of his office to enrich his family and friends; the same who had menaced Maryland, Pennsylvania, and North Carolina; obstinate and impatient of contradiction, ignorant of business, and disposed to cruelty in defence of authority.

To these was now added Charles Townshend, who was selected for the administration of the colonies. About his schemes there was no disguise. No man in the house of commons was thought to know America so well; no one was so resolved on making a thorough change in its constitutions and government. Halifax and Townshend, in 1753, had tried to establish order in the New World by the prerogative, and had signally failed; the new system was to be derived from the transcendental power of the British parliament. America, which had been the occasion of the war, became at the peace the great subject of consideration; and the minister who was charged with its government took the lead in the cabinet and in the house of commons.

The total remittance of revenue from all the colonies, on an average of thirty years, had not reached nineteen hundred pounds a year, and the establishment of officers necessary to collect that pittance cost more than seven thousand pounds a year. The object was now a substantial American revenue, to be disposed of under the sign manual of the king. The ministry would tolerate no further "the disobedience of long time to royal instructions," nor bear with the claim of "the lower houses of provincial assemblies" to the right of deliberating on their votes of supply, like the parliament of Great Britain. It was announced "by authority" that there were to be "no more requisitions from the king," but, instead of them, an immediate taxation of the colonies by the British legislature.

The first charge upon that revenue was to be the civil list, that all the royal officers in America, the judges in every court not less than the executive, might be superior to the assemblies, and dependent on the king's pleasure alone for their appointment to office, their continuance in it, and the amount and payment of their emoluments; so that the corps of persons in the public employ might be a civil garrison, set to sustain the authority of Great Britain.

The charters were obstacles, which, in the opinion of Charles Townshend, should give way to one uniform system of government. The republics of Connecticut and Rhode Island, which Clarendon had cherished and every ministry of Charles II. had spared, were no longer safe. By a new territorial arrangement of provinces, Massachusetts was to be curtailed, as well as made more dependent on the king.

This arbitrary policy required an American standing army, to be maintained by those whom it was to oppress. To complete the system, the navigation acts were to be strictly enforced. These most eventful measures were entered upon without any observation on the part of the historians and writers of memoirs of the hour. The ministry itself was not aware of what it was doing.

The first opposition proceeded from the general assembly of New York. In the spirit of loyalty and the language of reverence, they pleaded with the king concerning the colonial court of judicature, which exercised the ample authorities of the two great courts of king's bench and common pleas, and also of the barons of the exchequer. They represented that this plenitude of uncontrolled power in persons who could not be impeached in the colony, and who, holding their offices during pleasure, were subject to the influence of governors, was to them an object of terror; and, from tenderness to the security of their lives, rights, and liberties, as well as fortunes, they prayed anxiously for leave to establish by law the independence and support of so important a tribunal. They produced, as an irrefragable argument, the example given in England after the accession of King William III.; they quoted the declaration of the present king himself, that he "looked upon the independency and uprightness of the judges as essential to the impartial administration of justice, one of the best securities to the rights and liberties of the subject, and as most conducive to the honor of the crown;" and they expressed confidence in his undiscriminating liberality to all his good subjects, whether at home or abroad. But the treasury board, at which Lord North had a seat, decided that the commission of the chief justice of New York, the amount of his salary, and the payment of it, should be at the king's pleasure. The system was to be universally introduced, and the judiciary of a continent to be placed for political purposes in dependence on the crown.

In March, Welbore Ellis, the successor of Charles Townshend as secretary at war, presented the army estimates for the year, including the proposition of twenty regiments for America. The country members would have grudged the expense; but Charles Townshend explained that these regiments were, for the first year only, to be supported by England, and ever after by the colonies themselves. With Edmund Burke in the gallery for one of his hearers, he dazzled country gentlemen by playing before their eyes the image of a revenue to be raised in America. The house of commons listened with complacency to a scheme which, at the expense of the colonies, would give twenty new places of colonels, that might be filled by members of their own body. On the report to the house, Pitt wished that more troops had been retained in service; and he called "the peace hollow and insecure, a mere armed truce for ten years." His support prevented opposition to the estimates.

Two days after, on the ninth of March 1763, Charles Townshend, from a committee of which Lord North was a member, brought forward a part of the scheme for raising a revenue in America by act of parliament. The existing duty on the trade of the continental colonies with the French and

Spanish islands was prohibitory, and had been regularly evaded by a treaty of connivance between the merchants on the one side and the custom-house officers and their English patrons on the other; for the custom-house officers were "quartered upon" by those through whom they gained their places. The minister proposed to reduce the duty and enforce its collection. "Short as the term was, it seemed probable that he would carry it through before the rising of parliament." A stamp act and other taxes were to follow.

At the same time, the usual "compensation for the expenses of the several provinces," according to their "active vigor and strenuous efforts," was voted without curtailment, and amounted to more than seven hundred thousand dollars. The appropriation was the most formal recognition that the colonies, even in the year when the war was carried on outside of their limits and remote from their frontier, had contributed to the common cause more than their equitable proportion.

Just then the people of Boston held their March town meeting in 1763. "We in America," said Otis, on being chosen its moderator, "have abundant reason to rejoice. The heathen are driven out and the Canadians conquered. The British dominion now extends from sea to sea, and from the great rivers to the ends of the earth. Liberty and knowledge, civil and religious, will be co-extended, improved, and preserved to the latest posterity. No constitution of government has appeared in the world so admirably adapted to these great purposes as that of Great Britain. Every British subject in America is, of common right, by act of parliament, and by the laws of God and nature, entitled to all the essential privileges of Britons. By particular charters, particular privileges are justly granted, in consideration of undertaking to begin so glorious an empire as British America. Some weak and wicked minds have endeavored to infuse jealousies with regard to the colonies; the true interests of Great Britain and her plantations are mutual; what God in his providence has united let no man dare attempt to pull asunder."

Meantime, Grenville would not be outdone by Townshend in zeal for British interests. He worshipped the navigation act as the palladium of his country's greatness; and regarded connivance at the breaches of it by the overflowing commerce of the colonies "with an exquisite jealousy." Placed at the head of the admiralty, he united his official influence, his knowledge of the law, and his place as a leader in the house of commons, to restrain American intercourse by grants of new powers to vice-admiralty courts, and by a curiously devised system, which should bribe the whole navy of England to make war on colonial trade. March had not ended when a bill was brought in giving authority to employ the ships, seamen, and officers of the navy as custom-house officers and informers. The measure was Grenville's own, and it was rapidly carried through; so that in three weeks it became lawful, from the mouth of the St. Lawrence to Cape Florida, for each commander of an armed vessel to stop and examine, and, in case of suspicion, seize any merchant ship approaching the colonies; while avarice was stimulated to do so by the hope of large emoluments, to be awarded by the vice-admiralty courts.

The supplies voted by the British parliament for the first year of peace amounted to seventy millions of dollars; the public charges pressed heavily on the lands and the industry of England, and additional sources of revenue were required. The ministry proposed and carried an excise on cider and perry, by its nature affecting only the few counties where the apple was much cultivated. Pitt opposed the tax as "intolerable," and brought ridicule upon Grenville; the cider counties were in a flame; the city of London, proceeding beyond all precedent, petitioned commons, lords, and king against the measure; the cities of Exeter and Worcester instructed their members to oppose it; the house of lords divided upon it; and two protests against it appeared on their journals. An English tax, which came afterward to be regarded as proper, met with turbulent resistance; no one uttered a word for America. The bill for raising a colonial revenue was quietly read twice, and committed; but on the twenty-ninth of March it was postponed; for Charles Townshend, seeing that the ministry was crumbling, made a timely retreat from the cabinet. A strong party was forming against the earl of Bute, whose majority in "the king's parliament" was broken. Nearly every member of the cabinet which he had formed was secretly or openly against him. "The ground I tread upon," said he, "is hollow;" and he might well be "afraid of falling." By his instances to retire, made a half year before, the king had been so troubled that he frequently sat for hours together leaning his head upon his arm without speaking; and when he consented to a change, it was on condition that in the new administration there should be no chief minister.

For a moment Grenville, to whom the treasury and the exchequer were offered, affected to be coy; and then gratefully accepted the "high and important situation" destined for him by the goodness of his sovereign and Lord Bute's friendship, promising not "to put any negative" upon those whom the king might approve as his colleagues in the ministry.

Bute next turned to Bedford, announcing the king's "abiding determination never to suffer those ministers of the late reign who had attempted to fetter and enslave him to come into his service while he lived to hold the sceptre." "Shall titles and estates," he continued, "and names like a Pitt, that impose on an ignorant populace, give this prince the law?" And he solicited Bedford to accept the post of president of the council, promising, in that case, the privy seal to Bedford's brother-in-law, Lord Gower.

While the answer was waited for, the youthful monarch in April confided the executive powers of government to a triumvirate, consisting of Grenville, Egremont, and Halifax. After making this arrangement, Bute resigned, having established, by act of parliament, a standing army in America, and bequeathing to his successor his pledge to the house of commons to provide for the support of that army, after the current year, by taxes on America.

George III. was revered by his courtiers as the ideal of a patriot king. The watchword of his friends was "a coalition of parties," in the spirit of dutiful obedience, so that he might himself select his ministers from among them all; and he came to the throne resolved "to begin to govern as soon as he should begin to reign."

Grenville, whose manners were never agreeable to the king, was chosen to take the place of Bute in the ministry, because, from his position, he seemed dependent on the court.

He remarked to the king that he had no party. Moreover, he loved office, loved it for its emoluments, and loved it inordinately, but not as a venal adventurer; and, in his quest of fortune, he retained the austerity that marked his character. His desire was for solid and sure places, a tellership in the exchequer or the profits of a light-house, the rich sinecures which English law and usages tolerated; and, even in the indulgence of his strongest passion, he kept a good name as a model of integrity and the enemy of corruption. It was his habit to hoard all his emoluments from public office; and he represented his parsimony as disinterestedness because it only enriched his children.

His personal deportment was formal and forbidding; and his apathy in respect of pleasure made him appear a paragon of sanctity. Bishops praised him for his constant attendance at the Sunday's morning service. He was not cruel; but the coldness of his nature left him incapable of compassion. He was not vengeful; when evil thoughts toward others rose up within him, they chiefly served to embitter his own peace.

Nor was he one of the king's friends, nor did he seek advancement by unworthy flattery of the court. A good lawyer and trained in the best liberal school of his day, it was ever his pride to be esteemed a sound whig, making the test of his consistency his unchangeable belief in the supremacy of parliament. It was by a thorough knowledge of the constitution of parliament and an indefatigable attention to all its business, that he rose to eminence through the laborious gradations of public service. Just before his death, after a service in the house of commons of about thirty years, he said, with pride, that to that house he owed all his distinction.

His self-conceit ascribed all his eminence to his own merits, which he never regarded as too highly rewarded. Gratitude, therefore, found no place in his nature; and he was so much like the bird that croaks while enjoying the fullest meal, that toward those who had benefited him most there remained in his heart something like a reproach for their not having succeeded in doing more. Yet Grenville wanted the elements of true statesmanship. His nature inclined him not to originate measures, but to amend and alter and regulate. He had neither salient traits, nor general comprehensiveness; neither the warm imagination which can arrange and vivify various masses of business, nor the sagacity which penetrates the springs of public action and foresees the consequences of measures. In a word, he was a dull, plodding pedant in politics; a painstaking, exact man of business. In his frequent, long, and tedious speeches, a trope rarely passed his lips; but he abounded in repetitions and self-justification. He would have made a laborious and an upright judge, or an impartial speaker of the house of commons; but, in an administration without a head, he could be no more than the patient and methodical executor of plans "devolved" upon him. The stubbornness with which he adhered to them sprung from pride and obstinacy, not from a commanding will, which never belonged to him.

With Bute's office, the new minister inherited the services of his own former *protégé*, Charles Jenkinson, a man of rare ability, who now became the principal secretary of the treasury. An Oxford scholar, without fortune, and at first destined for the church, he entered life on the side of the whigs; but, using an opportunity of becoming known to George III. while prince of Wales, devoted himself to his service. He remained always a friend and a favorite of the king. Engaged in the most important scenes of political action, and rising to the highest stations, he moved as noiselessly as a shadow; and history was hardly aware of his presence. He had the singular talent of conducting delicate and disagreeable personal negotiations so as to retain the friendship of those whom he seemed commissioned to wound. Except at first, when still very poor, he never showed a wish for office, but waited till it seemed to seek him. His old age was one of dignity, cheered by the unabated regard of the king, the political success of one son, and the affectionate companionship of another. The error of his life was his conduct respecting America; the thorough measures which Charles Townshend rashly counselled, which George Grenville feebly resisted, Jenkinson carried forward with quiet decision.

Townshend, while he took care to retain the favor of the king, declined to act under George Grenville. The duke of Bedford advised a return to the old whig aristocracy. The scheme of taxing the colonies was laid over for the next session; but the king, each house of parliament, and nearly everybody in Great Britain, wished to throw a part of the public burdens on the increasing opulence of the New World.

In the midst of the confusion, Grenville set about confirming himself in power by diligence in the public business. He meant well for the public service, and was certainly indefatigable. For one of the joint secretaries of the treasury he selected an able and sensible lawyer, Thomas Whately. For his secretary as chancellor of the exchequer he chose Richard Jackson, and the choice is strong proof that, though he entered upon his task in ignorance of the colonies, yet his intentions were fair; for Jackson was a liberal member of the house of commons, a good lawyer, not eager to increase his affluent fortune, frank, independent, and abhorring intrigue. He was, moreover, well acquainted with the state of America, and exercised a sound judgment on questions of colonial administration. His excellent character led Connecticut and Pennsylvania to make him their agent, and he was always able to combine affection for England with fidelity to his American employers.

To a mind like Grenville's, the protective system had irresistible attractions. He saw in trade the foundation of the wealth and power of his country, and he wished by regulations and restrictions to advance the commerce which really owed its superiority to the greater liberty of the English people. He prepared to recharter the bank of England; to connect it still more closely with the funding system; to sustain the credit of the merchants under the revulsion consequent on peace; to increase the public revenue, and to expend it with frugality. America, with its new acquisitions, Florida, the valley of the Mississippi, and Canada, lay invitingly before him. The enforcing of the acts of trade was peculiarly his own policy, and was the first leading feature of his administration. An American revenue was his second great object, and it was his purpose so to divide the public burdens between England and America, as to diminish the motive to emigrate from Great Britain and Ireland.

In less than a month after Bute's retirement, Egremont

asked the advice of the lords of trade on the organization of governments in the newly acquired territories, the military force to be kept up in America, and in what mode least burdensome and most palatable to the colonies they could contribute toward the support of the additional expense which must attend their civil and military establishment.

The head of the board of trade was the earl of Shelburne. He was at that time not quite six-and-twenty years old, had served creditably in the seven years' war as a volunteer, and, on his return, was appointed aide-de-camp to George III.

While his report was waited for, Grenville, through Charles Jenkinson, began his system of retrenchment by an order to the commander-in-chief of the forces in America to withdraw the allowance for victualling the regiments stationed in the cultivated parts of America. This expense was to be met in future by the colonies.

## CHAPTER IV.

PONTIAC'S WAR. THE TRIUMVIRATE MINISTRY CONTINUED.

MAY–SEPTEMBER 1763.

THE western territory, of which England believed itself in possession, was one continuous forest, interrupted only by rocks or prairies or waters, or an Indian cleared field for maize. The English came into the illimitable waste as conquerors, and here and there in the solitudes, all the way from Niagara to the falls of the St. Mary and the banks of the St. Joseph's, a log fort with a picketed enclosure was the emblem of their pretensions. In their haste to supplant the French, they were blind to danger, their posts were often left dependent on the Indians for supplies, and were too remote from each other for mutual support. The smaller garrisons consisted only of an ensign, a sergeant, and perhaps fourteen men. Yet, feeble as they were, they alarmed the red man, for they implied the design to occupy the country which for ages had been his own. His canoe could no longer quiver on the eddying current of the St. Mary's, or pass into the clear waters of Lake Huron, or paddle through the strait that connects Lakes Huron and Erie, or be carried across the portage to the waters of the Ohio, without passing the British flag. What right to his forest could the English derive from victories over the French? The native race must vindicate their right to their own heritage.

The conspiracy began with the lower nations, and spread from the Niagara and the Alleghanies to the Mississippi and Lake Superior. It was discovered in March 1763, by the officer in command at Miami, who, "after a long and troublesome" interview, obtained from the Miami chiefs the bloody belt, which was then in the village and was to have been sent forward to the tribes on the Wabash.

On receiving the news, Amherst prepared re-enforcements, and threatened that the mischief should end in the destruction of the Indians. But Pontiac, "the king and lord of all the North-west"—a Catawba prisoner, as is said, adopted into the clan of the Ottawas and elected their chief; respected, and in a manner adored, by all the nations around him; a man of "integrity and humanity" according to the morals of the wilderness; dauntless and fertile in resources—persevered in the design of recovering the land of the Senecas and all west of it by a confederacy of Indian nations.

Of the remote north-western settlements, Detroit was the largest and the most important. The deep, majestic river, more than a half mile broad, carried its vast flood calmly and noiselessly between strait and well-defined banks through a country whose rising grounds and meadows, woodlands festooned with prolific vines, plains yielding maize and wheat and every product of the garden, were so mingled together that nothing was left to desire. The climate was mild and the air salubrious. The forests were a natural park, stocked with buffaloes, deer, quails, partridges, and wild turkeys. Waterfowl of delicious flavor hovered along its streams, which invited the angler by a great variety of fish, especially the white fish, the richest of them all. The cheerful region attracted alike white men and savages. About sixty French families, seated on both banks of the river, occupied farms, which were about three or four acres wide upon the river and eighty acres deep; by light labor as herdsmen and with the plough they drew abundance from the soil, and traffic with the Indians brought them affluence.

The English fort, of which Gladwin was the commander, was a stockade, about twenty feet high and twelve hundred yards in circumference, enclosing, perhaps, eighty houses. It stood within the limits of the present city, on the river bank, commanding a wide prospect for nine miles above and below; and was garrisoned by about one hundred and twenty men and eight officers. Two slightly armed vessels lay in the river. The nation of the Pottawatomies dwelt about a mile below the fort; on the Canadian side the cabins of the Wyandots were a little below the English; of the Ottawas, five miles above them.

After a preliminary visit to lull suspicion, Pontiac came, on the seventh of May 1763, with about three hundred warriors, carrying arms under their blankets. While they were seated in council he was to speak, holding a belt white on one side and green on the other; and his turning the belt was to be the signal for beginning a general massacre. But Gladwin, aware of his purpose, was so well on his guard and took such precautions that the interview passed off without harm.

On the morning of the same day, an English party who were sounding the entrance of Lake Huron were killed. On the afternoon of the ninth began the siege of the garrison, which had not on hand provisions enough for three weeks. "The first man that shall bring them provisions, or anything else, shall suffer death:" such was Pontiac's proclamation. On the tenth the fort was summoned to capitulate. Not till after Gladwin had obtained the needed supplies did he break off the parley. The garrison was in high spirits, though outnumbered by the besiegers fivefold.

The rovers of the wilderness, though unused to enterprises requiring time and assiduity, blockaded the place closely. The French inhabitants were divided in their sympathies. Pontiac made one of them his secretary, and supplied his wants by requisitions upon them all. Emissaries were sent even to Illinois to ask for a French officer to conduct the siege. The savages of the West took part in the hatred of the English. "Be of good cheer, my father," were the words of one tribe after another to the commander at Fort Chartres; "do not desert thy children: the English shall never come here so long as a red man lives." But the French officers in Illinois desired to execute the treaty of Paris with loyalty.

On the sixteenth, a party of Indians appeared before the gate of Fort Sandusky. Ensign Paulli, the commander, admitted seven of them—four Hurons and three Ottawas—as old acquaintances and friends. They sat smoking, till one of them raised his head as a signal, on which the two that were next Paulli seized and tied him fast without uttering a word.

As they carried him out of the room he saw the garrison, lying one here and one there; the sergeant, in his garden, which he had been planting. The traders were killed, and their stores plundered. Paulli was taken to Detroit. On the twenty-fifth, a party of Pottawatomies from Detroit appeared near the fort at the mouth of the St. Joseph's, saying: "We are come to see our relatives and wish them a good morning." A cry was suddenly heard in the barracks; "in about two minutes," Schlosser, the commanding officer, was seized, and eleven out of a garrison of fourteen were massacred.

At Fort Pitt twenty boats had been launched to bear the English to the country of the Illinois. On the twenty-seventh, bands of Mingoes and Delawares, the bitterest enemies of the English, exchanged with English traders three hundred pounds' worth of skins for powder and lead, and then suddenly went away, as if to intercept any attempt to descend the river. An hour before midnight of the same day the chiefs of the Delawares sent a message to Fort Pitt recounting the attacks on the English posts, and added: "A party is coming to cut you and your people off; make the best of your way to some place of safety, as we would not desire to see you killed in our town." The next day Indians scalped a family, sparing neither woman nor child, and left a tomahawk in sign of war. The passes to the eastward were so watched that it was difficult to keep up any intercourse, while the woods resounded with the wild halloos which announced successive murders.

Near Fort Wayne, just where the canal which unites the waters of Lake Erie and the Wabash now leaves the waters of the Maumee, stood Fort Miami. On the twenty-seventh, Holmes, its commander, knowing that the fort at Detroit had been attacked, put his men on their guard; but an Indian woman came to him, saying that a squaw in a cabin, but three hundred yards off, was ill, and wished him to bleed her. He went on the errand of mercy, and was shot on the way. The sergeant who followed was taken prisoner; the soldiers, nine in number, capitulated.

On the thirtieth, the besieged at Detroit saw a fleet of boats sweeping round the point. They flocked to the bastions to welcome friends; but the death-cry of the Indians announced that an English detachment from Niagara had, two nights previously, been attacked on the beach near the mouth of Detroit river and utterly defeated, a part turning back to Niagara, the larger part falling into the hands of the savages.

At eight o'clock in the night of the last day of May the war-belt reached the Indian village near Fort Ouatanon, just below Lafayette, in Indiana; the next morning the commander was lured into an Indian cabin and bound, and his garrison surrendered. The French, moving the victors to clemency by gifts of wampum, received the prisoners into their houses.

West of the straits at Michilimackinac, two acres on the main land, enclosed with pickets, gave room for the cabins of a few traders, and a fort with a garrison of about forty souls. On the second day of June, the Ojibwas, who dwelt on a plain near the fort, assembled to play ball. In this game each man has a bat curved like a crosier, and ending in a racket. Posts are planted apart on the open prairie. At the beginning of the game the ball is placed midway between the goals. The eyes of the players flash, their cheeks glow. A blow is struck; all crowd with merry yells to renew it, the fleetest in advance now driving the ball home, now sending it sideways, with one unceasing passionate pursuit. On that day the squaws entered the fort, and remained there. Etherington, the commander, with one of his lieutenants, stood outside of the gate, watching the game, fearing nothing. The Indians had played from morning till noon, when, throwing the ball close to the gate, they came behind the two officers, and seized and carried them into the woods, while the rest rushed into the fort, snatched their hatchets, which their squaws had kept hidden under their blankets, and in an instant killed an officer, a trader, and fifteen men. The rest of the garrison and all the English traders were made prisoners, and robbed of everything they had; but the French traders were not harmed.

On the eighteenth, the fort of Le Bœuf was attacked. Its gallant officer kept off the enemy, till at midnight the Indians succeeded in setting the block-house on fire; but he escaped with his garrison into the woods, while the enemy believed them buried in the flames. The fort at Venango was consumed, never to be rebuilt; and not one of its garrison was left alive to tell the story of its destruction. Presque Isle, now Erie, had a garrison of four-and-twenty men, and could most easily have been relieved. On the twenty-second, after a two days' defence, the commander, out of his senses with terror, capitulated, giving up the sole chance of saving them. He, with a few others, was carried in triumph to Detroit.

Nor was it the garrisoned stockades only that encountered the fury of the savages. They struck down more than a hundred traders in the woods, scalping every one of them, quaffing their blood, horribly mutilating their bodies. They prowled round the cabins on the border; and their tomahawks fell alike on the laborer in the field and the child in the cradle. They menaced Fort Ligonier, the outpost of Fort Pitt; they passed the mountains, and spread death even to Bedford. About five hundred families, from the frontiers of Maryland and Virginia, fled before them to Winchester.

In Virginia, nearly a thousand volunteers, at the call of the lieutenant-governor, hastened to Fort Cumberland and to the borders; and the lieutenant-governor of Maryland gave aid. The legislature of Pennsylvania was ready to arm and pay the farmers and reapers on the frontier, to the number of seven hundred, as a resident force for the protection of the country, but refused to place them under the orders of the British general; and the consequent invectives of officers of the army brought upon Pennsylvania once more the censure of the king for its "supine and neglectful conduct," and confirmed the purpose of keeping up a regular army in America through taxes by parliament.

The fortifications of Fort Pitt had never been finished, and heavy rains had opened it on three sides; but the brave Ecuyer, its commander, with no engineer or artificers except a few shipwrights, raised a rampart of logs around the fort above the old one, palisaded the interior area, and took all possible precautions. The post had a garrison of three hundred and thirty men, and gave asylum to more than two hundred women and children.

On the twenty-first, a large party of Indians made a vigorous though fruitless assault on Fort Ligonier. The next day Fort Pitt was approached by savages, who killed one man and wounded another. In the night of the twenty-third, they reconnoitred the fort, and in a conference, held after midnight, a second time "warned them to go home." "All your strong places in our country from this eastward," said Turtle's Heart, a principal warrior of the Delawares, "are burnt and cut off. Six different nations are ready to attack you. They have agreed to permit you and your people to pass safely. Therefore, brother, we desire you to set off to-morrow, as great numbers of Indians are coming here, and after two days we shall not be able to do anything with them for you."

The commander gave for answer that three English armies were on the march to the frontier of Virginia, to Fort Pitt, and to the North-west.

A schooner, with a re-enforcement of sixty men, reached Detroit in June. At daybreak of the twenty-ninth of July, the garrison was gladdened by the arrival of Dalyell, an aide-de-camp to Amherst, with a detachment of two hundred and sixty men, who had passed the besiegers under cover of the night. After but one day's rest, Dalyell proposed a midnight sally. He was cautioned that the Indians were on their guard; but the express instructions of Amherst were on his side. Gladwin reluctantly yielded; and, half an hour before three o'clock on the last morning of July, Dalyell marched out with two hundred and forty-seven chosen men, while two boats followed along shore to protect the party and bring off the wounded and dead. They proceeded in double file, along the great road by the river side, for a mile and a half, then, forming into platoons, they advanced a half mile farther, when they suddenly received from the Indians a destructive fire, and could escape only by an inglorious retreat. Twenty of the English were killed and forty-two wounded, leaving to a rivulet the name of The Bloody Run. Dalyell fell while attempting to bring off the wounded; his scalp became one more ornament to the red man's wigwam.

This victory encouraged the confederates; two hundred recruits joined the forces of Pontiac, and the siege of Detroit was kept up by bands of more than a thousand men.

In July, the Delawares and Shawnees, in the name of their own tribes and of the north-western Indians, for the third time summoned the garrison of Fort Pitt to retire. "Brothers," said they, "you have towns and places of your own. You know this is our country. All the nations over the lakes are soon to be on their way to the forks of the Ohio. Here is their wampum. If you return quietly to your wise men, this is the farthest they will go. If not, see what will be the consequence."

The next day, Ecuyer gave answer: "You suffered the French to settle in the heart of your country; why would you turn us out of it now? I will not abandon this post; I have warriors, provisions, and ammunition in plenty to defend it three years against all the Indians in the woods. Go home to your towns, and take care of your women and children."

No sooner was this answer received than the united forces of the Delawares, Shawnees, Wyandots, and Mingoes beset the fort, and, from such shelter as they could find or make, they kept up a discharge of musketry and threw fire arrows, though with little injury to the English, who were under cover. This continued through July, when they suddenly vanished.

At that time Lieutenant-Colonel Henry Bouquet, a Swiss by birth, in the British service, an officer of large experience and superior merit, who had the command at Philadelphia, was making his way to relieve Fort Pitt, with about five hundred men, chiefly Highlanders, driving a hundred beeves and twice that number of sheep, with powder, flour, and provisions on pack-horses and in wagons drawn by oxen. Between Carlisle and Bedford they passed the ruins of mills, deserted cabins, fields ripe for the harvest but without a reaper, and everywhere the signs of death.

The commander at Ligonier could give no intelligence of the condition of Fort Pitt; all the expresses for the previous month had been killed or forced to return. Leaving the wagons at Ligonier, Bouquet, on the fourth, proceeded with the troops and about three hundred and fifty pack-horses. At one o'clock on the fifth, the savages attacked the advance-guard; but two companies of Highlanders drove them from their ambuscade. The savages returned, and were again repelled; but grew to be so numerous that they at last hung on every side of the English, who would have been cut to pieces but for their cool behavior. Night intervened, during which the English remained on Edge Hill, a mile to the east of Bushy Run.

All that night hope cheered the red men. Morning dawned only to show the English party that they were encircled. If they should advance, their convoy and wounded men would have fallen a prey to the enemy; if they should remain quiet, they would be picked off one by one. With happy sagacity, Bouquet feigned a retreat. The red men hurried to charge with the utmost daring, when two Highland companies, that had lain hid, fell upon their flank; others met them in front, and put them to flight. But Bouquet in the two actions lost, in killed and wounded, about one fourth of his men, and almost all his horses, so that he was obliged to destroy his stores. The following night the English encamped at Bushy Run, and in four days more arrived at Pittsburg.

Before news of this last conflict with the red men could reach New York, the wrath of Amherst against "the bloody villains" had burst all bounds. His orders were: "I will have no accommodation with the savages until they have felt our just revenge. I would have every measure taken for their destruction." "Whoever kills Pontiac shall receive from me a reward of one hundred pounds." "Take no prisoners, but put to death all that fall into your hands."

Had this spirit prevailed, the war would have become an endless series of alternate murders, in which the more experienced Indian excelled the white man. In September, the Senecas, against whom Amherst had specially directed unsparing hostilities, lay in ambush for one of his convoys about three miles below Niagara Falls; and, on its passing over the carrying-place, fell upon it with such suddenness and vigor that but eight wounded men escaped with their lives, while seventy-two were victims to the scalping-knife.

The first effective measures toward a general pacification proceeded from the French in Illinois. De Neyon, the French officer at Fort Chartres, sent belts and messages and peace-pipes to all parts of the continent, exhorting the many nations of savages to bury the hatchet and take the English by the hand, for a representative of the king of France would be seen among them nevermore.

VOL. III.-

## CHAPTER V.

THE TREASURY ENTER A MINUTE FOR AN AMERICAN STAMP-TAX. MINISTRY OF GRENVILLE.

MAY–SEPTEMBER 1763.

THE savage warfare was relentlessly raging when, in May and June, the young statesman, to whom the forms of office had referred the subject of the colonies, was devising plans for organizing governments in the newly acquired territories. Of an Irish family, and an Irish as well as an English peer, Shelburne naturally inclined to limit the legislative authority of the parliament of Great Britain over the outlying dominions of the crown. The world gave him credit for great abilities; and, except the lawyers who had been raised to the peerage, he was the best speaker in the house of lords.

For the eastern boundary of New England, Shelburne hesitated between the Penobscot and the St. Croix; on the north-east, he adopted the crest of the water-shed dividing the streams tributary to the St. Lawrence river from those flowing into the Bay of Fundy, or the Atlantic Ocean, or the Gulf of St. Lawrence, south of Cape Rosières, designating the line on a map, which is still preserved. At the south, the boundary of Georgia was extended to its present limit.

Of Canada, General Murray proposed to make a military colony, and to include within it the lands on the Ohio and the lakes, in order to overawe the older colonies. Shelburne, in a more liberal spirit, desired to restrict that province by a line drawn from the intersection of the parallel of forty-five degrees north with the St. Lawrence to the east end of Lake Nipising. This advice was rejected by Egremont, who insisted on a plan like that of Murray; but Shelburne enforced his own opinion, and the new government did not include the domain, which was to be reserved for the Indians.

It fell to Jenkinson, the principal secretary of the treasury, to prepare the plans for taxing America. In addition to the numerous public reports and correspondence, information was sought from men who were held in England worthy of trust in all situations, and the exaggerated accounts given by the officers who had been employed in America dispelled every doubt of its ability to bear a part in the national expenses. Ellis, for several years governor of Georgia, looked up to as one of the ablest men that had been employed in America of whose interests he made pretensions to a thorough knowledge, a favorite of Halifax and the confidential friend of Egremont, had no small share in introducing the new system, and bore away sinecure offices for his reward.

McCulloh, a crown officer in North Carolina, and agent for an English land company, furnished a brief state of the taxes usually raised in the old settled colonies, and gave assurance that a stamp-tax on the continental colonies would, at a moderate computation, produce sixty thousand pounds per annum, and twice that sum if extended to the West Indies. He renewed the proposition which he had made eight years before to Halifax, for gaining an imperial revenue by issuing a currency of exchequer bills for the use of America.

The triumvirate ministry had neither popularity nor weight in parliament. To strengthen his government, the king, conforming to the views sketched by Bute in the previous April, but against the repeated advice of his three ministers, directed Egremont to invite Lord Hardwicke to enter the cabinet, as president of the council. "It is impossible for me," said Hardwicke, at an interview on the first day of August, "to accept an employment, while all my friends are out of court." "The king," said Egremont, "cannot bring himself to submit to take in a party in gross, or an opposition party." "A king of England," answered Hardwicke, "at the head of a popular government, especially as of late the popular scale has grown heavier, will sometimes find it necessary to bend and ply a little; not as being forced, but as submitting to the stronger reason, for the sake of himself and his government. King William, hero as he was, found himself obliged to this conduct; so had other princes before him, and so did his majesty's grandfather, King George II., who thanked me for advising him to it."

This wise answer was reported to the king, who, disregarding the most earnest dissuasions of Grenville, reserved to himself ten days for reflection before choosing his part. Egremont, in great anger, was ready to concert with Grenville how to maintain themselves in office, in spite of the king's wishes, by employing "absolute necessity and fear;" but Grenville went into the country to await the king's decision. On the third, Halifax and Egremont harangued the king for half an hour or more, pressing him, on the instant, to resolve either to support the existing administration or to form another from its adversaries. The king all the while preserved absolute silence. But now wishing to be rid of Egremont, Shelburne was commissioned to propose a coalition between Pitt and Temple on the one side, and the duke of Bedford on the other.

The anger of Bedford toward Bute had ripened into hatred. He was therefore willing to enter the ministry, but on condition of Bute's exclusion from the king's counsels and presence, and Pitt's concurrence in a coalition of parties and the maintenance of the present relations with France. Pitt had no objection to a coalition of parties, and could not but acquiesce in the peace, now that it was made; but Bedford had been his strongest opponent in the cabinet, had contributed to force him into retirement, and had negotiated the treaty which he had so earnestly arraigned. For Pitt to have accepted office with Bedford would have been glaringly inconsistent with his declared opinions, and his engagements with the great whig families in opposition. "If I suffer force to be put upon me by the opposition," said the king, after mature deliberation, "the mob will try to govern me next;" and he decided to stand by the ministry. But, just at that moment, news came that Egremont was dying of a stroke of apoplexy.

"Your government," said the duke of Bedford to the king, "cannot stand; you must send to Mr. Pitt and his friends;" advice which Grenville never forgave. On Saturday, the twenty-seventh, Grenville went to the king and found Pitt's servants waiting in the court. He passed two long hours of agony and bitterness in the ante-chamber, incensed and humiliated on finding himself at the mercy of the brother-in-law whom he had deserted. The king, in his interview with Pitt, assuming to himself the formation of a ministry, proceeded upon the plan of defeating faction by a coalition of parties, and offered the great commoner his old place of secretary of state. "I cannot abandon the friends who have stood by me," said Pitt; and he declined to accept office without them. Nor did he fail to comment on the infirmities of the peace, and to declare that "the duke of Bedford should have no efficient office whatever." The king, with self-possession, combated several of these demands, said now and then that his honor must be consulted, and reserved his decision till a second interview.

Confident that those who made the overture must carry it through, Pitt summoned Newcastle, Devonshire, Rockingham, and Hardwicke to come to London as his council. But the king had no thought of yielding to his "hard terms." "Rather than submit to them," said he to Grenville, in the greatest agitation, "I would die in the room I now stand in."

On the twenty-ninth, at the second audience, Pitt still insisted on a thorough change of administration. The king closed the debate of nearly two hours by saying: "I see this won't do. My honor is concerned, and I must support it." A government formed out of the minority who had opposed the peace seemed to the king an offence to his conscience and a wound to his honor. "The house of commons," said Pitt, on taking leave, "will not force me upon your majesty, and I will never come into your service against your consent."

Events now shaped themselves. First of all, Bute, having disobliged all sides, went to the country in September, with the avowed purpose of absolute retirement. His retreat was his own act, and not a condition to be made the basis of a new ministry. As a protection against the duke of Bedford, he desired that Grenville might be armed with every degree of power. Next Lord Shelburne withdrew from office. Bedford, doubly irritated at being proscribed by Pitt whom he had proposed as minister, accepted the post which was pressed upon him by his own set of friends, by Grenville, and by the king.

From seemingly accidental causes there arose within ten days, out of a state of great uncertainty, a compact and well-cemented ministry. The king, in forming it, stood on the solid ground of the constitution. The last great question in parliament was on the peace, and was carried in its favor by an overwhelming majority. The present ministers had made or supported that peace, and so were in harmony with parliament. If they were too little favorable to liberty, the fault lay in the system on which parliament was chosen; they adequately represented the British constitution of that day, and needed nothing but cordial union among themselves and with the king to last for a generation.

Of the secretaries of state, Halifax, as the elder, had his choice of departments, and took the southern, " on account of the colonies; " and the earl of Hillsborough, like Shelburne an Irish as well as an English peer, was placed at the head of the board of trade.

One and the same spirit was at work on each side of the Atlantic. From Boston, Bernard renewed the clamor for the establishment of an independent civil list, sufficient to pay enlarged salaries to the crown officers. He acknowledged that " the compact between the king and the people was in no colony better observed than in that of the Massachusetts Bay," that " its people in general were well satisfied with their subordination to Great Britain," that " their former prejudices, which made them otherwise disposed, were wholly, or almost wholly, worn off." And yet he persistently urged on the British government the subversion of the charter of Massachusetts, which was the bond of its loyalty. For its council, which was elected annually by a carefully devised and successful method, he, with ceaseless importunity, entreated the government to substitute a body " resembling as near as possible the house of lords; " its members to be appointed for life, with some title, as baronet or baron; composed of people of consequence, willing to look up to the king for honor and authority.

New England towns, under grants from Wentworth, the governor of New Hampshire, rose up on both sides of the Connecticut and extended to the borders of Lake Champlain; but New York, under its old charter to the duke of York, disputed with New Hampshire the jurisdiction of the country between the river and the lake. The British government regarded the contest with indifference, till Colden urged the board of trade to annex to New York all of Massachusetts and of New Hampshire west of the Connecticut river. "The New England governments," he reasoned, "are all formed on republican principles, and those principles are zealously inculcated in the minds of their youth. The government of New York, on the contrary, is established as nearly as may be after the model of the English constitution. Can it, then, be good policy to diminish New York, and enlarge the power and influence of the others?"

The assembly of South Carolina was engaged in the defence of "its most essential privilege," for Boone, its governor, claimed exclusive authority to administer the required oaths, and, on occasion of administering them, assumed the power to reject members whom the house declared duly elected and returned, "thereby taking upon himself to be the sole judge of elections." The "arbitrary and imperious" governor was too clearly in the wrong to be sustained; but the controversy lasted long enough to train the statesmen of South Carolina to systematical opinions on the rights of their legislature, and on the king's power in matters of their privilege.

No sooner was the ministry established than Grenville, as the head of the treasury, proceeded to redeem the promise made to the house of commons of an American revenue. On the morning of the twenty-second day of September, three lords of the treasury, George Grenville, Lord North, and one Hunter who completed the number requisite for the transaction of business, held a board in Downing street; and, without hesitancy or discussion, they adopted a minute directing Jenkinson to "write to the commissioners of the stamp duties to prepare the draft of a bill to be presented to parliament for extending the stamp duties to the colonies." The next day Jenkinson accordingly wrote to them "to transmit to him the draft of an act for imposing proper stamp duties upon his majesty's subjects in America and the West Indies."

Who was the author of the American stamp-tax? At a later day Jenkinson assured the house of commons that, "if the stamp act was a good measure, the merit of it was not due to Grenville; if it was a bad one, the ill policy did not belong to him;" but he never confessed to the house where the blame or the merit could rest more justly. In his late old age he delighted to converse freely, with the son he loved best, on every topic connected with his long career, save only on the one subject of the contest with America; on that he maintained an inflexible and total silence.* But, though Jenkinson proposed the American tax while private secretary to Bute, and brought it with him into the treasury for adoption by Bute's successor, he was but a subordinate, without power of direction or a seat in council. Nor does the responsibility for the measure attach to Bute, for the ministry which had forced him into absolute retirement would not have listened to his advice in the smallest matter; nor to the king, for they boasted of being free from sycophancy to the court. Hunter, one of the lords of the treasury, who ordered the minute, was but a cipher, and Lord North, who supported the stamp act, at a later day told the house of commons that he took the propriety of passing it very much upon the authority of Grenville.

From the days of King William there was a steady line of precedents of opinion that America should, like Ireland, provide in whole, or at least in part, for the support of its military establishment. It was one of the first subjects of consideration on the organization of the board of trade. It again employed the attention of the servants of Queen Anne. It was still more seriously considered in the days of George I.; and when, in the reign of George II., the duke of Cumberland was at the head of American military affairs, it was laid down as a necessity that a revenue sufficient for the purpose must be provided. The ministry of Bute resolved to raise such a revenue, for which Charles Townshend pledged the government. Parliament wished it; so did the king. Almost all sorts and conditions of men repeatedly made it known that they desired it.

For half a century or more the king had sent executive orders or requisitions. But upon these each colonial legislature claimed a right of freely deliberating, and, as there were nearly twenty different governments, it was held that they

* Communicated to me by that son.

never would come to a common result. The need of some central power was asserted. To give the military chief a dictatorial authority to require subsistence for the army was suggested by the board of trade in 1696, in the days of King William and Locke, was more deliberately considered in 1721, was favored by Cumberland, and was one of the arbitrary proposals put aside by Pitt. To obtain the revenue through a congress of the colonies was at one time the plan of Halifax; but, if the congress was of governors, their decision would be only consultatory, and have no more weight than royal instructions; and, if the congress was a representative body, it would claim and exercise the right of free discussion. To support a demand for a revenue by stringent coercive measures was beyond the power of the prerogative, under the system established at the revolution. Once when New York failed to make appropriations for the civil service, a bill was prepared to be laid before parliament, giving the usual revenue, and this bill, having received the approbation of the great whig lawyers, Northey and Raymond, was the precedent which overcame Grenville's scruples about taxing the colonies without first allowing them representatives. It was settled that there must be a military establishment in America of twenty regiments; that, after the first year, its expenses must be defrayed by America; that the several American colonies themselves, with their various charters, never would agree to vote such a revenue, and that parliament must do it.

It remained to consider what tax parliament should impose, and here all agreed that the first object of taxation was foreign and intercolonial commerce. But that resource, under the navigation acts, would not produce enough. A poll-tax was common in America; but, applied by parliament, would fall unequally upon the colonies holding slaves. The difficulty in collecting quit-rents proved that a land-tax would meet with formidable obstacles. An excise was thought of, but held in reserve. An issue of exchequer bills, to be kept in circulation as the currency of the continent, would have conflicted with the policy of acts of parliament against the use of paper money in the colonies. Nearly everybody who reasoned on the subject decided for a stamp-tax, as certain of collection, and in

America, where lawsuits were frequent, as likely to be very productive. A stamp act had been proposed to Sir Robert Walpole; it had been thought of by Pelham; it had been almost resolved upon in 1755; it had been pressed upon Pitt; it was a part of the system adopted in the ministry of Bute. Knox, the agent of Georgia, defended it as least liable to objection. The agent of Massachusetts, through his brother, Israel Mauduit, who had Jenkinson for his fast friend and often saw Grenville, favored raising money in that way, because it would occasion less expense of officers, and would include the West India islands, and, speaking for his constituents, he made a merit of cheerful "submission" to the ministerial policy.

One man in Grenville's office, and one man only, did indeed give him sound advice: Richard Jackson, his secretary for the exchequer, advised him to lay the project aside, and formally declined to take any part in preparing or supporting it.

In this way George Grenville, in September 1763, was led to adopt the measure which was "devolved upon him," brought it into form, and consented that it should be "christened by his name." He doubted the propriety of taxing colonies without allowing them representatives; but he loved power and placed his hopes on the favor of parliament, which at that day contemplated the increased debt of England with terror, knew not that the resources of the country were increasing in a still greater proportion, and insisted on throwing a part of the public burdens upon America.

## CHAPTER VI.

ENFORCEMENT OF THE ACTS OF NAVIGATION.  GRENVILLE'S ADMINISTRATION CONTINUED.

OCTOBER 1763–APRIL 1764.

TAXING America by parliament was to be the close of a system of colonial "measures," founded, as Grenville believed, "on the true principles of policy, of commerce, and of finance." He, said those who paid him court, is not like some of his predecessors, ignorant of the importance of the colonies; nor, like others, impotently neglectful of their concerns; nor diverted by meaner pursuits from attending to them; England is now happy in a minister who sees that the greatest wealth and maritime power of Great Britain depend on the use of its colonies, and who will make it his highest object to form " a well-digested, consistent, wise, and salutary plan of colonization and government."

The extent of the American illicit trade was very great; it was thought that, of a million and a half pounds of tea consumed annually in the colonies, not more than one tenth part was sent from England. Grenville held that the contraband was stolen from the commerce and from the manufactures of Great Britain, against the principles of colonization and the provisions of the law. It pleased his severe vanity to be the first and only minister to insist on enforcing the laws, which usage and corruption had invalidated; and this brought him in conflict with the spirit which Otis had aroused in Boston, and which equally prevailed among the descendants of the Dutch of New York. The island of Manhattan lies convenient to the sea, sheltered by other islands from the ocean; having safe anchorage in deep water for many miles along its shores, inviting the commerce of continents, of the near tropical islands, and of the world. To-day [1850], its ships, swift, safe, and beautiful in their forms, exceed in amount of tonnage nearly twice over all the commercial marine of Great Britain at the moment of Grenville's schemes. Between its wharfs and the British harbors its packets run to and fro, swiftly and regularly, like the weaver's shuttle, weaving the band that joins nations together in friendship. Its imports of foreign produce are in value equal twice-told to all that was imported into the whole island of Great Britain in 1763. Nor does a narrow restrictive policy shut out the foreigner; its port is lively with the display at the mast-head of the flag of every civilized nation of the earth; in its streets may be heard every language that is spoken from the steppes of the Ukraine to the Atlantic. Grenville would have interdicted direct foreign commerce and excluded every foreign vessel. American independence, like the great rivers of the country, had many sources; but the head-spring which colored all the stream was the colonial mercantile system.

Reverence for that system was deeply branded into Grenville's mind. It was his "idol," and he adored it as "sacred." He held that colonies are only settlements made in distant parts of the world for the improvement of trade; that they would be intolerable except on the conditions contained in the acts of trade and navigation; that those who, from the increase of contraband, had apprehensions that they may break off their connection with the mother country saw not half the evil; that, wherever the acts of navigation are disregarded, the connection is broken already. Nor did this monopoly seem to him a wrong; he claimed for England the exclusive trade with its colonies, as the exercise of an indisputable right which every state, in exclusion of all others, has to the services of its own subjects. In pursuit of this object his zeal was indefatigable.

All officers of the customs in the colonies were ordered to their posts; their numbers were increased; they were provided with "new and ample instructions, enforcing in the strongest manner the strictest attention to their duty;" every officer that faltered was instantly to be dismissed.

Nor did Grenville fail to perceive that "the restraint and suppression of practices which had long prevailed would certainly encounter great difficulties in such distant parts of the king's dominions;" the royal authority was therefore called into action. The governors were to make the suppression of the forbidden trade with foreign nations the constant and immediate object of their care. All officers, both civil and military and naval, in America and the West Indies, were to give their co-operation. "We depend," said a memorial from the treasury, "upon the sea-guard as the likeliest means for accomplishing these great purposes;" and that sea-guard was to be extended and strengthened as far as the naval establishments would allow. To complete the whole, and this was a favorite part of Grenville's scheme, a new and uniform system of courts of admiralty was to be established. On the next day after this memorial was presented, the king in council gave his sanction to the system.

Forthwith orders were directed to the commander-in-chief in America that the troops under his command should give their assistance to the officers of the revenue for the effectual suppression of contraband trade. Admiral Colville, the naval commander-in-chief on the coasts of North America from the river St. Lawrence to Cape Florida and the Bahama islands, became the head of a new corps of revenue officers. Each captain of his squadron had custom-house commissions and a set of instructions from the lords commissioners of the admiralty for his guidance; and other instructions were given them by the admiral, to enter the harbors or lie off the coasts of America, to qualify themselves by taking the usual custom-house oaths to do the office of custom-house officers, and to seize such persons as were suspected by them to be engaged in illicit trade.

The promise of large emoluments in case of forfeitures stimulated their irregular vivacity to enforce laws which had become obsolete, and they pounced upon American property as they would have done in war upon prize-money. From the first their acts were equivocal, and they soon came to be as illegal as they were oppressive. There was no redress. An appeal to the privy council was costly and difficult; and besides, when, as happened before the end of the year, an officer had to defend himself on an appeal, the suffering colonists were exhausted by delay and expenses, while the treasury took care to indemnify their agent.

In forming the new territory into provinces, the fear of danger from large states led to the division of Florida; for it was held to be good policy to enhance the difficulties of union among the colonies by increasing the number of independent governments.

The boundary of Massachusetts, both on the east and on the north, was clearly defined, extending on the east to the St. Croix, and on the north leaving to the province of Quebec no more than the narrow strip from which the water flows into the St. Lawrence.

For Canada, or the province of Quebec as it was called, the narrower boundaries which had lately been established were retained. All British territory west of Lake Nipising, and west of the Alleghanies, was shut against the emigrant, from the fear that colonies in so remote a region could not be held in dependence. England by war had conquered the West, and a ministry had come which dared not make use of the conquest. Some even advised to abandon the monument to Pitt's name at the head of the Ohio, and to bring to this side of the mountains all the settlers beyond them. "The country to the westward, quite to the Mississippi, was intended to be a desert for the Indians to hunt in and inhabit."

But there was already at Detroit the indestructible seed of a commonwealth. The long-protracted siege drew near its end. The belts sent in all directions by the French reached the nations on the Ohio and Lake Erie. The Indians were assured that their old allies would depart; the garrison in the Peorias was withdrawn; fort Massiac was dismantled, and its cannon sent to St. Genevieve, the oldest settlement of Europeans in Missouri. The missionary Forget retired. At Vincennes, the message to all the nations on the Ohio was explained to the Piankeshaws, who accepted the belts and the calumets.

The courier who took the belt to the north offered peace to all the tribes wherever he passed; and to Detroit, where he arrived on the last day of October, he bore a letter of the nature of a proclamation, informing the inhabitants of the cession of Canada to England; another, addressed to twenty-five nations by name, to all the red men, and particularly to Pontiac, chief of the Ottawas; a third to the commander, expressing a readiness to surrender to the English all the forts on the Ohio and east of the Mississippi. The next morning, Pontiac sent to Gladwin that he accepted the peace which his father, the French, had despatched to him, and desired that the past might be forgotten on both sides. Friendly words were exchanged, though the formation of a definitive treaty of peace was referred to the commander-in-chief. The savages dispersed to their hunting-grounds.

Nothing could restrain the Americans from peopling the wilderness. To be a freeholder was the ruling passion of the New England man. Marriages were early and fruitful. The sons, as they grew up, skilled in the use of the axe and the rifle, would, one after another, move from the old homestead; and, with a wife, a yoke of oxen, a cow, and a few husbandry tools, build a small hut in some new plantation, and, by tasking every faculty of mind and body, secure independence. Such were they who began to dwell in the forests between the Penobscot and the St. Croix, or in the New Hampshire grants on each side of the Green Mountains, or in the valley of Wyoming, to which Connecticut laid claim.

In defiance of reiterated royal mandates, Virginian adventurers seated themselves on the New river, near the Ohio; and not even the terrors of border wars with the savages "could stop the enthusiasm of running backward to hunt for fresh lands."

Hunters from Carolina gave names to the streams and ridges of Tennessee, annually passed the Cumberland Gap, and chased game in the basin of the Cumberland river. From the Holston river to the head-springs of the Kentucky and of the Cumberland there dwelt not one red man. It was the neutral forest that divided the Cherokees from the Five Nations and their dependants. The lovely region had been left for untold years the paradise of wild beasts, which had so filled the valley with their broods that a thrifty hunter could, in one season, bring home peltry worth sixteen hundred dollars.

When, in July, possession was taken of Florida, its inhabitants, of every age and sex, men, women, children, and servants, numbered but three thousand; and, of these, the men were nearly all in the pay of the Catholic king. The possession of it had cost him nearly two hundred and thirty thousand dollars annually; and now it was accepted by England as a compensation for Havana. Most of the people, receiving from the Spanish treasury indemnity for their losses, had migrated to Cuba, taking with them the bones of their saints and the ashes of their distinguished dead.

The western province of Florida extended to the Mississippi, on the line of latitude of thirty-one degrees. On the twentieth of October, the French surrendered the post of Mobile, with its brick fort, which was fast crumbling to ruins. A month later, the slight stockade at Tombigbee, in the west of the Chocta country, was delivered up. In a congress of the Catawbas, Cherokees, Creeks, Chicasas, and Choctas, held on the tenth of November, at Augusta, the governors of Virginia and the colonies south of it were present, and the peace with the Indians of the South and South-west was ratified. The head man and chiefs of the upper and lower Creek nations, whose warriors were thirty-six hundred in number, agreed to extend the frontier of the settlement of Georgia. From this time dates its prosperity; its commerce in ten years increased almost fivefold.

For these vast regions Grenville believed he was framing a perfect system of government, and confidently prepared to meet parliament. His opponents were divided. Newcastle and his friends selected as their candidate for the place of chancellor Charles Yorke, through whom the ways of thinking of Lord Mansfield would have prevailed in Westminster Hall; but Pitt would never hear of it, and dismissed the dream that any solid union on revolution principles was possible under the old whigs, who fought alike against king and people.

On the first night of the session, in the debate on the king's speech and the address, Pitt spoke with great ability; Grenville, in answering him, contrasted his own plans of economy with the profusion which had marked the conduct of the war, and was excessively applauded. The king repeated to him the praises bestowed on the superiority of talent and judgment which he had shown. Barré, the gallant associate of Wolfe, was dismissed from the army for his votes, and Conway from the army and from his place in the bed-chamber. Shelburne was not to remain the king's aide-de-camp.

The house of commons readily voted the supplies necessary for the military establishment in the colonies; and this was followed by a renewed grant of the land-tax, which, at four shillings in the pound, produced a little more than two million pounds sterling. "I never will consent," said Grenville, "to continue that high tax after the second year of peace;" and he promised its reduction to three shillings in the pound, an easement to the landed interest of five hundred thousand pounds. Huske, the new member for Malden, a native of New Hampshire, educated at Boston, affirmed that the colonies were well able to pay annually taxes to that amount, and was heard by the house with great attention and joy.

In England, the force of opposition was broken. Charles Yorke came penitently to Grenville to mourn over his mistake in resigning office, and Grenville felt himself so strong as to dare to slight him. Even Charles Townshend's manifest desire of taking a place passed unheeded. Nothing was feared from the opposition in England. Who could forebode danger from a cause on trial in a county court in Virginia?

Tobacco was the legalized currency of Virginia. In 1755, and again in 1758, years of war and of distress, the legislature indulged the people in the alternative of paying their public dues, including the dues to the established clergy, in money, at the fixed rate of twopence for the pound of tobacco. All but the clergy acquiesced in the law. At their instance, its ratification was opposed by the bishop of London, who remarked on "the great change in the temper of the people of Virginia in the compass of a few years, and the diminution of the prerogative of the crown." "The rights of the clergy and the authority of the king," said he, "must stand or fall together;" and the act was negatived by the king in council. The "Twopenny Act" became, therefore, null and void from the beginning; and it remained only to ascertain by a jury in Virginia the amount of damages which the complainants had sustained.

Patrick Henry was engaged to plead against "the parsons," whose cause was become a contest between the prerogative and the people of Virginia. When a boy, he had learned something of Latin; of Greek, the letters; but nothing methodically. It had been his delight to wander alone with the gun or the angling-rod; or, by some sequestered stream, to enjoy the ecstasy of meditative idleness. He married at eighteen; attempted trade; toiled unsuccessfully as a farmer; then, with buoyant mind, resolved on becoming a lawyer; and, answering questions by the aid of six weeks' study of Coke upon Littleton and the Statutes of Virginia, he gained a license as a barrister. For three years the novice dwelt under the roof of his father-in-law, an inn-keeper near Hanover court-house, ignorant of the science of law, and slowly learning its forms.

On the first day of December 1763, as Patrick Henry entered the court before which he had never spoken, he saw on the bench more than twenty clergymen, the most learned men in the colony; and the house was filled and surrounded by a multitude. To the select jury which had been summoned, Maury, "the parson" whose cause was on trial, made objections; for he thought them of "the vulgar herd," and three or four of them dissenters of the sect called "New Lights." "They are honest men," said Henry, "and therefore unexceptionable;" and, the court being satisfied, "they were immediately called to the book and sworn."

The course of the trial was simple. The contract was that Maury should be paid sixteen thousand pounds of tobacco: the act of 1758 fixed its value at twopence a pound; in 1759, it had been worth thrice that sum. The king had disallowed the act of 1758. The counsel for the clergy briefly explained the standard of their damages, and gave a high-wrought eulogium on their benevolence.

The forest-born orator, in reply, built his argument on the natural right of Virginia to self-direction in her affairs, against the prerogative of the crown and the civil establishment of the church, against monarchy and priestcraft. The act of 1758, having every characteristic of a good law, and being of general utility, could not, consistently with the original compact between king and people, be annulled. "A king who annuls or disallows laws of so salutary a nature, from being the father of his people degenerates into a tyrant and forfeits all right to obedience." At this assertion the opposing counsel cried out to the bench: "The gentleman has spoken treason." Royalists in the crowd raised a confused murmur of "treason, treason, treason." "The harangue," thought one of the hearers, "exceeds the most seditious and inflammatory of the most seditious tribunes in Rome." The patriot, as he proceeded, defined the use of an established church and of the clergy in society: "When they fail to answer those ends," thus he addressed the jury, "the community have no further need of their ministry, and may justly strip them of their appointments. In this particular instance, by obtaining the negative of the law in question instead of acquiescing in it, they ceased to be useful members of the state, and ought to be considered as enemies of the community." "Instead of countenance, they very justly deserve to be punished with signal severity." "Except you are disposed yourselves to rivet the chains of bondage on your own necks, do not let slip the opportunity now offered of making such an example of the reverend plaintiff as shall hereafter be a warning to himself and his brothers not to have the temerity to dispute the validity of laws authenticated by the only sanction which can give force to laws for the government of this colony, the authority of its own legal representatives, with its council and governor."* The jury promptly rendered a verdict of a penny damages. A motion for a new trial was refused: an appeal was granted; but, the verdict being received, there was no redress. "The crime of which Henry is guilty," wrote Maury, "is little, if any, inferior to that which brought Simon Lord Lovat to the block." For "the vindication of the king's injured honor and authority," he urged the punishment of the young Virginian; and a list was furnished of witnesses who could insure his conviction.

In quest of business, Patrick Henry removed to the county

---

* The report of Henry's speech is taken from a very long letter written by Rev. James Maury himself to Rev. John Camm, 12 December, 1763. MS.

of Louisa; but he loved the greenwood better even than before; and, as he strolled through the forest, with his ever-ready musket in his hand, his mind was ripening for duty, he knew not how, by silent communion with nature.

Vague rumors prevailed of new commercial and fiscal regulations, to be made by act of parliament; and yet Americans refused to believe that the British legislature would wilfully overthrow their liberty. No remonstrance was prepared against the impending measures, of which the extent was kept secret. Massachusetts, in January 1764, with a view to effect the greatest possible reduction of the duty on foreign West Indian products, elected Hutchinson as its joint agent with Mauduit. But, before he could leave the province, the house began to distrust him, and, by a majority of two, excused him from the service. Its next choice fell on Grenville's secretary, Richard Jackson.

When the crown officers in America learned that the taxes which they had so long and so earnestly recommended were to be applied exclusively to the support of the army, they shrunk from upholding obnoxious measures which to them were to bring no profit. In their view, a parliamentary regulation of colonial charters and a certain and sufficient civil list, laid upon perpetual funds, should take precedence of all other business. But when Halifax urged the payment of their salaries directly from England, in accordance with the system which he had been maturing since 1748, Grenville would not consent to it; and, though Halifax, at a formal interview, at which Hillsborough and Jenkinson were present, became extremely heated and eager,[*] he remained inflexible.

Nor would he listen to the suggestion that the revenue to be raised in America should constitute a fund to be disposed of under the sign manual of the king; he insisted that it should be paid into the receipt of the exchequer, to be regularly appropriated by parliament. Nor did he take part in the schemes which were on foot to subvert the charters of the colonies, control their domestic governments, and confer paramount authority on military officers in America; though he did not, indeed, insist that the ministry should conform to his opinions.

[*] Diary in Grenville Papers, i. 48.

When he proposed the taxation of America by the British parliament, he had but one object: to rivet the support of the landlords of England, whose favor secured majorities in parliament and with them a firm tenure of office.

For a moment, the existence of the ministry itself was endangered. In closing the session of 1763, the king had arrogated merit for the peace which Frederic of Prussia had concluded after having been left to himself by England. Wilkes, in number forty-five of the "North Briton," exposed the error of statement. The king, thinking that one of his subjects had given him the lie, applied to the ministry for protection; and under a general warrant, issued by Halifax, one of the secretaries of state, Wilkes was arrested; but, on the plea that his privilege as a member of parliament had been violated, he had been set at liberty by the popular chief justice, Pratt; and the cry for Wilkes and liberty was heard in all parts of the British dominions. Now, in February 1764, all parties joined in expelling Wilkes from parliament, yet general warrants were undoubtedly illegal; Grenville knew that they were illegal, and the house of commons was invited to declare them so. But Grenville changed the issue by insisting that a single branch of the legislature ought not to declare law; and, in a house of four hundred and fifty, the ministry escaped censure but by a majority of only fourteen. In the account of the division sent by Grenville to the king, marks of being dispirited were obvious; the king instantly answered "that, if he would but hide his feelings, and speak with firmness the first occasion that offered, he would find his numbers return." The opportunity came in March with the presentation of the budget.

Grenville had been "made to believe" that the Americans were able to contribute to the revenue, and he had little reason to think them so stubborn as to refuse the payment of a tax. There was not "the least disposition in the agents of the colonies to oppose it;" and the agent of Massachusetts had made a merit of his submission. Thomas Pownall, "the fribble" who had been governor of Massachusetts, and is remembered as one who grew more and more liberal as he grew old, openly contended for an American revenue, to "be raised by customs on trade, a stamp duty, a moderate land-tax in lieu of quit-rents, and an excise." Cecilius Calvert, the secretary of Maryland, had for years watched the ripening of the measure, and could not conceal his joy at its adoption.

Yet there were motives enough to make Grenville reluctant to propose a stamp-tax for America. Jackson, his secretary, would never be privy to any measures taken with respect to it, after having formally declined giving any other advice on the subject than that which he had always given, to lay the project aside. Lord Hillsborough, then first lord of the board of trade, who as yet retained enough of the spirit of an Irishman to disapprove a direct taxation of a dependency of the British empire by a British act of parliament, gave advice against the stamp act, and to the last withheld from it his support. Moreover, the traditions of the whig party, whose principles Grenville claimed to represent, preserved the opinions of Sir Robert Walpole, and questioned the wisdom of deriving a direct parliamentary revenue from America. "Many members of the house of commons declared against the stamp duty, while it was mere matter of conversation;" nor could Grenville have been ignorant that Pitt had in vain been urged to extend it to the colonies.

The Americans in London unanimously denied the right of the British parliament, in which their country was not represented, to grant their property to the crown. This questioning of the power of parliament irritated the minister; as a thorough whig, he maintained that the parliament of England is in all cases supreme; he knew "no other law, no other rule." But the force of the objection derived from the want of a colonial representation did not escape his consideration. Regarding the house of commons as a representative body, in his inner mind he recognised, and to one friend he confessed, the propriety of allowing to America a representation in the body by which it should be taxed, and wished that parliament would couple the two measures.

Under these circumstances Thomas Penn, one of the proprietaries of Pennsylvania, Allen, a loyal American, then its chief justice under a proprietary appointment, and Richard Jackson, the agent of its people and of Connecticut, obtained an interview with Grenville. They reasoned against a system of direct taxation of America by parliament. The stamp duty, they said, was an internal regulation; and they entreated him to wait till some sort of consent to it should be given by the assemblies, to prevent a tax of that nature from being laid without the consent of the colonies. Grenville's colleagues did not share his scruples; but he was accustomed to balance opinions, and desired to please all parties. He persisted, therefore, in the purpose of proposing a stamp-tax; but, from "tenderness" to the colonies, and at the risk of being scoffed at by the whole Bedford party, he agreed to postpone the tax for a year. In this his enemies said that he did but "allow time for mooting the question of right and preparing in the colonies an opposition to the law."

He looked about for palliatives to reconcile America to his new regulations. In doing this, he still continued within the narrow limits of protection. The British consumption of foreign hemp amounted in value to three hundred thousand pounds a year. The bounties on hemp and flax, first given in the time of Queen Anne, having never been called for, had been suffered to drop. The experiment was renewed; and a liberal bounty was granted on hemp or undressed flax imported from America. But it was expected that no American would be "so unreasonable or so rash" as to establish linen manufactories there, even of "the coarser kinds" of linens; for the exigencies of the state required that Great Britain should disappoint American establishments of manufactures as "contrary to the general good."

To South Carolina and Georgia special indulgence was shown; following the line of precedent, rice, though an enumerated commodity, was, on the payment of a half subsidy, allowed to be carried directly to any part of America south of those colonies; so that the broken and mowburnt rice might be sold as food for negroes.

The boon that was to mollify New England was concerted with Israel Mauduit, acting for his brother, the agent of Massachusetts; and was nothing less than the whale fishery. In vain had Great Britain striven to compete with the Dutch in that branch of industry. Grenville gave up the unsuccessful attempt, and sought a rival for Holland in British America, which had hitherto lain under the double discouragement of being excluded from the benefit of a bounty and of having the products of its whale fishing taxed unequally. He now adopted the plan of gradually giving up the bounty to the British whale fishery, which would be a saving of thirty thousand pounds a year to the treasury, and of relieving the American fishery from the inequality of the discriminating duty, except the old subsidy, which was scarcely one per cent. It was done with a conviction that "the American whale fishery, freed from its burden, would soon totally overpower the British." So this valuable branch of trade, which produced annually three hundred thousand pounds, and which would give employment to many shipwrights and other artificers, and to seamen, was resigned to America.

After these preparations, on the ninth day of March 1764, George Grenville made his appearance in the house of commons, as chancellor of the exchequer, to unfold his first budget. He did it with art and ability. He boasted that the revenue was managed with more frugality than in the preceding reign; he explained his method of funding the debt. The demands from Germany, which had amounted to nearly nine millions of pounds, he had settled for about thirteen hundred thousand pounds. The landgrave of Hesse, whose demands exceeded seventeen hundred thousand pounds, was put off with a payment of one hundred and fifty thousand pounds. The taxes of Great Britain exceeded, by three millions of pounds, what they were in 1754, before the war; yet the present object was only to make the colonies maintain their own army. Till the last war, they had never contributed to the support of an army at all. Beside the taxes on trade, which were immediately to be enacted, Grenville gave notice in the house that it was his intention, in the next session, to bring in a bill imposing stamp duties in America; and the reasons for giving such notice were because he understood some people entertained doubts of the power of parliament to impose internal taxes in the colonies, and because he was not so wedded to a stamp act as to be unwilling to give it up for any one that might appear more eligible; or, if the colonies themselves thought any other mode would be more expedient, he should have no objections to come into it by act of parliament. The opposition were called upon, if they thought it fitting, to deny the right of the legislature to impose any tax, internal or external, on the colonies; and upon a solemn question, asked in a full house, there was not one negative. "As we are stout," said Beckford, "I hope we shall be merciful." No one else made a reply.

On the fourteenth of March, Jenkinson, from a committee on which he had for his associates Grenville and Lord North, reported a bill modifying and perpetuating the act of 1733, with some changes to the disadvantage of the colonies; an extension of the navigation acts, making England the storehouse of Asiatic as well as of European supplies; a diminution of drawbacks on foreign articles exported to America; imposts in America, especially on wines; a revenue duty instead of a prohibitory duty on foreign molasses; an increased duty on sugar; various regulations to sustain English manufactures, as well as to enforce more diligently the acts of trade; a prohibition of all trade between America and St. Pierre and Miquelon.

The bill was rapidly carried through its several stages, was slightly amended, on the fourth of April was agreed to by the lords, and on the next day was approved by the king. "These new taxes," wrote Whately, the joint secretary of the treasury, "will certainly not be sufficient to defray that share of the American expense which America ought and is able to bear. Others must be added." The act had for the first time the title of "granting duties in the colonies and plantations of America; for the first time it was asserted, in the preamble, that it was just and necessary that a revenue should be raised there."

When the agents waited upon Grenville, to know what could be done to avert the stamp act, he answered: "I have proposed the resolution in the terms that parliament has adopted, from a real regard and tenderness for the subjects in the colonies. It is highly reasonable they should contribute something toward the charge of protecting themselves, and in aid of the great expense Great Britain put herself to on their account. No tax appears to me so easy and equitable as a stamp duty; it will fall only upon property, will be collected by the fewest officers, and will be equally spread over America and the West Indies. What ought particularly to recommend it is the mode of collecting it, which does not require extraordinary powers of entering houses, or extend a sort of influence which I never wished to increase. The colonists now have it in their power, by agreeing to this tax, to establish a precedent for their being consulted before any tax is imposed on them by parliament; for their approbation of it being signified to parliament next year, when the tax comes to be imposed, will afford a forcible argument for the like proceeding in all such cases. If they think any other mode of taxation more convenient to them, and make any proposition of equal efficacy with the stamp duty, I will give it all due consideration." To a considerate and most respectable merchant, a member of the house of commons, who was making a representation against proceeding with the stamp act, Grenville answered: "If the stamp duty is disliked, I am willing to change it for any other equally productive. If you object to the Americans being taxed by parliament, save yourself the trouble of the discussion, for I am determined on the measure." The colonists were apprised that not a single member of either house doubted the right of parliament to impose a stamp duty or any other tax upon them; and the king, at the prorogation, gave to what he called "the wise regulations" of Grenville his "hearty approbation."

It was said that "the great minister," who was taking "pains to understand the interests" of the plantations, and with "firmness and candor" entering seriously upon regulating their affairs, was about to unite them indissolubly with the mother country by one comprehensive commercial system, and by "interweaving their administration into the British administration."

## CHAPTER VII.

HOW AMERICA RECEIVED THE PLAN OF A STAMP-TAX. GRENVILLE'S ADMINISTRATION CONTINUED.

APRIL–DECEMBER 1764.

No sooner was parliament up than Jenkinson pressed Grenville to forward the American stamp act by seeking that further information, the want of which he had assigned as a reason for delay. Meantime, the officers of France, as they made their last journey through Canada and down the valley of the Mississippi, and on every side received the expressions of passionate attachment from the many tribes of red men, cast a look of regret upon the magnificent empire which they were ceding. But Choiseul saw futurity better. In April 1764, he issued the order for the transfer of the island of New Orleans and all Louisiana to Spain. He did it without mental reserve, foreseeing that the whole colonial system would be changed. In the same year he sent Pontleroy, a lieutenant in the navy, to travel through America in the guise of an Acadian wanderer, and report on the political condition of its people. While England was taxing America by act of parliament, France was counting its steps toward independence.

The world was rising up against superstition and authority over mind; the oppression of industry was passing away, not less than the oppression of free thought. The use of reason was no longer held to be presumption, but a duty, and the very end of creation. "Everything that I see," wrote Voltaire, in April 1764, "is scattering the seeds of a revolution, which will come inevitably. Light has so spread from neighbor to neighbor, that on the first occasion it will kindle and burst forth. Happy are the young, for their eyes shall see it." The impulse to the revolution was to proceed from the New World. "If the colonist is taxed without his consent," said the press of New York, "he will, perhaps, seek a change." "The ways of Heaven are inscrutable," wrote Richard Henry Lee, of Virginia, privately to a friend; "this step of the mother country, though intended to secure our dependence, may produce a fatal resentment and be subversive of that end." "If the colonies do not now unite," wrote Dyer, of Connecticut, from England, "they may bid farewell to liberty, burn their charters, and make the best of thraldom."

Before it was known that the bill had passed, the alarm was given in Boston, at its town-meeting in May 1764, by Samuel Adams, a native of the place, a provincial statesman of a clear and logical mind, which, throughout a long life, imparted consistency to his public conduct. His will resembled well-tempered steel, which may ply, but will not break. Bred as a Calvinist of the straitest sect, his riper judgment confirmed him in his creed. On church government he adhered to the Congregational forms, as most friendly to civil and religious liberty; was a member of the church; and the austere purity of his life witnessed the sincerity of his profession. Evening and morning his house was a house of prayer; and no one more revered the Christian sabbath. He was a tender husband, an affectionate parent, and could vividly enjoy conversation with friends; but the walls of his modest mansion never witnessed anything inconsistent with the discipline of the man whose desire for his birthplace was that "Boston might become a Christian Sparta."

For his political creed, he held the opinions of the fathers of New England, that the colonies and England had a common king, but separate and independent legislatures. When, in consequence of an act of the British parliament overruling the laws of the colony, his father's estate had been taken, he defended the supremacy of colonial laws within colonial limits, and by success gratified alike his filial piety and his love of country.

He was at this time near two-and-forty years of age; poor, and so contented with poverty that men censured him as "wanting wisdom to estimate riches at their just value." But he was frugal and temperate; and his prudent and industrious wife was endowed with the best faculties of a New England woman, so that the small resources, which men of the least opulent class would have deemed an imperfect support, satisfied his wants. Yet such was the union of dignity with economy that whoever visited him saw around him every circumstance of propriety. Above all, he combined with poverty a stern and incorruptible integrity.

Already famed as a political writer, employing wit and sarcasm as well as energy of language and earnestness, no one had equal influence over the popular mind. The blandishments of flattery could not lull his vigilance, nor sophistry deceive his penetration, nor difficulties discourage his decision, nor danger appall his fortitude. He had an affable and persuasive address, which could reconcile conflicting elements and promote harmony in action. He never, from jealousy, checked the advancement of others; and in accomplishing great deeds he took to himself no praise. Seeking fame as little as fortune, and office less than either, he aimed steadily at the good of his country and the best interests of mankind. Trials only nerved him for severer struggles; his sublime hope was as unfaltering as if it sprung from insight into the divine decrees. For himself and for others, he held that all sorrows and losses were to be encountered, rather than that liberty should perish. Such was his devotion, such his inflexibility and courage, he may be called the last of the Puritans, destined to win for his country "the victory of endurance born."

On his motion and in his words, Boston, while it still set forth its acknowledged dependence upon Great Britain, and the ready submission of its merchants to all just and necessary regulations of trade, asserted its rights and privileges. "There is no room for delay," said the town to its representatives. "Those unexpected proceedings may be preparatory to more extensive taxation; for, if our trade may be taxed, why not our lands and everything we possess? If taxes are laid upon us in any shape, without our having a legal representation where they are laid, are we not reduced from the character of free subjects to the miserable state of tributary slaves? This annihilates our charter right to govern and tax ourselves. We claim British rights, not by charter only; we are born to them. Use your endeavors that the weight of the other North American colonies may be added to that of this province, that by united application all may happily obtain redress."

At New York, when the English packet arrived tardily in June, all expressed their resentment in the strongest manner. "I will wear nothing but homespun," exclaimed one citizen; "I will drink no wine," said another, angry that wine must pay a new duty; "I propose," cried a third, "that we dress in sheepskins with the wool on." "It appears plainly," said the gentle Robert R. Livingston, "that these duties are only the beginning of evils. The stamp duty, they tell us, is deferred, till they see whether the colonies will take the yoke upon themselves, and offer something else as certain. They talk, too, of a land-tax, and to us the ministry appears to have run mad;" and looking forward to resistance, "We in New York," he added, "shall do as well as our neighbors; the God of heaven, whom we serve, will sanctify all things to those who love him and strive to serve him."

The legislature of Massachusetts was then in session. The Boston instructions, drawn by Samuel Adams, formed the corner-stone of its policy. In pursuance of them, James Otis prepared "a state" of the case for the instruction of the colonial agent in London. By the laws of nature and of nations, the voice of universal reason and of God, by statute law and the common law, this memorial claimed for the colonists the absolute rights of Englishmen: personal security and liberty; the rights of property; the power of local legislation, subject only to the king's negative, as in Ireland; and the sole power of taxing themselves. "The authority of the parliament of Great Britain," such were the words of this paper, "is circumscribed by bounds, which, if exceeded, their acts become mere power without right, and consequently void." "Acts of parliament against natural equity or against the fundamental principles of the British institutions are void." "The wild wastes of America have been turned into pleasant habitations; little villages in Great Britain into manufacturing towns and opulent cities; and London itself bids fair to become the metropolis of the world. These are the fruits of commerce and liberty. The British empire, to be perpetuated, must be built on the principles of justice."

The assembly repudiated the concessions of their agent. Their silence had rather been the silence of "despair." They protested against "the burdensome scheme of obliging the colonies to maintain a standing army," as in conflict with the constitution and against reason. They rehearsed their services during the last war. Still incredulous, they demand: "Can it be possible that duties and taxes shall be assessed without the voice or consent of an American parliament? If we are not represented, we are slaves." "Ireland," they cried, connecting the questions of American and Irish liberty, "was a conquered country, yet no duties have been levied by the British parliament on Ireland." "Prohibitions of trade are neither equitable nor just; but the power of taxing is the grand barrier of British liberty. If this is once broken down, all is lost." "In a word," say they, representing truly the point of resistance at which America was that year ready to halt, "a people may be free, and tolerably happy, without a particular branch of trade; but, without the privilege of assessing their own taxes, they can be neither."

On the twenty-fifth of June, Otis, Cushing, Thacher, Gray, and Sheafe, as the committee for corresponding with the other colonies, sent a circular letter to them all, exposing the danger that menaced their "most essential rights," and desiring "their united assistance."

On the other hand, Bernard sought to ingratiate himself in England by sending to his superiors a scheme of American polity which he had employed years in maturing. He urged on the cabinet that a general reformation of the American governments was not only desirable, but necessary; that the colonies enjoyed their separate legislatures not as a right, but as a contingent privilege; that parliament could modify their governments as it should see fit; that its power to impose port duties, and levy internal taxes in the colonies, was not to be disputed; and, if requisitions were neglected, the power ought to be exercised; that there should be for the colonies a certain, sufficient, and independent civil list; that there should be an American nobility for life, to mediate between the king and the people; that the American charters were suited only to the infancy of states, and should be abolished, and one form of government established for all America by parliament. Of the paper containing this advice, Bernard sent copies to the ministry, carefully concealing from America his treacherous solicitations.

Suspecting the designs of Bernard, Otis, in July, spoke thus through the press. "The British constitution comes nearest the idea of perfection of any that has been reduced to practice. Let parliament lay what burdens they please on us, it is our duty to submit and patiently bear them till they will be pleased to relieve us. If anything fall from my pen that bears the least aspect but that of obedience, duty, and loyalty to the king and parliament, the candid will impute it to the agony of my heart.

"Government is founded not on force, as was the theory of Hobbes; nor on compact, as was the theory of Locke and of the revolution of 1688; nor on property, as was asserted by Harrington. It springs from the necessities of our nature, and has an everlasting foundation in the unchangeable will of God. Man came into the world and into society at the same instant. There must exist in every earthly society a supreme sovereign, from whose final decision there can be no appeal but directly to heaven. This supreme power is originally and ultimately in the people; and the people never did in fact freely, nor can rightfully, make an unlimited renunciation of this divine right. Kingcraft and priestcraft are a trick to gull the vulgar. The happiness of mankind demands that this grand and ancient alliance should be broken off forever.

"The omniscient and omnipotent Monarch of the universe has, by the grand charter given to the human race, placed the end of government in the good of the whole. The form of government is left to the individuals of each society; its whole superstructure and administration should be conformed to the law of universal reason. There can be no prescription old enough to supersede the law of nature and the grant of God Almighty, who has given all men a right to be free. If every prince since Nimrod had been a tyrant, it would not prove a right to tyrannize. The administrators of legislative and executive authority, when they verge toward tyranny, are to be resisted; if they prove incorrigible, are to be deposed.

"The first principle and great end of government being to provide for the best good of all the people, this can be done only by a supreme legislative and executive ultimately in the people, or whole community, where God has placed it; but the difficulties attending a universal congress gave rise to a right of representation. Such a transfer of the power of the whole to a few was necessary; but to bring the powers of all into the hands of one or some few, and to make them hereditary, is the interested work of the weak and the wicked. Nothing but life and liberty are actually hereditable. The grand political problem is to invent the best combination of the powers of legislation and execution: they must exist in the state, just as in the revolution of the planets; one power would fix them to a centre, and another carry them off indefinitely; but the first and simple principle is EQUALITY and THE POWER OF THE WHOLE.

"The best writers on public law contain nothing that is satisfactory on the natural rights of colonies. Even Grotius and Puffendorf establish the matter of right on the matter of fact. Their researches are often but the history of ancient abuses; and the American admiralty courts learn of them to determine controversies by the rules of civil and feudal law. To be too fond of studying them is a ridiculous infatuation. The British colonists do not hold their liberties or their lands by so slippery a tenure as the will of the prince. Colonists are men, the common children of the same Creator with their brethren of Great Britain.

"The colonists are men: the colonists are therefore free born; for, by the law of nature, all men are free born, white or black. No good reason can be given for enslaving those of any color. Is it right to enslave a man because his color is black, or his hair short and curled like wool, instead of Christian hair? Can any logical inference in favor of slavery be drawn from a flat nose or a long or a short face? The riches of the West Indies, or the luxury of the metropolis, should not have weight to break the balance of truth and justice. Liberty is the gift of God, and cannot be annihilated.

"Nor do the political and civil rights of the British colonists rest on a charter from the crown. Old Magna Charta was not the beginning of all things, nor did it rise on the borders of chaos out of the unformed mass. A time may come when parliament shall declare every American charter void; but the natural, inherent, and inseparable rights of the colonists, as men and as citizens, can never be abolished.

"There is no foundation for distinction between external and internal taxes; if parliament may tax our trade, they may lay stamps, land-taxes, tithes, and so indefinitely; there are no bounds. But such an imposition of taxes in the colonies, whether on trade or on land, on houses or ships, on real or personal, fixed or floating property, is absolutely irreconcilable with the rights of the colonists as British subjects and as men. Acts of parliament against the fundamental principles of the British constitution are void.

"Yet the colonists know the blood and treasure independence would cost. They will never think of it till driven to it as the last fatal resort against ministerial oppression, which will make the wisest mad and the weakest strong. The world is at the eve of the highest scene of earthly power and grandeur that has ever yet been displayed to the view of mankind. Who will win the prize is with God. But human nature must and will be rescued from the general slavery that has so long triumphed over the species."

Reasoning for his country and for the race, Otis brought into the conscious intelligence of the people the elemental principles of free government and human rights.

This book was reprinted in England. Lord Mansfield, who read it, rebuked those who spoke of it with contempt. But they rejoined: "The man is mad." "What then?" answered Mansfield, in parliament. "One madman often makes many. Massaniello was mad: nobody doubted it; yet, for all that, he overturned the government of Naples."

But Otis was a prophet, not the leader of a party; full of sagacity in his inspirations, unsteady in conduct. His colleague, Oxenbridge Thacher, was less enthusiastic and more consistent. Connection with Great Britain was to him no blessing, if Great Britain would impose burdens unconstitutionally. He vindicated the right of resisting arbitrary taxation by the frequent example of the British parliament; and he dwelt on the danger to the inhabitants of England if the ministers could disfranchise a million and a half of subjects in America.

"Here," said Mayhew, as he lamented the cold adhesion of the timid good, and for himself trod the thorny path of resistance to the grandeurs of the world, "there are many who 'see the right, and yet the wrong pursue.' But it is my fixed resolution, notwithstanding many discouragements, in my little sphere to do all I can, that neither the republic nor the churches of New England may sustain any injury." Men began to enter into an agreement not to use a single article of British manufacture, not even to wear black clothes for mourning. To encourage the growth and manufacture of wool, nearly all Boston signed a covenant to eat no lamb.

While the people heartened one another in the conviction that taxation by parliament was tyranny, Hutchinson addressed the secretary of the chancellor of the exchequer, saying: "The colonists claim a power of making laws, and a privilege of exemption from taxes, unless voted by their own representatives. In Rome, not only the colonies when first planted, but the provinces when changed into colonies, were freed from taxes for the Roman exchequer of every sort. In modern Europe, the inhabitants of Britain only are free, and the inhabitants of British colonies only feel the loss of freedom; and they feel it more sensibly, because they thought it doubly secured as their natural right and their possession by virtue of the most solemn engagements. Nor are the privileges of the people less affected by duties laid for the sake of the money arising from them than by an internal tax.

"The colonies have an interest distinct from the interest of the nation; and shall the parliament be at once party and judge? Is it not a continual question, What can be done to make the colonies further beneficial to the nation? And nobody adds, consistently with their rights. You consider us as your property, to improve in the best way you can for your advantage.

"None of the colonies, except Georgia and Halifax, occasioned any charge to the crown or kingdom in the settlement of them. The people of New England fled for the sake of civil and religious liberty; multitudes flocked to America with this dependence, that their liberties should be safe. They and their posterity have enjoyed them to their content, and therefore have endured with greater cheerfulness all the hardships of settling new countries. No ill use has been made of these privileges; but the dominion and wealth of Great Britain have received amazing addition. Surely the services we have rendered the nation have not subjected us to any forfeitures.

"I know it is said the colonies should contribute to their own defence and protection. But, during the last war, they annually contributed so largely that the parliament was convinced the burden would be insupportable, and from year to year made them compensation; in several of the colonies, for several years together, more men were raised, in proportion, than by the nation. In the trading towns, one fourth part of the profit of trade, besides imposts and excise, was annually paid to the support of the war and public charges; in the country towns, a farm which would hardly rent for twenty pounds a year paid ten pounds in taxes. If the inhabitants of Britain had paid in the same proportion, there would have been no great increase of the national debt.

"Nor is there occasion for any national expense in America. For one hundred years together, the New England colonies received no aid in their wars with the Indians when the Indians were assisted by the French. Those governments now molested are as able to defend their respective frontiers, and had rather do the whole of it by a tax of their own raising, than pay their proportion in any other way.

"Moreover, it must be prejudicial to the national interest to impose parliamentary taxes. The advantages promised by an increase of the revenue are all delusive. You will lose more than you gain. Britain already reaps the profit of all their trade, and of the increase of their substance. By cherishing their present turn of mind, you will serve your interest more than by your present schemes."

The argument of Hutchinson, Conway read at the time, and pronounced it "very sensible and unanswerable against passing the stamp act;" but the pusillanimous man entreated his correspondent to conceal his confession from those whom it would displease. To his friends in America he used to say that there was no ground for the distinction between the duties on trade and internal taxes; that, if the parliament intended to go on, there would be a necessity to dispute the distinction; "for," said he, "they may find duties on trade enough to drain us thoroughly." And to members of the legislature of Massachusetts from whom he had ends to gain, he denied utterly the right of parliament to tax America.

The appeals of the colonies were made in the spirit of loyalty. The wilderness was still ringing with the war-whoop of the savage, the frontiers were red with blood, while the colonies, at the solicitations of Amherst and of Gage, his successor, were lavishing their treasure to secure the West to Great Britain. In July, eleven hundred men, composed chiefly of provincial battalions from New Jersey, New York, and Connecticut, that of Connecticut led by Colonel Israel Putnam, the whole under the command of Bradstreet, reached Niagara.

There, in August, the Senecas, to save their settlements from imminent destruction, brought in prisoners, and ratified a peace. Half way from Buffalo to Erie, Bradstreet, conforming to his orders from Gage, settled a treaty with deputations from the nations dwelling between Lake Erie and the Ohio.

At Detroit, in September, he was welcomed by the Hurons. On the seventh, the Ottawas and Ojibwas, seating themselves on the ground for a congress, cashiered all their old chiefs, and the young warriors shook hands with the English as with brothers. The Miamis asked for peace in the names of their wives and children, and these, the Pottawatomies, the Sacs, and the Missisagas, attached their seals to a treaty in which Pontiac, though absent, was included. By its conditions the Indian country was made a part of the royal dominions; its tribes were bound to render aid to the English troops, and in return were promised protection. Indian murderers and plunderers, as well as British deserters, were to be delivered up; all captives to be restored. English families were assured of a welcome. A detachment took possession of Mackinaw.

In the same month, in pursuance of the new methods of government, "an impost of four and a half per cent in specie, on produce shipped from Grenada," began to be levied, "by virtue of the prerogative royal;" and this order was justified on the ground that Grenada was a conquered island, in which customs had been collected by the most Christian king.

In Canada arbitrary taxation was the only French usage which was retained. By an ordinance of the seventeenth of September, all the laws, customs, and forms of judicature of a populous and long-established colony were in one hour overturned; and English laws, even the penal statutes against Catholics, all unknown to the Canadians, and unpublished, were introduced in their stead. "A general presentment," said Thurlow, "was lodged against all the inhabitants of the colony as papists."

The improper choice and the number of the civil officers sent over from England increased the disquietude of the colony. The ignorant, the greedy, and the factious were appointed to offices which required integrity, knowledge, and abilities. The judge pitched upon to conciliate the minds of seventy thousand foreigners to the laws and government of Great Britain was taken from a jail, and was entirely unacquainted with the civil law and the language of the people. The attorney-general, with regard to the language, was not better qualified. Other principal offices were given by patent to men of interest in England, who let them out to the best bidders, none of whom understood the language of the natives, but all, in their turn, hired such servants as would work at the cheapest rate, without much inquiry how the work was done. As no salary was annexed to these patent places, the value of them depended upon the fees, which the governor was ordered to establish equal to the fees in the richest ancient colonies; nor could he restrain the officers who lived by fees from running them up to extortion. When he checked them in their profits, he was regarded as their enemy, nor was there any chance for harmony in the government, unless all should become equally corrupt.

The supreme court of judicature took to itself all causes, civil and criminal. The chicanery and expensiveness of Westminster Hall were introduced into the impoverished province; and English justice and English offices seemed to the poor Canadians an ingenious device to drain them of the little substance which was still left to them. In the one hundred and ten rural parishes there were but nineteen Protestant families. The rest of the Protestants were a few half-pay officers, disbanded soldiers, traders, mechanics, and publicans, who resided in Quebec and Montreal; most of them followers of the army, of low education; all, with their fortunes to make, and little solicitous about the means. "I report them," wrote Murray, "to be, in general, the most immoral collection of men I ever knew." Yet out of these, and these alone, though they were but about four hundred and fifty in number, magistrates were to be made and juries composed; for all Catholics were disfranchised. The meek and unresisting province was given over submissively to hopeless oppression. The history of the world furnishes no instance of so rash injustice.

In September, letters were received in New York, announcing a similar most cruel and unjust exercise of the prerogative in the region which now forms the state of Vermont. The king in council, misled by the entreaties of some of the crown officers of New York who were greedy of the wealth to be gained through the land grants of a province, had, at the instance of Halifax, dismembered New Hampshire, and annexed to New York the country north of Massachusetts and west of Connecticut river. The decision was declaratory of the boundary; and it was therefore held by the royalists that the grants made under the sanction of the royal governor of New Hampshire were annulled. Many of the lands for which the king had received the price, and which were already occupied and cultivated, were granted in the king's name anew, and the former purchasers were compelled to redeem them, or take the risk of eviction.

After the return of Bradstreet from Lake Erie and Detroit, it was desirable to show a strong force in the midst of the red men on the Ohio. The regular army could furnish scarcely five hundred men, most of them Highlanders. Pennsylvania, at her own charge, added a thousand, and Virginia contributed a corps of volunteers. These in October took up the march, under Bouquet, for the heart of Ohio. Virginia volunteers formed the advance-guard, the axe-men followed to clear three paths. On each flank, the soldiers marched in single file; in the centre, two deep, followed by the convoy of well-laden pack-horses and droves of sheep and oxen; a party of light horsemen came next; Virginia volunteers brought up the rear. Many who had lost children or friends went with the army to search for them in the wilderness.

A little below the mouth of Sandy Creek, chiefs and warriors of the Senecas, the Delawares, and the Shawnees lighted the council-fire, smoked the calumet, and entreated peace. At the close of the speech, the Delaware chiefs delivered up eighteen white prisoners, and eighty-three small sticks as pledges for the return of so many more. To insure the performance of their promises, Bouquet marched farther into their country; and, at the junction of the White Woman and the Tuscarawas, in the centre of the Indian villages, he made an encampment that had the appearance of an English town.

There the Shawnees, the most violent and warlike of all the tribes, accepting the terms of peace with dejected sullenness, promised by their orator, Red Hawk, to collect all captives from the lower towns, and restore them in the spring; and there the nearer villages delivered up their white prisoners. Mothers recognised their children; sisters and brothers, scarcely able to recover the accent of their native tongue, learned to know that they had the same parents. Whom the Indians spared they loved. They had not taken the little ones and the captives into their wigwams without receiving them into their hearts, and adopting them into their tribes and families. At parting with them, the red men shed torrents of tears, and entreated the white men to show kindness to those whom they restored. From day to day they visited them in the camp; they gave them corn and skins. As the English returned to Pittsburg, they followed to hunt for them and bring them provisions. A young Mingo would not be torn from a young woman of Virginia, whom he had taken as his wife. Some of the children had learned to love their savage friends, and wept at leaving them. Some of the captives could not be brought away but in bonds. Some, who were not permitted to remain, clung to their dusky lovers at parting; others invented means to escape to the wigwams of their chosen warriors.

With the wilderness pacified, with the French removed, an unbounded career of happiness and tranquillity seemed opening upon the British empire. Never was there a moment when the affections of the colonists struggled more strongly toward England, or when she could more easily have secured to herself all the benefits of their trade, as well as their good-will; but the new regulations, and the announcement of the determination of the British parliament to impose further taxes on America, drove them toward independence.

At that moment the spirit of resistance was nowhere so strong as in New York. Its assembly, in September, in their address to the governor, claimed for their constituents "that great badge of English liberty, the being taxed only with their own consent." This "exclusive right," of which the loss would bring "basest vassalage," they, in October, represented to the king as a right which "had received the royal sanction;" and they enumerated, as their grievances, "involuntary taxes," the "acts of trade," the substitution of a judge in a vice-admiralty court for the trial by jury, the restraint on the use of the credit of the colony by act of parliament. These complaints they repeated in a manifesto to the house of lords, to whom they further "showed" that "the supreme power lodged in a single person" is less fearful than a constitution in which one part of the community holds the right forever to tax and legislate for the other. If the constitution of Great Britain gives to parliament that right, then, they say, "it is the most unequal constitution that ever existed; and no human foresight or contrivance can prevent its final consummation in the most intolerable oppression."

In a petition and representation to the house of commons, they pleaded that they had never refused, and promised that they never would refuse, to hearken to a just requisition from the crown. They appealed to their records, as evidence of their untainted loyalty and their exercise of their political privileges without abuse. "An exemption from the burden of ungranted and involuntary taxes must be the grand principle of every free state. Without such a right vested in themselves, exclusive of all others, there can be no liberty, no happiness, no security, nor even the idea of property. Life itself would become intolerable. We proceed with propriety and boldness to inform the commons of Great Britain, who, to their infinite honor, in all ages asserted the liberties of mankind, that the people of this colony nobly disdain the thought of claiming that exemption as a privilege. They challenge it, and glory in it as their right. The thought of independency upon the supreme power of the parliament we reject with the utmost abhorrence. The authority of the parliament of Great Britain to model the trade of the whole empire, so as to subserve the interest of her own, we are ready to recognise in the most extensive and positive terms; but the freedom to drive all kinds of traffic, in subordination to and not inconsistent with the British trade, and an exemption from all duties in such a course of commerce, is humbly claimed by the colonies as the most essential of all the rights to which they are entitled as colonists, and connected in the common bond of liberty with the free sons of Great Britain. For, since all impositions, whether they be internal taxes, or duties paid for what we consume, equally diminish the estates upon which they are charged, what avails it to any people by which of them they are impoverished?" And they deprecated the loss of their rights as likely "to shake the power of Great Britain."

Connecticut, in its October session, in a methodical statement, with divisions and subdivisions, and a just enumeration of its services in the war, demonstrated that "charging stamp duties, or other internal duties, by authority of parliament, would be such an infringement of the rights, privileges, and authorities of the colonies, that it might be humbly and firmly trusted, and even relied upon, that the supreme guardians of the liberties of the subject would not suffer the same to be done."

At the opening of an October session of the general court of Massachusetts, Thacher, of the house, offered an address to the king, lords, and commons, in which exemption from taxation by an act of parliament was claimed as a right. To this the council, misled by the pretended patriotism of Hutchinson, made resistance. After long altercations between the two branches, the house joined in a memorial, which left out the assertion of right, and asked for the continuance of the privileges heretofore enjoyed. Hardly was the business disposed of when the petition of New York came to their knowledge, and put them to shame.

The people of Rhode Island, headed by Stephen Hopkins, the governor of their own choice, would not admit any just authority in parliament to enact even the laws of trade. They elected Hopkins, Daniel Jenckes, and Nicholas Brown their committee of correspondence. These, in their circular of the twelfth of October, expressed their wish "that some method could be hit upon for collecting the sentiments of each colony, and for uniting and forming the substance of them all into one common defence of the whole." Rhode Island, in its petition to the king, claimed "by right the essential privilege not to part with their property but by laws to which they have consented."

Pennsylvania had failed to make liberal grants for the public service, only because its proprietaries had interposed their negative, unless their own estates should be wholly or partially exempted from taxation. They were, moreover, the landlords of all the inhabitants, and yet the judges, who were to decide all questions between them and their tenants, were of their own appointment and held office only during their own good pleasure. To escape from the perpetual intervention of the interest of the proprietaries in public affairs, Franklin, with the great body of the Quakers as well as royalists, desired that the province should become a royal government. Dickinson, though ever the opponent of the scandalous selfishness of the proprietaries, earnestly resisted the proposal; for he saw that "the province must stake on the event liberties that ought to be immortal;" and desired to see an olive-leaf, at least, brought to them from the king before they should quit their ark. On the other side, Joseph Galloway, a royalist at heart, urged their just complaints against the proprietaries.

A petition for the change was adopted by a large majority; but, when in summer the policy of Grenville with regard to the American stamp act was better understood, a new debate arose, in which Franklin took the lead. It was argued that, during the war, the people of Pennsylvania had granted more than their proportion, and were ever ready to grant sums suitable to their abilities and zeal for the service; that, therefore, the proposition of taxing them in parliament was both cruel and unjust; that, by the constitution of the colonies, their business was with the king, and never, in any way, with the chancellor of the exchequer; that they could not make any proposition to Grenville about taxing their constituents by parliament, since parliament had no right to tax them at all; that the notice which they had received bore no marks of being the king's order, or made with his knowledge; that the king had always accompanied his requisition with good words, but that the financier, instead of making a decent demand, had sent a menace that they should certainly be taxed, and had only left them the choice of the manner; and they "resolved, that as they always had, so they always should, think it their duty to grant aid to the crown, according to their abilities, whenever required of them in the usual constitutional manner."

At the elections in autumn, the proprietary party, representing that "the king's little finger would be found heavier than the proprietaries' whole loins," succeeded, by a majority of about twenty votes among near four thousand, in defeating Franklin's return as the representative of Philadelphia. But the new assembly, on the twenty-sixth of October, elected him their agent, and he forthwith sailed for England.

On the last day of October, the assembly of North Carolina, in an address to their governor, used these words: "We observe our commerce circumscribed in its most beneficial branches, diverted from its natural channel, and burthened with new taxes and impositions laid on us without our privity or consent, and against what we esteem our inherent right and exclusive privilege of imposing our own taxes."

On the fourteenth of November, the council and burgesses of Virginia, acting in perfect harmony, and admitting the veto power vested in the crown, sent this entreaty to the king: "Protect your people of this colony in the enjoyment of their ancient and inestimable right to be governed by such laws respecting their internal polity and taxation as are derived from their own consent—a right which, as men, and descendants of Britons, they have ever quietly possessed, since, by royal permission and encouragement, they left the mother kingdom to extend its commerce and dominion."

In their memorial to the lords spiritual and temporal, they said: "Our ancestors brought with them every right they could claim in their mother kingdom, and their descendants cannot be deprived of those rights without injustice; the power in the British parliament to tax the colonies was never before constitutionally assumed; duty to themselves and their posterity lays your memorialists under the necessity of endeavoring to establish their constitution upon its proper foundation."

To the British house of commons Virginia alone addressed a REMONSTRANCE. It was written by George Wythe, and was equally explicit in claiming that Virginians held the rights of Englishmen as inherent rights, impossible to be renounced or forfeited by their removal hither; that these rights had been established by charter and by unbroken usage; that a contrary system would break up the commercial connection between Great Britain and her colonies and compel the colonists to supply their wants by their own manufactures. "It is to be hoped that the commons will not prosecute a measure which those who must suffer under it could not but look upon as fitter for exiles driven from their native country after ignominiously forfeiting its favor and protection, than for the posterity of loyal Britons; the exercise of anti-constitutional power even in this remote corner might be dangerous in its example."

In the midst of the strife about taxation, Colden planned the prostration of the influence of the lawyers and great landholders by insisting that in all cases, even in the common law courts, and without a writ of error, there lay the right to appeal from the verdict of a jury to the king. To the earl of Halifax he signalized the lawyer John Morin Scott as an incendiary; and entreated the removal of Justice Robert R. Livingston, who refused appeals from the verdict of juries.

From Massachusetts, Bernard, in November, urged that the proper time was come for the "new arrangement of New England" by the king in parliament. The two "republics" of Connecticut and Rhode Island were to be dissolved; New York was to be bounded on the east by Connecticut river; Massachusetts to embrace the country from the Connecticut to the

Piscataqua. Another colony, with Falmouth—now Portland—as its capital, might extend to the Penobscot, and yet another to the St. John's. A modification of the charter of Massachusetts, an order of nobility for life, and places of profit with sure emoluments, would place the king's authority "upon a rock."

In Connecticut, the aged Johnson, then enjoying "sweet retirement" in Stratford, thought it no sin to pray to God that "the monstrously popular constitution" of Connecticut might be changed; that the government at home might make but "one work" of bringing "all the colonies under one form of government," confidently hoping that the first news in the spring would be bishops for America, and all charter governments dependent immediately on the king.

On the eleventh of December, the board of trade represented to the king that the legislature of Massachusetts by its votes in June, of New York by its address to Colden in September, had been guilty "of the most indecent disrespect to the legislature of Great Britain." This the privy council reported to be "a matter of the highest consequence to the kingdom;" and Halifax received orders on "the time and manner of laying the papers before parliament." Having thus made sure in advance of the support of vast majorities, the ministry retired to enjoy the Christmas holidays in country-houses, where wealth, and intelligence, and tradition, combined to give to aristocratic hospitality its greatest grace, abundance, and refinement.

## CHAPTER VIII.

THE TWELFTH PARLIAMENT OF GREAT BRITAIN PASSES THE AMERICAN STAMP-TAX. GRENVILLE'S ADMINISTRATION CONTINUED.

JANUARY–APRIL 1765.

AT the opening of the year 1765, the people of New England were reading the history of the first sixty years of the colony of Massachusetts, by Hutchinson. Nothing so much revived the ancestral spirit which a weariness of the gloomy superstitions, mixed with Puritanism, had long overshadowed. All hearts ran together in the study of the character of New England's fathers; and liberty became the dearer, as men were reminded through what sorrow and self-denial and cost of life it had been purchased.

"I always," said John Adams, "consider the settlement of America with reverence and wonder, as the opening of a grand scene and design in Providence for the illumination of the ignorant and the emancipation of the slavish part of mankind all over the earth." This vision was drawing near its fulfilment. On the tenth of January, the king, opening the session of parliament, presented the American question as one of "obedience to the laws and respect for the legislative authority of the kingdom."

In the debates on the forces to be kept up in the navy and the army, Charles Townshend advocated the largest numbers; "for the colonies," said he, "are not to be emancipated." In private, the arguments in behalf of America were urged with persuasive earnestness. The London merchants found that America was in their debt to the amount of four millions of pounds sterling. Grenville sought to relieve their fears by the profuse offer of bounties to the Americans, as offsets to the intended taxation. "If one bounty," said he to them, "will not do, I will add two; if two will not do, I will add three." He wished to act smoothly in the matter; but was resolved "to establish as undoubted the authority of the British legislature in all cases whatsoever."

The agents of the colonies had several meetings, and on Saturday, the second of February, Franklin, with Ingersoll, Jackson, and Garth, as agents for Pennsylvania, Connecticut, and South Carolina, waited on the minister, to remonstrate in behalf of America against taxation of the colonies by parliament. "I have really been made to believe," he replied, "that, considering the whole circumstances of the mother country and the colonies, the latter can and ought to pay something to the common cause. I know of no better way than that now pursuing to lay such tax. If you can tell of a better, I will adopt it." Franklin pleaded for the usual method, by the king's requisition, through the secretary of state; and he put into his hands the pledge of Pennsylvania to respect the demand, when so made. "Can you agree," rejoined Grenville, "on the proportions each colony should raise?" To this they could only answer no, on which he remarked that the stamp act would adapt itself to the number and increase of the colonies. Jackson pointed out the danger that, when the crown should have a civil list and support for a standing army from their money, independent of their assemblies, the assemblies would soon cease to be called together. "No such thing is intended," replied Grenville, warmly, addressing himself to the Americans. "I have pledged my word for offering the stamp bill to the house, and I cannot forego it; they will hear all objections, and do as they please. I wish you may preserve moderation in America. Resentments indecently expressed on one side of the water will naturally produce resentments on the other. You cannot hope to get any good by a controversy with the mother country. With respect to this bill, her ears will always be open to every remonstrance expressed in a becoming manner."

The decorum of Grenville was not preserved by the government; Soame Jenyns, the oldest member of the board of trade, published authoritatively the views of his patrons.

He mocked at the "absurdity" of Otis, and "the insolence" of New York and Massachusetts. "The arguments of America," said he, "mixed up with patriotic words, such as liberty, property, and Englishmen, are addressed to the more numerous part of mankind, who have ears, but no understanding," and he met them with jesting levity.

"It is to be hoped," so he concluded, "all parties and factions, all connections, every member of the British parliament, will most cordially unite to support this measure, which every man who has any property or common sense must approve, and which every English subject ought to require of an English administration."

A dispute had arisen in West Florida between the half-frantic governor, Johnstone, and the commanding officer. Johnstone insisted on the subordination of the military to the civil power: the occasion was seized to proclaim its supremacy in America. The continent was divided into a northern and southern district, each with its brigadier, beside a commander-in-chief for the whole; and, on the morning of the sixth of February, Welbore Ellis, secretary of war, who, at the request of Halifax, had taken the king's pleasure on the subject, made known the king's intention "that the orders of his commander-in-chief, and under him of the brigadiers-general commanding in the northern and southern departments, in all military matters, should be supreme, and be obeyed by the troops as such in all the civil governments of America." In the absence, and only in the absence, of the general and of the brigadiers, the civil governor might give the word. And these instructions, which concentrated undefined power in the hands of the commander-in-chief, rested on the words of the commission which Hardwicke had prepared for governing the troops in time of war. From this measure Grenville had kept aloof.

At a few hours later on the same day, George Grenville proposed to the house of commons, in committee on ways and means, fifty-five resolutions, embracing the details of a stamp act for America, and making all offences against it cognizable in the courts of admiralty, without any trial by jury.

To prove the fitness of the tax, he argued that the colonies had a right to demand protection from parliament, and parliament, in return, had a right to enforce a revenue from the colonies; that protection implied an army, an army must receive pay, and pay required taxes; that, on the peace, it was found necessary to maintain a body of ten thousand men, at a cost exceeding three hundred thousand pounds, most of which was a new expense; that the duties and taxes already imposed or designed would not yield more than one hundred thousand pounds, so that England would still have to advance two thirds of the new expense; that it was reasonable for the colonies to contribute this one third part of the expense necessary for their own security; that the debt of England was one hundred and forty millions sterling, of America but eight hundred thousand pounds; that the increase of annual taxes in England, within ten years, was three millions, while all the establishments of America, according to accounts which were produced, cost the Americans but seventy-five thousand pounds.

The charter clause under which a special exemption was claimed for Maryland was read; and he argued that that province, upon a public emergency, is subject to taxation, in like manner with the rest of the colonies, or the sovereignty over it would cease. If it were otherwise, why is it bound at present by several acts affecting all America, and passed since the grant of its charter? Besides, all charters, he insisted, are under the control of the legislature.

"The colonies claim, it is true," he continued, "the privilege, which is common to all British subjects, of being taxed only with their own consent, given by their representatives; and may they ever enjoy the privilege in all its extent; may this sacred pledge of liberty be preserved inviolate to the utmost verge of our dominions, and to the latest pages of our history. I would never lend my hand toward forging chains for America, lest, in so doing, I should forge them for myself. But the remonstrances of the Americans fail in the great point of the colonies not being represented in parliament, which is the common council of the whole empire, and as such is as capable of imposing internal taxes as impost duties, or taxes on intercolonial trade, or laws of navigation."

Beckford, a member for London, a friend of Pitt, and a large owner of West India estates, without disputing the supreme authority of parliament, declared his opinion that "taxing America for the sake of raising a revenue would never do." Jackson, who had concerted with Grenville to propose an American representation in parliament, spoke and voted against the resolutions. "The parliament," he argued, "may choose whether they will tax America or not; they have a right to tax Ireland, yet do not exercise that right. Still stronger objections may be urged against their taxing America. Other ways of raising the moneys there requisite for the public service exist, and have not yet failed; but the colonies, in general, have with alacrity contributed to the common cause. It is hard all should suffer for the fault of two or three. Parliament is undoubtedly the universal, unlimited legislature of the British dominions, but it should voluntarily set bounds to the exercise of its power; and, if the majority think they ought not to set these bounds, then they should give a share of the election of the legislature to the American colonies, otherwise the liberties of America, I do not say will be lost, but will be in danger; and they cannot be injured without danger to the liberties of Great Britain."

Grenville had urged the house not to suffer themselves to be moved by resentment. One member, however, referred with asperity to the votes of New York and Massachusetts; and it was generally held that America was as virtually represented in parliament as the great majority of the inhabitants of Great Britain.

Isaac Barré, the companion and friend of Wolfe, sharer in the capture of Louisburg and Quebec, without denying the power of parliament to tax America, derided the idea of virtual representation. "Who of you, reasoning upon this subject," he cried, putting his hand to his breast, "feels as warmly from the heart for the Americans as you would for yourselves, or as you would for the people of your own native country?" and he taunted the house with its ignorance of American affairs.

The charge of ignorance called upon his feet Charles Townshend. He insisted that the colonies had borne but a small proportion of the expenses of the last war, and had yet obtained by it immense advantages at a vast expense to the mother country. "And now," said he, "will these American children, planted by our care, nourished up to strength and opulence by our indulgence, and protected by our arms, grudge to contribute their mite to relieve us from the heavy burden under which we lie?"

With eyes darting fire and outstretched arm, Barré uttered an unpremeditated reply: "*They planted by* YOUR *care!* No: your oppressions planted them in America. They fled from your tyranny to a then uncultivated, unhospitable country, where they exposed themselves to almost all the hardships to which human nature is liable; and, among others, to the cruelties of a savage foe, the most subtle, and, I will take upon me to say, the most formidable of any people upon the face of God's earth; and yet, actuated by principles of true English liberty, they met all hardships with pleasure, compared with those they suffered in their own country from the hands of those who should have been their friends. *They nourished up by* YOUR *indulgence!* They grew by your neglect of them. As soon as you began to care about them, that care was exercised in sending persons to rule them in one department and another, who were, perhaps, the deputies of deputies to some members of this house, sent to spy out their liberties, to misrepresent their actions, and to prey upon them; men whose behavior on many occasions has caused the blood of those SONS OF LIBERTY to recoil within them; men promoted to the highest seats of justice, some who, to my knowledge, were glad, by going to a foreign country, to escape being brought to the bar of a court of justice in their own. *They protected by* YOUR *arms!* They have nobly taken up arms in your defence; have exerted a valor, amid their constant and laborious industry, for the defence of a country whose frontier was drenched in blood, while its interior parts yielded all its little savings to your emolument. And believe me—remember I this day told you so—the same spirit of freedom which actuated that people at first will accompany them still. But prudence forbids me to explain myself further. God knows I do not at this time speak from motives of party heat; what I deliver are the genuine sentiments of my heart. However superior to me in general knowledge and experience the respectable body of this house may be, yet I claim to know more of America than most of you, having seen and been conversant in that country. The people, I believe, are as truly loyal as any subjects the king has; but a people jealous of their liberties, and who will vindicate them, if ever they should be violated. But the subject is too delicate; I will say no more."

As Barré spoke, Ingersoll, of Connecticut, joint agent for that province, sat in the gallery. Delighted with the speech, he made a report of it, which the next packet carried across the Atlantic. The lazy posts of that day brought it in nearly three months to New London, in Connecticut; and it was printed in the newspaper of that village. May had not shed its blossoms before the words of Barré were as household words in every New England town. Midsummer saw them circulate through Canada, in French; and the continent rung from end to end with the cheering name of the SONS OF LIBERTY. But, at St. Stephen's, the members only observed that Townshend had received a heavy blow. The opponents of the measure, who were chiefly Irishmen, or holders of estates in Ireland, or holders of West India estates, dared not risk a division on the merits of the question, but about midnight, after a languid debate of seven hours, Beckford moved an adjournment, which Sir William Meredith seconded; and it was carried against America by two hundred and forty-five to forty-nine. Conway and Beckford alone were said to have denied the power of parliament; and it is doubtful how far it was questioned even by them.

While this debate was proceeding, faith in English liberty was conquering friends for England in new regions. The people of Louisiana, impatient of being transferred from France, would gladly have exchanged the dominion of Spain for that of England. Officers from West Florida reached Fort Chartres, preparatory to taking possession of the country, which was still delayed by the discontent of the Indians. With the same object, Croghan and a party descended the Ohio from Pittsburg. A plan was formed to connect Mobile and Illinois. The governor of North Carolina believed that, by pushing trade up the Missouri, a way to the great western ocean would be discovered, and an open trade to it be established. So wide was the territory, so vast the interests, for which the British parliament was legislating!

On the seventh of February, Grenville, Lord North, and Jenkinson, with others, were ordered to bring in a stamp bill for America, which on the thirteenth was introduced by Grenville, and read the first time without a syllable of debate. Among the papers that were to be stamped, it enumerated the several instruments used in the courts of episcopal jurisdiction; for he reasoned that one day such courts might be established in America. On the fifteenth, merchants trading to Jamaica offered a petition against it, and prayed to be heard by counsel. "No counsellor of this kingdom," said Fuller, formerly chief justice of Jamaica, "would come to the bar of this house and question its authority to tax America. Were he to do so, he would not remain there long." It was the rule of the house "to receive no petition against a money bill;" and the petition was withdrawn.

Next, Sir William Meredith, in behalf of Virginia, presented a paper, in which Montague, its agent, interweaving expressions from the votes of the assembly of the Old Dominion, prayed that its house of burgesses might be continued in the possession of the rights and privileges they had so long and uninterruptedly enjoyed, and might be heard. Against this, too, the same objection existed. But Virginia found an advocate in Conway. Indignant at his recent dismissal from the army, as he rose in opposition to Grenville, his cheeks flushed, and he was tremulous from emotion.

"Shall we shut our ears," he argued, "against the representations which have come from the colonies, and for receiving which we, with an affectation of candor, allotted sufficient time? The light which I desire, the colonists themselves alone can give. The practice of receiving no petitions against money bills is but one of convenience, from which, in this instance, if in no other, we ought to vary; for from whom, unless from themselves, are we to learn the circumstances of the colonies, and the fatal consequences that may follow the imposing of this tax? The question regards two millions of people, none of whom are represented in parliament. Gentlemen cannot be serious when they insist on their being virtually represented. Will any man in this house get up and say he is one of the representatives of the colonies?"

"The commons," said Gilbert Elliot, "have maintained against the crown and against the lords their right of solely voting money without the control of either, any otherwise than by a negative; and will you suffer your colonies to impede the exercise of those rights?"

"Can there be a more declared avowal of your power," retorted Conway, "than a petition submitting this case to your wisdom, and praying to be heard before your tribunal against a tax that will affect them in their privileges, which you at least have suffered, and in their property which they have acquired under your protection? From a principle of lenity, of policy, and of justice, I am for receiving the petition of a people from whom this country derives its greatest commerce, wealth, and consideration."

In reply, Charles Yorke entered into a very long and most elaborate defence of the bill, resting his argument on the supreme and sovereign authority of parliament. With a vast display of legal erudition, he insisted that the colonies were but corporations; their power of legislation was but the power of making by-laws, subject to parliamentary control. Their charters could not convey the legislative power of Great Britain, because the prerogative could not grant that power. The charters of the proprietary governments were but the king's standing commissions; the proprietaries were but his hereditary governors. The people of America could not be taken out of the general and supreme jurisdiction of parliament.

The authority of Yorke was decisive: less than forty were willing to receive the petition of Virginia. A third from South Carolina; a fourth from Connecticut, though expressed in the most moderate language; a fifth from Massachusetts, though silent about the question of "right"—shared the same refusal. That from New York no one could be prevailed upon to present. That from Rhode Island, offered by Sherwood, its faithful agent, claimed by their charter, under a royal promise, equal rights with their fellow-subjects in Great

Britain, and insisted that the colony had faithfully kept their part of the compact; but it was as little heeded as the rest. The house of commons would neither receive petitions nor hear counsel.

All the efforts of the agents of the colonies were fruitless. "We might," said Franklin, "as well have hindered the sun's setting." "We have power to tax them," said one of the ministry, "and we will tax them." "The nation was provoked by American claims of legislative independence, and all parties joined in resolving by this act to settle the point." Within doors, less resistance was made to the act than to a common turnpike bill.

"The affair passed with so very little noise that in town they scarcely knew the nature of what was doing."

On the twenty-seventh, the house of commons sent up the stamp act to the house of lords. In that body, Rockingham was silent; Temple and Lyttelton both approved the principle of the measure, and the right asserted in it. Had there existed any doubt concerning that right, they were of opinion it should then be debated, before the honor of the legislature was engaged to its support. On the eighth of March, the bill was agreed to by the lords, without having encountered an amendment, debate, protest, division, or single dissentient vote.

The king was too ill to ratify the act in person. To a few only was the nature of his affliction known. At the moment of passing the stamp act George III. was crazed; so, on the twenty-second of March, it received the royal assent by a commission. The sovereign of Great Britain, whose soul was wholly bent on exalting the prerogative, taught the world that a bit of parchment bearing the sign of his hand, scrawled in the flickering light of clouded reason, could, under the British constitution, do the full legislative office of the king. Had he been a private man, his commission could have given validity to no instrument whatever.

It was thought "prudent to begin with small duties and taxes, and to advance in proportion as it should be found the colonies would bear." For the present, Grenville attempted nothing more than to increase the revenue from the colonial post-office by reducing the rate of postage in America.

His colleagues desired to extend the mutiny act to America, with power to billet troops on private houses. Clauses for that purpose had been strongly recommended by Gage. They had neither the entire conviction nor the cordial support of Grenville; so that they were introduced and carried through, by the secretary at war, as a separate measure. In their progress, provincial barracks, inns, ale-houses, barns, and empty houses were substituted by the merchants and agents for private houses; but there remained a clause to compel the colonies to furnish the troops with various articles; and the sums needed for the purpose were "required to be raised in such manner as the public charges for the province are raised." Thus the billeting act contained, what had never before been heard of, a parliamentary requisition on the colonies.

Bounties were at the same time granted on the importation of deals, plank, boards, and timber from the plantations. Coffee of their growth was exempted from an additional duty; their iron might be borne to Ireland; their lumber to Ireland, Madeira, the Azores, and Europe south of Cape Finisterre; the prohibition on exporting their bar iron from England was removed; the rice of North Carolina was as much liberated as that of South Carolina; and rice might be warehoused in England for re-exportation without advancing the duties. It was further provided that the revenue to be derived from the stamp act should not be remitted to England, but constitute a part of the sum to be expended in America.

Grenville resolved to select the stamp officers for America from among the Americans. The friends and agents of the colonies were invited to make the nominations; and they did so, Franklin among the rest.

"You tell me," said the minister, "you are poor, and unable to bear the tax; others tell me you are able. Now take the business into your own hands; you will see how and where it pinches, and will certainly let us know it, in which case it shall be eased."

Not one of the American agents in England "imagined the colonies would think of disputing the stamp-tax with parliament at the point of the sword." "It is our duty to submit," had been the words of Otis. "We yield obedience to the act granting duties," had been uttered by the legislature of Massachusetts. "If parliament, in their superior wisdom, shall pass the act, we must submit," wrote Fitch, the governor of Connecticut, elected by the people, to Jackson. "It can be of no purpose to claim a right of exemption," thought Hutchinson. "It will fall particularly hard on us lawyers and printers," wrote Franklin to a friend in Philadelphia, never doubting it would go into effect, and looking for relief to the rapid increase of the people of America. Knox, the agent for Georgia, wrote publicly in its favor.

Thomas Pownall, who had been so much in the colonies, and really had an affection for them, congratulated Grenville in advance "on the good effects he would see derived to Great Britain and to the colonies from his firmness and candor in conducting the American business." The act seemed sure to enforce itself. Unless stamps were used, marriages would be null, notes of hand valueless, ships at sea prizes to the first captors, suits at law impossible, transfers of real estate invalid, inheritances irreclaimable, newspapers suppressed. Of all who acted with Grenville in the government, he never heard one prophesy that the measure would be resisted. "He did not foresee the opposition to it, and would have staked his life for obedience."

It was held that the power of parliament, according to the purest whig principles, was established over the colonies; but, in truth, the stamp act was the harbinger of American independence, and the knell of the unreformed house of commons.

## CHAPTER IX.

### THE DAY-STAR OF THE AMERICAN UNION.

#### April–July 1765.

This is the moment when the power of the British oligarchy, under the revolution of 1688, was at its culminating point. The ministry esteemed the supreme power of parliament established firmly and forever. The colonists could not export the chief products of their industry—neither sugar, nor tobacco, nor cotton, nor indigo, nor ginger; nor fustic, nor other dyeing woods; nor molasses, nor rice, with some exceptions; nor beaver, nor peltry of any kind; nor copper ore, nor pitch, nor tar, nor turpentine, nor masts, nor yards, nor bowsprits, nor coffee, nor pimento, nor cocoanuts, nor whale-fins, nor raw silk, nor hides, nor skins, nor pot and pearl ashes—to any place but Great Britain, not even to Ireland. No foreign ship might enter a colonial harbor. Salt might be imported from any place into New England, New York, Pennsylvania, and Quebec; wines might be imported from the Madeiras and the Azores, but were to pay a duty in American ports for the British exchequer; and victuals, horses, and servants might be brought from Ireland. In all other respects, Great Britain was not only the sole market for the products of America, but the only storehouse for its supplies.

Lest the colonists should multiply their flocks of sheep and weave their own cloth, they might not use a ship, nor a boat, nor a carriage, nor even a pack-horse, to carry wool, or any manufacture of which wool forms a part, across the line of one province to another. They could not land wool from the nearest islands, nor ferry it across a river, nor even ship it to England. A British sailor, finding himself in want of clothes in their harbors, might not buy there more than forty shillings' worth of woollens.

Where was there a house in the colonies that did not possess and cherish the English Bible? And yet to print that Bible in British America would have been a piracy; and the Bible, though printed in German and in a native savage dialect, was never printed there in English till the land became free.

That the country, which was the home of the beaver, might not manufacture its own hats, no man in the plantations could be a hatter or a journeyman at that trade unless he had served an apprenticeship of seven years. No hatter might employ a negro or more than two apprentices. No American hat might be sent from one plantation to another, or be loaded upon any horse, cart, or carriage for conveyance.

America abounded in iron ores of the best quality, as well as in wood and coal; slitting-mills, steel furnaces, and plating forges, to work with a tilt hammer, were prohibited in the colonies as "nuisances."

While free labor was debarred of its natural rights, the slave-trade was encouraged with unrelenting eagerness; and in the year that had just expired, from Liverpool alone seventy-nine ships had borne from Africa to the West Indies and the continent more than fifteen thousand three hundred negroes, two thirds as many as the first colonists of Massachusetts.

And now, in addition to colonial restrictions and the burdens attached to them, the British parliament had enacted a new system of taxes on America for the relief of the British exchequer. A duty was to be collected on foreign sugar, molasses, indigo, coffee, Madeira wine, imported directly into any of the plantations in America; also a duty on Portuguese and Spanish wines, on eastern silks, on eastern calicoes, on foreign linen cloth, on French lawn, though imported directly from Great Britain; on British colonial coffee shipped from one plantation to another. Nor was henceforward any part of the old subsidy to be drawn back on the export of foreign goods of Europe or the East Indies, and on the export of white calicoes and muslins a still higher duty was to be exacted and retained. And stamp duties were to be paid throughout all the

British American colonies on and after the first day of the coming November.

These laws were to be enforced, not by the regular authorities only, but by naval and military officers, irresponsible to the civil power in the colonies. The penalties and forfeitures for breach of the revenue laws were to be decided in courts of vice-admiralty, without the interposition of a jury, by a single judge, who had no support whatever but from his share in the profits of his own condemnations.

But, if the British parliament can tax America, it may tax Ireland and India, and hold the wealth of the East and of the West at the service of its own oligarchy. As the relation of the government to its outlying dominions would become one of power and not of right, it could not but employ its accumulated resources to make itself the master of the ocean and the oppressor of mankind. "This system, if it is suffered to prevail," said Oxenbridge Thacher, of Boston, "will extinguish the flame of liberty all over the world."

Massachusetts had been led to rely on the inviolability of English freedom and on the equity of parliament; and, when the blow fell, "the people looked upon their liberties as gone." "Tears," said Otis, "relieve me a moment;" and, repelling the imputation " that the continent of America was about to become insurgent," " it is the duty of all," he added, "humbly and silently to acquiesce in all the decisions of the supreme legislature. Nine hundred and ninety-nine in a thousand of the colonists will never once entertain a thought but of submission to our sovereign, and to the authority of parliament in all possible contingencies." "They undoubtedly have the right to levy internal taxes on the colonies." "From my soul, I detest and abhor the thought of making a question of jurisdiction."

Hutchinson was only "waiting to know what more parliament would do toward raising the sums which the colonies were to pay," and which as yet were not half provided for. As chief justice, he charged "the jurors and people" of the several counties to obey. Nor did the result seem doubtful. There could be no danger but from union; and "no two colonies," said he, "think alike; there is no uniformity of measures; the bundle of sticks thus separated will be easily broken." "The stamp act," he assured the ministry, five weeks after the news of its passage, "is received among us with as much decency as could be expected; it leaves no room for evasion, and will execute itself."

In Boston, at the annual election of representatives in May, men called to mind the noble sentiments which had been interwoven into the remonstrances of New York, and were imbittered at the thought that their legislature had been cajoled by Hutchinson into forbearing to claim exemption from taxation as a right. While the patriots censured the acquiescence of Otis, as a surrender of their liberties, the friends of government jeered at him as a Massaniello and a madman. In the gloom that was thickening around him, he repelled merited reproaches like one who could find no consolation. But the town of Boston never ceased to cherish the most genial of its patriots so long as he retained enough of the light of reason to be sensible of its support.

At first the planters of Virginia foreboded universal ruin from the stamp act; but soon they resolved that the act should recoil on England: articles of luxury of English manufacture were banished; and threadbare coats came into fashion. A large provincial debt enforced the policy of thrift. The legislature of Virginia was then assembled, and the electors of Louisa county had just filled a vacancy in their representation by making choice of Patrick Henry, though he had resided among them scarcely a year. Devoted to their interest, he never flattered the people, and was never forsaken by them. As he took his place, not yet acquainted with the forms of business in the house or with its members, he saw the time for the enforcement of the stamp-tax drawing near, while all the other colonies, through timid hesitation or the want of opportunity, remained silent; and cautious loyalty hushed the experienced statesmen of his own. Many of the assembly had made the approaching close of the session an excuse for returning home; but Patrick Henry, a burgess of but a few days, unadvised and unassisted, in an auspicious moment, of which the recollection cheered him to his latest day, came forward in the committee of the whole house; and while Thomas

Jefferson, a young collegian, from the mountain frontier, stood outside of the closed hall, eager to catch the first tidings of resistance, and George Washington, there is no cause to doubt, was in his place as a member, he maintained by resolutions that the inhabitants of Virginia inherited from the first adventurers and settlers of that dominion equal franchises with the people of Great Britain; that royal charters had declared this equality; that taxation by themselves, or by persons chosen by themselves to represent them, was the distinguishing characteristic of British freedom and of the constitution; that the people of that most ancient colony had uninterruptedly enjoyed the right of being thus governed by their own laws respecting their internal polity and taxation; that this right had never been forfeited, nor given up, and had been constantly recognised by the king and people of Great Britain.

It followed from these resolutions, and Patrick Henry so expressed it in a fifth supplementary one, that the general assembly of the whole colony have the sole right and power to lay taxes on the inhabitants of the colony, and that any attempt to vest such power in any other persons whatever tended to destroy British as well as American freedom. It was still further set forth, yet not by Henry, in two resolutions, which, though they were not officially produced, equally embodied the mind of the younger part of the assembly, that the inhabitants of Virginia were not bound to yield obedience to any law designed to impose taxation upon them other than the laws of their own general assembly; and that any one who should, either by speaking or writing, maintain the contrary, should be deemed an enemy to the colony.

A stormy debate arose, and many threats were uttered. Robinson, the speaker, already a defaulter, Peyton Randolph, the king's attorney, and the frank, honest, and independent George Wythe, a lover of classic learning, accustomed to guide the house by his strong understanding and single-minded integrity, exerted all their powers to moderate the tone of "the hot and virulent resolutions;" while John Randolph, the best lawyer in the colony, "singly" resisted the whole proceeding. But, on the other side, George Johnston, of Fairfax, reasoned with solidity and firmness; and Henry flamed with impassioned zeal. Lifted beyond himself, "Tarquin," he cried, " and Cæsar, had each his Brutus; Charles I., his Cromwell; and George III."—"Treason!" shouted the speaker; "treason! treason!" was echoed round the house; while Henry, fixing his eye on the first who interrupted him, continued without faltering, "may profit by their example!"

Swayed by his words, the committee of the whole showed its good-will to the spirit of all the resolutions enumerated, but the five offered by Patrick Henry were alone reported to the house; and on Thursday, the thirtieth of May, having been adopted by small majorities, the fifth by a vote of twenty to nineteen, they became a part of the public record. "I would have given five hundred guineas for a single vote," exclaimed the attorney-general aloud as he came out past Jefferson. But Henry "carried all the young members with him." That night, thinking his work done, he rode home; but the next day, in his absence, an attempt was made to strike all the resolutions off the journals, and the fifth, but only the fifth, was blotted out. The lieutenant-governor, though he did not believe new elections would fall on what he esteemed cool, reasonable men, dissolved the assembly; but the four resolutions which remained on the journals, and the two others on which no vote had been taken, were published in the newspapers throughout America as the avowed sentiment of the Old Dominion.

This is the "way the fire began." "Virginia rang the alarum bell for the continent."

At the opening of the legislature of Massachusetts, Oliver, who had been appointed stamp distributor, was, on the joint ballot of both branches, re-elected councillor by a majority of but three out of about one hundred and twenty votes. More than half the representatives voted against him.

On the day on which the resolves of Virginia were adopted, and just as the speech of Barré acquainted all the people that within parliament itself they had been hailed as the "Sons of Liberty," a message from Governor Bernard informed the new legislature of Massachusetts that "the general settlement of the American provinces, though it might necessarily produce some regulations disagreeable from their novelty, had been long ago proposed, and would now be prosecuted to its utmost completion; that submission to the decrees of the supreme legislature, to which all other powers in the British empire were subordinate, was the duty and the interest of the colonies; that this supreme legislature, the parliament of Great Britain, was happily the sanctuary of liberty and justice; and that the prince who presided over it realized the idea of a patriot king."

Contrary to usage, the house made no reply; but, on the sixth of June, James Otis advised the calling of an American congress, which should consist of committees from each of the thirteen colonies, to be appointed respectively by the delegates of the people, without regard to the other branches of the legislature. Such an assembly had never existed; and the purpose of deliberating upon the acts of parliament was equally novel. The tories sneered at the proposal as visionary and impracticable; but the representatives of Massachusetts shared the creative instinct of Otis. Assuring unanimity by even refusing to consider the question of their exclusive right to originate measures of internal taxation, they sent letters to every assembly on the continent, proposing that committees of the several assemblies should meet at New York, on the first Tuesday of the following October, "to consult together" and "consider of a united representation to implore relief." They elected Otis and two others of their own members for their delegates.

At the same time, the province increased its strength by perseverance in appropriating annually fifty thousand pounds toward discharging its debt; and so good was its credit, and so affluent its people, that the interest on the remaining debt was reduced from six to five per cent by a public subscription among themselves.

Before the proceedings in Virginia and Massachusetts were known in New York, where the reprint of the stamp act was hawked about the streets as the "folly of England and the ruin of America," a freeman of that town, discussing the policy of Grenville, and the arguments on which it rested, demonstrated that they were leading alike to the reform of the British parliament and the independence of America.

"It is not the tax," said he, "it is the unconstitutional manner of imposing it, that is the great subject of uneasiness to the colonies. The minister admitted in parliament that they had in the fullest sense the right to be taxed only by their own consent, given by their representatives; and grounds his pretence of the right to tax them entirely upon this, that they are virtually represented in parliament.

"It is said that they are in the same situation as the inhabitants of Leeds, Halifax, Birmingham, Manchester, and several other corporate towns; and that the right of electing does not comprehend above one tenth part of the people of England.

"And in this land of liberty, for so it WAS our glory to call it, are there really men so insensible to shame as before the awful tribunal of reason to mention the hardships which some places in England are obliged to bear without redress, as precedents for imposing still greater hardships and wrongs upon America?

"It has long been the complaint of the most judicious in England, as the greatest misfortune to the nation, that its people are so unequally represented. Time and change of circumstances have occasioned defects in the rules or forms of choosing representatives for parliament. Some large towns send none to represent them, while several insignificant places, of only a few indigent persons, whose chief support is the sale of their votes, send many members. Seats are purchased with the nation's money; and a corrupt administration, by bribing others with places and pensions, can command a majority in the house of commons that will pass what laws they please. These evils are too notorious to escape general observation, and too atrocious to be palliated. Why are not these crying grievances redressed? Only because they afford the greatest opportunities for bribery and corruption.

"The fundamental principle of the English constitution is reason and natural right. It has within itself the principle of self-preservation, correction, and improvement. That there are towns, corporations, and bodies of people in England in similar circumstances as the colonies, shows that some of the people in England, as well as those in America, are injured and oppressed, but shows no sort of right for the oppression.

Those places ought to join with the Americans in remonstrances to obtain redress of grievances.

"Our adherence to the English constitution is on account of its real excellence. It is not the mere name of English rights that can satisfy us. It is the reality that we claim as our inheritance, and would defend with our lives.

"The great fundamental principles of a government should be common to all its parts and members, else the whole will be endangered. If, then, the interest of the mother country and her colonies cannot be made to coincide, if the same constitution may not take place in both, if the welfare of the mother country necessarily requires of the colonies a sacrifice of their right of making their own laws and disposing of their own property by representatives of their own choosing, then the connection between them ought to cease; and sooner or later it must inevitably cease.

"There never can be a disposition in the colonies to break off their connection with the mother country so long as they are permitted to have the full enjoyment of those rights to which the English constitution entitles them. They desire no more; nor can they be satisfied with less."

These words embodied the sober judgment of New York. They were caught up by the impatient colonies, were reprinted in nearly all their newspapers, were approved of by their most learned and judicious statesmen, and even formed part of the instructions of South Carolina to its agent in England.

Thus revolution proceeded. Virginia marshalled resistance, Massachusetts entreated union, New York pointed to independence.

The summons for the congress had gone forth from Massachusetts when the resolves of Virginia were published to the world. "They have spoken treason," said the royalists. "Is it treason," retorted others, "for the deputies of the people to assert their rights, or to give them away?" "Oh! those Virginians," cried Oxenbridge Thacher, from his death-bed, where, overplied by public exertions, he was wasting away with a hectic, "those Virginians are men; they are noble spirits. I long to speak in court against tyranny words that shall be read after my death." "Why," said one of his friends, "are not our rights and liberties as boldly asserted by every government in America as by Virginia?" "Behold," cried another, "a whole continent awakened, alarmed, restless, and disaffected." Everywhere, from north to south, through the press, in letters, or as they met in private for counsel or in groups in the street, the "Sons of Liberty" told their griefs to one another, and planned retaliation or redress.

"No good reason can be given," observed the more calm among them, "why the colonies should not modestly and soberly inquire what right the parliament of Great Britain has to tax them." "We were not sent out to be slaves," they continued, citing the example of ancient Greece and the words of Thucydides; "we are the equals of those who remained behind. Americans hold equal rights with those in Britain, not as conceded privileges, but inherent and indefeasible." "We have the rights of Englishmen," was the common voice, "and as such we are to be ruled by laws of our own making, and tried by men of our own condition."

"If we are Englishmen," said one, "on what footing is our property?" "The great Mr. Locke," said another, "lays it down that no man has a right to that which another may take from him;" and a third, proud of his respect for the law, sheltered himself under the words of the far-famed Coke: "The lord may tax his villein, high or low; but it is against the franchises of the land for freemen to be taxed but by their own consent in parliament." "If the people in America are to be taxed by the representatives of the people in England, their malady," said Hopkins, of Rhode Island, "is an increasing evil, that must always grow greater by time." "When the parliament once begins," such was the discourse at Boston, "there is no drawing a line." "And it is only the first step," repeated the New York owners of large estates; "a land-tax for all America will be thought of next."

"It is plain," said even the calmest, "Englishmen do not regard Americans as brothers, and equals, but as subordinates, bound to submit to oppression at their pleasure." "A bill was even prepared," thus men warned each other against new dangers, "that authorized quartering British soldiers upon

American private families." "And is not our property seized," they further exclaimed, "by men who cry, 'give, give,' and never say, 'enough,' and thrown into a prerogative court to be forfeited without a jury?"

"There is not silver enough in the colonies to pay for the stamps," computed patriot financiers, "and the trade by which we could get more is prohibited." "And yet," declared the merchants of New York, "we have a natural right to every freedom of trade of the English." "To tax us, and bind our commerce and restrain manufactures," reasoned even the most patient, "is to bid us make brick without straw." "The northern colonies will be absolutely restricted from using any articles of clothing of their own fabric," predicted one colony to another. And men laughed as they added: "Catching a mouse within his majesty's colonies with a trap of our own making will be deemed, in the ministerial cant, an infamous, atrocious, and nefarious crime." "A colonist," murmured a Boston man, who had dipped into Grenville's pamphlet, "cannot make a horseshoe or a hobnail but some ironmonger of Britain shall bawl that he is robbed by the 'American republican.'" "They are even stupid enough," it was said in Rhode Island, "to judge it criminal for us to become our own manufacturers."

"We will eat no lamb," promised the multitude, seeking to retaliate; "we will wear no mourning at funerals." "We will none of us import British goods," said the traders in the towns. The inhabitants of North Carolina set up looms for weaving their own clothes, and South Carolina was ready to follow the example. "The people," wrote Lieutenant-Governor Sharpe, of Maryland, "will go on upon manufactures." "We will have homespun markets of linens and woollens," passed from mouth to mouth, till it found its way across the Atlantic, and alarmed the king in council; "the ladies of the first fortune shall set the example of wearing homespun." "It will be accounted a virtue in them to wear a garment of their own spinning." "A little attention to manufactures will make us ample amends for the distresses of the present day, and render us a great, rich, and happy people."

When the churchmen of New York preached loyalty to the king as the Lord's anointed, "The people," retorted William Livingston, "are the Lord's anointed. Though named 'mob' and 'rabble,' the people are the darling of Providence." Was the Bible quoted as demanding deference to all in authority? "This," it was insisted, "is to add dulness to impiety;" for "tyranny is no government." From the pulpit, Mayhew, of Boston, taught: "The gospel promises liberty and permits resistance."

And then patriots would become maddened with remembering that "some high or low American had had a hand in procuring every grievance." "England," it was said, "is deceived and deluded by place-men and office-seekers." "Yes," exclaimed the multitude, "it all comes of the horse-leeches." When "the friends to government" sought to hush opposition by terror of parliament, the answer was: "You are cowards, you are parricides."

"Power is a sad thing," wrote the Presbyterians of Philadelphia: "our mother should remember we are children, and not slaves." "When all Israel saw that the king hearkened not unto them," responded the Calvinists of the North, "the people answered the king, saying: 'What portion have we in David? what inheritance in the son of Jesse? To your tents, O Israel! Now see to thine own house, David!'" "Who cares," reasoned the more hardy, "whether George or Louis is the sovereign, if both are alike?" "The beast of burden," continued others, "asks not whose pack it carries." "I would bear allegiance to King George," said one who called himself a lover of truth, "but not be a slave to his British subjects."

"But the members of parliament," argued the royalists, "are men of wisdom and integrity, and incapable of dealing unjustly." "One who is bound to obey the will of another," retorted Hopkins, "is as really a slave, though he may have a good master, as if he had a bad one; and this is stronger in politic bodies than in natural ones."

"It is an insult on the most common understanding," thought James Habersham, of Georgia, and every American from Savannah to Maine, "to talk of our being virtually represented in parliament." "It is an insult on common sense to say it," repeated the Presbyterian ministers of the middle states. "Are persons chosen for the representatives of London and

Bristol in like manner chosen to be the representatives of Philadelphia or Boston? Have two men chosen to represent a poor English borough that has sold its votes to the highest bidder any pretence to say that they represent Virginia or Pennsylvania? And have four hundred such fellows a right to take our liberties?"

But it was argued again and again: "Manchester, Birmingham, and Sheffield, like America, return no members." "Why," rejoined Otis, and his answer won applause in England, "why ring everlasting changes to the colonists on them? If they are not represented, they ought to be." "Every man of a sound mind," he continued, "should have his vote." "Ah, but," replied the royalists, holding Otis to his repeated concessions, "you own that parliament is the supreme legislature; will you question its jurisdiction?" And his answer was on the lips of all patriots, learned and unlearned: "Lord Coke declares that it is against Magna Charta and against the franchises of the land for freemen to be taxed but by their own consent."

Thus opinion was echoed from mind to mind, as the sun's rays beam from many clouds, all differing in tints, but every one taking its hue from the same fire. In the midst of the gloom, light broke forth from the excitement of a whole people. Associations were formed in Virginia, as well as in New England, to resist the stamp act by all lawful means. Hope began to rise that American rights and liberties might safely be trusted "to the watchfulness of a united continent."

The insolence of the royal officers provoked to insulated acts of resistance. The people of Rhode island, angry with the commander of a ship-of-war who had boarded their vessels and impressed their seamen, seized his boat, and burned it on Newport common. Men of New England, "of a superior sort," had obtained of the government of New Hampshire a warrant for land down the western slope of the Green Mountains, on a branch of the Hoosic, twenty miles east of the Hudson river. They formed already a community of sixty-seven families, in as many houses, with an ordained minister, their own municipal officers, three several public schools, their meeting-house among the primeval forests of beech and maple; in a word, they enjoyed the flourishing state which springs from rural industry, intelligence, and piety. They called their village Bennington. The royal officers at New York disposed anew of that town, as well as of others near it, so that the king was known to the settlers near the Green Mountains chiefly by his agents, who had knowingly sold his lands twice over. In this way Bennington was made a battle-ground for independence.

But there was no present relief for America unless union could be perfected. Union was the hope of Otis—union that "should knit and work into the very blood and bones of the original system every region, as fast as settled." Yet how comprehensive and how daring the idea! The traditions of the board of trade branded it as "mutinous." Massachusetts had proceeded timidly, naming for its delegates to the proposed congress the patriot Otis, with two others who were "friends to government."

Virginia was ready to convince the world that her people were firm and unanimous in the cause of liberty, but its newly elected assembly was not suffered by Fauquier to come together. New Jersey received the circular letter of Massachusetts on the twentieth of June, the last day of the session of its legislature. The speaker, a friend to the British government, at first inclined to urge sending delegates to the proposed congress; but, on some "advice" from the governor, changed his mind, and the house, in the hurry preceding the adjournment, rather from uncertainty than the want of good-will, unanimously declined the invitation. The assembly of New Hampshire seemed to approve, but did not adopt it. "Nothing will be done in consequence of this intended congress," wrote Bernard, in July; and he seized the opportunity to press "more and more" upon the government at home "the necessity of taking into their hands the appointment of the American civil list," as well as changing the council of the province. Even the liberal governor of Maryland reported "that the resentment of the colonists would probably die out; and that, in spite of the violent outcries of the lawyers, the stamp act would be carried into execution."

But, far away toward the lands of the sun, the assembly of South Carolina was in session; and, on the twenty-fifth of July, debated the circular from Massachusetts. Many objections were made to the legality, the expediency, and most of all to the efficiency of the proposed measure; and many eloquent words were uttered, especially by the youthful John Rutledge, when the subject, on the deliberate resolve of a small majority, was referred to a committee, of which Christopher Gadsden was the chairman. He was a man of deep and clear convictions; thoroughly sincere; of an unbending will and a sturdy, impetuous integrity, which drove those about him, like a mountain torrent dashing on an over-shot wheel, though sometimes clogging with back-water from its own violence. He possessed not only that courage which defies danger, but that persistence which neither peril nor imprisonment nor the threat of death can shake. Full of religious faith, and at the same time inquisitive and tolerant, methodical, yet lavish of his fortune for public ends, he had in his nature nothing vacillating or low, and knew not how to hesitate or feign. After two legislatures had held back, South Carolina, by "his achievement," pronounced for union. "Our state," he used to say, "was the first, though at the extreme end, and one of the weakest, as well internally as externally, to listen to the call of our northern brethren in their distresses. Massachusetts sounded the trumpet, but to Carolina is it owing that it was attended to. Had it not been for South Carolina, no congress would then have happened. She was all alive, and felt at every pore." And when we count up those who, above others, contributed to the great result of union, we are to name the inspired "madman," James Otis, and the unwavering lover of his country, Christopher Gadsden.

Otis now seemed to himself to hear the prophetic song of the "Sibyls" chanting the spring-time of a "new empire."

## CHAPTER X.

### THE BATTLE BETWEEN THE KING AND THE DUKE OF BEDFORD.

#### April–July 1765.

There was but one desire in the king's heart stronger than that of taxing America; it was, to govern as well as to reign in Britain. While America was consolidating its union, divisions that could not be healed planted confusion in the councils of its oppressors. No sooner had the king recovered from the illness, of which the true nature was kept secret even from the members of his cabinet, than, bearing in mind that the heir to the throne was an infant of but two years old, he contemplated the contingency of his own incapacity or death, and resolved on framing a plan for a regency. For this purpose he turned away from his ministers and took the aid of Lord Holland. In consequence, Grenville, on the twenty-eighth of April, "with a firm and steady countenance," and at very great length, expostulated with him on his withholding confidence from his ministers. The king at first started and professed surprise; and, as the conversation proceeded, grew "exceedingly agitated and disturbed, changed countenance, and flushed so much that the water stood in his eyes from the excessive heat of his face;" but he neither denied nor admitted the charge; used no words of anger, of excuse, or of softening; and only put on a smile, when, at a "late hour," the tedious minister "made his bow."

When the offended ministers received orders to prepare the bill for a regency, they thought to win popularity and fix in the public mind their hostility to Bute by disqualifying the princess dowager. So they restrained the choice of the regent "to the queen or any other person of the royal family." The king approved the minute entirely, not knowing that, in the opinion of Bedford, Grenville, Halifax, and Sandwich, his own family did not include his mother.

On the second reading of the bill for the regency in the house of lords, it was asked: "Who are the royal family to whom the selection is restrained?" "The royal family are those who are in the order of succession, one after another," answered Bedford, unmasking the malice in which the bill had been conceived.

The king, who had never intended to appoint his mother regent, authorized the employment of words of which the meaning would admit of no dispute. At the next sitting, Halifax used this permission so indiscreetly that the queen dowager appeared to be excluded from those eligible to the regency by the express authority of her son. The ministry had not intended so much; they had circumvented the king, and used his name to put a brand upon his mother. Bute's friends were thunderstruck, while the duke of Bedford almost danced for joy.

The king's natural affection was very strong; he suffered the utmost agitation, even to tears; and declared that Halifax "had surprised him into the message." When, on the fifth of May, he admitted Grenville, he colored, complained of the disregard to his mother as an offence to her which he could not bear; and, with the embarrassment of a man who begs a favor which he fears may be denied, entreated its removal. Grenville obstinately refused to make the necessary motion; but, with no good grace, consented that the name of the princess dowager should be inserted in the house of commons by one of her own servants.

The ministers pursued the desperate conflict with the king, believing themselves strong enough to compel their sovereign to conform in all things to their advice, and the fate of the American stamp act depended on the issue. Bedford spoke to him defiantly; Grenville asked earnestly that the king's ministers should be suffered to retire, or be seen manifestly to possess his favor. But they drew out no satisfactory answer, though Grenville was led to believe that his own services would be required, even should his old enemy, the duke of Bedford, be dismissed.

On the thirteenth, the king, in his impatience of ministers who did not love each other and only agreed to give him the law, authorized his uncle, the duke of Cumberland, to open negotiations with Pitt, Temple, and the great whig families, for constructing a new administration, with Charles Townshend as one of the secretaries of state, and Northumberland, Bute's son-in-law, at the head of the treasury. Pitt refused the terms offered, but yet without closing the door to other offers. Edmund Burke, as he watched the negotiations with impatient desire, complained of Pitt's hesitancy, and derided his "fustian." Rockingham and Newcastle were eager for the proposed change. Temple and Grafton were summoned to town. Of Grafton, Cumberland asked if a ministry could be formed out of the minority, without Pitt, and received for answer that "nothing so formed could be stable." The wings of popularity were on Pitt's shoulders.

A new complication arose from a riot. At the sitting in which the regency bill, with the amendment rehabilitating the princess dowager, was accepted by the house of lords, it so happened that a bill came up raising the duties on silks, for the benefit of English weavers. In the commons it had been countenanced by Grenville, and it had the approval of the king. But Bedford, having, like Edmund Burke, more liberal views of political economy, spoke on the side of freedom of trade, and the bill was refused a second reading. The next day the silk-weavers went in a large body to Richmond to petition the king for redress.

On the fourteenth, the king, on his way to accept the act for a regency, found himself followed by a crowd of weavers, who beset the house of parliament, vowing vengeance against Bedford, and stoning his chariot. The next day they paraded the streets of London. Bedford repaired with complaints to the king, and Grenville remonstrated; but the king's emotion betrayed his purpose of changing the government.

On Friday, the weavers, threatening death to the duke of Bedford, assembled in the evening round his house, which they might have sacked and destroyed but for the timely arrival of an armed force. Persons of all parties hastened to Bedford house to mark their abhorrence of the riot and their joy at its suppression. The dismissing of Bedford at such a moment had the aspect of inviting the mob to dictate a ministry. Public sympathy turned on his side. "To attempt changing the government," said Lord Mansfield, "is madness, infatuation, and utter ruin to the king's authority forever." The house of lords warmly took up the cause of the ministers. The ministry had never been, and was not then, a thoroughly united body; now, however, Bedford gaining the lead, insisted that they all should act in perfect union; and Grenville, concealing his well-founded distrust of his colleagues, gave and received promises to withstand the court with inseparable fidelity.

But the king had the impatience of offended pride, excited by sleeplessness and disease. Ready to yield every point to Pitt and Temple, he said to the duke of Cumberland, in the kindest terms and most explicit words: "I put myself in this affair wholly into your hands."

Early, therefore, on the nineteenth, the prince hastened to visit Pitt, inviting Temple to join them at a later hour. His journey was a public proclamation of its design. While the royal envoy was negotiating with the great commoner at Hayes, Grenville, Bedford, Halifax, and Sandwich, confident that no new ministry could be formed, each by himself expostulated with the king.

The duke of Bedford reminded him "how very unfaithfully the conditions which the king himself had proposed had been kept," and added: "Since I can no longer be useful, I entreat you not to lose a moment in replacing us all; for the harmony which has subsisted between us does and will continue." "Thus," says the duke, "I left him." Bedford was blunt, as suited his open nature; warm, as one who felt himself wronged; excited, as the bravest man might have been after the risk of having his house torn down over his family. Unabashed, he meant to be plain-spoken, but not to be insolent; and, if he had been so, he did not know it. He went about vowing vengeance on the courtiers who had exposed him to unworthy treatment. "I can depend," said he, "on all my friends as well as colleagues. There have been examples of new ministries that have not been able to last more than four-and-twenty hours."

Meantime, Pitt was saying to the royal envoy at Hayes: "I am ready to go to St. James's if I can carry the constitution with me." In reply, the duke of Cumberland declared, on the king's authority, that he might choose in a new ministry the station which should best suit his own failing health; might direct the foreign policy of England at his pleasure; might procure the condemnation of general warrants, a peerage for Pratt, and the restoration of Conway and other officers who had been dismissed for their opinions; might chalk out a list of such persons as he would wish to fill all the posts of business, and might name Temple for the treasury. In the conduct of this negotiation no obstacle arose from the palace. But the wayward Temple began to estrange himself from his brother-in-law, and was reconciled to Grenville, his brother and apparent heir. "I did not want inducements," said he, "to accept of the great post that presented itself as a supplicant at my gate;" but he refused to royalty the small alms which it begged, and, without the concurrence of Temple, Pitt saw in his way difficulties which he could not overcome.

The ministry now resolved to brave and put down the still obstinate resistance of the king. Exaggerating the danger from the continuance of the riots, Halifax, on the twentieth, obeying Bedford, wrote to the king to appoint the marquis of Granby to the command in chief, in place of Cumberland; while the king, in violation of the constitution, privately ordered Cumberland to act as captain-general.

The king was in despair; and, though the old ministry was sustained by parliament, and at that moment by public opinion, he would have put "in their places any mortal who could have carried on business." Cumberland hated Grenville; but he knew no remedy, and advised his nephew to submit.

The king, who for many days had not slept two hours in twenty-four, next attempted to divide the ministers. Referring to the differences that had existed between Grenville and members of the cabinet, he said: "You never have displeased me; I did not mean to have removed you; I know nothing that could induce me to do it;" and he sought to draw from him a promise to remain in his service. But Grenville chose to stand by his colleagues, and, after meeting them, reported in their name that "before they should again undertake his affairs they must lay before him some questions." "Questions!" said he, abruptly; "conditions you mean, sir; what are they?"

On Wednesday, Grenville, in behalf of the four, communicated to their sovereign the terms offered him for his capitulation. They were that he should renew assurances against Bute's meddling in state affairs; dismiss Mackenzie, Bute's brother, from his employment and place; treat Lord Holland, the adviser of the plan for the regency bill, in the same manner; appoint Granby commander-in-chief in place of Cumberland; and leave to the ministers the settlement of the government in Ireland. Terms more humiliating could not have been devised.

On the next day, Grenville called to receive the king's submission. Of the insult to be offered to his uncle, he obtained a modification; and no one was made commander-in-chief. He struggled to retain Mackenzie in the office of the privy seal in Scotland. Grenville was obstinate. "But I passed to him my royal word," said the king, falling into great agitation; "I should disgrace myself if I dismissed him." "In that case, sir," replied Grenville, "we must decline coming in." The king surrendered; but he was so deeply moved that his physicians were ordered to attend him; his gloom revealed grief at his heart; on the following Sunday the usual drawing-room was omitted; and his mind was so convulsed that he would not take the sacrament.

Grenville, in apparently confident security, continued his schemes of colonial revenue, and made a representation "that the Canadians were subject to taxation by virtue of his prerogative." The king, quivering with wounded pride at the affront received from his ministers, thwarted their suggestions about appointments to office, frowned on those whom they promoted, and publicly showed regard to his friends whom they had displaced. This the duke of Bedford would not brook. On the twelfth of June, being resolved on an immediate explanation, he bluntly recapitulated to his sovereign what had passed between him and his ministers on their resuming their functions, when he had promised them his support. "Has this promise," he demanded, "been kept?

On the contrary, are not almost all our bitter enemies countenanced in public? I hope your majesty will give your countenance to your ministers; or else give your authority where you are pleased to give your favor."

The king, who was resolved to interpret the discourse of Bedford as a resignation, summoned Pitt on the nineteenth to a personal interview. It continued for three hours. Pitt declared himself against the measures that had been adopted to restrain the American colonies from trade with the Spanish islands, and against the taxation of the colonies by act of parliament, which nothing but extreme illness had prevented him from opposing in the house of commons, and of which he foreboded the fatal consequences. The discussion was renewed on the twenty-second, when, having obtained satisfaction as to measures and as to men, he renewed to Lord Temple the invitation to assist in forming an administration. On receiving the news, Temple privately communicated its substance to Grenville, and with a predetermined mind repaired to Pitt. The two were at variance on no important measure except the stamp act. On that there appeared an antagonism of opinion, which divided them for the rest of their lives. Temple refused to take office. Pitt was alike wounded and embarrassed. Lord Temple was his brother-in-law; had, in the time of his retiring from the office of paymaster, helped him with his purse; had twice gone into a ministry with him, and twice faithfully retired with him. The long discussion that ensued deeply affected both; but Temple inflexibly resisted Pitt's judgment and most earnest remonstrance; he would not consent to supplant the brother whose present measures he applauded, and with whom he had just been reconciled. As they parted, Pitt said, pathetically, in the words of a Roman poet: "You, brother, bring ruin on me and on yourself, and on the people and the peers and your country."

"Nervous and trembling," Temple went in to the king and declined "entering his service in any office." "I am afraid," he added—and it was the king himself who repeated the remark—"I foresee more misfortunes in your majesty's reign than in any former period of history." Pitt made his excuses to the king, who "parted from him very civilly," and, with grief and disappointment in his heart, he retired into Somersetshire.

The ministry of Grenville seemed established more firmly than before. The most wary gave in their adhesion; even Charles Yorke went to Grenville and declared his support. "Our cause is in your hands," said the Bedfords to Grenville, "and you will do it justice." This was the moment of his greatest pride; he was at the head of the treasury; he had defeated his sovereign's efforts to change the ministry; he was owned by the Bedfords as their savior and protector. His ambition, his vanity, and his self-will were gratified.

The king had been complaining of the little business done, and of "the neglect of the colonies and new conquests;" Grenville applied himself earnestly to American measures. Bishops were to be engrafted on a plan for an ecclesiastical establishment in Canada. He proposed a reform in the courts of admiralty; in the following days, he, with Lord North, settled the emoluments of the officers charged with carrying into execution the American stamp act; made an enumeration of the several districts for inspection; provided for supplying vacant places among the stamp distributors; and on the ninth of July consulted about removing incidental objections to the measure, in which he gloried as his own.

But the duke of Cumberland had succeeded in forming an administration out of the remnants of the old whig aristocracy and their successors; and, on the tenth, Grenville was summoned to St. James's to surrender the seals of his office. "I beseech your majesty," he said, "as you value your own safety, not to suffer any one to advise you to separate or draw the line between your British and American dominions. Your colonies are the richest jewel of your crown. If any man should venture to defeat the regulations laid down for the colonies by a slackness in the execution, I shall look upon him as a criminal and the betrayer of his country."

The conditions on which the new ministry came into power did not extend beyond the disposal of offices. They introduced no projects of reform; they gave no pledges in behalf of liberty. The old duke of Newcastle was the type of the administration, though he took only the post of privy seal, with the patronage of the church. The law adviser of its choice, as attorney-general, was Charles Yorke, whose opinions coincided with those of Mansfield. The duke of Cumberland had a seat in the cabinet as its mediator with the king.

The post of head of the treasury was assigned to the marquis of Rockingham. He was an inexperienced man of five-and-thirty, possessing no great natural abilities, of a feeble constitution and a nervous timidity which made him almost incapable of speaking in public; acquainted with race-courses and the pedigree of horses; unskilled in the finances of his country, and never before proposed for high office. But he had clear and sagacious sense and good feeling, unshaken fortitude, integrity, kindness of nature, and an honest and hearty attachment to moderated liberty. His virtues were his arts, and they were his talents. Had he been untitled and less opulent, he never would have been heard of; but, being high in rank, of vast wealth, and generous without wastefulness, he was selected, at the moment when the power of the oligarchy was passing its culmination, to lead its more liberal branch; and such was his own ambition of being first in place, such his sincerity, such his fidelity to his political connections, that from this time till the day of his death he remained their standard-bearer.

His deficiencies in knowledge and in rhetoric the minister compensated by selecting as his secretary and intimate friend Edmund Burke, who had recently left the service of one of the opposite party, and renounced a pension bestowed by Halifax. It was characteristic of that period for a man like Rockingham to hold for life a retainer like Edmund Burke; and never did a true-hearted, kindly, and generous patron find one more faithful. He brought to his employer, and gave up to his party, all that he had: boundless stores of knowledge, especially respecting the colonies; wit, philosophy, imagination, gorgeous eloquence, unwearied industry, mastery of the English tongue; and a most accomplished intellect. His ambition was fervid, yet content with the applause of the aristocracy. His political training had brought him in contact with the board of trade, and afterward with the government of Ireland, the country of his birth. His writings are a brilliant picture of the British constitution as it existed in the best days of the eighteenth century; and his genius threw lustre over the decline of the party which he served. No man more thoroughly hated oppression; but he possessed neither experience in affairs nor tranquil judgment, nor the rule over his own spirit: so that his genius wrought much evil to his country and to Europe, even while he rendered noble service to the cause of commercial freedom, to Ireland, and to America.

The seals of the northern department of state were conferred on the duke of Grafton, a young man of respectable abilities, yet impaired by fondness for pleasure; a ready speaker, honest and upright, naturally inclining to the liberal side. He had little sagacity, but he meant well; and, in after years, preferred to record his errors of judgment rather than to leave in doubt the sincerity of his character. This is he to whom the poet Gray, in verse adulatory but not venal, flung praise as to one who, on the wild waves of public life, kept the steady course of honor. In his college vacations, he had seen Pitt at Stowe, and been fascinated by his powers; he took office in the hope that the ministry might adopt the great commoner as its chief.

Conway, who had been arbitrarily dismissed from military office, was suggested as Grafton's associate. But "thinking men foresaw" peril to the stamp act, from "intrusting its execution to one of the very few persons who had opposed the passing of it;" and the king wished to consign that office, which included the administration of the colonies, to Charles Townshend, by whom it had so long been coveted. Who can tell how America would have fared under him, in an administration whose patron was the victor at Culloden? But, though the king in person used every argument to prevail with him, he declined to join in a system which he compared to "lutestring, fit only for summer wear." Even so late as on the ninth of July, the king, who had reserved the place of secretary at war for Conway, renewed his entreaties; but the persistent refusal of Townshend, who held fast to his lucrative office of paymaster, threw the seals of the southern department and America, at the very last moment, into the hands of Conway.

The new secretary, like Shelburne and Edmund Burke, was an Irishman, and therefore disposed to have "very just notions" of the colonies. His temper was mild and moderate; in his inquiries he was reasonable and accurate; and it was his desire to unite both countries in affection as well as interest. But he was diffident and hesitating. He seemed to be inflexibly proud, and was not firm; to be candid, and was only scrupulous. His honesty, instead of nerving his will, kept him forever a skeptic. He would in battle walk up to the cannon's mouth with imperturbable courage; but in the cabinet his mind was in a perpetual seesaw, balancing arguments, and never reaching fixed conclusions, unless his sense of honor was touched, or his gentle disposition was invigorated by his humanity. The necessity of immediate action was sure to find him still wavering. He was fond of doing right, but the time for doing it passed before he could settle what it was; and the man who was now appointed to guide the mind of the house of commons never could make up his own.

The ministry would have restored Shelburne to the presidency of the board of trade; but he excused himself, because Rockingham, on taking office, had given no pledges but as to "men." "Measures, not men, will be the rule of my conduct," said Shelburne, in concurrence with Pitt; and thus the two branches of the liberal aristocracy gained their watchwords. The one was bound to provide for its connection, the other to promote reform. There could be no progress of liberty in England but from the union of the aristocratic power of the one with the popular principle of the other. The refusal of Shelburne left the office to the young earl of Dartmouth, whom the poet Cowper described as the "one who wears a coronet and prays."

A peerage was conferred on Pratt, who took the name of Camden, though Rockingham was averse to his advancement. But it was through Rockingham himself that Lord George Sackville, who had been convicted of cowardice on the field of battle and degraded while Pitt was minister, was restored to a seat at the council board, and raised to one of the lucrative vice-treasurerships of Ireland.

Thus was an administration, whose policy had been sanctioned by large and increasing majorities in parliament, and by the most cordial approbation of the king, avowedly turned out, to gratify his personal disgust at its exercising its constitutional right to control him in the use of the court favor. The new cabinet did not include one man of commanding ability, nor had it a single measure to propose to the crown, to the nation, or to the colonies; and, in parliament, its want of debating talent stamped its character with weakness. Grenville sullenly predicted that every day would produce difficulties in the colonies and with foreign powers.

"Within the last twelve years," wrote Voltaire at that time, "there has been a marked revolution in the public mind. Light is certainly spreading on all sides." George III., without intending it, promoted the revolution which Voltaire awaited.

The agents of the colonies, seeing among the ministry some who had been their friends, took courage to solicit relief; but for many weeks Franklin admitted no hope of success. An order in council, sanctioned by Lord Dartmouth—perhaps the worst order ever proposed by the board of trade, so bad that it was explained away by the crown lawyers as impossible to have been intended—permitted appeals to the privy council from any verdict given by any jury in the courts of New York; while the treasury board prepared to collect in Canada, by the king's authority, the same revenue which had been collected there under the government of Louis XV.; and completed the arrangements for executing the stamp act.

## CHAPTER XI.

AMERICA REPELS ITS STAMP-TAX. ADMINISTRATION OF ROCKINGHAM.

AUGUST–SEPTEMBER 1765.

SIX weeks and more before the change of ministry was known in Boston, Jared Ingersoll, of Connecticut, late agent for that province, now its stamp-master, arrived there from England; and the names of the stamp distributors were published on the eighth of August. The craftily devised policy of employing Americans failed from the beginning. "It will be as in the West Indies," clamored the people; "there the negro overseers are the most cruel." "Had you not rather," said a friend of Ingersoll, "these duties should be collected by your brethren than by foreigners?" "No," answered Professor Dagget, of New Haven. "If the ruin of your country is decreed, are you free from blame for taking part in the plunder?"

"North American Liberty is dead," it was said in one of the newspapers of Boston; "but happily she has left one son, prophetically named Independence, now the hope of all when he shall come of age." But why wait? asked the impatient. "Why should any stamp officers be allowed in America at all?" "I am clear in this point," declared Mayhew, "that no people are under a religious obligation to be slaves if they are able to set themselves at liberty." "The stamp act," it was said universally in Boston, "is arbitrary, unconstitutional, and a breach of charter. Let it be of short duration. There are two hundred thousand inhabitants in this province, and by computation about two millions in America. It is too late for us to be dragooned out of our rights. We may refuse submission, or at least the stamp officers will be afraid to stab their country." If every one of them could be forced to resign, the statute which was to execute itself would perish from the beginning. Boston must lead the way.

It was already known there that the king, desirous of changing his ministry, had sent for William Pitt; and the crowd that kindled the bonfire in King street on the birthday of the prince of Wales rent the air with "God bless our true British king! Heaven preserve the prince of Wales! Pitt and liberty for ever!" And high and low, rich and poor, joined in the chorus: "Pitt and liberty!"

The daybreak of Wednesday, the fourteenth of August, saw the effigy of Oliver, the stamp distributor for Boston, tricked out with emblems of Bute and Grenville, swinging on the bough of an elm, the pride of the neighborhood, known as the Great Tree, standing near what was then the entrance to the town. The pageant had been secretly prepared by Boston mechanics, true-born SONS OF LIBERTY: Benjamin Edes, the printer; Thomas Crafts, the painter; John Smith and Stephen Cleverly, the braziers; and the younger Avery; Thomas Chase, a hater of kings; Henry Bass and Henry Welles. The passers-by stopped to gaze on the grotesque show, and their report collected thousands. Hutchinson, as chief justice, ordered the sheriff to remove the images. "We will take them down ourselves at evening," said the people.

Bernard summoned his council. "The country, whatever may be the consequence," said some of them, "will never submit to the execution of the stamp act." The majority spoke against interfering with the people. Bernard and Hutchinson were still engaged in impotent altercations with their advisers, when, just after dark, an "amazing" multitude, moving in the greatest order and following the images borne on a bier, after passing down the main street, marched directly through the old state house and under the council-chamber itself, shouting at the top of their voices: "Liberty, property, and no stamps." Giving three huzzas of defiance, they next, in Kilby street, demolished the frame of a building which they thought Oliver destined for a stamp office, and with the wooden trophies made a funeral pyre for his effigy in front of his house on Fort Hill.

"The stamp act shall not be executed here," exclaimed one who spoke the general sentiment. "Death to the man who offers a piece of stamped paper to sell!" cried others. "All the power of Great Britain," said a third, "shall not oblige us to submit to the stamp act." "We will die upon the place first," declared even the sober-minded. "We have sixty thousand fighting-men in this colony alone," wrote Mayhew. "And we will spend our last blood in the cause," repeated his townsmen.

Hutchinson directed the colonel of the militia to beat an alarm. "My drummers are in the mob," was his answer. With the sheriff, Hutchinson went up to disperse the crowd. "Stand by, my boys," cried a ringleader; "let no man give way;" and Hutchinson, as he fled, was obliged to run the gauntlet, not escaping without one or two blows. At eleven, the multitude repaired to the Province House, where Bernard lived, and after three cheers they dispersed quietly.

"We have a dismal prospect before us," said Hutchinson, the next morning, anticipating "tragical events in some of the colonies." "The people of Connecticut," reported one whose name is not given, "have threatened to hang their distributor on the first tree after he enters the colony." "If Oliver," wrote Bernard, "had been found last night, he would certainly have been murthered." "If he does not resign," thought many, "there will be another riot to-night, and his house will be pulled down about his ears." So the considerate self-seeker, seasonably in the day-time, "gave it under his own hand" that he would not serve as stamp officer, while Bernard, deserting his post as guardian of the public peace, hurried to the castle, and did not cease trembling even within its walls. At night, a bonfire on Fort Hill celebrated the people's victory. Several hundred men gathered round the house of Hutchinson. "Let us but hear from his own mouth," said their leader, "that he is not in favor of the stamp act, and we will be easy;" but Hutchinson evaded a reply.

The governor, just before his retreat, ordered a proclamation for the discovery and arrest of the rioters. "If discovery were made," wrote Hutchinson, "it would not be possible to commit them." "The prisons," said Mayhew, "would not hold them many hours. In this town, and within twenty miles of it, ten thousand men would soon be collected together on such an occasion." And on the next Lord's Day but one, before a crowded audience, choosing as his text, "I would they were even cut off which trouble you; for, brethren, ye have been called unto liberty," he preached fervidly in behalf of civil and religious freedom. "I hope," said he, "no persons among ourselves have encouraged the bringing such a burden as the stamp act on the country."

The distrust of the people fell more and more upon Hutchinson. "He is a prerogative man," they cried. "He grasps at all the important offices in the state." "He himself holds four, and his relations six or seven more." "He wiped out of the petition of Massachusetts every spirited expression." "He prevailed to get a friend of Grenville made agent for the colony." "He had a principal hand in projecting the stamp act." "He advised Oliver against resigning." "He granted writs of assistance, which are no better than general warrants." "He took depositions against the merchants as smugglers."

The rougher spirits wrought one another into a frenzy. At nightfall, on the twenty-sixth, a bonfire in front of the old state house collected a mixed crowd. They first burned all the records of the hated vice-admiralty court; next ravaged the house of the comptroller of the customs; and then, giving Hutchinson and his family barely time to escape, split open his doors with broadaxes, broke his furniture, scattered his plate and ready money, his books and manuscripts, and at daybreak left his house a ruin.

The coming morning, the citizens of Boston, in town-meeting, expressed their "detestation of these violent proceedings," and pledged themselves to "suppress the like disorders for the future." "I had rather lose my hand," said Mayhew, "than encourage such outrages;" and Samuel Adams agreed with him. But they, and nearly all the townsmen, and the whole continent, applauded the proceedings of the fourteenth of August; and the elm, beneath which the people had on that day assembled, was named "the Tree of Liberty."

The officers of the crown were terror-stricken. The attorney-general did not dare to sleep in his own house, nor two nights together in the same place; and for ten days could not be found. Several persons, who thought themselves obnoxious, left their houses and removed their goods. Hutchinson fled to the castle, wretched from agitation of mind. His despair dates from that moment. He saw the dilemma in which England had placed herself; "if parliament should make concessions, their authority would be lost; if they used force, affection was alienated forever."

"We are not bound to yield obedience," voted the freemen of Providence, repeating the resolves of Virginia. The patriots of Rhode Island, remembering the renowned founders of the colonies, thanked God that their pleasant homes in the western world abounded in the means of "defence." "That little turbulent colony," reported Gage, "raised their mob likewise." And on the twenty-eighth day of August, after destroying the house and furniture of one Howard, who had written, and of one Moffat, who had spoken in favor of the power of parliament to tax America, they gathered round the house of their stamp officer, and, after a parley, compelled him to resign.

At New York, the lieutenant-governor expressed a wish to the general for aid from the army. "You shall have as many troops as you shall demand, and can find quarters for," replied Gage; and he urged Colden to the exertion of the civil power. "The public papers," he continued, "are crammed with treason, and the people excited to revolt." But, meantime, MacEvers, the stamp officer of New York, resigned; "for," said he, "if I attempt to receive the stamps, my house will be pillaged." "MacEvers is terrified," said Colden to a friend; "but I shall not be intimidated; and the stamps shall be delivered in proper time."

On the morning of Monday, the twenty-sixth of August, a number of "the asserters of British American privileges" met in Annapolis, to show their detestation of the stamp act and their dislike of Zachariah Wood, a native of the province and the newly arrived stamp distributor for Maryland. Among the foremost of the gathering was Samuel Chase, a young lawyer of the age of twenty-four, already a member of the Maryland legislature. An effigy of Wood, arrayed as a malefactor, was placed in a one-horse cart, paraded through the streets till noon, with the bells tolling a solemn knell, scourged at the whipping-post, put in the pillory, hung on a gibbet, and then set on fire from a tar-barrel. On the second of September, a party of four or five hundred pulled down a house which he was repairing, as was believed, for the sale of the stamps. Shaking with terror, yet unwilling to part with an office which promised wealth, he fled from the colony to the fort of New York. The Maryland lawyers were of opinion that the stamp-tax must be declared invalid by the courts of Maryland, as a breach of chartered rights. One man published his card, refusing to pay taxes to which he had not consented. All resolved to burn the stamp paper on its arrival in Annapolis; and the governor wrote home that he had no power to prevent it.

On the third of September, Coxe, the stamp officer for New Jersey, renounced his place.

On the fifth, Bernard, at Boston, whose duty it was, after the resignation of Oliver, to take possession of the stamped papers that might arrive, set forth to a very full council that "he had no warrant whatsoever to unpack a bale of them or to order any one else to do so; and it could not be conceived that he should be so imprudent as to undertake the business."

On the ninth, a ship entered Boston, bringing news of the change of ministry, which created great joy and the sanguine expectation of the speedy repeal of the stamp act. "If Astræa were not fled," said Mayhew, "there might be grounds for the hope;" and the colonies, mingling doubt with hope, persisted in showing that the act would bring ills on Great Britain itself. George Meserve, the stamp distributor for New Hampshire, arriving in the same vessel, resigned his office before stepping on land; and, on his return to Portsmouth, repeated his resignation on the parade, in the presence of a great multitude.

Assured of the protection of Fitch, the governor of Connecticut, who at heart was a lukewarm royalist, Ingersoll sought to reason the people into forbearance. "The act," said he, "makes it your interest to buy the stamps. When I undertook the office, I meant a service to you." He was answered: "It was decreed our Saviour should suffer; but was it better for Judas Iscariot to betray him, so that the price of his blood might be saved by his friends?" The multitude, surrounding his house, demanded if he would resign. "I know not," he replied, "if I have power to resign;" but he promised, if stamps came to him, to reship them, or leave his doors open to the people to do with them as they would.

New Haven, his own town, spoke out with authority in town-meeting. On Tuesday, the seventeenth, they elected as one of their representatives Roger Sherman, one of the great men of his time. They next, by public vote, "earnestly desired Ingersoll to resign his stamp office immediately." "I shall await," said Ingersoll, "to see how the general assembly is inclined." But the cautious people were anxious to save their representatives from a direct conflict with the British parliament, lest it should provoke the forfeiture of their charter; and already several hundreds of them, particularly three divisions from Norwich, from New London, and from Windham and adjacent towns, had come out on horseback, with eight days' provisions, resolved to scour the colony till their stamp officer should be unearthed and reckoned with.

To save his house from the peril of an attack, Ingersoll rode out from New Haven in company with the governor, intending to place himself under the protection of the legislature, which was to convene on Thursday, at Hartford. On Thursday morning he set forward alone. Two or three miles below Wethersfield he met an advanced party of four or five; half a mile farther, another of thirty; and soon the main body of about five hundred men, farmers and freeholders, all bearing long and large staves, white from being freshly rinded, all on horseback, two abreast, preceded by three trumpeters, and led by two militia officers in full uniform. They opened and received him; and then, to the sound of trumpets, rode forward through the alluvial farms that grace the banks of the "lovely" Connecticut, till they came into Wethersfield. There in the broad main street, twenty rods wide, in the midst of neat dwelling-houses, and of a people that owned the soil and themselves held the plough, in the very heart of New England culture, where the old Puritan spirit, as it had existed among "the best" in the days of Milton, had been preserved with the least admixture, the cavalcade halted, and bade their stamp-master resign. "Is it fair," said he, "that the counties of New London and Windham should dictate to all the rest of the colony?" "It don't signify to parley," they answered; "here are a great many people waiting, and you must resign." "I wait," said he, "to know the sense of the government." Entering a house with a committee, he sent word to the governor and assembly of his situation; and for three hours kept the people at bay by evasive proposals. "This delay," said several of the members, "is his artifice to wheedle the matter along till the assembly shall get ensnared in it." "I can keep the people off no longer," said the leader, coming up from below, with a crowd following in the passage. "It is time to submit," thought Ingersoll; and saying, "The cause is not worth dying for," he publicly resigned, making a written declaration that it was his own free act, without any equivocation or mental reservation. "Swear to it," said the crowd; but from that he excused himself. "Then," cried they, "shout 'Liberty and property' three times;" and, throwing his hat into the air, he shouted, "Liberty and property, liberty and property, liberty and property," on which the multitude gave three loud huzzas.

After dinner, a cavalcade, by this time numbering near one thousand men, escorted him along the road, studded with farm-houses, from Wethersfield into Hartford, and dismounted within twenty yards of the hall where the assembly was sitting. The main body, led by Durkee, with their white cudgels in their hands, marched in ranks, four abreast, to the sound of trumpets, round the court-house, and formed a semicircle. Ingersoll then read the paper which he had signed within the hearing of the legislature. This was succeeded by the cry of "liberty and property," and three cheers, soon after which the people, having done their work thoroughly, rode home to their several villages.

There the Calvinist ministers nursed the flame of piety and of civil freedom. Of that venerable band, none did better service than the American-born Stephen Johnson, pastor of the first church of Lyme. "Bute, Bedford, and Grenville," said he to the people, "will be had in remembrance by Americans as an abomination, execration, and curse. These measures tend to a very fatal civil war; and France and Spain will make advantage of the crisis. If they are pursued, this people cannot bear it, till they have lost the memory of their dear fathers and their affection to their posterity. They will call to mind revolution principles, such as 'where there is a right, there is a remedy.' Their uneasiness is not the sudden heat of passion, from the novelty of the tax; but is the more deep rooted the more attentively it is considered.

"The advocates for these measures seem to be counsellors of Rehoboam's stamp. Instead of hearing the cries and redressing the grievances of a most loyal and injured people, they are for adding burden upon burden, till they make the little finger of his present majesty a thousand times heavier than the loins of his good grandfather, and would bind all fast with a military chain. Such counsels ended in Israel in such a revolt and wide breach as could never be healed. That this may end in a similar event is not impossible to the providence of God, nor more improbable to Britons than five years ago this stamp-tax was to Americans."

During these acts of compulsory submission, and while Boston, in a full town-meeting, unanimously asked the pictures of Conway and Barré for Faneuil Hall, the lords of the treasury in England, Rockingham, Dowdeswell, and Lord John Cavendish being present, held meetings almost daily, to carry the stamp act into effect; they completed the lists of stamp officers, provided for the instant filling of vacancies that might result from death or neglect, signed warrants for the expense of preparing the American stamps, and enjoined each governor to superintend and assist their distribution. These minutes might have had their excuse in the principle that there existed no power to dispense with the law of the land; but Dartmouth, from the board of trade, adopting the measure of corruption which Grenville had resisted, proposed to make the government of each province independent of its provincial legislature for its support.

Everything implied confidence in the obedience of the colonies, yet every one of them was resolved to run all hazards rather than submit. When they were asked, "What will you do after the first of November?" "Do?" they replied, "do as we did before." "Will you violate the law of parliament?" "The stamp act," repeated every one over and over, "is against

Magna Charta; and Lord Coke says an act of parliament against Magna Charta is for that reason void."

In a more solemn tone, the convictions and purposes of America found utterance through the press. John Adams, of Massachusetts, a fiery Protestant, claiming intellectual freedom as the birthright of man, at once didactic and impetuous, obeying the impulses of "a heart that burned for his country's welfare," summoned the whole experience of the human race, and human nature herself, to bear witness that, through the increase and diffusion of intelligence, the world was advancing toward the establishment of popular power. He set liberty and knowledge in opposition to authority and ignorance; America to Europe; the modern principle of popular freedom to the middle age and its tyrannies; the New World over against the Old.

"The people," thus he continued, "the populace, as they are contemptuously called, have rights antecedent to all earthly government; rights that cannot be repealed or restrained by human laws; rights derived from the great Legislator of the universe." Tracing the gradual improvement of human society from the absolute monarchy of the earliest ages, and from the more recent tyrannies of the canon and the feudal law, he saw in the reformation the uprising of the people, under the benign providence of God, against the confederacy of priest-craft and feudalism, of spiritual and temporal despotism.

"This great struggle," these are his words, "peopled America. Not religion alone, a love of universal liberty projected, conducted, and accomplished its settlement. After their arrival here, the Puritans formed their plan, both of ecclesiastical and civil government, in direct opposition to the canon and feudal systems. They demolished the whole system of diocesan episcopacy. To render the popular power in their new government as great and wise as their principles of theory, they endeavored to remove from it feudal inequalities, and establish a government of the state, more agreeable to the dignity of human nature than any they had seen in Europe.

"Convinced that nothing could preserve their posterity from the encroachments of the two systems of tyranny but knowledge diffused through the whole people, they laid very early the foundations of colleges, and made provision by law that every town should be furnished with a grammar school. The education of all ranks of people was made the care and expense of the public, in a manner unknown to any other people, ancient or modern; so that a native American who cannot read and write is as rare an appearance as a comet or an earthquake.

"There seems to be a direct and formal design on foot in Great Britain to enslave all America. Be it remembered, Liberty must at all hazards be defended. Rulers are no more than attorneys, agents, and trustees for the people; and, if the trust is insidiously betrayed or wantonly trifled away, the people have a right to revoke the authority that they themselves have deputed, and to constitute abler and better agents. We have an indisputable right to demand our privileges against all the power and authority on earth.

"The true source of our sufferings has been our timidity. Let every order and degree among the people rouse their attention and animate their resolution. Let us study the law of nature, the spirit of the British constitution, the great examples of Greece and Rome, the conduct of our British ancestors, who have defended for us the inherent rights of mankind against kings and priests. Let us impress upon our souls the ends of our own more immediate forefathers in exchanging their native country for a wilderness. Let the pulpit delineate the noble rank man holds among the works of God. Let us hear that consenting to slavery is a sacrilegious breach of trust. Let the bar proclaim the rights delivered down from remote antiquity; not the grants of princes or parliaments, but original rights, coequal with prerogative and coeval with government, inherent and essential, established as preliminaries before a parliament existed, having their foundations in the constitution of the intellectual and moral world, in truth, liberty, justice, and benevolence. Let the colleges impress on the tender mind the beauty of liberty and virtue, and the deformity and turpitude of slavery and vice, and spread far and wide the ideas of right and the sensation of freedom. No one of any feeling, born and educated in this happy country, can consider the usurpations that are meditating for all our countrymen and all their posterity without the utmost agonies of heart and many tears."

These words expressed the genuine sentiments of New England; and extracts from them were promptly laid before the king in council. In Maryland, Daniel Dulany, an able lawyer, not surpassed in ability by any of the crown lawyers in the house of commons, "a patriot counsellor, inclined to serve the people," discussed the propriety of the stamp act not before America only, but seeking audience of England. He admitted that the colonies were subordinate to the supreme national council; that the British parliament had the unquestionable right to legislate on their trade; that trade may frequently be most properly regulated by duties on imports and exports; that parliament is itself to determine what regulations are most proper; and that, if they should produce an incidental revenue, they are not therefore unwarrantable.

But, in reply to the arguments of the crown lawyers and the ministerial defenders of the stamp act, he argued, with minute and elaborate learning, that the late regulations for the colonies were not just, because the commons of England, in which the Americans were neither actually nor virtually represented, had no right, by the common law or the British constitution, to give and grant the property of the commons in America; that they were rightfully void, as their validity rested only on the power of those who framed them to carry them into effect; that they were not lenient, the taxes imposed being excessive and unequal; that they were not politic, as Great Britain, by the acts of trade, already took all from the colonies, and could but drive them to observe the strictest maxims of frugality, and to establish manufactures of leather, cotton, wool, and flax; that they were not consistent with charters, which were the original compacts between the first emigrants to America and the crown; that they were against all precedents of the previous legislation of the British parliament; that they were equally against the precedents of legislation for Ireland, which was as subject to Great Britain as were the colonies; that they were against the judgment of former British ministers, whose requisitions for revenue were uniformly transmitted to the colonies to tax themselves.

"There may be a time," he added, "when redress may be obtained. Till then, I shall recommend a legal, orderly, and prudent resentment to be expressed in a zealous and vigorous industry. A garment of linsey-woolsey, when made the distinction of patriotism, is more honorable than the plumes and the diadem of an emperor without it. Let the manufacture of America be the symbol of dignity and the badge of virtue, and it will soon break the fetters of distress."

So wrote Dulany, the champion of the day, pleading for exemption from taxes imposed without consent; promoting repeal, but beating back revolution. In the British parliament, William Pitt took most honorable notice of his words, and adopted them as the groundwork of his own reasoning.

"This unconstitutional method of taxation," observed Washington, at Mount Vernon, of the stamp act, "is a direful attack upon the liberties of the colonies, will be a necessary incitement to industry, and for many cogent reasons will prove ineffectual. Our courts of judicature," he added, "must inevitably be shut up; and, if so, the merchants of Great Britain will not be among the last to wish for its repeal."

Enlightened by discussions, towns and legislatures made their declaration of rights, following one another like a chime of bells.

In Georgia, the great majority of the representatives, at the instance of their speaker, against the will of the governor, came together on the second of September; and, though they doubted their power, at such a voluntary meeting, to elect delegates to the congress, they sent an express messenger to New York to promise their adhesion to its results; "for," said they, "no people, as individuals, can more warmly espouse the common cause than do the people of this province."

Farther north, on the ninth, the assembly of Pennsylvania, disregarding the wishes of Galloway, its speaker, accepted the plan for a congress by a majority of one. At the same time, it recognised the indispensable duty to grant requisite aids cheerfully and liberally, but only in a constitutional way, through its own assembly.

Next in time, the assembly of Rhode Island not only joined the union, but unanimously directed all the officers of the colony to proceed in their duties as usual, without regard to the stamp act, and engaged to indemnify them and save them harmless.

In the same month, Delaware, by the spontaneous act of the representatives of each of its counties; Connecticut, with the calm approval of its assembly; Maryland, with the consent of every branch of its legislature—successively elected delegates to the general American congress.

In Massachusetts, Boston, under the guidance of Samuel Adams, arraigned the stamp act and its courts of admiralty as contrary to the British constitution, to the charter of the province, to the common rights of mankind, and built "the warmest expectations" on the union of the colonies in Congress. A week later, the town of Braintree, led by John Adams, declared "the most grievous innovation of all" to be "the extension of the power of courts of admiralty, in which one judge presided alone, and, without juries, decided the law and the fact; holding his office during the pleasure of the king, and establishing that most mischievous of all customs, the taking of commissions on all condemnations."

To the legislature which convened on the twenty-fifth, Bernard drew a frightful picture of the general outlawry and rising of the poor against the rich which were to ensue if stamps were not used; recommended to the assembly not to dispute "the right of the parliament of Great Britain to make laws for her American colonies," however they might deny the expediency of the late exercise of that power; and, shirking the responsibility of action, he put the "arduous business" of executing the stamp act into their hands, that it might become a provincial concern.

It was a matter of the greatest moment that the town of Boston elected Samuel Adams their representative, in the place made vacant by the death of Thacher. On the morning on which the new member took his seat he found the legislature adopting resolves that all courts should do business without stamps, on which Bernard, in a fright, prorogued it till nine days before the first of November.

The continent watched with the intensest anxiety the conduct of New York, the head-quarters of the standing forces in

America, having a septennial assembly, a royal council, ships-of-war near its wharfs, and within the town itself a fort mounting many heavy cannon. There the authority of the British government was concentrated in the hands of Gage, the general, whose military powers, as ample as those of a viceroy, extended over all the colonies, but who was owned by the royalists to be wanting in "capacity." He was "extremely exasperated" at the course of events in Massachusetts, thought Bernard pusillanimous, and was at a loss what to do. At New York he called upon the civil power to exert itself more efficiently. "All civil authority is at an end," answered Colden; "the presence of a battalion is the only way to prevent mischief." "It will be more safe for the government," interposed the council of the province, "to show a confidence in the people." But Colden, emboldened by the arrival of two artillery companies from England,* put the fort in a state of offence and defence, and boasted alike to Conway and Amherst that he had "effectually discouraged" sedition. "I will cram the stamps down the throats of the people with the end of my sword," cried the braggart James, major of artillery, as he busied himself with bringing into the fort more field-pieces, as well as powder, shot, and shells. "If they attempt to rise, I," he gave out, "will drive them all out of the town for a pack of rascals, with four-and-twenty men." "The people here will soon come to better temper, after taxes become more familiar to them," wrote an officer who had been sent to America on a tour of observation. But the press of New York, from denying the right of parliament to tax the colonies, proceeded to doubt its legislative authority over America altogether. On the twenty-first day of September, "The Constitutional Courant," a paper defending that principle, made its appearance, and "JOIN OR DIE" was its motto. "Join or Die" was echoed from one end of the continent to the other.

* Colden to Amherst, 10 Oct. 1765. MS.

## CHAPTER XII.

THE STAMP ACT LEADS AMERICA TO UNION. ADMINISTRATION OF ROCKINGHAM.

OCTOBER–DECEMBER 1765.

THE cry was the harbinger of an American congress. The delegates of South Carolina—Gadsden, who never practiced disguise; the upright and eloquent John Rutledge; Lynch, who combined good sense, patriotism, and honesty with conciseness of speech and dignity of manner—arrived first at its place of meeting. In New Jersey, where the lawyers were resolved to forego all business rather than purchase a stamp, a little delay in the organization of its house of representatives gave them time to imitate the example of Delaware.

While they were waiting, on the third day of October, the last stamp officer north of the Potomac, the stubborn John Hughes, a Quaker of Philadelphia, as he lay ill in his house, heard the beating of muffled drums through the city, the ringing of the muffled state house bell, and the trampling feet of the people assembling to demand his resignation. His illness obtained for him some forbearance; but his written promise was extorted not to do anything that should have the least tendency to put the stamp act into execution in Pennsylvania or Delaware; and he announced to the governor his "resignation." "If Great Britain can or will suffer such conduct to pass unpunished," thus he wrote to the commissioners of stamps, "a man need not be a prophet, nor the son of a prophet, to see clearly that her empire in North America is at an end."

On Monday, the seventh of October, delegates chosen by the house of representatives of Massachusetts, Rhode Island,

Connecticut, Pennsylvania, Maryland, and South Carolina; delegates named by a written requisition from the individual representatives of Delaware and New Jersey, and the legislative committee of correspondence of New York, met at New York in congress. New Hampshire, though not present by deputy, agreed to abide by the result, and they were gladdened during their session by the arrival of the messenger from Georgia, sent near a thousand miles by land to obtain a copy of their proceedings.

The members of this first union of the American people were elected by representatives of each separate colony; and, notwithstanding great differences in the respective population and extent of territory of the several colonies, they recognised each other as equals "without the least claim of pre-eminence one over the other."

The congress entered directly on the consideration of the safest groundwork on which to rest the collective American liberties. Should they build on charters or natural justice, on precedents and fact or abstract truth, on special privileges or universal reason? Otis was instructed by Boston to support not only the liberty of the colonies, but chartered rights; and Johnson, of Connecticut, submitted a paper, which pleaded charters from the crown. But Robert R. Livingston, of New York, "the goodness of whose heart set him above prejudices, and equally comprehended all mankind," would not place the hope of America on that foundation; and Gadsden, of South Carolina, spoke against it with irresistible impetuosity. "A confirmation of our essential and common rights as Englishmen," thus he himself reports his sentiments, "may be pleaded from charters safely enough; but any further dependence upon them may be fatal. We should stand upon the broad common ground of those natural rights that we all feel and know as men, and as descendants of Englishmen. I wish the charters may not ensnare us at last by drawing different colonies to act differently in this great cause. Whenever that is the case, all will be over with the whole. There ought to be no New England man, no New-Yorker, known on the continent, but all of us Americans."

These views prevailed; and, in the proceedings of the congress, the argument for American liberty from loyal grants was avoided. This is the first great step toward independence. Dummer had pleaded for colony charters; Livingston, Gadsden, and the congress of 1765 provided for American self-existence and union, by claiming rights that preceded charters and would survive their ruin.

And how would that union extend? What nations would be included in the name of Americans? Even while congress were deliberating, the prairies of Illinois, the great eastern valley of the Mississippi, with all its solitudes in which futurity would summon the eager millions of so many tongues to build happy homes, passed from the sway of France into the temporary custody of England.

The French officers had, since the peace, been ready loyally to surrender the country to the English. But the Illinois, the Missouri, and the Osage tribes would not consent. At a council held in the spring of 1765, at Fort Chartres, the chief of the Kaskaskias, turning to the English officer, said: "Go hence, and tell your chief that the Illinois and all our brethren will make war on you if you come upon our lands; that these lands are ours; that no one else can claim them, not even the other red men; that we will have no English here; and that this is the mind of all the red men. Go, and never return, or our wild warriors will make you fall."

But when Fraser, who arrived from Pittsburg, brought proofs that their elder brothers, the Senecas, the Delawares, and the Shawnees, had made peace with the English, the Kaskaskias said: "We follow as they shall lead." "I waged this war," said Pontiac, "because, for two years together, the Delawares and Shawnees begged me to take up arms against the English. So I became their ally, and was of their mind;" and, plighting his word for peace, he kept it with integrity.

A just curiosity may ask how many persons of foreign lineage had gathered in the valley of the Illinois since its discovery by the missionaries. Fraser was told that there were of white men, able to bear arms, seven hundred; of white women, five hundred; of their children, eight hundred and fifty; of negroes of both sexes, nine hundred. The banks of the Wabash, we learn from another source, were occupied by about one hundred and ten French families, most of which were at Vincennes. Fraser sought to overawe the French traders with the menace of an English army that was to come among them; but they pointed to the Mississippi, beyond which they would be safe from English jurisdiction. As he embarked for New Orleans, Pontiac again gave him assurances of continuing peace if the Shawnees and other nations on the Ohio would recall their war-belts.

With Croghan, an Indian agent, who followed from Fort Pitt, the Illinois nations agreed that the English should take possession of all the posts which the French formerly held; and Captain Stirling, with one hundred men of the forty-second regiment, was detached down the Ohio, to relieve the French garrison. At Fort Chartres, St. Ange, who had served for fifty years in the wilderness, gave them a friendly reception; and on the morning of the tenth of October he surrendered to them the left bank of the Mississippi.

Some of the French crossed the river, so that at St. Genevieve there were at least five-and-twenty families, while St. Louis, whose origin dates from the fifteenth of February 1764, and whose skilfully chosen site attracted the admiration of the British commander, already counted about twice that number, and ranked as the leading settlement on the western side of the Mississippi. In the English portion of the distant territory, the government then instituted was the absolute rule of the British army, with a local judge to decide all disputes among the inhabitants according to the customs of the country, yet subject to an appeal to the military chief.

The Duke de Choiseul, then minister of the marine and the colonies, repressed regrets at the retirement of France from the valley of the Mississippi. He predicted to his sovereign the nearness of the final struggle between England and its dependencies, and urged that France should prepare for the impending crisis by increasing its naval force.

The inexperienced ministers of England had been suddenly brought to the administration of an empire. Of the men whose support they needed, many were among the loudest clamorers for the stamp-tax. So orders were given to Bernard in Massachusetts and to governors elsewhere, in cases of a vacancy, to act as stamp distributors; and the resolves of Virginia were reserved for the consideration of the parliament which had passed the stamp act by a vote of five to one. Nothing was promised to America but relief to trade, where it was improperly curbed. To rouse the ministry from its indifference, Thomas Hollis, who perceived in the "ugly squall," that had just reached them, the forerunner of the general hurricane, waited on Rockingham with the accounts which he had received from Mayhew, that the stamp act and the power given to the admiralty courts to dispense with juries were detested "as instances of grievous oppression, and scarce better than downright tyranny," not by Boston only, but by the people throughout the continent; that the tax could never be carried into execution unless by at least one considerable army in each province, at the hazard of the destruction of the American colonies, or their entire revolt and loss. The ministry shrunk from enforcing by arms the law which a part of them in their hearts disapproved; and, on the twenty-fourth of October, the eighth day before the time for the stamp act to go into effect, Conway, by advice of the privy council, sent letters to the American governors and to the general, exhorting to "persuasive methods" and "the utmost prudence and lenity."

The conduct of America was regulated by the congress at New York, in which no colony was better represented than South Carolina. Her delegation gave a chief to two of the three great committees, and in all that was done well her mind visibly appeared. The difficult task of defining the rights and "setting forth the liberty" which America "ought to enjoy" led the assembly to debate for two weeks "on liberty, privileges, and prerogative." In these debates, "not one appeared to be so complete a master of every subject, or threw so much light on every question, as James Otis," of Boston.

It was proposed to "insist upon a repeal of all acts laying duties on trade, as well as the stamp act." "If we do not make an explicit acknowledgment of the power of Britain to regulate our trade," said the too gentle Livingston, "she will never give up the point of internal taxation." But he was combated with great heat, till the congress, by the hand of Rutledge, of South Carolina, erased from the declaration of rights the unguarded concession; and the restrictions on American commerce, though practically acquiesced in, were enumerated as grievances.

Still, Gadsden and Lynch were not satisfied. With vigorous dialectics they proceeded, from a denial of the power of parliament in America, to deny the propriety of approaching either house with a petition. "The house of commons," reasoned Gadsden, "refused to receive the addresses of the colonies when the matter was pending; besides, we neither hold our rights from them nor from the lords." But, yielding to the majority, Gadsden suppressed his opposition; "for," said he, "union is most certainly all in all."

The carefully considered documents, in which the congress embodied the demands of America, dwell mainly on the right to trial by jury in opposition to the extension of the admiralty jurisdiction, and the right to freedom from taxation except through the respective colonial legislatures. These were promulgated in the declaratory resolutions, with the further assertion that the people of the colonies not only are not, but, from their local circumstances, never can be, represented in the house of commons in Great Britain; that taxes never have been, and never can be, constitutionally imposed on the colonies but by their respective legislatures; that all supplies to the crown are free gifts; and that for the people of Great Britain to grant the property of the colonists was neither reasonable nor consistent with the principles or spirit of the British constitution. The same immunities were claimed, in the address to the king, as "inherent rights and liberties," of which the security was necessary to the "most effectual connection of America with the British empire." They formed the theme of the memorial to the house of lords, mingled with complaints of the "late restrictions on trade."

The congress purposely employed a different style in the address to the house of commons, insisting chiefly on the disadvantages the new measure might occasion, as well to the mother country as to the colonies. They disclaimed for America the "impracticable" idea of a representation in any but American legislatures. Acknowledging "all due subordination to the parliament of Great Britain," and extolling the

"English constitution as the most perfect form of government," the source of "all their civil and religious liberties," they argued that, in reason and sound policy, there exists a material distinction between the exercise of a parliamentary jurisdiction in general acts of legislation for the amendment of the common law or the regulation of trade through the whole empire, and the exercise of that jurisdiction by imposing taxes on the colonies; from which they, therefore, entreated to be relieved.

While the congress were still weighing each word and phrase which they were to adopt, a ship laden with stamps arrived. At once all the vessels in the harbor lowered their colors. The following night papers were posted up at the doors of every public office and at the corners of the streets, in the name of the country, threatening the first man that should either distribute or make use of stamped paper. "Assure yourselves," thus the stamp distributors were warned, "the spirit of Brutus and Cassius is yet alive." The people declared: "We will not submit to the stamp act upon any account or in any instance." "In this, we will no more submit to parliament than to the divan at Constantinople." "We will ward it off till we can get France or Spain to protect us." From mouth to mouth flew the words of John Adams: "You have rights antecedent to all earthly government; rights that cannot be repealed or restrained by human laws; rights derived from the great Legislator of the universe." In the midst of this intense excitement, the congress brought its deliberations to a close. Ruggles, of Massachusetts, full of scruples and timidities, and Ogden, of New Jersey, who insisted that it was better for each province to petition separately for itself, pretended that the resistance to the stamp act through all America was treason, argued strenuously in favor of the supreme authority of parliament, and, cavilling to the last at particular expressions, refused to sign the papers prepared by the congress. "Union," said Dyer, of Connecticut, "is so necessary, disunion so fatal, in these matters, that, as we cannot agree upon any alteration, they ought to be signed as they are, by those who are authorized to do so."

On the morning of the twenty-fifth, the anniversary of the

accession of George III., the congress assembled for the last time; and the delegates of six colonies, being empowered to do so—namely, all the delegates from Massachusetts, except Ruggles; all from New Jersey, except Ogden; all those of Rhode Island; all of Pennsylvania but Dickinson, who, though absent, adhered; all of Delaware; and all of Maryland; with the virtual assent of New Hampshire, Connecticut, New York, South Carolina, and Georgia—set their hands to the papers, by which the colonies became, as they expressed it, "a bundle of sticks, which could neither be bent nor broken."

On the day on which the congress consummated the union, the legislature which first proposed it, cheered and invigorated by the presence of Samuel Adams, embodied in their reply to Bernard, the opinion on the power of parliament, from which the colony was never to recede.

"Your excellency tells us," they said, "that the province seems to be upon the brink of a precipice! To despair of the commonwealth is a certain presage of its fall. The representatives of the people are awake to the sense of its danger, and their utmost prudence will not be wanting to prevent its ruin.

"Of the power of parliament there undoubtedly are boundaries. The church, in the name of the sacred Trinity, in the presence of King Henry III. and the estates of the realm, solemnly denounced that most grievous sentence of excommunication against all those who should make statutes contrary to the liberties of Magna Charta, or observe them being made. Such acts as infringed upon the rights of that charter were always repealed. We have the same confidence in the rectitude of the present parliament. To require submission to an act as a preliminary to granting relief from the unconstitutional burdens of it supposes such a wanton exercise of mere arbitrary power as ought never to be surmised of the patrons of liberty and justice.

"The charter of the province invests the general assembly with the power of making laws for its internal government and taxation; and this charter has never yet been forfeited.

"There are certain original inherent rights belonging to the people which the parliament itself cannot divest them of: among these is the right of representation in the body which exercises the power of taxation. There is a necessity that the subjects of America should exercise this power within themselves; for they are not represented in parliament, and indeed we think it impracticable.

"To suppose an indisputable right in parliament to tax the subjects without their consent includes the idea of a despotic power.

"The people of this province have a just value for their inestimable rights, which are derived to all men from nature, and are happily interwoven in the British constitution. They esteem it sacrilege ever to give them up; and, rather than lose them, they would willingly part with everything else.

"The stamp act wholly cancels the very conditions upon which our ancestors, with much toil and blood and at their sole expense, settled this country and enlarged his majesty's dominions. It tends to destroy that mutual confidence and affection, as well as that equality, which ought ever to subsist among all his majesty's subjects in this wide and extended empire; and, what is the worst of all evils, if his majesty's American subjects are not to be governed according to the known and stated rules of the constitution, their minds may, in time, become disaffected."

In addition to this state paper, which was the imprint of the mind of Samuel Adams and had the vigor and polished elegance of his style, the house adopted "the best, and the best digested series of resolves," prepared by him, "to ascertain the just rights of the province," which the preamble said "had been lately drawn into question" by the British parliament.

The answer of the house was regarded in England as the ravings of "a parcel of wild enthusiasts:" in America, nothing was so much admired through the whole course of the controversy; and John Adams, who recorded at the time the applause which it won, said that, of all the politicians of Boston, "Samuel Adams had the most thorough understanding of liberty and her resources in the temper and character of the people, though not in the law and the constitution, as well as the most habitual radical love of it, and the most correct, genteel, and artful pen." "He is a man," he continued, "of refined policy, steadfast integrity, exquisite humanity, genteel erudition, obliging, engaging manners, real as well as professed piety, and a universal good character, unless it should be admitted that he is too attentive to the public, and not enough so to himself or his family. He is always for softness and prudence, where they will do; but is stanch, and stiff, and strict, and rigid, and inflexible in the cause."

The firmness of the new legislator was sustained by the people of Boston; and the vacillation of Otis, which increased with his infirmities, ceased to be of importance. Massachusetts never again discussed with the British ministry the amount of a tax, or the inexpediency of taxation by parliament, or the propriety of an American representation in that body.

"I am resolved to have the stamps distributed," wrote Colden to the British secretary, the day after the congress adjourned. Officers of the navy and army, with great alacrity, gave him every assistance, and ridiculed the thought that the government would repeal the stamp act, as the most singular delusion of party spirit. His son, whom he appointed temporary distributor, wrote on the same day to the commissioners of stamps, soliciting to hold the place permanently; for, he assured them, "in a few months the act would be quietly submitted to."

On the thirty-first of October, Colden and all the royal governors took the oath to carry the stamp act punctually into effect. In Connecticut, which in its assembly had already voted American taxation by a British parliament to be "unprecedented and unconstitutional," Dyer, of the council, entreated Fitch not to take an oath, which was contrary to that of the governor to maintain the rights of the colony. But Fitch had urged the assembly to prosecute for riot the five hundred that coerced Ingersoll at Wethersfield, had said that the act must go down, that forty regulars could guard the stamp papers; that the American conduct would bring from home violent measures and the loss of charters, and he resolved to comply; on which Pitkin, Trumbull, and Dyer rose with indignation and left the room. The governor of Rhode Island stood alone among the governors in his refusal to take the oath to support the stamp act.

But, either quietly of themselves, or at the instance of the people, amid shouts and the ringing of bells and the firing of cannon, or, as in Virginia, with rage changing into courtesy on the prompt submission of the stamp-master, or, as at Charleston, with the upraising of the flag of liberty surmounted by a branch of laurel, everywhere the officers resigned. There remained not one person duly commissioned to distribute stamps.

Something more was needed to incline England to relent; and the merchants of New York, coming together on the last day of October, unanimously bound themselves to send no new orders for goods or merchandise; to countermand all former orders, and not even to receive goods on commission, unless the stamp act be repealed. A city, which was the chosen home of navigation, renounced all commerce; a people, who as yet had no manufactures, gave up every comfort from abroad, rather than continue trade at the peril of freedom. A committee of intercolonial correspondence was raised, and Isaac Sears, with Lamb, Mott, Wiley, and Robinson, sent expresses to invite the people of the neighboring governments to join in the league, justly confident they would follow the example of New York.

Friday, the first morning of November—the day on which the stamp act was to take effect—broke upon a people unanimously resolved on nullifying it. From New Hampshire to the far South the day was introduced by the tolling of muffled bells; minute-guns were fired, and pennants hoisted at half-staff; or a eulogy was pronounced on liberty and its knell sounded, and then again the note changed as if she were restored to life; and, while pleasure shone on every countenance, men shouted confusion to her enemies. Children, hardly able to speak, caught up the general chorus, and went along the streets merrily carolling, "Liberty, property, and no stamps."

The publishers of newspapers which appeared on Friday bore the brunt in braving the penalties of the act. Honor, then, to the ingenious Benjamin Mecom, the bold-hearted editor at New Haven, who on that morning, without apology or concealment, issued the "Connecticut Gazette," filled with patriotic appeals; for, said he, "the press is the test of truth, the bulwark of public safety, the guardian of freedom, and the people ought not to sacrifice it."

Nor let the true lovers of their country pass unheeded the grave of Timothy Green, one of an illustrious family of printers, himself publisher of the "New London Gazette," which had always modestly and fearlessly defended his country's rights; for, on the same day, his journal came forth without stamps, and gave to the world a paper from the incomparable Stephen Johnson, of Lyme.

"The hearts of Americans," so it ran, "are cut to the quick by the act; we have reason to fear very interesting and terrible consequences, though by no means equal to tyranny or slavery. But what an enraged, despairing people will do, when they come to see and feel their ruin, time only can reveal." "The liberty of free inquiry is one of the first and most fundamental of a free people. They may publish their grievances: they have an undoubted right to be heard and relieved. The American governments or inhabitants may associate for the mutual defence of their birthright liberties. It is the joy of thousands that there is union and concurrence in a general congress. We trust they will lay a foundation for another congress. Shut not your eyes to your danger, O my countrymen! Do nothing to destroy or betray the rights of your posterity; do nothing to sully or shade the memory of your noble ancestors. Let all the governments and all the inhabitants in them unitedly resolve to a man, with an immovable stability, to sacrifice their lives and fortunes before they will part with their invaluable freedom. It will give you a happy peace in your own breasts, and secure you the most endeared affection, thanks, and blessing of your posterity; it will gain you the esteem of all true patriots and friends of liberty through the whole realm; yea, and as far as your case is known, it will gain you the esteem and the admiration of the whole world."

The conduct and the language of the "Gazette" animated the patriots within its sphere; and he who would single out the region where at that time patriotism burned with the purest flame can find none surpassing the county of New London. The royalists of New York, like Bernard at Boston, railed at

Connecticut as a land of republicans, and at Yale college as "a seminary of democracy."

In New York "the whole city rose up as one man in opposition to the stamp act." The sailors came from their shipping; "the people flocked in," as Gage thought, "by thousands;" and the leader of the tumult was Isaac Sears. At the corners of streets, at the doors of the public offices, placards threatened all who should receive or deliver a stamp, or delay business for the want of one.

Colden retired within the fort, and drew from the Coventry ship-of-war a detachment of marines. He would have fired on the people, but was menaced with being hanged, like Porteus of Edinburgh, upon a sign-post, if he did so. In the evening a torch-light procession, carrying a scaffold and two images, one of the governor, the other of the devil, came from the Fields, now the Park, down Broadway, to within ten or eight feet of the fort, knocked at its gate, broke open the governor's coach-house, took out his chariot, carried the images upon it through the town, and returned to burn them, with his own carriages and sleighs, before his eyes, on the Bowling Green, under the gaze of the garrison on the ramparts and of all New York gathered round about. "He has bound himself," they cried, "by oath to be the chief murderer of our rights." "He was a rebel in Scotland, a Jacobite." "He is an enemy to his king, to his country and mankind." At the same time, a party of volunteers sacked the house occupied by James, and bore off the colors of the royal regiments.

On the second of November, Colden gave way. The council called in question his authority to distribute the stamps, and unanimously advised him to declare that he would do nothing in relation to them, but await the arrival of the new governor; and his declaration to that effect, duly authenticated, was immediately published. But the confidence of the people was shaken. "We will have the stamp papers," cried Sears to the multitude, "within four-and-twenty hours;" and the crowd expressed their adherence by shouts. "Your best way," added Sears to the friends of order, "will be to advise Lieutenant-Governor Colden to send the stamp papers from the fort to the inhabitants." To appease their wrath, Colden invited Kennedy to receive them on board the Coventry. "They are already lodged in the fort," answered Kennedy, unwilling to offend the people.

The common council of New York next interposed, and asked that the stamped paper should be delivered into their custody. Colden pleaded his oath, and the still greater contempt into which the government would fall by the concession; but the council answered that his power was unequal to the protection of the inhabitants. Gage, being appealed to, avowed the belief that a fire from the fort would be the signal for "an insurrection" and "the commencement of a civil war." So the head of the province of New York and the military chief of all America capitulated to the municipal body which represented the people. The stamps were taken to the city hall; the city government restored order; the press continued its activity; and in all the streets was heard the shout of "liberty, property, and no stamps."

The thirst for revenge rankled in Colden's breast. "The lawyers of this place," so he reported to the secretary of state, "are the authors and conductors of the present sedition; if judges be sent from England, with an able attorney-general and solicitor-general, to make examples of some very few, this colony will remain quiet;" and, in other letters, he pointed plainly to John Morin Scott, Robert R. Livingston, and William Livingston as suitable victims.

When Moore, the new governor, arrived, he dismantled the fort, and suspended his power to execute the stamp act. The assembly confirmed the doings of its committee at the congress.

In New Jersey, Ogden was disavowed by his constituents and burned in effigy. The assembly, by a unanimous vote, accepted his resignation as speaker, and thanked the two faithful delegates who had signed the proceedings of the congress. Of those proceedings, New Hampshire, by its assembly, signified its entire approbation. The people of Georgia approved the adhesion of their representatives, and its governor was met by "the same rebellious spirit as prevailed at the North."

The delegates of South Carolina were received by their assembly on the twenty-sixth of November. On that morning the papers of the congress, the declaration of rights, and the addresses were read; in an evening session, they were adopted without change, by a vote which wanted but one of being unanimous; they were signed by the speaker, and put on board the Charming Charlotte, a fine ship riding in the harbor with its sails bent; and the next morning, while the assembly were signifying, in the most ample manner, their satisfaction at the conduct of their agents, it stood away with swelling canvas for England. "Nothing will save us," wrote Gadsden, "but acting together; the province that endeavors to act separately must fall with the rest, and be branded besides with everlasting infamy."

The people of North Carolina would neither receive a stamp-man, nor tolerate the use of a stamp, nor suffer its ports to be closed. Its legislature was so long prorogued that it could not join in the application of the congress; but, had there been need of resorting to arms, "its whole force was ready to join in protecting the rights of the continent." The same spirit pervaded the country. Wherever a jealousy was roused that a stamp officer might exercise his functions, the people were sure to compel him to renew his resignation.

The colonies began to think of permanent union. "JOIN OR DIE" became more and more their motto. At Windham, in Connecticut, the freemen, in a multitudinous assembly, agreed with one another "to keep up, establish, and maintain the spirit of union and liberty;" and, for that end, they recommended monthly county conventions, and a general meeting of the colony.

At New London, the inhabitants of the county of that name, holding a mass meeting in December, unanimously decided, in carefully prepared resolves, that every form of rightful government originates from the consent of the people; that, if the limits of lawful authority are passed, they may reassume the authority which they had delegated; and that, if there is no other mode of relief against the stamp act and similar acts, they must reassume the natural rights and authority with which they were invested by the laws of nature and of God. These principles were adopted at various village gatherings, and became the political platform of Connecticut.

In New York, the validity of the British navigation acts was more and more openly impugned, and the merchants claimed a right to every freedom of trade enjoyed in England. When the general applied for the supplies, which the province was enjoined by the British mutiny act to contribute for the use of the troops quartered among them, the assembly would pay no heed to an act of parliament to which they themselves had given no assent; and, in the general tumult, their refusal passed almost unnoticed.

Everywhere the fixed purpose prevailed that "the unconstitutional" stamp act should not go into effect. Nothing less than its absolute repeal would give contentment, much as England was loved. The greatest unanimity happily existed; and all were bent on cherishing it forever. Here was something new in the affairs of men. Never had the people of provinces extending over so vast a continent, and so widely sundered from one another, been thus cordially bound together in one spirit and one resolve. In all their tumults, they deprecated the necessity of declaring independence; but they yet more earnestly abhorred and rejected unconditional submission. Still satisfied with the revolution of 1688 and its theory of security to liberty and property, they repelled the name of "republican" as a slander on their loyalty; but they spurned "passive obedience." Nothing on earth, they insisted, would deprive Great Britain of her transatlantic dominions but her harboring ungenerous suspicions, and thereupon entering into arbitrary and oppressive measures. "All eyes were turned on her with hope and unbounded affection," with apprehension and firmness of resolve. "Pray for the peace of our Jerusalem," said Otis, from his heart, fearing "the parliament would charge the colonies with presenting petitions in one hand and a dagger in the other." Others thought "England would look with favor on what was but an old English spirit of resentment at injurious treatment." They trusted that "the united voice of this very extensive continent," uttering "the sober opinions of all its inhabitants," would be listened to, so that Great Britain and America might once more enjoy "peace, harmony, and the greatest prosperity." "Every moment is tedious," wrote South Carolina to its agent in London: "should you have to communicate the good news we wish for, send it to us, if possible, by a messenger swifter than the wind."

## CHAPTER XIII.

HAS PARLIAMENT THE RIGHT TO TAX AMERICA? ADMINISTRATION OF ROCKINGHAM.

DECEMBER 1765–JANUARY 1766.

THE stamp act, said George Grenville, when, emaciated, exhausted, and borne down by disappointment, he spoke in the house of commons for the last time before sinking into the grave, "the stamp act was not found impracticable. Had I continued in office, I would have forfeited a thousand lives if the act had been found impracticable." "If the administration of this country had not been changed," the Bedford party long persisted in asserting, "the stamp-tax would have been collected in America with as much ease as the land-tax in Great Britain." Lord North professed to be of the same opinion.

Many of the landed aristocracy regarded the colonies as in an open rebellion, which ought to be checked in the beginning; the mercantile people were for redressing their grievances. Successive administrations had listened to schemes of coercive taxation; but no minister before Grenville had attempted to carry them into effect. Grenville declared the paramount authority of parliament throughout the British dominions to be the essence of the revolution of 1688; but the British constitution was in its idea more popular than in its degenerate forms; a large and growing party in England insisted that, by revolution principles, property is sacred against every exaction without consent, and demanded for its inhabitants a more equal share in the national council. In the new ministry, Northington, the chancellor, and Charles Yorke, the attorney-general, insisted on the right to tax America, while Grafton and Conway inclined to abdicate the pretended right, and Rockingham declared himself ready to repeal a hundred stamp acts rather than run the risk of such confusion as would be caused by enforcing one.

Nor was the argument for the stamp act in harmony with the convictions of reflecting Englishmen. Its real authors insisted that protection and obedience are correlative duties; that Great Britain protected America, and, therefore, America was bound to obedience. But this is the doctrine of absolute monarchy, not of the British constitution.

The colonists had a powerful ally in the love of liberty, which was to the true Englishman a habit of mind, grafted upon a proud but generous nature. His attachment to it was stronger than the theory of the absolute power of a parliament, of which an oligarchy influenced the choice and controlled the deliberations. America divided English sympathies by appealing with steadfast confidence to the cherished principles of English liberty in their ideal purity.

It is the glory of England that the rightfulness of the stamp act was in England itself a subject of dispute. It could have been so nowhere else. The king of France taxed the French colonies as a matter of course; the king of Spain collected a revenue by his own will in Mexico and Peru, in Cuba and Porto Rico, and wherever he ruled; the states general of the Netherlands had no constitutional scruples about imposing duties on their outlying possessions. To England exclusively belongs the honor that between her and her colonies the question of right could arise; it is still more to her glory, as well as to her happiness and freedom, that in that contest her success was not possible. Her principles, her traditions, her liberty, her constitution, all forbade that arbitrary rule should become her characteristic. The shaft aimed at her new colonial policy was tipped with a feather from her own wing.

The night before the stamp act was to have gone into effect, the duke of Cumberland, all weary of life which for him had been without endearments, died suddenly on his way to a cabinet council on American affairs; and his influence perished with him. Weakened by his death, the ministry showed itself less and less settled in its policy. On the third of October, they had agreed that the American question was too weighty for their decision, and that parliament should be consulted; and yet they postponed the meeting of parliament till there had been time to see if the stamp act would execute itself. To Franklin, who was unwearied in his efforts to promote its repeal, no hope was given of relief; and, though the committee of merchants, who on the twelfth of December waited on Rockingham, Dowdeswell, Conway, and Dartmouth, were received with dispassionate calmness, it was announced that the right to tax Americans could never be given up, and that a suspension was "the most that could be expected."

The king looked upon the matter as undoubtedly the most serious that ever came before parliament. He was "highly provoked" by the riots in New York; and the surrender of the stamps to the municipality of the city seemed to him "greatly humiliating." When, on the seventeenth of December, 1765, he opened parliament, he was impatient to receive a minute report of all that should occur.

The address moved in the house of lords only gave a pledge "to do everything which the exigency of the case might require." The earl of Suffolk, a young man of five-and-twenty, proposed "to enforce the legal obedience of the colonies, and their dependence on the sovereign authority of the kingdom."

Grafton resisted the amendment, avoiding the merits of the question till the house should be properly possessed of it by the production of papers. Of these, Dartmouth added that the most important related to New York, and had been received within four or five days. Rockingham was dumb. Shelburne alone, unsupported by a single peer, intimated plainly his inclination for a repeal of the law. "Before we resolve upon rash measures," said he, "we should consider first the expediency of the law, and next our power to enforce it. The wisest legislators have been mistaken. The laws of Carolina, though planned by Shaftesbury and Locke, were found impracticable, and are now grown obsolete. The Romans planted colonies to increase their power; we, to extend our commerce. Should the regiments in America, at Halifax or Pensacola, embark at once upon the same destination, and no intervening accident disappoint the expedition, what could be effected against colonies so populous and of such magnitude and extent? The colonies may be ruined first, but the distress will end with ourselves."

Halifax, Sandwich, Gower, even Temple, Lyttelton, and Bedford, joined in saying: "Protection, without dependence and obedience, is a solecism in politics. The connection between Great Britain and her colonies is that of parent and child. For the parent not to correct the undutiful child would argue weakness. The duty to enforce obedience cannot be given up, because the relation cannot be destroyed. The king cannot separate his colonies any more than any other part of his dominions from the mother country, nor render them independent of the British legislature. The laws and constitution of the country are prior and superior to charters, many of which were issued improvidently and ought to be looked into.

"The colonies wish to be supported by all the military power of the country without paying for it. They have been for some time endeavoring to shake off their dependence. Pennsylvania, in 1756, refused to assist government, though the enemy was at their gates; and afterward, in their manner of granting aid, they encroached on the king's prerogative. The next attempt of the colonies will be to rid themselves of the navigation act, the great bulwark of this country, and, because they can thus obtain their commodities twenty-five per cent cheaper, they will buy of the French and Dutch, rather than of their fellow-subjects. They do not condescend to enter into explanations upon the stamp act, but object to its principle and the power of making it; yet the law was passed very deliberately, with no opposition in this house, and very little in the other. The tax, moreover, is light, and is paid only by the rich, in proportion to their dealings. The objections for want of representation are absurd. Who are affected by the duties on hardware but the people of Manchester, Birmingham, and Leeds? And how are they represented?

"But suppose the act liable to exceptions: is this a time to discuss them? When the pretender was at Derby, did you then enter upon a tame consideration of grievances? What occasion is there for papers? The present rebellion is more unnatural, and not less notorious, than that of 1745. The king's governors have been hanged in effigy, his forts and generals besieged, and the civil power annulled or suspended. Will you remain inactive till the king's governors are hanged in person? Is the legislature always to be dictated to in riot and tumult? The weavers were at your doors last year, and this year the Americans are up in arms, because they do not like what you have passed.

"Why was not parliament called sooner? Why are we now called to do nothing? The house is on fire: shall we wait till it is burnt down before we interpose? Resist at the threshold. First repress the rebellion, and then inquire into grievances. Ministers may be afraid of going too far on their own authority; but will they refuse assistance when it is offered them? We serve the crown by strengthening its hands."

Northington, the chancellor, argued from the statute-book that, as a question of law, the dependence of the colonies had been fully declared in the reign of William III., and he "lustily roared" that "America must submit." Lord Mansfield endeavored to bring the house to unanimity by recommending the ministry to assent to the amendment; "for," said he, "the question is most serious, and not one of the ordinary matters agitated between the persons in and out of office." Failing to prevent a division, he went away without giving a vote. The opposition was thought to have shown great ability, and to have expressed the prevailing opinion of the house of lords, as well as of the king. But the king's friends, unwilling to open a breach through which Bedford and Grenville could storm the cabinet, divided against the amendment.

In the house of commons, though the new ministers were not yet re-elected, Grenville, enraged at seeing an act of his ministry set at naught, moved to consider North America as "resisting the laws by open and rebellious force." Cooke, the member from Middlesex, showed the cruelty of fixing the name of rebels on all. Charles Townshend asserted with vehemence his approbation of the stamp act, and leaned toward the opinion of Grenville. "Sooner," said he, "than make our colonies our allies, I should wish to see them returned to their primitive deserts." Norton dwelt much on the legislative authority of parliament to tax all the world under British dominion. Some one said that Great Britain had long arms. "Yes," it was answered, "but three thousand miles is a long way to extend them." Especially it is observable that Lord George Sackville, just rescued from disgrace by Rockingham, desired to enforce the stamp act.

The amendment was withdrawn. When, three days later, Grenville divided the house, he had only thirty-five votes against seventy-seven. Baker, in the debate, chid him as the author of all the trouble in America; but he threw the blame from himself upon parliament. Out of doors there was a great deal of clamor that repealing the stamp act would be a surrender of sovereignty; but others held the attempt at coercion to be the ruinous side of the dilemma.

While opinion in England was still unformed, the colonies were proceeding with their system of resistance. "If they do not repeal the stamp act, we will repeal it ourselves," said Otis, who, nine months before, had counselled submission. The first American ship that ventured to sea with a rich cargo, and without stamp papers, was owned by the Boston merchant, John Hancock. In the Savannah river, a few British ships took stamped clearances; but this continued only till the people had time to understand one another and to interfere. In South Carolina, the lieutenant-governor, pleading the necessity of the case, sanctioned opening the port of Charleston.

At New York, the men-of-war detained vessels ready for sea till the people rose in anger; then the naval commander, becoming alarmed by the danger of riots, left the road from New York to the ocean free.

In Rhode Island, all public officers, judges among the rest, continued to transact business. In New York, the judges would willingly have held their terms, but were restrained by a menace of dismissal from office. In Boston, the people dealt first with Andrew Oliver, who had received his commission as stamp-man. On the day when the king was proceeding in state to the house of lords to open parliament, the "true-born Sons of Liberty" placed Oliver at the head of a long procession, with Mackintosh, a leader in the August riots, at his side, and, on the cold wet morning, escorted him to Liberty Tree, to stand in the rain under the very bough on which he had swung in effigy. There, in the presence of two thousand men, he declared in a written paper, to which he publicly set his name, that he would never directly or indirectly take any measures to enforce the stamp act, and, with the multitude for witnesses, he, upon absolute requisition, made oath to this pledge before Richard Dana, a justice of the peace. At this, the crowd gave three cheers, and, when Oliver spoke to them with a smile, they gave three cheers more.

On the evening of the next day, as John Adams sat ruminating, in his humble mansion at Quincy, on the interruption of his career as a lawyer, a message came that Boston, at the instance of Samuel Adams, had joined him, with Gridley and Otis, to sustain their memorial to the governor and council for opening the courts. It fell to him, on the evening of the twentieth, to begin the argument. "The stamp act," he reasoned, "is invalid; it is not in any sense our act; we never consented to it. A parliament in which we are not represented had no legal authority to impose it; and, therefore, it ought to be waived by the judges as against natural equity and the constitution." Otis spoke with great learning and zeal on the duties and obligations of judges. Gridley dwelt on the inconvenience of the interruption of justice. "Many of the arguments," said Bernard, in reply, "are very good ones to be used before the judges, but there is no precedent for the interference of the governor and council. In England, the judges would scorn directions from the king on points of law."

The town voted the answer unsatisfactory. Otis proposed to invite the governor to call a convention of the members of both houses of the legislature; if the governor should refuse, then to call one themselves, by requesting all the members to meet; and John Adams came round to this opinion.

"The king," thus the young lawyer mused at his own fireside, "is the fountain of justice. Protection and allegiance are reciprocal. If we are out of the king's protection, we are discharged from our allegiance. The ligaments of government are dissolved, the throne abdicated." Otis, quoting Grotius and the English lawyers of 1688, assured the public that, "if a king lets the affairs of a state run into disorder and confusion, his conduct is a real abdication;" that, unless business should proceed as usual, there "would be a release of subjects from their allegiance."

America must unite and prepare for resistance. In New York, on Christmas day, the lovers of liberty pledged themselves "to march with all despatch, at their own costs and expense, on the first proper notice, with their whole force, if required, to the relief of those who should or might be in danger from the stamp act or its abettors." Before the year was up, Mott, one of the New York committee of correspondence, arrived with others at New London, to ascertain how far New England would adopt the same covenant.

"If the great men are determined to enforce the act," said John Adams, on New Year's day 1766, "they will find it a more obstinate war than the conquest of Canada and Louisiana." "GREAT SIR," said Edes and Gill through their newspaper to the king, printing the message in large letters, "RETREAT, OR YOU ARE RUINED."

The press of Philadelphia widely diffused the words: "None in this day of liberty will say that duty binds us to yield obedience to any man or body of men, forming part of the British constitution, when they exceed the limits prescribed by that constitution. The stamp act is unconstitutional, and no more obligatory than a decree of the divan of Turkey."

Encouraged by public opinion, the Sons of Liberty of New York, on the seventh of January, resolved that "there was safety for the colonies only in the firm union of the whole;" that they themselves "would venture their lives and fortunes effectually to prevent the stamp act." On the following night, the ship, which arrived from London with ten more packages of stamps for New York and Connecticut, was searched from stem to stern, and the packages were seized and carried in boats up the river to the ship-yards, where, by the aid of tar-barrels, they were thoroughly consumed.

The resolutions of New York were carried swiftly to Connecticut. The town of Wallingford voted a fine of twenty shillings on any of its inhabitants "that should use or improve any stamped vellum or paper;" its Sons of Liberty were ready "to oppose the unconstitutional stamp act to the last extremity, even to take the field." The county of New London, meeting at Lyme, declared "the general safety and privileges of all the colonies to depend on a firm union;" and they appointed Major John Durkee to correspond with the Sons of Liberty in the adjoining provinces. Israel Putnam, the brave patriot of Pomfret—whose people derived their connection with England from a compact, their freedom from God and nature—rode from town to town through the eastern part of Connecticut to see what number of men could be relied upon, and gave out that he could lead forth ten thousand.

Massachusetts spoke through its house of representatives, which convened in the middle of January. They called on impartial history to record their glorious stand even against an act of parliament, and that the union of all the colonies was upon a motion made in their house. Insisting that "the courts of justice must be open, open immediately," they voted, sixty-six against four, that the shutting of them was not only "a very great grievance, requiring immediate redress," but "dangerous to his majesty's crown."

Bernard, who consulted in secret a "select council," unknown to the law, in which the principal advisers were Hutchinson and Oliver, opposed all concession. Tranquillity, he assured the secretary of state, could not be restored by "lenient methods." "There will be no submission," reported he, "until there is a subjection. The people here occasionally talk very high of their power to resist Great Britain; but it is all talk. They talk of revolting from Great Britain in the most familiar manner, and declare that, though the British forces should possess themselves of the coast and maritime towns, they never will subdue the inland. But nothing can be more idle. New York and Boston would both be defenceless to a royal fleet; and, they being possessed by the king's forces, no other town or place could stand out. A forcible subjection is unavoidable, let it cost what it will. The forces, when they come, should be respectable enough not to encourage resistance, that, when the people are taught they have a superior, they may know it effectually. I hope that New York, as well upon account of its superior rank and greater professions of resistance, and of its being the head-quarters, will have the honor of being subdued first."

## CHAPTER XIV.

WILLIAM PITT INTERVENES. ROCKINGHAM'S ADMINISTRATION CONTINUED.

### JANUARY 1766.

SIR JEFFREY AMHERST, in his advice to the ministry, strenuously opposed the repeal of the stamp act. During the recess of parliament, Egmont, Conway, Dowdeswell, Dartmouth, and Charles Yorke met at the house of Rockingham. To modify, but not to repeal the American tax, and to enact the penalty of high treason against any one who, by speaking or writing, should impeach the legislative authority of parliament, were measures proposed in this assembly; but they did not prevail. The ministry could form no plan of mutual support, and decided nothing but the words of the speech. The world looked from them to a private man at Bath, unconnected and poor, vainly seeking relief from infirmities that would have crushed a less hopeful mind. The cabinet, therefore, yielding to Grafton and Conway, requested Pitt's advice as to the measures proper to be taken with regard to America, and expressed a desire, now or at any future time, for his reception among them as their head. To this vague and indefinite offer of place, unsanctioned by the king, Pitt answered that he would support those, and those only, who acted on true revolution principles. "My resolution," said he, "is taken; and, if I can crawl or be carried, I will deliver my mind and heart upon the state of America."

On the fourteenth of January 1766, the king acquainted parliament that "matters of importance had happened in America, and orders had been issued for the support of lawful authority." "Whatever remained to be done, he committed to their wisdom."

The lords, in their reply, which was moved by Dartmouth, pledged their "utmost endeavors to assert and support the king's dignity, and the legislative authority of the kingdom over its colonies." The friends of the king and of the late ministry willingly agreed to words which seemed to imply the purpose of enforcing the stamp act.

The house of commons was very full. The address submitted for their adoption was of no marked character, yet the speeches of its proposers indicated the willingness of the administration to repeal the American tax. In the course of a long debate, Pitt entered most unexpectedly, having arrived in town that morning.

The adherents of the late ministry took great offence at the tenderness of expression respecting America. Nugent insisted that the honor of the kingdom required the execution of the stamp act, unless its rightfulness was acknowledged and its repeal solicited as a favor. He expostulated on the ingratitude of the colonies. He computed the expense of the troops employed in America for what he called its defence at ninepence in the pound of the British land-tax, while the stamp act would not raise a shilling a head on the Americans; "but," said he, "a peppercorn, in acknowledgment of the right, is of more value than millions without."

The eyes of all the house turned toward Pitt as he rose in his place; the Americans present in the gallery gazed at him as at the appearance of their good "angel, or savior."

"I approve the address in answer to the king's speech; for it decides nothing, and leaves every member free to act as he will. The notice given to parliament of the troubles was not early, and it ought to have been immediate.

"I speak not with respect to parties. I stand up in this place single, unsolicited, and unconnected. As to the late ministry," and he turned scornfully toward Grenville, who sat within one of him, "every capital measure they have taken is entirely wrong. To the present ministry, to those, at least, whom I have in my eye," looking at Conway and the lords of the treasury, "I have no objection. Their characters are fair. But pardon me, gentlemen; youth is the season for credulity; confidence is a plant of slow growth in an aged bosom. By comparing events with each other, reasoning from effects to causes, methinks I discover traces of overruling influences.

"It is long," he continued, "since I have attended in parliament. When the resolution was taken in the house to tax America, I was ill in bed. If I could have endured to have been carried in my bed, so great was the agitation of my mind for the consequences, I would have solicited some kind hand to have laid me down on this floor, to have borne my testimony against it. It is now an act that has passed. I would speak with decency of every act of this house, but I must beg indulgence to speak of it with freedom. The subject of this debate is of greater importance than ever engaged the attention of this house, that subject only excepted, when, nearly a century ago, it was a question whether you yourselves were to be bond or free. The manner in which this affair will be terminated will decide the judgment of posterity on the glory of this kingdom, and the wisdom of its government during the present reign.

"As my health and life are so very infirm and precarious that I may not be able to attend on the day that may be fixed by the house for the consideration of America, I must now, though somewhat unseasonably, leaving the expediency of the stamp act to another time, speak to a point of infinite moment, I mean to the right. Some seem to have considered it as a point of honor, and leave all measures of right and wrong, to follow a delusion that may lead us to destruction. On a question that may mortally wound the freedom of three millions of virtuous and brave subjects beyond the Atlantic ocean, I cannot be silent. America, being neither really nor virtually represented in Westminster, cannot be held legally or constitutionally or reasonably subject to obedience to any money bill of this kingdom. The colonies are equally entitled with yourselves to all the natural rights of mankind and the peculiar privileges of Englishmen; equally bound by the laws, and equally participating of the constitution of this free country. The Americans are the sons, not the bastards, of England. As subjects, they are entitled to the common right of representation, and cannot be bound to pay taxes without their consent.

"Taxation is no part of the governing power. The taxes

are a voluntary gift and grant of the commons alone. In an American tax, what do we do? We, your majesty's commons of Great Britain, give and grant to your majesty—what? Our own property? No. We give and grant to your majesty the property of your majesty's commons in America. It is an absurdity in terms.

"There is an idea, in some, that the colonies are virtually represented in this house. They never have been represented at all in parliament; they were not even virtually represented at the time when this law, as captious as it is iniquitous, was passed to deprive them of the most inestimable of their privileges. I would fain know by whom an American is represented here? Is he represented by any knight of the shire, in any county of this kingdom? Would to God that respectable representation was augmented to a greater number. Or will you tell him that he is represented by any representative of a borough—a borough which, perhaps, no man ever saw? This is what is called the rotten part of the constitution. It cannot endure the century. If it does not drop, it must be amputated. The idea of a virtual representation of America in this house is the most contemptible that ever entered into the head of a man. It does not deserve a serious refutation.

"The commons of America, represented in their several assemblies, have ever been in possession of the exercise of this their constitutional right, of giving and granting their own money. They would have been slaves if they had not enjoyed it.

"And how is the right of taxing the colonies internally compatible with that of framing regulations without number for their trade? The laws of this kind, which parliament is daily making, prove that they form a body separate from Great Britain. While you hold their manufactures in the most servile restraint, will you add a new tax to deprive them of the last remnants of their liberty? This would be to plunge them into the most odious slavery, against which their charters should protect them.

"If this house suffers the stamp act to continue in force, France will gain more by your colonies than she ever could have done if her arms in the last war had been victorious.

"I never shall own the justice of taxing America internally until she enjoys the right of representation. In every other point of legislation, the authority of parliament is, like the north star, fixed for the reciprocal benefit of the parent country and her colonies. The British parliament, as the supreme governing and legislative power, has always bound them by her laws, by her regulations of their trade and manufactures, and even in a more absolute interdiction of both. The power of parliament, like the circulation from the human heart, active, vigorous, and perfect in the smallest fibre of the arterial system, may be known in the colonies by the prohibition of their carrying a hat to market over the line of one province into another, or by breaking down a loom in the most distant corner of the British empire in America; and, if this power were denied, I would not permit them to manufacture a lock of wool or a horseshoe or a hobnail. But, I repeat, the house has no right to lay an internal tax upon America, that country not being represented.

"I know not what we may hope or fear from those now in place; but I have confidence in their good intentions. I could not refrain from expressing the reflections I have made in my retirement, which I hope long to enjoy, beholding, as I do, ministries changed one after another, and passing away like shadows."

A pause ensued as he ceased, when Conway rose and spoke: "I not only adopt all that has just been said, but believe it expresses the sentiments of most, if not all, the king's servants, and wish it may be the unanimous opinion of the house. I have been accidentally called to the high employment I bear; I can follow no principles more safe or more enlightened than those of the perfect model before my eyes; and I should always be most happy to act by his advice, and even to serve under his orders. Yet, for myself and my colleagues, I disclaim an overruling influence. The notice given to parliament of the troubles in America was not early, because the first accounts were too vague and imperfect to be worth its attention."

"The disturbances in America," replied Grenville, who by this time had recovered self-possession, "began in July, and now we are in the middle of January; lately they were only occurrences; they are now grown to tumults and riots; they border on open rebellion; and, if the doctrine I have heard this day be confirmed, nothing can tend more directly to a revolution.

"External and internal taxes are the same in effect, and only differ in name. That this kingdom is the supreme legislative power over America cannot be denied: and taxation is a part of that sovereign power. It is one branch of the legislation. It has been, and it is, exercised over those who are not, who were never, represented. It is exercised over the India company, the merchants of London, the proprietors of the stocks, and over many great manufacturing towns. It was exercised over the palatinate of Chester and the bishopric of Durham, before they sent any representatives to parliament. I appeal for proof to the preambles of the acts which gave them representatives, the one in the reign of Henry VIII., the other in that of Charles II." He then quoted the statutes exactly, and desired that they might be read; which being done, he resumed.

"To hold that the king, by the concession of a charter, can exempt a family or a colony from taxation by parliament, degrades the constitution of England. If the colonies, instead of throwing off entirely the authority of parliament, had presented a petition to send to it deputies elected among themselves, this step would have marked their attachment to the crown and their affection for the mother country, and would have merited attention.

"The stamp act is but the pretext of which they make use to arrive at independence. It was thoroughly considered, and not hurried at the end of a session. It passed through the different stages in full houses, with only one division on it. When I proposed to tax America, I asked the house if any gentleman would object to the right; I repeatedly asked it, and no man would attempt to deny it. Protection and obedience are reciprocal. Great Britain protects America; America is bound to yield obedience. If not, tell me when the Americans were emancipated? When they want the protection of this kingdom, they are always ready to ask it. That protection has always been afforded them in the most full and ample manner. The nation has run itself into an immense debt to give it them; and, now that they are called upon to contribute a small share toward an expense arising from themselves, they renounce your authority, insult your officers, and break out, I might almost say, into open rebellion.

"The seditious spirit of the colonies owes its birth to the factions in this house. We were told we trod on tender ground; we were bid to expect disobedience. What was this but telling the Americans to stand out against the law, to encourage their obstinacy with the expectation of support from hence? Let us only hold out a little, they would say; our friends will soon be in power.

"Ungrateful people of America! Bounties have been extended to them. When I had the honor to serve the crown, while you yourselves were loaded with an enormous debt of one hundred and forty millions sterling, and paid a revenue of ten millions sterling, you have given bounties on their lumber, on their iron, their hemp, and many other articles. You have relaxed, in their favor, the act of navigation, that palladium of British commerce. I offered to do everything in my power to advance the trade of America. I discouraged no trade but what was prohibited by act of parliament. I was above giving an answer to anonymous calumnies; but in this place it becomes me to wipe off the aspersion."

As Grenville ceased, several members got up; but the house clamored for Pitt, who seemed to rise. A point of order was decided in his favor, and the walls of St. Stephen's resounded with "Go on! go on!"

"Gentlemen," he exclaimed in his fervor, while floods of light poured from his eyes, and the crowded assembly stilled itself into breathless silence; "sir," he continued, remembering to address the speaker, "I have been charged with giving birth to sedition in America. They have spoken their sentiments with freedom against this unhappy act, and that freedom has become their crime. Sorry I am to hear the liberty of speech in this house imputed as a crime; but the imputation shall not discourage me. It is a liberty I mean to exercise. No gentleman ought to be afraid to exercise it. It is a liberty by which the gentleman who calumniates it might and ought to have profited. He ought to have desisted from his project. The gentleman tells us America is obstinate; America is almost in open rebellion. I rejoice that America has resisted." At the word, the whole house started as though the shock of an electric spark from the wire had run through them all.

"I rejoice that America has resisted. If its millions of inhabitants had submitted, taxes would soon have been laid on Ireland; and, if ever this nation should have a tyrant for its king, six millions of freemen, so dead to all the feelings of liberty as voluntarily to submit to be slaves, would be fit instruments to make slaves of the rest.

"I come not here armed at all points with law cases and acts of parliament, with the statute-book doubled down in dogs' ears, to defend the cause of liberty; if I had, I would myself have cited the two cases of Chester and Durham, to show that, even under arbitrary reigns, parliaments were ashamed of taxing a people without their consent, and allowed them representatives. Why did the gentleman confine himself to Chester and Durham? He might have taken a higher example in Wales, that was never taxed by parliament till it was incorporated. I would not debate a particular point of law with the gentleman; but I draw my ideas of freedom from the vital powers of the British constitution, not from the crude and fallacious notions too much relied upon, as if we were but in the morning of liberty. I can acknowledge no veneration for any procedure, law, or ordinance that is repugnant to reason and the first elements of our constitution; and," he added, sneering at Grenville, who was once so much of a republican as to have opposed the whigs, "I shall never bend with the pliant suppleness of some who have cried aloud for freedom, only to have an occasion of renouncing or destroying it.

"The gentleman tells us of many who are taxed, and are not represented—the India company, merchants, stockholders, manufacturers. Surely, many of these are represented in other capacities. It is a misfortune that more are not actually represented. But they are all inhabitants, and as such are virtually represented. Many have it in their option to be actually represented. They have connection with those that elect, and they have influence over them.

"Not one of the ministers who have taken the lead of government since the accession of King William ever recommended a tax like this of the stamp act. Lord Halifax, educated in the house of commons, Lord Oxford, Lord Orford, a great revenue minister, never thought of this. None of these ever dreamed of robbing the colonies of their constitutional rights. That was reserved to mark the era of the late administration.

"The gentleman boasts of his bounties to America. Are those bounties intended finally for the benefit of this kingdom? If they are, where is his peculiar merit to America? If they are not, he has misapplied the national treasures.

"If the gentleman cannot understand the difference between internal and external taxes, I cannot help it. But there is a plain distinction between taxes levied for the purposes of raising revenue and duties imposed for the regulation of trade for the accommodation of the subject, although in the consequences some revenue may accidentally arise from the latter.

"The gentleman asks, When were the colonies emancipated? I desire to know when they were made slaves. But I do not dwell upon words. The profits to Great Britain from the trade of the colonies, through all its branches, is two millions a year. This is the fund that carried you triumphantly through the last war. The estates that were rented at two thousand pounds a year threescore years ago are at three thousand pounds at present. You owe this to America. This is the price that America pays you for her protection. And shall a miserable financier come with a boast that he can fetch a peppercorn into the exchequer to the loss of millions to the nation? I dare not say how much higher these profits may be augmented. Omitting the immense increase of people in the northern colonies by natural population and the migration from every part of Europe, I am convinced the whole commercial system may be altered to advantage. Improper restraints have been laid on the continent in favor of the islands. Let acts of parliament in consequence of treaties remain; but let not an English minister become a custom-house officer for Spain or for any foreign power.

"The gentleman must not wonder he was not contradicted when, as the minister, he asserted the right of parliament to tax America. There is a modesty in this house which does not choose to contradict a minister. I wish gentlemen would get the better of it. If they do not, perhaps," he continued, glancing at the coming question of the reform of parliament, "the collective body may begin to abate of its respect for the representative. Lord Bacon has told me that a great question will not fail of being agitated at one time or another.

"A great deal has been said without doors of the strength of America. It is a topic that ought to be cautiously meddled with. In a good cause, on a sound bottom, the force of this country can crush America to atoms. If any idea of renouncing allegiance has existed, it was but a momentary frenzy; and, if the case was either probable or possible, I should think of the Atlantic sea as less than a line dividing one country from another. The will of parliament, properly signified, must forever keep the colonies dependent upon the sovereign kingdom of Great Britain. But on this ground of the stamp act, when so many here will think it a crying injustice, I am one who will lift up my hands against it. In such a cause your success would be hazardous. America, IF she fell, would embrace the pillars of the state, and pull down the constitution along with her.

"Is this your boasted peace? Not to sheathe the sword in its scabbard, but to sheathe it in the bowels of your brothers, the Americans? Will you quarrel with yourselves, now the whole house of Bourbon is united against you? The Americans have not acted in all things with prudence and temper. They have been driven to madness by injustice. Will you punish them for the madness you have occasioned? Rather let prudence and temper come first from this side. I will undertake for America that she will follow the example.

>Be to her faults a little blind;
>Be to her virtues very kind.

"Upon the whole, I will beg leave to tell the house what is really my opinion. It is that the stamp act be repealed, absolutely, totally, and immediately; that the reason for the repeal be assigned, because it was founded on an erroneous principle. At the same time, let the sovereign authority of this country over the colonies be asserted in as strong terms as can be devised, and be made to extend to every point of legislation, that we may bind their trade, confine their manufactures, and exercise every power whatsoever, except that of taking their money out of their pockets without their consent.

"Let us be content with the advantages which Providence has bestowed upon us. We have attained the highest glory and greatness; let us strive long to preserve them for our own happiness and that of our posterity."

Thus he spoke, with fire unquenchable; "like a man inspired;" greatest of orators, for his words opened the gates of futurity to a better culture. There was truth in his arguments, that were fitly joined together and blazed with light, so that his closely woven speech was as the links of a chain cable in a thunder-storm, along which the lightning pours its flashes. Men in America, for the moment, paid no heed to the assertion of parliamentary authority to bind manufactures and trade; it was enough that the great commoner had, in the house of commons, thanked God that America had resisted.

On the next day, Grafton advised the king to send for Pitt. Had this been done, and had his opinion on American affairs prevailed, who can tell into what distant age the question of American independence would have been adjourned? But, at seven o'clock in the evening of the sixteenth, Grafton was suddenly summoned to the palace. The king was in that "extreme agitation" which afflicted him when he was thwarted; and, avowing designs leading to a change of ministry of a different kind, he commanded the duke to carry no declaration from him to Pitt. Two hours later, he gave an audience to Charles Townshend, whom he endeavored, though ineffectually, to persuade to take a principal part in forming a new administration. The duke of Grafton, nevertheless, himself repaired to Pitt, and sought his confidence. "The differences in politics between Lord Temple and me," said the commoner, "have never till now made it impossible for us to act on one plan. The difference upon this American measure will, in its consequences, be felt for fifty years at least." He proposed to form a proper system with the younger and better part of the ministry, if they would willingly co-operate with him. Honors might be offered the duke of Newcastle, but not a place in the cabinet. "I see with pleasure," said he, "the present administration take the places of the last. I came up upon the American affair, a point on which I feared they might be borne down."

Of this conversation Grafton made so good a use that, on the eighteenth, by the king's direction, he and Rockingham waited on Pitt, who once more expressed his readiness to join the ministry, yet with some "transposition of places." At the same time he dwelt on the disgrace brought on the nation by the recall of Lord George Sackville to the council, declaring over and over that his lordship and he could not sit at the council board together.

But no sooner had Pitt consented to renounce his connection with Temple and unite with the ministry than Rockingham threw in objections, alike of a personal nature and of principle. The speechless prime minister, having tasted the dignity of chief, did not wish to be transposed; and the principle of "giving up all right of taxation over the colonies," on which the union was to have rested, had implacable opponents in his own private secretary and in himself. "If ever one man lived more zealous than another for the supremacy of parliament and the rights of the imperial crown, it was Edmund Burke." He was the advocate "of an unlimited legislative power over the colonies." "He saw not, how the power of taxation could be given up without giving up the rest." If Pitt was able to see it, Pitt "saw further than he could." His wishes were "very earnest to keep the whole body of this authority perfect and entire." He was "jealous of it;" he was "honestly of that opinion;" and Rockingham, after proceeding so far, and finding in Pitt all the encouragement that he expected, let the negotiation drop. Conway and Grafton were compelled to disregard their own avowals on the question of the right of taxation; and the ministry conformed to the opinion of Mansfield, Charles Yorke, and Edmund Burke.

Neglected by Rockingham, hated by the aristocracy, and feared by the king, Pitt pursued his career alone. In confidential intercourse he inquired if fleets and armies could reduce America, and heard from a friend that the Americans would not submit, that they would still have their woods and liberty. Thomas Hollis sent to him the "masterly" essay of John Adams on the canon and feudal law; he read it, and pronounced it "indeed masterly."

Of the papers from the American congress, Conway did not scruple to present the petition to the king; and George Cooke, the member for Middlesex, was so pleased with the one to the commons that, on the twenty-seventh, he offered it to the house, where he read it twice over. Jenkinson opposed receiving it, as did Nugent and Welbore Ellis. "The American congress at New York," they argued, "was a dangerous and federal union, unconstitutionally assembled without any requisition on the part of the supreme power."

"It is the evil genius of this country," replied Pitt, "that has riveted among them the union now called dangerous and federal. The colonies should be heard. The privilege of having representatives in parliament, before they can be taxed internally, is their birthright. This question, being of high concern to a vast empire rising beyond the sea, should be discussed as a question of right. If parliament cannot tax America without her consent, the original compact with the colonies is actually broken. The decrees of parliament are not infallible; they may be repealed. Let the petition be received as the first act of harmony, and remain to all posterity on the journals of this house."

Conway adhered to the opinions of Pitt on the subject of taxation, but thought the rules of the house forbade the reception of the petition.

Sir Fletcher Norton, in great heat, denounced the distinction between internal and external taxation, as a novelty unfounded in truth, reason, or justice, unknown to their ancestors, whether as legislators or judges; a whim that might serve to point a declamation, but abhorrent to the British constitution. "Expressions," said he, "have fallen from that member now, and on a late similar occasion, which make my blood run cold even at my heart. I say, he sounds the trumpet to rebellion. Such language in other days, and even since the morning of freedom, would have transported that member out of this house into another, with more leisure for better reflections." Pitt silently fixed his eye on him, with an air of contempt, from which Norton knew no escape but by an appeal for protection to the speaker.

Edmund Burke, speaking for the first time in the house of commons, advocated the reception of the petition, as in itself an acknowledgment of the jurisdiction of the house, while Charles Townshend, in a short speech, treated the line drawn between external and internal taxation as "the ecstasy of madness."

An hour before midnight, Lord John Cavendish avoided a defeat on a division by moving the orders of the day, while Conway assured the American agents of his good-will, and the speaker caused the substance of the petition to be entered on the journals.

The reading of papers and examination of witnesses continued during the month, in the utmost secrecy. The evidence, especially of the riots in Rhode Island and New York, produced a very unfavorable effect. On the last day of January, Bedford and Grenville were asked if, on Bute's opening the door, they were ready to negotiate for a change of administration; and they both sent word to the king that his order would be attended to, with duty and respect, through "whatever channel it should come."

Had Pitt acceded to the administration, he would have made the attempt to convince the nation of the expediency of "giving up all right of taxation over the colonies." Left to themselves, with the king against them and the country gentlemen wavering, the ministers, not perceiving the concession to be a sign of expiring power, introduced a resolution that "the king in parliament has full power to bind the colonies and people of America in all cases whatsoever."

## CHAPTER XV.

**PARLIAMENT AFFIRMS ITS RIGHT TO TAX AMERICA. ROCKINGHAM'S ADMINISTRATION CONTINUED.**

### THE THIRD OF FEBRUARY 1766.

It was the third day of February when the duke of Grafton offered in the house of lords the resolution, which was in direct contradiction to his wishes. Shelburne proposed to repeal the stamp act, and avoid the question of right.

"If you exempt the American colonies from one statute or law," said Lyttelton, "you make them independent communities. If opinions of this weight are to be taken up and argued upon through mistake or timidity, we shall have Lycurguses and Solons in every coffee-house, tavern, and gin-shop in London. Many thousands in England who have no vote in electing representatives will follow their brethren in America in refusing submission to any taxes. The commons will with pleasure hear the doctrine of equality being the natural right of all; but the doctrine of equality may be carried to the destruction of this monarchy."

Lord Temple treated as a jest his brother-in-law's distinction in regard to internal taxation. "Did the colonies, when they emigrated, keep the purse only, and give up their liberties?" He cited Shakespeare to prove that "who steals a purse steals trash;" then, advising the lords to firmness toward the colonies, he concluded with an admonition from Tacitus.

"The question before your lordships," said Camden, "concerns the common rights of mankind. The resolution now proposed gives the legislature an absolute power of laying any tax upon America. In my opinion, my lords, the legislature had no right to make this law. When the people consented to be taxed, they reserved to themselves the power of giving and granting by their representatives. The colonies, when they emigrated, carried their birthright with them; and the same spirit of liberty still pervades the new empire." He proceeded to show, from the principles and precedents of English law, that none could be taxed unless by their representatives; that the clergy, the counties palatine, Wales, Calais, and Berwick, were never taxed till they sent members to parliament; that Guernsey and Jersey send no members, and are not taxed; and, dwelling particularly on the case of Ireland, he cited the opinion of Chief Justice Hale, that Great Britain had no power to raise subsidies in Ireland. But, supposing the Americans had no exclusive right to tax themselves, he maintained it would be good policy to give it them. This he argued as a question of justice; for, in the clashing interests of the mother country and the colonies, every Englishman would incline against them. This, too, he supported, as the only means of maintaining their dependence; for America felt that she could better do without England than England without America; and he reminded the house that inflexibility lost to the court of Vienna the dominion of the Low Countries.

He reasoned in a strain which Pitt called divine. With Benjamin Franklin for one of his listeners, Northington very shortly replied: "I cannot sit silent, upon doctrines being laid down so new, so unmaintainable, and so unconstitutional. In every state there must be a supreme dominion; every government can arbitrarily impose laws on all its subjects, by which all are bound; and resistance to laws that are even contrary to the benefit and safety of the whole is at the risk of life and fortune. I seek for the constitution of this kingdom no higher up than the revolution, as this country never had one before; and, in the reign of King William, an act passed, avowing the power of this legislature over the colonies. The king cannot suspend the stamp act; he is sworn by his coronation oath to do the contrary. If you should concur as to the expediency of repeal, you will have twelve millions of your subjects of Great Britain and Ireland at your doors, not making speeches, but using club law.

"These favorite Americans have sent deputies to a meeting

of their states at New York, by which"—and, as he spoke, he appealed personally to Mansfield and Camden—"I declare, as a lawyer, they have forfeited all their charters. The colonies are become too big to be governed by the laws they at first set out with. They have therefore run into confusion, and it will be the policy of this country to form a plan of laws for them. If they withdraw allegiance, you must withdraw protection; and then the petty state of Genoa or the little kingdom of Sweden may run away with them."

Next rose Mansfield, to whose authority the house of lords paid greater deference than to that of any man living. Though he entered public life as a whig, he stood ready to serve the cause of power, even without sharing it. Cautious even to timidity, his understanding was clear, but his heart was cold. The childless man had been unsuccessful in love, and formed no friendships. His vast accumulations of knowledge, which a tenacious memory stored up in its hundred cells, ever came forward at his summons. His lucid arrangement assisted to bring conviction; and he would expound the intricacies of law, or analyze reasonings and evidence, with an intelligent smile on his features that spoke plainly the perfect ease with which he did it. Ornament seemed to flow so naturally from his subject that, while none could speak with more elegance, it seemed impossible for him to speak with less. His countenance was beautiful, inspiring reverence and regard; his eye gleamed with light; his voice was acutely clear, yet varied and musical. He had been a member of the cabinet when the plan of the stamp act was adopted; his legal opinion lay at its foundation; and he now vindicated its rightfulness, of which he saw that the denial invoked the reform of the British constitution.

"My lords," said he, in reply to Camden, "I shall speak to the question strictly as a matter of right. I shall also speak to the distinctions which have been taken, without any real difference, as to the nature of the tax; and I shall point out, lastly, the necessity there will be of exerting the force of the superior authority of government, if opposed by the subordinate part of it.

"I am extremely sorry that the question has ever become necessary to be agitated, and that there should be a decision upon it. No one in this house will live long enough to see an end put to the mischief which will be the result of the doctrine that has been inculcated; but the arrow is shot, and the wound already given.

"All arguments fetched from Locke, Harrington, and speculative men, who have written upon the subject of government, the law of nature, or of other nations, are little to the purpose; for we are not now settling a new constitution, but finding out and declaring the old one.

"The doctrine of representation seems ill-founded; there are twelve millions of people in England and Ireland who are not represented. The parliament first depended upon tenures; representation by election came by the favor of the crown, and the notion now taken up, that every subject must be represented by deputy, is purely ideal. The doctrine of representation never entered the heads of the great writers in Charles I.'s time against ship money or other illegal exertions of the prerogative, nor was the right of representation claimed in the petition of rights at the era of the revolution.

"There can be no doubt that the inhabitants of the colonies are as much represented in parliament as the greatest part of the people of England are represented, of whom, among nine millions, there are eight who have no votes in electing members of parliament. Every objection, therefore, to the dependency of the colonies upon parliament, which arises to it upon the ground of representation, goes to the whole present constitution of Great Britain; and I suppose it is not meant to new model that too! For what purpose, then, are arguments drawn from a distinction in which there is no real difference, of a virtual and actual representation? A member of parliament, chosen by any borough, represents not only the constituents and inhabitants of that particular place, but he represents the inhabitants of every other borough in Great Britain. He represents the city of London and all other the commons of this land, and the inhabitants of all the colonies and dominions of Great Britain.

"The colonists, by the condition on which they emigrated, settled, and now exist, are more emphatically subjects of Great Britain than those within the realm; and the British legislature have, in every instance, exercised their right of legislation over them without any dispute or question, till the fourteenth of January last.

"Our colonies emigrated under the sanction of the crown and parliament, upon the terms of being subjects of England. They were modelled gradually into their present forms by charters, grants, and statutes; but they were never so emancipated as to become their own masters. The very idea of a colony implies subordination and dependence, to render allegiance for protection. The charter colonies were under the authority of the privy council. In the nineteenth year of James I., a doubt, as thrown out in the house of commons, whether parliament had anything to do with America, was immediately answered by Coke. The rights of Maryland were, by charter, coextensive with those of any bishop of Durham; and Durham was taxed by parliament before it was represented. The commonwealth parliament passed a resolution to declare and establish the authority of England over its colonies. The charter of Pennsylvania, who have preposterously taken the lead, is stamped with every badge of subordination, and a particular saving as to all English acts of parliament. Could the king's bench vacate the Massachusetts charter, and yet the parliament be unable to tax them? Do they say this, when they themselves acquiesced in the judgment, and took a new charter?

"Let the advocates for America say how far the sovereignty of the British parliament should go, and where it should stop. Did the Americans keep the right of the purse only, and not of their persons and their liberties?

"But if there was no express law, or reason founded upon any necessary inference from an express law, yet the usage alone would be sufficient to support that authority of England over its colonies; for have they not submitted, ever since their first establishment, to the jurisdiction of the mother country? In all questions of property, the appeals from them have been to the privy council here; and such causes have been determined, not by their laws, but by the law of England. They have been obliged to recur very frequently to the jurisdiction here to settle the disputes among their own governments.

"Acts of parliament have been made not only without a

doubt of their legality, but with universal applause, the great object of which has been to centre the trade of the colonies in the bosom of that country from which they took their original. The navigation act shut up their intercourse with foreign countries. Their ports have been made subject to customs and regulations, which have cramped and diminished their trade; and duties have been laid affecting the very inmost parts of their commerce. The legislature have even gone so low as to restrain the number of hatters' apprentices in America, and have, in innumerable instances, given the forfeitures to the king. Yet all these have been submitted to peaceably; and no one ever thought till now of this doctrine, that the colonies are not to be taxed, regulated, or bound by parliament. This day is the first time we have heard of it in this house.

"The noble lord who quoted so much law, and denied upon those grounds the right of the parliament of Great Britain to lay internal taxes upon the colonies, allowed at the same time that restrictions upon trade and duties upon the ports were legal. But I cannot see a real difference in this distinction; a tax on tobacco, either in the ports of Virginia or London, is a duty laid upon the inland plantations of Virginia, wheresoever the tobacco grows. The legislature properly interposed for the purpose of a general taxation, as the colonies would never agree to adjust their respective proportions among themselves.

"The colonies must remain dependent upon the jurisdiction of the mother country, or they must be totally dismembered from it, and form a league of union among themselves against it, which could not be effected without great violences. No one ever thought the contrary, till now the trumpet of sedition has been blown.

"If the disturbances should continue for a great length of time, force must be the consequence, an application adequate to the mischief, and arising out of the necessity of the case. The difference between a superior and subordinate jurisdiction is, the whole force of the legislature resides collectively in the superior jurisdiction; and, when it ceases to reside, the whole connection is dissolved. It will indeed be to very little purpose that we sit here enacting laws or making resolutions if the inferior will not obey them, or if we neither can nor dare enforce them; for then, of necessity, the matter comes to the sword. If the offspring are grown too big and too resolute to obey the parent, you must try which is the strongest, and exert all the powers of the mother country to decide the contest.

"There may be some mad, enthusiastic, or ill-designing people in the colonies, yet I am convinced that the greatest bulk, who have understanding and property, are still well affected to the mother country. The resolutions in the most of the assemblies have been carried by small majorities, and in some by one or two only. You have many friends still in the colonies; take care that you do not, by abdicating your own authority, desert them and yourselves, and lose them forever. You may abdicate your right over the colonies: take care how you do so, for such an act will be irrevocable. Proceed, then, my lords, with spirit and firmness, and, when you shall have established your authority, it will then be a time to show your lenity."

The house of lords accepted the words of Mansfield as unanswerable; and, when the house divided, only five peers— Camden, Shelburne, the young Cornwallis, destined to a long and checkered career, Torrington, and Paulet—went down below the bar. These five began a strife for reform, which the child that was unborn would rue or would bless. The rest of the peers, one hundred and twenty-five in number, saw with derision the small number of the visionaries. As for Camden, they said Mansfield had utterly prostrated him.

In the commons, the resolution was presented by Conway, who, at the time of passing the stamp act, had denied the right of parliament to impose the tax, and twice within twenty days had reiterated that opinion. He now treated the question of power as a point of law, which parliament might take up. For himself, he should never be for internal taxes. He would sooner cut off his right hand than sign an order for sending out a force to maintain them. Yet he begged not to be understood to pledge himself for future measures, not even for the repeal of the stamp act.

Dowdeswell, the chancellor of the exchequer, defended the

proposition in its fullest extent. Parliament might change the charters of the colonies, and, much more, might tallage them; though, in point of policy, justice, or equity, it was a power that ought to be exercised in the most extraordinary cases only.

Barré moved to strike out from the resolution the words "in all cases whatsoever." He was seconded by Pitt, and sustained by Beckford. They contended that American taxation by parliament was against the spirit of the British constitution; against the authority of Locke and the principles of the revolution of 1688; against the right of the colonists to enjoy English liberty; against the inherent distinction between taxation and legislation, which pervaded modern history; against the solemn compacts which parliament itself had recognised as existing between the crown and the colonies; against the rights of the American assemblies, whose duty it ever is to obtain redress of material grievances before making grants of money, and whose essence would be destroyed by a transfer from them of the powers of taxation; against justice, for Great Britain could have interests conflicting with those of the colonies; against reason, for the assemblies of the colonists could know their own abilities and circumstances better than the commons of England; against good policy, which could preserve America only as Rome had preserved her distant colonies, not by the number of its legions, but by lenient magnanimity.

Only three men, or rather Pitt alone, "debated strenuously the rights of America" against more than as many hundred; and yet the house of commons, half-conscious of the fatality of its decision, seemed to shrink from pronouncing its opinion. Edmund Burke argued for England's right in such a manner that the strongest friends of power declared his speech to have been "far superior to that of every other speaker;" while Grenville, Yorke, and all the lawyers—Richard Hussey, who yet was practically for humanity and justice; Blackstone, the commentator on the laws of England, though he disliked internal taxation of America by parliament; the selfish, unscrupulous, unrelenting Wedderburn—filled many hours with solemn arguments for England's unlimited supremacy. They persuaded one another and the house that the charters which kings had granted were, by the unbroken opinions of lawyers, from 1689, subordinate to the good-will of the houses of parliament; that parliament, for a stronger reason, had power to tax.

It was further contended that representation was not the basis of the authority of parliament, and did not exist; that the kingdom and colonies were one empire; that the colonies enjoyed the opportunity of taxing themselves as an indulgence; that duties and impositions, taxes and subsidies, were all one; and, as kingdom and colonies were one body, parliament had the right to bind the colonies by taxes and impositions, alike internal and external, in all cases whatsoever.

So the watches of the long winter's night wore away; and at about four o'clock in the morning, when the question was called, less than ten voices—some said five or four, some said but three—spoke out in the minority; "and the resolution passed for England's right to do what the treasury pleased with three millions of freemen in America." The Americans were henceforward excisable and taxable at the mercy of parliament. Grenville stood acquitted; the rightfulness of his policy was affirmed; and he was judged to have proceeded in conformity with the constitution.

It was decided, as a question of law, that irresponsible taxation was not a tyranny, but a vested right; that parliament held legislative power, not as a representative body, but in absolute trust. It had grown to be a fact that the house of commons was no longer responsible to the people; and this night it was held to be the law that it was not and never had been responsible; that the doctrine of representation was not in the bill of rights. The tory party, with George III. at its head, accepted from Burke and Rockingham the creed which Grenville claimed to be the whiggism of the revolution of 1688, and Mansfield the British constitution.

The new toryism was the child of modern civilization. It carried its pedigree no further back than the revolution of 1688, and was but a coalition of the king and the aristocracy upon the basis of the established law. By law, the house of Hanover held the throne; by law, the English church was established, with a prayer-book and a creed as authorized by parliament, and with such bishops as the crown gave leave to choose; by law, the Catholics and dissenters were disfranchised, and none but conformers to the worship of the legal church could hold office or sit in the legislature; by law, the house of commons was lifted above responsibility to the people; by law, the colonies were "bound" to be taxed at mercy. The tory party took the law as it stood, and set itself against reform. Henceforward its leaders and lights were to be found not among the representatives of mediæval traditions. It was a new party, of which the leaders and expounders were to be new men. The moneyed interest, so firmly opposed to the legitimacy and aristocracy of the middle age, was to become its ally. Mansfield was its impersonation, and would transmit it, through Thurlow, to Eldon and the Boston-born Copley.

It is the office of law to decide questions of possession. Woe hangs over the land where the absolute principles of private right are applied to questions of public law, and the effort is made to bar the progress of the undying race by the despotic rules which ascertain the property of evanescent mortals. Humanity smiled at the parchment chains which the lawyers threw around her, even though those chains were protected by a coalition of the army, the navy, the halls of justice, a corrupt parliament, and the crown. The new tory party created a new opposition. The non-electors of Great Britain were to become as little content with virtual representation as the colonists. Already the press of London gave to the world a very sensible production, showing the equity and practicability of a more equal representation throughout the whole British dominions; and a scheme for a general parliament, to which every part of them should send one member for every twenty thousand of its inhabitants.

## CHAPTER XVI.

### THE REPEAL OF THE STAMP ACT. ADMINISTRATION OF ROCKINGHAM.

#### FEBRUARY–MAY 1766.

THE Sons of Liberty, acting spontaneously, were steadily advancing toward an organization which should embrace the continent. In February, those in Boston and many towns of Massachusetts, of Portsmouth in New Hampshire, acceded to the association of Connecticut and New York, and joined in urging a continental union. In Connecticut the patriots of Norwich welcomed the plan; and a convention of almost all the towns of Litchfield county resolved that the stamp act was unconstitutional, null, and void, and that business of all kinds should go on as usual. The hum of domestic industry was heard more and more: young women would get together, and merrily and emulously drive the spinning-wheel from sunrise till dark; and every day the humor spread for being clad in homespun.

Cheered by the zeal of New England, the Sons of Liberty of New York sent circular letters as far as South Carolina, inviting to the formation of a permanent continental union. But the summons was not waited for. The people of South Carolina grew more and more hearty against the stamp act. "We are a very weak province," reasoned Christopher Gadsden, "yet a rich growing one, and of as much importance to Great Britain as any upon the continent; and a great part of our weakness, though at the same time 'tis part of our riches, consists in having such a number of slaves among us; and we find in our case, according to the general perceptible workings of Providence, where the crime most commonly, though slowly, yet surely, draws down a similar and suitable punishment, that slavery begets slavery. Jamaica and our West India islands demonstrate this observation, which I hope will not be our case now, whatever might have been the consequence, had the fatal attempt been delayed a few years longer, when we had drunk deeper of the Circean draught, and the measures of our iniquities were filled up. I am persuaded, with God's blessing, we shall not fall, nor disgrace our sister colonies at this time."

The associated freeholders and inhabitants of several of the counties of North Carolina mutually plighted their faith and honor that they would, at any risk whatever, and whenever called upon, unite, and truly and faithfully assist each other to the best of their power in preventing entirely the operation of the stamp act.

In the Ancient Dominion, men pledged themselves to one another for the same purpose, with equal ardor; and, in case an attempt should be made to arrest an associate, they bound themselves, at the utmost risk of their lives and fortunes, to restore such associate to liberty. The magistrates composing the court for Northampton unanimously decided that the stamp act did not bind the inhabitants of Virginia, and that no penalties would be incurred by those who should transact business as before. The great lawyer, Edmund Pendleton, of Caroline county, gave the opinion that "the stamp act was void for want of constitutional authority in parliament to pass it."

On Tuesday, the fourth of February, the party of Bedford and the old ministry of Grenville coalesced with the friends of prerogative in the house of lords to exercise over the colonies the power which it had just been resolved that parliament rightfully possessed. The ministry desired to recommend to them to compensate the sufferers by the American riots. The new tory party, by a vote of sixty-three to sixty, changed the recommendation into a parliamentary requisition.

The next morning, Rockingham and Grafton, much irritated, went to court and proposed the removal from office of one or two of those most hostile to their ministry; but the king refused his assent.

On the night of the fifth, the same question came up in the house of commons, where Pitt spoke at length, with tact and gentleness; and the house, with considerable unanimity, contented itself with changing the proposition of the ministry into a resolution declaratory of its opinion.

The house of lords nevertheless persevered; and, on the sixth, it attracted the world to witness its proceedings. To keep up appearances, Bute rose and declared that "the king would not blame him or other lords for obeying the dictates of their conscience on important affairs of state." Encouraged by this indirect promise of the king's good-will, the new coalition, after a solemn debate, carried a vote of fifty-nine against fifty-four in favor of executing the stamp act. For the house of lords now to consent to its repeal would in some sort be an abdication of its co-ordinate authority with the commons.

The evening of that same day, Grenville made a motion for the execution of all acts. With instant sagacity, Pitt seized the advantage thus offered, and called on the house not to order the enforcement of the stamp act before they had decided the question of repeal. The request was reasonable, was pressed by him with winning candor and strength of argument, and commended itself to the good sense and generous feeling of the independent members.

"I shudder at the motion," cried the aged General Howard, while the crowded house listened as if awed into silence; "I hope it will not succeed, lest I should be ordered to execute it. If ordered to draw my sword, before I would imbrue my hands in the blood of my countrymen, who are contending for English liberty, I would sheathe it in my own body." Nugent argued that giving way would infuse the spirit of resistance into the Irish. Charles Townshend praised the general purport of Grenville's proposal, and yet censured him vehemently for anticipating the decision of the house. Grenville remained obdurate, and denounced curses on the ministers who should sacrifice the sovereignty of Great Britain over her colonies. He had expected great support; and now, though Lord Granby and all the Scotch lords and the king's friends voted with him, the motion was rejected, in a very full house, by more than two to one.

The king, when informed of this great majority, was more deeply affected than ever before; and authorized Lord Strange, chancellor of the duchy of Lancaster, " to say that he was for a modification of the stamp act, but not for a repeal of it."

On the same day, Bedford and Grenville went to an interview with Bute, for whom it was a proud moment to find his aid solicited by his bitterest enemies. He desired that the past might be buried in oblivion, and that all honest men might unite; but he refused to enter upon any conference on the subject of a new administration. The duke of York interposed his offices, and bore to the king the duke of Bedford's " readiness to receive the royal commands, should his majesty be inclined to pursue the modification instead of the total repeal of the stamp act." But the king, who was resolved not to receive Grenville again as his chief minister, disregarded the offer.

Such were the auspices when, on the thirteenth, Benjamin Franklin was summoned to the bar of the house of commons. The occasion found him full of hope and courage, though he had among his interrogators Grenville and Charles Townshend, and the house of commons for listeners. Choiseul, too, was sure to learn and to weigh all that he should utter.

In answer to questions, Franklin declared that America could not pay the stamp-tax for want of gold and silver, and from want of post-roads and means of sending stamps back into the country; that there were in North America about three hundred thousand white men from sixteen to sixty years of age; that the inhabitants of all the provinces together, taken at a medium, doubled in about twenty-five years; that their demand for British manufactures increased much faster; that in 1723 the whole importation from Britain to Pennsylvania was but about fifteen thousand pounds sterling, and had already become near half a million; that the exports from the province to Britain could not exceed forty thousand pounds; that the balance was paid from remittances to England for American produce, carried to our own islands or to the French, Spaniards, Danes, and Dutch in the West Indies, or to other colonies in North America, or to different parts of Europe, as Spain, Portugal, and Italy; that these remittances were greatly interrupted by new regulations, and by the English men-of-war and cutters stationed all along the coast in America; that the last war was really a British war, commenced for the defence of a purely British trade and of territories of the crown, and yet the colonies contributed to its expenses beyond their proportion, the house of commons itself being the judge; that they were now imposing on themselves many and very heavy taxes, in part to discharge the debts and mortgages on all their taxes and estates then contracted; that if, among them all, Maryland, a single province, had not contributed its proportion, it was the fault of its government alone; that they had never refused, and were always willing and ready to do what could reasonably be expected from them; that, before 1763, they were of the best temper in the world toward Great Britain, and were governed at the expense only of a little pen, ink, and paper; they allowed the authority of parliament in laws except such as should lay internal duties, and never disputed it in laying duties to regulate commerce, and considered that body as the great bulwark and security of their liberties and privileges; but that now their temper was much altered, and their respect for it lessened; and, if the act is not repealed, the consequence would be a total loss of the respect and affection they bore to this country, and of all the commerce that depended on that respect and affection.

"Do you think it right," asked Grenville, "that America should be protected by this country, and pay no part of the expense?" "That is not the case," answered Franklin; "the colonies raised, clothed, and paid during the last war twenty-five thousand men, and spent many millions." "Were you not reimbursed by parliament?" rejoined Grenville. "Only what, in your opinion," answered Franklin, "we had advanced beyond our proportion; and it was a very small part of what we spent. Pennsylvania, in particular, disbursed about five hundred thousand pounds; and the reimbursements, in the whole, did not exceed sixty thousand pounds."

"Do you think the people of America would submit to pay the stamp duty if it was moderated?" "No, never. They will never submit to it." And when the subject was brought up a second and a third time, and one of Grenville's ministry asked, "May not a military force carry the stamp act into execution?" Franklin answered: "Suppose a military force sent into America; they will find nobody in arms; what are they then to do? They cannot force a man to take stamps who chooses to do without them. They will not find a rebellion: they may, indeed, make one."

"How would the Americans receive a future tax, imposed on the same principle with that of the stamp act?" "Just as they do this; they would not pay it," was the answer. "What will be the opinion of the Americans on the resolutions of this house and the house of lords, asserting the right of parliament to tax the people there?" "They will think the resolutions unconstitutional and unjust." "How would they receive an internal regulation, connected with a tax?" "It would be objected to. When aids to the crown are wanted, they are, according to the old established usage, to be asked of the assemblies, who will, as they always have done, grant them freely. They think it extremely hard that a body in which they have no representatives should make a merit of giving and granting what is not its own, but theirs, and deprive them of a right which is the security of all their other rights." "Is not the post-office, which they have long received, a tax as well as a regulation?" interposed Grenville to Franklin, the deputy post-master for America; and Charles Townshend repeated the question. "No," replied Franklin, "the money paid for the postage of letters is merely a remuneration for a service."

"But if the legislature should think fit to ascertain its right to lay taxes, by any act laying a small tax contrary to their opinion, would they submit to pay the tax?" "An internal tax, how small soever, laid by the legislature here on the people there, will never be submitted to. They will oppose it to the last." "The people," he made answer to the same question under many forms, "will pay no internal tax by parliament."

"Is there any kind of difference," continued Grenville's ministry, "between external and internal taxes to the colony on which they may be laid?" "The people," argued Franklin, "may refuse commodities, of which the duty makes a part of the price; but an internal tax is forced from them without their consent. The stamp act says we shall have no commerce, make no exchange of property with each other, neither purchase nor grant, nor recover debts, nor marry, nor make our wills, unless we pay such and such sums; and thus it is intended to extort our money from us, or ruin us by the consequences of refusing to pay it." "But suppose the external duty to be laid on the necessaries of life?" continued Grenville's ministry. And Franklin amazed them by his true answer: "I do not know a single article imported into the northern colonies but what they can either do without or make themselves. The people will spin and work for themselves, in their own houses. In three years there may be wool and manufactures enough."

"Does the distinction between internal and external taxes exist in the charter of Pennsylvania?" asked a friend of Grenville. "No," said Franklin, "I believe not." "Then," asked Charles Townshend, "may they not, by the same interpretation of their common rights as Englishmen, as declared by Magna Charta and the Petition of Right, object to the parliament's right of external taxation?" And Franklin answered instantly: "They never have hitherto. Many arguments have been lately used here to show them that there is no difference; and that, if you have no right to tax them internally, you have none to tax them externally, or make any other law to bind them. At present, they do not reason so; but, in time, they may be convinced by these arguments."

On the twentieth, while the newspapers of New York were reiterating the resolves of the Sons of Liberty, that they would venture their lives and fortunes to prevent the stamp act from taking place, that the safety of the colonies depended on a firm union of the whole, the ministers, at a private meeting of their supporters, settled the resolutions of repeal which even Charles Townshend was present to accept, and which, as Burke believed, he intended to support by a speech.

The next day between four and five hundred members attended. Pitt was ill, but his zeal was above disease. "I must get up to the house as I can," said he; "when in my place, I feel I am tolerably able to remain through the debate, and cry ay to the repeal with no sickly voice;" and, through the huzzas of the lobby, he hobbled into the house on crutches, swathed in flannels.

Conway moved for leave to bring in a bill for the repeal of the American stamp act. It had interrupted British commerce; jeoparded debts to British merchants; stopped one third of the manufactures of Manchester; increased the rates on land by throwing thousands of poor out of employment. The act, too, breathed oppression. It annihilated juries, and gave vast power to the admiralty courts. The lawyers might decide in favor of the right to tax; but the conflict would ruin both countries. In three thousand miles of territory, the English had but five thousand troops, the Americans one hundred and fifty thousand fighting men. If they did not repeal the act, France and Spain would declare war, and protect the Americans. The colonies, too, would set up manufactories of their own. Why, then, risk the whole for so trifling an object?

Jenkinson, on the other side, moved a modification of the act, insisting that the total repeal, demanded as it was with menaces of resistance, would be the overthrow of British authority in America. In reply to Jenkinson, Edmund Burke spoke in a manner unusual in the house, connecting his argument with a new kind of political philosophy.

About eleven, Pitt rose. He conciliated the wavering by allowing good ground for their apprehensions, and, acknowledging his own perplexity in making an option between two ineligible alternatives, he pronounced for repeal, as due to the liberty of unrepresented subjects, and in gratitude to their having supported England through three wars. He spoke with an eloquence which expressed conviction, and with a suavity of manner which could not offend even the warmest friends of the act.

"The total repeal," replied Grenville, "will persuade the colonies that Great Britain confesses itself without the right to impose taxes on them, and is reduced to make this confession by their menaces. Do the merchants insist that debts to the amount of three millions will be lost, and all fresh orders be countermanded? Do not injure yourselves from fear of injury; do not die from the fear of dying. With a little firmness, it will be easy to compel the colonists to obedience. America must learn that prayers are not to be brought to Cæsar through riot and sedition."

Between one and two o'clock on the morning of the twenty-second of February the division took place. Only a few days before, Bedford had confidently predicted the defeat of the ministry. The king, the queen, the princess dowager, the duke of York, Lord Bute, desired it. The scanty remains of the old tories; all the followers of Bedford and Grenville; the king's friends; every Scottish member except Sir Alexander Gilmore and George Dempster; Lord George Sackville; Oswald, Sackville's colleague as vice-treasurer for Ireland; Barrington, the paymaster of the navy—were all known to be in the opposition.

The lobbies were crammed with upward of three hundred men, representing the trading interests of the nation, trembling and anxious, as they waited to learn the resolution of the house. Presently it was announced that two hundred and seventy-five had voted for the repeal of the act, against one hundred and sixty-seven for softening and enforcing it. The roof of St. Stephen's rung with the long-continued shouts and cheerings of the majority.

When the doors were thrown open, and Conway went forth, there was an involuntary burst of gratitude from the grave multitude which beset the avenues; they gathered round him like children round a parent, like captives round a deliverer. As Grenville moved along, swelling with rage and mortification, they pressed on him with hisses. But, when Pitt appeared, the crowd reverently pulled off their hats; and their applause touched him with tender and lively joy. Many followed his chair home with benedictions.

He felt no illness after his immense fatigue. It seemed as if the gratitude of a rescued people, and the gladness of thousands, now become his own, had restored him to health; but his heartfelt and solid delight was not perfect till he found himself in his own house, with the wife whom he loved, and the children, who all partook of the overflowing pride of their mother. This was the earliest great political lesson received by his second son, then not quite seven years old, the eager and impetuous William, who rejoiced that he was not the eldest-born, but could serve his country in the house of commons, like his father.

The king treated with great coolness all his servants who voted for the repeal. "We have been beaten," said Bedford to the French minister; "but we made a gallant fight."

With the Scottish members, elected as they then were by a dependent tenantry, or in boroughs by close corporations, the mind of Scotland was as much at variance as the intelligence of France with Louis XV. Adam Smith, at Glasgow, was teaching the youth of Scotland the natural right of industry to freedom; Reid was constructing a system of philosophy, based upon the freedom of the active powers of man; and now, at the relenting "of the house of commons concerning the stamp act," "I rejoice," said Robertson, the illustrious historian, "from my love of the human species, that a million of men in America have some chance of running the same great career which other free people have held before them. I do not apprehend revolution or independence sooner than these must and should come."

America was firm in her resistance to the stamp act. Massachusetts, Rhode Island, and Maryland had opened their courts. From New York, the governor reported that "every one around him was an abettor of resistance." A merchant, who had signed a stamped bond for a Mediterranean pass, was obliged to stand forth publicly, and ask forgiveness before thousands. The people of Woodbridge, in New Jersey, recommended "the union of the provinces throughout the continent." Delegates from the Sons of Liberty in every town of Connecticut met at Hartford in convention, demonstrating by their example the facility with which America could organize independent governments; they declared for "perpetuating the union" as the only security for liberty. "A firm union of all the colonies" was the watchword of Rhode Island, adopted in a convention of the county of Providence; and it was resolved to oppose the stamp act, even if it should tend to "the destruction of the union" of America with Great Britain. At Boston, Joseph Warren, a young man whom nature had adorned with grace and manly beauty and a courage that bordered on rash audacity, uttered the new war-cry of the world, "FREEDOM AND EQUALITY." "Death," said he, "with all its tortures, is preferable to slavery." "The thought of independence," said Hutchinson, despondingly, "has entered the heart of America."

Virginia had kindled the flame; Virginia now, by the hand of Richard Bland, through the press, claimed for America freedom from all parliamentary legislation, and pointed to independence as a remedy for a refusal of redress.

"The colonies," said he, "are not represented in parliament; consequently every act of parliament that imposes internal taxes upon the colonies is an act of power, and not of right? Whenever I have strength, I may renew my claim; or my son, or his son may, when able, recover the natural right of his ancestor. Oppression has produced very great and unexpected events. The Helvetic confederacy, the states of the United Netherlands, are instances in the annals of Europe of the glorious actions a petty people, in comparison, can perform when united in the cause of liberty."

On the fourth came on the last reading of the bill declaratory of the absolute power of parliament to bind America, as well as that for the repeal of the stamp act. Pitt moved to leave out the claim of right in all cases whatsoever, and reaffirmed that the parliament had no right to tax America while unrepresented. The amendment was rejected; and henceforward it became the law of the British land, that the British parliament was rightfully possessed of universal and absolute legislative power over America.

The final debate on the repeal ensued. "I doubt," said Pitt, who that night spoke most pleasingly, "I doubt if there could have been found a minister who would have dared to dip the royal ermine in the blood of the Americans." Every one felt that Pitt would soon be at the head of affairs. He had spoken throughout the winter with the dignity of conscious pre-eminence; and, being himself of no party, he had no party banded against him. At midnight, the question was disposed of by a vote of two hundred and fifty against one hundred and twenty-two. The Rockingham ministry sanctioned the principles of Grenville, and adopted, half-way, the policy of Pitt. On the next day, Conway, and more than one hundred and fifty members of the house of commons, carried the bill up to the house of lords, where Temple and

Lyttelton did not suffer it to receive its first reading without debate.

On the seventh, the declaratory bill was to have its second reading. "When I spoke last on this subject," said Camden, "I was indeed replied to, but not answered. As the affair is of the utmost importance, and its consequences may involve the fate of kingdoms, I took the strictest review of my arguments; I re-examined all my authorities, fully determined, if I found myself mistaken, publicly to give up my opinion; but my searches have more and more convinced me that the British parliament have no right to tax the Americans.

"My position is this; I repeat it; I will maintain it to my last hour: taxation and representation are inseparable.

"Taxation and representation are coeval with, and essential to, this constitution. I wish the maxim of Machiavel was followed—that of examining a constitution, at certain periods, according to its first principles; this would correct abuses and supply defects. I wish the times would bear it, and that the representative authority of this kingdom was more equally settled."

The speech printed in the following year found an audience in America; but, in the house of lords, Mansfield compared it to words spoken in Nova Zembla, which are said to be frozen for a month before anybody can get at their meaning; and then, with the loud applause of the peers, he insisted that the stamp act was a just assertion of the proposition that the parliament of Great Britain has a right to tax the subjects of Great Britain in all the dominions of Great Britain in America. But he treated the bill from the house of commons to ascertain the right of England over America with scorn, as an absurdity from beginning to end, and rendering the legislature ridiculous and contemptible. "It is," said he, "a humiliation of the British legislature to pass an act merely to annul the resolutions of a lower house of assembly in Virginia." "It is only assertion against assertion; and whether it rests in mere declaration, or is thrown into the form of a law, it is still a claim by one only, from which the other dissents; and, having first denied the claim, it will very consistently pay as little regard to an act of the same authority." Yet the bill was passed, with its two clauses: the one affirming the authority of parliament over America, in all cases whatsoever; and the other declaring the opposite resolutions of the American assemblies to be null and void.

On the eleventh, the bill for the repeal of the stamp act was read a second time. The house of lords was full. Ten peers spoke against the repeal, and the lords sat between eleven and twelve hours, which was later than ever was remembered. Once more Mansfield and Camden exerted all their powers on opposite sides, while Temple indulged in personalities, aimed at Camden. The duke of Bedford closed the debate, and the house of lords divided. For subduing the colonies, if need be, by sword or fire, there appeared sixty-one, including the duke of York and several of the bishops; in favor of the repeal, there were seventy-three; but, adding the voices of those absent peers who voted by proxy, the ministry prevailed by one hundred and five against seventy-one. Northington voted for the repeal, pleading his unwillingness to act on such a question against the house of commons.

Immediately the protest which Lyttelton had prepared against committing the bill was produced, and signed by thirty-three peers, with Bedford at their head. Against the total repeal of the stamp act it maintained that such a strange and unheard-of submission of king, lords, and commons to a successful insurrection of the colonies would make the authority of Great Britain contemptible; that the reason assigned for their disobeying the stamp act extended to all other laws, and, if admitted, must set them absolutely free from obedience to the power of the British legislature; that any endeavor to enforce it hereafter, against their will, would bring on the contest for their total independence, rendered, perhaps, more dangerous and formidable from the circumstances of the other powers of Europe; that the power of taxation, to be impartially exercised, must extend to all the members of the state; that the colonies were able to share the expenses of the army, now maintained in them at the vast expense of almost a shilling in the pound land-tax, annually remitted from England for their special protection; that parliament was the only supreme legislature and common council empowered to act for all; that its laying a general tax on the American colonies was not only right, but expedient and necessary; that it was "a most indispensable duty to ease the gentry and people of this kingdom, as much as possible, by the due exertion of that great right of taxation without an exemption of the colonies."

The protesting peers further opposed the repeal of the stamp act, "because," say they, "this concession tends to throw the whole British empire into a state of confusion, as the plea of our North American colonies, of not being represented in the parliament of Great Britain, may, by the same reasoning, be extended to all persons in this island who do not actually vote for members of parliament."

To this famous Bedford protest a larger number of peers than had ever before signed a protest hastened in that midnight hour to set their names. Among them were four in lawn sleeves. It is the deliberate manifesto of the party which was soon to prevail in the cabinet and in parliament, and to rule England for two generations. It is the declaration of the new tory party in favor of the English constitution as it was, against any countenance to the extension of suffrage, the reform of parliament, and the effective exercise of private judgment.

On the seventeenth, the bill passed without a further division; but a second protest, containing a vigorous defence of the policy of Grenville, and breathing in every line the sanguinary desire to enforce the stamp act, was introduced by Temple, and signed by eight-and-twenty peers. Five of the bench of bishops were found ready, in the hour of conciliation, to record on the journals of the house their unrelenting enmity to measures of peace. Nor was the apprehension of a great change in the fundamental principles of the constitution concealed. "If we pass this bill against our opinion," they said, meaning to assert, and with truth, that it was so passed, "if we give our consent to it here, without a full conviction that it is right, merely because it has passed the other house, by declining to do our duty on the most important occasion which can ever present itself, and when our interposition, for many obvious reasons," alluding to the known opinion of the king, "would be peculiarly proper, we in effect annihilate this branch of the legislature, and vote ourselves useless." The people of

England had once adopted that opinion. It was certain that the people of America were already convinced that the house of lords had outlived its functions, and was for them become worse than "useless."

The next morning the king went in state to Westminster, and gave his assent to what, ever after, he regarded as the well-spring of all his sorrows—"the fatal repeal of the stamp act." He returned amid the shouts and huzzas of the applauding multitude. There was a public dinner of the friends of America in honor of the event; Bow bells were set a-ringing; and the ships on the Thames displayed all their colors. At night, a bonfire was kindled, and houses illuminated all over the city. An express was despatched to Falmouth with letters to different provinces, to transmit the news of the repeal as rapidly as possible to the colonies; nor was it at that time noticed that the ministry had carried through the mutiny bill, with the obnoxious American clauses of the last year; and that the king, in giving his assent to the repeal of the stamp act, had given his assent to the act declaratory of the supreme power of parliament over America, in all cases whatsoever.

While swift vessels hurried with the news across the Atlantic, the cider act was modified by the ministry, with the aid of Pitt; general warrants were declared illegal; and Edmund Burke, already famed for "most shining talents" and "sanguine friendship for America," was consulting merchants and manufacturers on the means of improving and extending the commerce of the whole empire. When Grenville, madly in earnest, deprecated any change in "the sacred act of navigation," Burke ridiculed him for holding any act sacred, if it wanted correction. Free ports were therefore established in Jamaica and in Dominica, which meant only that British ports were licensed to infringe the acts of navigation of other powers. Old duties, among them the plantation duties, which had stood on the statute-book from the time of Charles II., were modified; and changes were made in points of detail, though not in principle. The duty on molasses imported into the plantations was fixed at a penny a gallon; that on British coffee, at seven shillings the hundred-weight; on British pimento, one half-penny a pound; on foreign cambric or French lawn, three shillings the piece, to be paid into the exchequer, and disposed of by parliament. The act of navigation was purposely so far sharpened as to prohibit landing non-enumerated goods in Ireland. Under instructions given by the former administration, the governor of Grenada claimed to rule the island by prerogative; and Sir Hugh Palliser, at Newfoundland, arrogated the monopoly of the fisheries to Great Britain and Ireland.

Great Britain not only gave up the stamp-tax, but defrayed the expenses of the experiment out of its sinking fund. The treasury asked what was to be done with the stamps in those colonies where the stamp act had not taken place; and they were ordered to be returned to England, where for near a century the curious traveller might see bags of them, cumbering the office from which they were issued.

A change of ministry was more and more spoken of. The nation demanded to see Pitt in the government; and Grafton and Conway continued to insist upon it. But Rockingham, who, during the repeal of the stamp act, had been dumb, was determined it should not be so; and Newcastle and Winchelsea and Egmont concurred with him. To be prepared for the change, and in the hope of becoming, under the new administration, secretary for the colonies, Charles Townshend assiduously courted the duke of Grafton. Pitt, on retiring to recruit the health which his unparalleled exertions in the winter had subverted, made a farewell speech, his last in the house of commons, wishing that faction might cease, and avowing his own purpose of remaining independent of any personal connections whatsoever.

The joy of the colonies was, for a time, unmixed with apprehension. Virginia voted a statue to the king, and an obelisk on which were to be engraved the names of those who, in England, had signalized themselves for freedom. "My thanks they shall have cordially," said Washington, "for their opposition to any act of oppression." The consequences of enforcing the stamp act, he was convinced, "would have been more direful than usually apprehended."

Otis, at a meeting at the town hall in Boston to fix a time for the rejoicings, told the people that the distinction between inland taxes and port duties was without foundation; and, as the parliament had given up the one, they had given up the other; and the merchants were fools if they submitted any longer to the laws restraining their trade, which ought to be free.

A bright day in May was set apart for the display of the public gladness, and the spot where resistance to the stamp act began was the centre of attraction. At one in the morning, the bell nearest Liberty Tree was the first to be rung; at dawn, colors and pendants rose over the house-tops all around it; and the steeple of the nearest meeting-house was hung with banners. During the day, all prisoners for debt were released by subscription. In the evening, the town shone as though night had not come; an obelisk on the common was brilliant with a loyal inscription; the houses round Liberty Tree exhibited illuminated figures of the king, of Pitt and Camden and Barré; and Liberty Tree was decorated with lanterns, till its boughs could hold no more.

Never was there a more rapid transition of a people from gloom to transport. They compared themselves to a bird escaped from the net of the fowler, and once more striking its wings in the upper air; or to Joseph, the Israelite, whom Providence had wonderfully redeemed from the bondage into which he was sold by his elder brethren.

The clergy from the pulpit joined in the fervent joy. "The Americans would not have submitted," said Chauncy. All the continent was cherishing the name of Pitt, the greatest statesman of England, the conqueror of Canada and the Ohio, the founder of empire, the apostle of freedom, "the genius and guardian of Britain and British America." "To you," said Mayhew, speaking to him across the ocean from the heart of the people, "grateful America attributes that she is reinstated in her former liberties. America calls you over and over again her father; live long in health, happiness, and honor; be it late when you must cease to plead the cause of liberty on earth."

## CHAPTER XVII.

THE CHARTER OF MASSACHUSETTS IN PERIL. THE FALL OF THE ROCKINGHAM WHIGS. THE EARL OF CHATHAM.

MAY–OCTOBER 1766.

THE repeal of the stamp act "planted thorns" under the pillow of the king who preferred losing the colonies to tempering the British claim of absolute authority over them. Their denial of that claim and their union were ascribed by his friends to the fatal compliance of his ministers, whose measures, they insisted, had prevailed "by artifices" against the real opinion of parliament, and "the coming hour" was foretold "when the British Augustus would grieve for the loss, not of a province, but of an empire; not of three legions, but of nations."

A reaction necessarily followed. Pitt had erected no stronger bulwark for America than the shadowy partition which divides internal taxation from imposts regulating commerce, and Rockingham had broken down this slight defence by declaring that the power of parliament extends of right to all cases whatsoever. But they who give absolute power give the abuse of absolute power; they who draw the bolts from the doors and windows let in the robber. When the opinions of Bedford and Grenville became sanctioned as just principles of constitutional law, the question that remained was but of the expediency of its exercise, and country gentlemen, if they had a right to raise a revenue from America, were sure that it was expedient to ease themselves of one fourth of their landtax by exercising the right. "The administration is dead, and only lying in state," was the common remark. Conway was eager to resign, and Grafton not only threw up his office, but, before the house of lords, called on the prime minister to be content with an inferior station, for the sake of accomplishing a junction with Pitt.

In May, on the resignation of Grafton, Conway, with his accustomed indecision, remained in office, but escaped from the care of America to the northern department. There appeared a great and general backwardness to embark with Rockingham. Lord North had hardly accepted a lucrative post before he changed his mind and excused himself. Lord Howe would not serve, unless under Pitt. Lord Hardwicke refused the place left vacant by Grafton; so did his brother, Charles Yorke; and so did Egmont, till at last it fell to the husband of Conway's stepdaughter, the liberal, self-confident duke of Richmond, who added grace and courtesy of manners to firm affections, but was swayed by an ambition that far outran his ability. He, too, shunned the conduct of American affairs, and they were made over to a new department of state, which Dartmouth was to accept. Once, to delay his fall, Rockingham suggested a coalition with the duke of Bedford. Female politicians, at their game of loo, divined the ruin of the ministry, and were zealots for governing the colonies by force.

In America, half-suppressed murmurs mingled with its transport. Taxation by parliament began to be compared with restrictions on industry and trade, and the latter were found to be "the more slavish thing of the two," and "the more inconsistent with civil liberty." The protesting lords had affirmed that, if the provinces might refuse obedience to one statute, they might to all; that there was no abiding-place between unconditional universal submission and independence. Alarmed that so desperate an alternative should be forced upon them, the colonists, still professing loyalty to a common sovereign, were driven nearer and nearer to a total denial of the power of the British legislature; but, for the present, they confined their case to the power of taxation. "I will freely spend nineteen shillings in the pound," said Franklin, "to defend my right of giving or refusing the other shilling; and, after all, if I cannot defend that right, I can retire cheerfully with my little family into the boundless woods of America, which are sure to afford freedom and subsistence to any man who can bait a hook or pull a trigger." "The Americans," said Thomson Mason, the ablest lawyer of that day in Virginia, "are hasty in expressing their gratitude, if the repeal of the stamp act is not at least a tacit compact that Great Britain will never again tax us. The different assemblies, without mentioning the proceedings of parliament, should enter upon their journals as strong declarations of their own rights as words can express. Thus one declaration of rights will stand against another, and matters will remain as they were, till some future weak minister, equally a foe to Britain and her colonies, shall, by aiming at popularity, think proper to revive the extinguished flame."

To the anxious colonies, Boston proposed union as the means of security. While within its own borders it sought "the total abolishing of slavery," and encouraged learning, as the support of the constitution and the handmaid of liberty, its representatives were charged to keep up a constant intercourse with the other English governments on the continent, to conciliate any difference that should arise; ever preferring their friendship and confidence to the demands of rigorous justice. Henceforth its watchword was union, which the rash conduct of the dismayed officers of the crown contributed to establish. Bernard was elated at having been praised in the house of lords by Camden for one set of his opinions, and quoted as an oracle in the Bedford protest for the other. There was even a rumor that he was to be made a baronet. His superciliousness rose with his sense of personal safety, and he boasted that, on the meeting of the legislature, he would play out his part as governor.

In choosing the new house in Massachusetts, many towns, stimulated by the "rhapsodies" of Otis, put firm patriots in the places of the doubtful and the timid. Plymouth sent James Warren, the brother-in-law of Otis; and Boston, at the suggestion of Samuel Adams, gave one of its seats to John Hancock, a popular young merchant, of large fortune. At their organization on the last Wednesday in May, the representatives elected James Otis their speaker, and Samuel Adams their clerk. Otis was still the most influential member of the house, had long been held in great esteem throughout the province, had been its delegate to the New York congress, and had executed that trust to universal acceptance. Though irritable, he was placable, and at heart was truly loyal to his king. Bernard ostentatiously negatived the choice. The negative, as unwise as it was unusual, excited undefined apprehensions of danger; but the house, deferring to legal right, acquiesced without complaint, and substituted as its speaker the respectable but irresolute Thomas Cushing.

In the afternoon of the same day, at the choice of the council, the four judges of the supreme court, of whom Hutchinson was the chief, the king's attorney, and Oliver, the secretary and late stamp-master, all members of the last year's board, were not re-elected, for, said Samuel Adams, "upon the principle of the best writers, a union of the several powers of government in one person is dangerous to liberty." The ballot had conformed strictly to the charter and to usage, and the successful candidates were men of prudence, uprightness, and loyalty. But Bernard "resented" the exclusion of the crown officers by negativing six of the ablest "friends of the people in the board." He had legally the power to do so, and the legislature submitted without a murmur.

Here the altercation should have terminated. But, on the following day, Bernard, an "abject" coward where courage was needed, and now insolent when he should have been conciliatory, undertook to force the election of Hutchinson and Oliver as the condition of an amnesty, and accused the house of having determined its votes from "private interests."

Concurrently, Rigby, as the leader of the Bedford party, on the third of June, proposed in the British house of commons an address to the king, censuring America for its "rebellious disposition," and pledging parliament to the coercion of the colonies.

From the ministerial benches, Charles Townshend, professing to oppose the motion, spoke substantially in its favor. "It has long been my opinion," said he, in conclusion, "that America should be deprived of its militating and contradictory charters, and its royal governors, judges, and attorneys be rendered independent of the people. I therefore expect that the present administration will, in the recess of parliament, take all the necessary previous steps for compassing so desirable an event. The madness and distractions of America have demanded the attention of the supreme legislature; and the colony charters have been considered, and by judges of the realm declared inconsistent and actually forfeited by the audacious and unpardonable resolves of subordinate assemblies. This regulation must no longer be trusted to accidental obedience. If I should differ in judgment from the present administration on this point, I now declare that I must withdraw, and not longer co-operate with persons of such narrow views in government; but I hope and expect otherwise, trusting that I shall be an instrument among them of preparing a new system."

Rigby was ably supported by Lord North and Thurlow; and especially by Wedderburn, who railed mercilessly at the ministers in a mixed strain of wit, oratory, and abuse: so that, notwithstanding a spirited speech from Conway and a negative to the motion without a division, America was taken out of their control and made the sport of faction.

The very same day on which Townshend proclaimed a war of extermination against American charters, similar threats were uttered at Boston. In communicating the circular letter from Conway, proposing "to forgive and forget" the incidents of the stamp act, and directing the several governors to "recommend" to the colonial legislatures an indemnification of all sufferers by the riots which it occasioned, Bernard renewed his complaints that the principal crown officers had been dropped from the council, and held out a menace of a change in the charter of the province, if Hutchinson should not be elected to the board.

"The requisition is founded upon a resolution of the house of commons," he continued, employing the word which that body, after debate, as well as Conway, had purposely avoided. "The authority with which it is introduced should preclude all disputation about complying with it."

Bernard's speeches fell on the ear of Samuel Adams as not less "infamous and irritating" than the worst "that ever came from a Stuart to the English parliament;" and, with sombre joy, he called the province happy in having for its governor one who left to the people no option but between perpetual watchfulness and total ruin.

"The free exercise of our undoubted privileges," replied the house, "can never, with any color of reason, be adjudged an abuse of our liberty. We have strictly adhered to the directions of our charter and the laws of the land. We made our election with special regard to the qualifications of the candidates. We cannot conceive how the assertion of our clear charter right of free election can tend to impeach that right or charter. We hope your excellency does not mean openly and publicly to threaten us with a deprivation of our charter privileges, merely for exercising them according to our best judgment."

"No branch of the legislature," insisted the council, "has usurped or interfered with the right of another. Nothing has taken place but what has been constitutional and according to the charter. An election duly made, though disagreeable to the chair, does not deserve to be called a formal attack upon government or an oppugnation of the king's authority."

Mayhew, of Boston, mused anxiously over the danger, which was now clearly revealed, till, in the morning watches of the next Lord's day, light dawned upon his active mind, and the voice of wisdom spoke from his warm heart, which was so soon to cease to beat. "You have heard of the communion of churches," he wrote to Otis; "while I was thinking of this in my bed, the great use and importance of a communion of colonies appeared to me in a strong light. Would it not be decorous for our assembly to send circulars to all the rest, expressing a desire to cement union among ourselves? A good foundation for this has been laid by the congress at New York; never losing sight of it may be the only means of perpetuating our liberties." The patriot uttered this great word of counsel on the morning of his last day of health in Boston. From his youth he had consecrated himself to the service of colonial freedom in the state and church; he died, overtasked, in the unblemished beauty of manhood, consumed by his fiery zeal, foreseeing independence. Whoever repeats the story of American liberty renews his praise.

The time for intercolonial correspondence was not come; but, to keep up a fellow-feeling with its own constituents, the house, setting an example to be followed by all representative bodies, opened a gallery for the public to attend its debates. It sent a grateful address to the king, and voted thanks to Pitt and to Grafton; and, among many others, to Conway and Barré, to Camden and Shelburne; to Howard, who had refused to draw his sword against the colonies; to Chesterfield, who left retirement for their relief. But, as to compensating the sufferers by the late disturbances, it upheld its right of deliberating freely, and would only promise at its next session to act as should then appear just and reasonable.

Connecticut, overjoyed at the repeal of the stamp act and expressing satisfaction at being connected with Great Britain, took the precaution to elect as its governor the discreet and patriotic William Pitkin, in place of the loyalist Fitch.

The legislature of South Carolina, retaining, like Georgia, its avowed sentiments on internal taxation, marked its loyalty by granting every requisition, even for doubtful purposes; at the same time, it asked for the pictures of Lynch, Gadsden, and Rutledge; and, on the motion of Rawlins Lowndes, remitted a thousand pounds toward a statue of Pitt. Still they felt keenly that they were undeservedly distinguished from their happier fellow-subjects in England by the unconstitutional tenure of their judges during the king's pleasure. They complained, too, that ships laden with their rice for ports north of Cape Finisterre were compelled, on their outward and return voyage, to touch at some port in England; and they prayed for modifications of the navigation act, which would equally benefit Great Britain and themselves.

At New York, on the king's birthday, the bells rang merry peals to the strains of martial music and the booming of artillery; the Fields near the Park were spread for feasting; and a tall mast was raised to George III., William Pitt, and Liberty. At night, enormous bonfires blazed; and all was as loyal and happy as though freedom had been brought back, with ample pledges for her stay.

The assembly came together in the best spirit. They passed over the claims of Colden, who was held to have been the cause of his own griefs; but resolved by a majority of one to indemnify James, who had given impartial testimony before the house of commons. They voted to raise on the Bowling

Green an equestrian statue of George III., and a statue of William Pitt, twice the preserver of his country. But the clause of the mutiny or billeting act, directing colonial legislatures to make specific contributions toward the support of the army, placed New York, where the head-quarters were established, in the dilemma of submitting immediately and unconditionally to the authority of parliament, or taking the lead in a new career of resistance. The rescript was, in theory, worse than the stamp act. For how could one legislative body command what another legislative body should enact? And, viewed as a tax, it was unjust, for it threw all the burden on the colony where the troops chanced to be collected. The requisition of the general, made through the governor, "agreeably to the act of parliament," was therefore declared to be unprecedented in its character and unreasonable in its amount; yet, in the exercise of the right of free deliberation, everything asked for was voted, except such articles as were not provided in Europe for British troops when in barracks.

The general and the governor united in accepting the grant; but, in reporting the affair, the well-meaning, indolent Moore reflected the opinions of the army, whose officers still compared the Americans to the rebels of Scotland, and wished them a defeat like that of Culloden. "My message," said he, at the end of his narrative, "is treated merely as a requisition made here; and they have carefully avoided the least mention of the act on which it is founded. It is my opinion that every act of parliament, when not backed by a sufficient power to enforce it, will meet with the same fate."

From Boston, Bernard, without any good reason, chimed in with the complainers. "This government," said he, "quickened and encouraged by the occurrences at New York, cannot recover itself by its own internal powers." "The making the king's council annually elective is the fatal ingredient in the constitution. The only anchor of hope is the sovereign power, which would secure obedience to its decrees, if they were properly introduced and effectually supported." And he gave himself no rest in soliciting the interposition of parliament and the change of the charter of Massachusetts.

The obnoxious clauses of the billeting act had been renewed inadvertently by ministers, who had designed to adopt a system of lenity. They proposed to remove Bernard from Massachusetts, in favor of Hutchinson, whom Conway had been duped into believing a friend to colonial liberty. Reviving against Spain the claim for the ransom of the Manillas, they suggested in lieu of it a cession of the island of New Orleans; though the Spanish ambassador took fire at the thought, saying: "New Orleans is the key to Mexico." With equally vain endeavors, they were forming new and milder instructions for the government of Canada, in the hope to combine respect for the municipal customs and religion of its old inhabitants with the safeguards of the English criminal law. The conquest of New France subjected to England one more country, whose people had not separated from the church of Rome; and the British government was soon compelled to take initiatory steps toward Catholic emancipation. Canadians, without altering their faith, were permitted to serve as jurors; and it was proposed to make them eligible as justices of the peace and as judges. But Northington, in very ill-humor, thrust forward vague objections; and, as his colleagues persevered, he repaired to the king to advise their change.

The time was come for the eclipse of the genius of William Pitt. Unrelenting disease and the labors of the winter session had wrecked his constitution. Yet had he remained out of place, and appeared at intervals in the house of commons, he would have left a name needing no careful and impartial analysis of facts for his apology. As it is, I have to record how vainly he labored to diminish the aristocratic ascendency in England, and guide a great people in the career of freedom. The charms of rural life in Somersetshire could not obliterate the memory of days when his life was the life of the British people. His eager imagination bore him back to the public world, though to him it was become a riddle, which not even the wisest interpreter could solve.

While he was in this tumult of emotions, a letter of the seventh of July was brought from the king's own hand, reminding him that his last words in the house of commons had been a declaration of freedom from party ties, and inviting him to form an independent ministry. The feeble invalid, whose feverishness inflamed his hopes, flew, as he expressed it, "on wings of expedition, to lay at the king's feet the poor but sincere offering of the remnant of his life, body, heart, and mind."

He arrived in London on Friday, the eleventh of July, by no means well; but fever bewildered his judgment and increased his self-confidence. On Saturday, he was barely able to have a short interview with the king, and obtain consent to take the actual administration as the groundwork of his own, even though Newcastle and Rockingham should retire. True to his affections, he next invited Temple, the beloved brother of his wife, the head of her family and their common benefactor, to become the first lord of the treasury. But Temple, who had connected himself with Grenville and the party of Bedford, refused to unite with the friends of Rockingham; and, having told the king "he would not go into the ministry like a child, to come out like a fool," he returned to Stowe, repeating this speech to the world, dictating a scurrilous pamphlet against his brother-in-law, and enjoying the notoriety of having been solicited to take office and been found impracticable.

The discussion with Temple and its issue aggravated the malady of Pitt. He was too ill on the eighteenth to see the king, or even the duke of Grafton; and yet, passing between all the factions of the aristocracy, he proceeded to form a ministry. Grafton, to whom, on the nineteenth, he offered the treasury, went directly to Charles Townshend, by whose assiduous court and rare abilities he had been "captivated," and found him "eager to give up the paymaster's place for the office of chancellor of the exchequer," which must have seemed to him "the readiest road to the upper seat." When informed of this proposal, Pitt said everything to dissuade him from taking such a man as his second, warning him of the many unexpected disappointments which he was preparing. But "I was weak enough, very unwisely, to persist in my desire," Grafton afterward wrote, more anxious to manifest the integrity of his intentions than to conceal the consequences of his advice. Pitt loved to oblige those in whom he confided, and gave way, though much against his inclination as well as his opinion; insisting, however, that Townshend was not to be called to the cabinet. On learning this exclusion, Townshend hesitated; but finally, on the twenty-sixth, pleading "the express commands" of the king, he acquiesced. "I sacrifice," said he, "with cheerfulness and from principle, all that men usually pursue." Affecting to trust that this merit would be acknowledged by posterity, he pledged himself, in every measure of business and every act of life, to cultivate Pitt's confidence and esteem; and to Grafton he said: "My plan is a plan of union with your grace; words are useless; God prosper our joint labors, and may our mutual trust, affection, and friendship grow from every act of our lives."

The lead in the house of commons was assigned to Conway, as one of the secretaries of state; the care of America, to the earl of Shelburne. The seals of the highest judicial office were confided to Camden, who had called taxing America by act of parliament, a robbery; Northington, the former chancellor, became president of the council; while the prime minister's own infirmities, which should have forbidden him to take office at all, made him reserve for himself the quiet custody of the privy seal. Taken as a whole, the cabinet, of which the members were Pitt, Camden, Grafton, Conway, Shelburne, and the now inactive Northington, was the most liberal that had been composed in England. "If ever a cabinet," wrote a sagacious observer, "can hope for the rare privilege of unanimity, it is this, in which Pitt will see none but persons whose imagination he has subjugated, whose premature advancement is due to his choice, whose expectations of permanent fortune rest on him alone."

Of the friends of Rockingham, Lord John Cavendish set the example of refusing to serve under Grafton; but he insisted to Conway that acts of civility would satisfy the heads of his party. At this suggestion, Pitt, on the twenty-seventh of July, went to pay Rockingham a visit of respect; and had passed the threshold, when the young chief of the great whig families refused to receive the venerable man of the people. But he was never afterward able to resume office, except with the friends of the minister he now insulted.

The old whig party, which in 1746 deserted the public service only to force its restoration on its own terms, which eleven years later kept England, in time of war, in a state of anarchy for ten weeks till its demands could be satisfactorily compromised, had, in 1765, owed office to the king's favor, and now fell powerless, when left to itself. The administration of Rockingham brought Cumberland into the cabinet; took the law from Mansfield; restored Lord George Germain to public life; and would willingly have coalesced with Bedford. Yet a spirit of humanity ruled its intentions and pervaded its measures, while most pernicious errors sprung from the attempt at a compromise with the principles of its predecessors. The rights of persons were confirmed by the condemnation of general warrants, and those friends of liberty who had run hazards in its cause were restored and upheld. The members of the government abstained from some of the worst methods of corruption usual to their party in its earlier days; they sold no employments and obtained no reversions. Opposed by placemen and pensioners, they had support in the increasing confidence and good-will of the nation. Still, they had entered the cabinet in violation of their essential doctrine, at the wish of the king superseding men who were dismissed only for maintaining privilege against prerogative; and, if they mitigated taxation in America by repealing the stamp act, they boasted of the increase of the revenue raised there from trade, renewed the unconstitutional method of making parliamentary requisitions on colonial assemblies, and in the declaratory act placed in the statute-book a law, tyrannical in principle, false in fact, and impossible in practice.

The incapacity of Pitt's new administration was apparent from its first day, when he announced to his astonished and disheartened colleagues his purpose of placing himself as the earl of Chatham in the house of lords. During the past year, such an elevation in rank had often been suggested. He was too much "shattered" to lead the commons; and he might wish to secure dignity for his age. But, in ceasing to be the great commoner, he veiled his superiority. "My friend," said Frederic of Prussia on hearing of it, "has harmed himself by accepting a peerage." "It argues," said the king of Poland, "a senselessness to glory to forfeit the name of Pitt for any title." "The strength of the administration," thought all his colleagues, "lay in his remaining with the commons." "There was but one voice among us," said Grafton, "nor, indeed, throughout the kingdom." The lion had left the forest, where he roamed as monarch, and had walked into a cage. His popularity vanished, and with it the terror of his name. He was but an English earl and the shadow of a prime minister; he no longer represented the British people. He had, moreover, offended the head of every faction, whose assistance he yet required; Camden had not the qualities of a great statesman; Grafton was indolent and easily misled; Conway always vacillated; Shelburne, his able and sincere friend, was disliked at court; and the king agreed with his minister in nothing but the wish to humble the aristocracy.

In August, just at the time of Chatham's taking office, Choiseul, having assigned the care of the navy to his brother, had resumed that of foreign affairs. He knew the gigantic schemes of colonial conquests which Pitt had formerly harbored, and weighed the probabilities of a new war against France and Spain. The agent whom he had sent, in 1764, on a tour of observation through the British colonies, was just returned, and reported how they abounded in corn, cattle, flax, and iron; in trees fit for masts; in pine timber, lighter than oak, easily wrought, not liable to split, and incorruptible; how the inhabitants, already numerous, and doubling their numbers every twenty years, were opulent, warlike, and conscious of their strength; how they followed the sea, especially at the North, and engaged in great fisheries; how they built annually one hundred and fifty vessels to sell in Europe and the West Indies, at the rate of seven pounds sterling the ton; and how they longed to throw off the restraints imposed on their navigation. New York stood at the confluence of two rivers, of which the East was the shelter to merchant vessels; its roadstead was a harbor, where a navy could ride at anchor. The large town of Philadelphia had rope-walks and busy ship-yards; manufactures of all sorts, especially of leather and of iron. In the province to which it belonged, the Presbyterians outnumbered the Quakers; and Germans openly declared that Pennsylvania would one day be called Parva Germania. In all New England there were no citadels, from the people's fear of their being used to compel submission to acts of parliament infringing colonial privileges. The garrison at Boston was in the service of the colony. The British troops were so widely scattered in little detachments as to be of no account. "England," reasoned the observer, "must foresee a revolution, and has hastened its epoch by relieving the colonies from the fear of France in Canada."

Choiseul read in the "Gazette" of Leyden the answer lately made by the assembly of Massachusetts to its governor, and learned with astonishment that colonies, which were supposed to have no liberties but by inference, spoke boldly and firmly of rights and a constitution.

Chatham in health would have mastered all difficulties, or fallen with dignity. Jealous of the Bourbon courts, he urged the improvement of the harbor of Pensacola, which, it was said, could shelter at least forty ships of the line, and hold in check the commerce of Vera Cruz.

The rival statesmen, with eyes fixed on America, competed for European alliances. No sooner had Chatham entered on the ministry than he rushed into the plan of a great northern league to balance the power of the Bourbons, and hastily invited Frederic of Prussia and Catharine of Russia to connect themselves intimately with England; but Frederic, doubting the permanency of his ministry, put the invitation aside. Choiseul was as superior in diplomacy as his opponent had been in war; and was establishing such relations with every power of Europe that, in the event of new hostilities respecting America, France would have Spain for its partner, and no enemy but England.

Chatham grew sick at heart, as well as decrepit. To be happy, he needed the consciousness of standing well with his fellow-men; but he whose voice had been a clarion to the Protestant world no longer enjoyed popularity at home, or influence abroad, or the trust of the colonies. The sense of his loneliness, on his return to power, crushed his vigor of will. The most imperative of statesmen knew not how to resolve. Once, at Grafton's earnest solicitation, Charles Townshend was permitted to attend a consultation on European alliances. The next day, Chatham, with the cheerful consent of the king, retreated to Bath; but its springs had no healing for him. He desired to control France by a northern union, and stood before Europe without one power as an ally. He loved to give the law to the cabinet, and was just admitting into it a restless intriguer, who would traverse his policy. He gloried in the confidence of his sovereign; and the king wanted nothing of him but "his name." He longed for the love of the people of England; and he had left them for an earldom. He would have humbled the aristocracy; and "the nobility" not only "hated him," but retained strength to overwhelm him.

Yet the cause of liberty was advancing, though Chatham had lost his way. Philosophy spread the knowledge of the laws of nature. The empress of Russia with her own hand minuted an edict for universal tolerance. "Can you tell me," writes Voltaire, in October, to D'Alembert, "what will come, within thirty years, of the revolution which is taking effect in the minds of men from Naples to Moscow? I, who am too old to hope to see anything, commend to you the age which is forming." But, though far stricken in years, Voltaire shall himself witness and applaud the greatest step in this progress; shall see insurgent colonies become a republic, and welcome its envoy to Paris and the academy of France.

Meantime, Choiseul dismissed from the council of his king all former theories about America, alike in policy and war; and looked more nearly into the condition of the British colonies, that his new system might rest on the surest ground.

## CHAPTER XVIII.

CHARLES TOWNSHEND USURPS THE LEAD IN GOVERNMENT.
ADMINISTRATION OF CHATHAM.

OCTOBER 1766 - MARCH 1767.

THE people of Massachusetts lulled themselves into the belief that they were "restored once more" to the secure enjoyment "of their rights and liberties;" but their secret enemies combined to obtain an American army and an American tribute, as necessary for the enforcement of the navigation acts, and even for the existence of government. When the soldiers stationed in New York had, in the night of the tenth of August 1766, cut down the flagstaff of the citizens, the general reported the ensuing quarrel as a proof of "anarchy and confusion," and the need of troops for the support of "the laws." Yet the New York association of the Sons of Liberty had dissolved itself; and all efforts to keep up "its glorious spirit" were subordinated to loyalty. "A few individuals" at Boston, having celebrated the anniversary of the outbreak against the stamp act, care was taken to report how healths had been drunk to Otis, "the American Hampden, who first proposed the congress;" "to the Virginians," who sounded the alarm to the country; to Paoli and the struggling Corsicans; to the spark of liberty that was thought to have been kindled in Spain. From Bernard, who made the restraints on commerce intolerable by claiming the legal penalty of treble forfeits from merchants whom his own long collusion had tempted to the infraction of a revenue law, came unintermitted complaints of illicit trade. At Falmouth, now Portland, an attempt to seize goods, under the disputed authority of writs of assistance, had been defeated by a mob; and the disturbance was made to support a general accusation against the province. At Boston, Charles Paxton, the marshal of the court of admiralty, came, with the sheriff and a similar warrant, to search the house of Daniel Malcom for a second time; but the stubborn patriot refused to open his doors, which they dared not break down, so doubtful were they of their right; and, when the altercation attracted a crowd, they withdrew, pretending to have been obstructed by a riotous assemblage. These incidents, by themselves of little moment, were secretly reported as a general rising against the execution of the laws of trade. But the cabal relied most on personal importunity; and, in October, the untiring Paxton, who had often visited England, and was known to possess as much of the friendship of Charles Townshend as a selfish client may obtain from an intriguing patron, was sent over by the colonial crown officers, with special authority to appear as the friend of Oliver and of Hutchinson.

We are drawing near the measures which compelled the insurrection of the colonies; but all the stars in their courses were harbingers of American independence. No sooner were the prairies of Illinois in the possession of England than Croghan, a deputy Indian agent, who from personal observation knew their value, urged their immediate colonization. Sir William Johnson, William Franklin the royalist governor of New Jersey, several fur-traders of Philadelphia, even Gage himself, eagerly took part in a project by which they were to acquire vast estates in the most fertile valley of the world. Their proposal embraced the territory bounded by the Mississippi, the Ohio, a line along the Wabash and Maumee to Lake Erie, and thence across Michigan, Green Bay, and the Fox river, to the mouth of the Wisconsin. The tract was thought to contain sixty-three millions of acres, the like of which could nowhere be found. Franklin favored the enterprise, which promised to America some new security for a mild colonial administration. It was the wish of Shelburne, who loved to take counsel with the great philosopher on the interests of humanity, that the valley of the Mississippi might be occupied by colonies enjoying English liberty. But the board of trade, to which Hillsborough had returned, insisted that emigrants to so remote regions would establish manufactures for themselves, and in the heart of America found a power which distance must emancipate. They adhered, therefore, to the proclamation of 1763, and to the range of the Alleghanies as the frontier of British settlements.

But the prohibition only set apart the great valley as the sanctuary of the unhappy, the adventurous, and the free; of those whom enterprise or curiosity, or disgust at the forms of life in the old plantations, raised above royal edicts; of the homeless, who would run all risks to take possession of the soil between the Alleghanies and the Ohio. The boundless West became the poor man's city of refuge, where the wilderness guarded his cabin as inviolably as the cliff or the cedar-top holds the eagle's eyrie. The few who occupied lands under grants from the crown could rely only on themselves for the protection of their property, and refused to pay quit-rents till their legal right should be acknowledged. The line of "straggling settlements" beyond the mountains extended from Pittsburg up the Monongahela and its tributaries to the banks of the Greenbrier and the New river, and to the well-known upper valley of the Holston, where the military path from Virginia led to the country of the Cherokees. Explorers or hunters went still farther to the west; for it is recorded that in 1766 "eight men were killed on Cumberland river."

In North Carolina, the people along the upland frontier, many of whom had sprung from Scotch-Irish Presbyterians, suffered from the illegal exactions of sheriffs and officials, whose pillaging was supported by the whole force of government. To meet this flood of iniquity, the most approved advice came from Herman Husbands, an independent farmer, who dwelt on Sandy Creek, where his fields of wheat and his "clover meadow" were the admiration of all observers. Each neighborhood throughout Orange county elected delegates to a general meeting, who were to "examine" into "abuses of power and into the public taxes, and inform themselves by what laws and for what uses they are laid."

In October, "the honest freeholders," about twelve in number, assembled on Enoe river, just outside of Hillsborough. But, to their repeated invitations to the officers to meet them, no answer came, except from Edmund Fanning. A favorite of

Governor Tryon, he was at that time the representative of the county, one of its magistrates, holding the highest commission under the crown in its militia, and was amassing a fortune by oppression as an attorney and extortion as registrar, loading titles to estates with doubts, and charging illegal prices for recording deeds. He was, above all others, justly obnoxious to the people, and his message to them ran that their proposition to inquire "judiciously" looked more like an insurrection than a settlement. "We meant," replied the meeting, "no more than wisefully, carefully, and soberly to examine the matter in hand." Their wrongs were flagrant and undeniable; and, since their "reasonable request" for explanations was unheeded, they resolved on "a meeting for a public and free conference yearly, and as often as the case might require," that so they might reap the profit of their right, under "the constitution, of choosing representatives and of learning what uses their money was called for." Yet how could unlettered farmers succeed against the undivided administrative power of the province? and how long would it be before some indiscretion would place them at the mercy of their oppressors? The apportionment of members of the colonial legislature was grossly unequal; the governor could create boroughs; the actual legislature, whose members were in part unwisely selected, in part unduly returned, rarely called together, and liable to be continued or dissolved at the pleasure of the executive, increased the poor man's burdens by voting an annual poll-tax to raise five thousand pounds, and the next year ten thousand more, to build a house for the governor at Newbern.

Moffat, of Rhode Island, asked of its legislature relief for his losses by the riot against the stamp act, founding his claim on the resolves of the British house of commons and the king's recommendation. "Neither of them," said the speaker of the assembly, "ought to influence the free and independent representatives of Rhode Island colony." Moffat had leave to withdraw his first petition and substitute an inoffensive one, which was received, but referred to a future session.

In Boston, the general court received like petitions. The form of its answer, in November, was suggested by Joseph Hawley, the member for Northampton. He was the only son of a school-master, himself married, but childless; a very able lawyer, of whose singular disinterestedness his native town still preserves the tradition. Content with a small patrimony, he lived in frugal simplicity, closing his house-door by a latch, without either bar or bolt. Inclined by temperament to moods of melancholy, his mind would again kindle with a brighter lustre, and be borne onward by resistless impulses. All parties revered his purity of life and ardent piety, and no man in his neighborhood equalled him in the public esteem. He opposed relief, except on condition of a general amnesty. "Of those seeking compensation," said he, "the chief is a person of unconstitutional principles, as one day or other he will make appear." The resolves of parliament were cited in reply. "The parliament of Great Britain," retorted Hawley, "has no right to legislate for us." At these words, Otis, rising in his place, bowed, and thanked him, saying: "He has gone further than I have as yet done in this house." For the first time the power of parliament was totally denied in a colonial legislature. "No representation, no taxation," had become a very common expression; the colonies began to cry: "No representation, no legislation." Having never shown bitterness of party spirit, Hawley readily carried the assembly with him, from their great opinion of his understanding and integrity; and a bill was framed, "granting compensation to the sufferers and pardon to the offenders," even to the returning of the fines which had been paid. A recess was taken, that members might consult their constituents. Before the adjournment complaint was made of the new zeal of Bernard in enforcing the navigation acts and sending to England injurious affidavits secretly taken. "I knew the time," interposed a member, "when the house would have readily assisted the governor in executing the laws of trade." "The times," replied Otis, "are altered; we now know our rights."

Meantime, Shelburne sought to recover the affections of the colonies. "Assure the assembly of Massachusetts," he said with "frankness" to their correspondent, "they may be perfectly easy about the enjoyment of their rights and privileges under the present administration." He enjoined moderation on every governor, and was resolved to make no appointments but of men of "the most generous principles." Through a letter to Bernard, whom he directed to pursue conciliatory measures, he invited the colonial legislature of itself to fall upon measures for terminating all local difficulties. The country people, as they read his words, agreed with one another that the compensation which he recommended should be made. "The king," said they, "has asked this of us as a favor; it would be ungenerous to refuse."

On the reassembling of the legislature, Hawley's bill prevailed by large majorities; yet it was voted that the sufferers had no just claim on the province, that the grant was of their own "free and good will," and not from deference to "a requisition." The governor assented to an act in which a colonial legislature exercised the prerogative of clemency; and Hutchinson, saying "Beggars must not be choosers," gave thanks at the bar of the house. But he nursed the feeling of revenge, and the next year, taking offence at some publication by Hawley, arbitrarily disbarred him in the superior court.

The patriots of New England did not doubt Shelburne's attention to its interests and respect for its liberties; but they were exquisitely sensitive to everything like an admission that the power of taxing them resided in parliament. Bernard was rebuked, because, with consent of council, he had caused the billeting act to be printed by the printer of the colony laws; and had made that act his warrant for furnishing supplies at the colony's expense to two companies of artillery, who, in stress of weather, had put into Boston. Otis attributed the taxing of America by parliament to Bernard's advice. The jealous legislature dismissed Richard Jackson from the service of the province, and the house elected the honest but aged Dennys de Berdt as its own particular agent.

This is the time from which Hutchinson dated the revolt of the colonies, and his correspondence and advice conformed to the opinion. Samuel Adams divined the evil designs, now so near their execution. He instructed De Berdt to oppose the establishment of a military force in America, as needless for protection and dangerous to liberty. "Certainly," said he, "the best way for Great Britain to make her colonies a real and lasting benefit is to give them all consistent indulgence in trade, and to remove any occasion of their suspecting that their liberties are in danger. While any act of parliament is in force which has the least appearance of a design to raise a revenue out of them, their jealousy will be awake."

In December, he wrote to the patriot most like himself, Christopher Gadsden, of South Carolina, inquiring whether the billeting act "is not taxing the colonies as effectually as the stamp act;" and protesting against a standing army, especially in time of peace, as dangerous to the civil community. "Surely," said he, "we cannot consent to their quartering among us; and how hard is it for us to be obliged to pay our money to subsist them!" Gadsden had already met patriots of South Carolina under the Live Oak, which was named their Tree of Liberty; had set before them the declaratory act, explained to them their rights, and leagued with them to oppose all foreign taxation.

At New York, the soldiery continued to irritate the people by insolent language, and by once more cutting down their flagstaff. Shelburne sought to reconcile their assembly to obedience to the billeting act, holding forth hope of a change of the law on a well-grounded representation of its hardship; and a prudent governor could have avoided a collision. But Moore was chiefly bent on establishing a play-house, against the wishes of the Presbyterians; and his thoughtless frivolity drove the house to a categorical conflict with the act of parliament, when they had really as an act of their own made "provision for quartering two battalions and one company of artillery." Their prudence secured unanimity in the assembly and among their constituents. In New York, as well as over all North America, the act declaratory of the absolute power of parliament was met by "the principle of the supreme power of the people in all cases whatsoever."

In England, a spirit was rising very different from that which had prevailed in the previous winter. "So long as I am in office," said Charles Townshend, on the floor of the house of commons, "the authority of the laws shall not be trampled upon." He did not fear to flatter the king, and court Grenville and Bedford; for Chatham was incurring the hatred of every branch of the aristocracy. Eight or nine whigs resigned their employments, on account of his headstrong removal of Lord Edgecombe from an unimportant post. Saunders and Keppel left the admiralty, and Keppel's place fell to Jenkinson. The Bedford party knew the weakness of the English Ximenes, and scorned his moderate bid for their support; but the king cheered him on "to rout out" the grandees of England, now "banded together." "Their unions," said Chatham, "give me no terrors;" "the king is firm, and there is nothing to fear."

To Shelburne, who was charged with the care of the colonies, Chatham gave his confidence and support. He claimed for the supreme government the right of dominion over the conquests in India, and the disposition of its territorial revenue; and, as Townshend crossed his plans by leaning to the East India company, early in December he proposed to Grafton the dismissal of Townshend as "incurable." Burke, indulging in derision of "the great person, so immeasurably high" as not to be reached by argument, travestied the litany in a solemn invocation to "the minister above." The next day, in the house of lords, Chatham marked his contempt of all such mockery by saying to the duke of Richmond: "When the people shall condemn me, I shall tremble; but I will set my face against the proudest connection of this country." "I hope," cried Richmond, "the nobility will not be browbeaten by an insolent minister;" and Chatham retorted the charge of insolence.

This is the last time during his ministry that he appeared in the house of lords. His broken health was unequal to the conflict which he had invited. On the eighteenth of December he repaired to Bath, with a nervous system so weak that he was easily fluttered and moved to tears; yet still he sent to the representatives of Massachusetts his friendly acknowledgment of their vote of gratitude.

Townshend saw his opportunity, and no longer concealed his intention. Knowing the king's dislike of Shelburne, he took advantage of his own greater age, his authority as the ablest orator in the house of commons, his long acquaintance with American affairs, and the fact that they turned chiefly on questions of finance, to assume their direction. His ambition deceived him into the hope of succeeding where Grenville had failed; and in concert with Paxton, from Boston, he was devising a scheme for a board of customs in America, and duties to be collected in its ports for an American civil list. He expected his dismissal, if Chatham regained health; and he saw the clearest prospect of advancement by setting his colleagues at defiance. He therefore prepared to solve the questions of Asia and America in his own way, and trod the ground which he had chosen with fearless audacity. On the twenty-sixth of January 1767, the house of commons, in committee of supply, considered the estimates for the land forces and garrisons in the plantations. Grenville seized the occasion to declaim on the repeal of the stamp act. He enforced the necessity of relieving Great Britain from a burden which the colonies ought to bear, and which with contingencies exceeded four hundred thousand pounds, reminding the country gentleman that this sum was nearly equal to one shilling in the pound of the land-tax. He spoke elaborately, and against Chatham was even more rancorous than usual.

"Administration," replied Townshend, "has applied its attention to give relief to Great Britain from bearing the whole expense of securing, defending, and protecting America and the West India islands; I shall bring into the house some propositions that I hope may tend, in time, to ease the people of England upon this head, and yet not be heavy in any manner upon the people in the colonies. I know the mode by which a revenue may be drawn from America without offence." As he spoke, the house shook with applause; "hear him!" "hear him!" now swelling loudest from his own side, now from the benches of the opposition. "I am still," he continued, "a firm advocate for the stamp act, for its principle, and for the duty itself, only the heats which prevailed made it an improper time to press it. I laugh at the absurd distinction between internal and external taxes. If we have a right to impose the one, we have a right to impose the other; the distinction is ridiculous in the opinion of everybody except the Americans." Looking up where the colony agents usually sat, he added: "I speak this aloud, that all you who are in the galleries may hear me; and, after this, I do not expect to have my statue erected in America." Then, laying his hand on the table in front of him, he declared to the house: "England is undone if this taxation of America is given up."

Grenville demanded of him to pledge himself to his declaration: he did so most willingly; and his promise received a tumultuous welcome.

Lord George Sackville pressed for a revenue that should be adequate; and Townshend engaged himself to the house to find a revenue, if not adequate, yet nearly sufficient to meet the military expenses, when properly reduced. The loud burst of rapture dismayed Conway, who sat in silent astonishment at the unauthorized but premeditated rashness of his colleague.

The next night, the cabinet questioned the insubordinate minister "how he had ventured to depart, on so essential a point, from the profession of the whole ministry;" and he browbeat them all. "I appeal to you," said he, turning to Conway, "whether the house is not bent on obtaining a revenue of some sort from the colonies." Not one of the ministry then in London had sufficient authority to advise his dismission; and nothing less could have stopped his measures.

In January 1767, the day after Townshend braved his colleagues, the legislature of Massachusetts convened. Hutchinson, having received compensation as a sufferer by the riots, restrained his ambition no longer, and took a seat in the council as though it of right belonged to the lieutenant-governor. The house resented his intrusion into an elective body of which he had not been chosen a member; the council, by a unanimous vote, denied his pretensions. The language of the charter was too explicit to admit of a doubt; yet Bernard urged the interposition of the central government.

With unshaken confidence in Hawley, Otis, and Samuel Adams, the people scanned every measure that could imply consent to British taxation. When the governor professed, "in pursuance of the late act of parliament," to have made provision at the colony's expense for troops which had recently touched at Boston harbor, they did not cease their complaints till they wrung from him the declaration that his supply "did not include articles prescribed by that act," but was "wholly conformable to the usage of the province." Upon this concession, the house acquiesced in the expenditure; and declared their readiness to grant of their own free accord such aids as the king's service should require.

Under the same act of parliament, Gage demanded of the governor of Connecticut quarters for one hundred and fifty-eight recruits; but that magistrate refused compliance till he should be duly authorized by the colonial assembly.

To check every aspiration after independence, Carleton, the able governor of Canada, advised to grant no legislative immunities to its people; to keep Crown Point and Ticonderoga in good repair; to have a citadel and place of arms in New York, as well as a citadel in Quebec; and to link the two provinces so strongly together that, on the beginning of an outbreak, ten or fifteen thousand men could be moved without delay from the one to the other, or to any part of the continent. No pains, no address, no expense, he insisted, would be too great for the object, which would divide the northern and southern colonies, as well as secure the public magazines.

Chatham could not suspend the act of parliament; but, through Shelburne, he enjoined the American commander-in-chief to make its burden as light, both in appearance and in reality, as was consistent with the public service. He saw that the imperfect compliance of New York would open a fair field to the arraigners of America; and, between his opinions as a statesman and his obligations as minister, he knew not what to propose. The declaratory act was as a barren fruit-tree, cumbering the earth only to spread a noxious shade.

Shelburne was aware that, if the Americans "should be tempted to resist in the last instance," France and Spain would no longer defer breaking the peace of which they began to number the days. Spain was resolved not to pay the Manilla ransom, was planning how to drive the English from the Falkland islands, and called on France to prepare to go to war in two years; "for Spain," said Grimaldi, "cannot longer postpone inflicting chastisement on English insolence." "This is the rhodomontade of a Don Quixote," said Choiseul.

Executive moderation might still have saved England from a conflict. Shelburne proceeded diligently to make himself master of each American question, and to prepare its solution. To form an American fund without exercising rigor in respect to quit-rents long due, he proposed to break up the system of forestalling lands by speculators, to require of the engrossing proprietors the fulfilment of the conditions of their grants, and to make all future grants on a system of quit-rents, which should be applied to defray the American expenses then borne by the British exchequer.

Relief to the mother country being thus derived from an income which had chiefly been squandered among favorites, he proposed to leave the Indian trade to be regulated under general rules by the respective provinces, at their own cost.

Resisting those who advised to concentrate the American army in the principal towns, he wished it posted on the frontiers, where its presence might be desired.

The people of America, even a majority of those who adhered to the church of England, feared an American episcopate, lest ecclesiastical courts should follow; Shelburne expressed his opinion openly that there was no occasion for American bishops.

He reprobated the political dependence of the judges in the colonies, and advised that their commissions should conform to the usage in England.

The grants of lands in Vermont, under the seal of New Hampshire, he confirmed; and this decision was not less prudent than just.

Massachusetts and New York were in controversy about limits, which had led to disputed land-titles and bloodshed on the border: instead of keeping the question open as a means of setting one colony against another, he directed that it should be definitively settled.

The billeting act for America, which the Rockingham ministry had continued till the twenty-fourth of March 1768, was contrary to the tenor of British legislation for Ireland, and to all former legislation for America. Shelburne disapproved its principle, and sought to reconcile the wants of the army with the rights of America, being resolved "not to establish a precedent, which might hereafter be turned to purposes of oppression."

The American continent was interested in the settlement of Canadian affairs; Shelburne listened to the hope of restoring tranquillity by calling an assembly that should assimilate to the English laws such of the French laws as it was necessary to retain, and by rendering the Canadian Catholics eligible to the assembly and council.

But the more Shelburne showed wise moderation, the more the court spoke of him as "an enemy." The king who was accustomed "to talk a great deal about America" told him plainly that the billeting act "should be enforced," though he declined "to suggest the mode." Besides, the dependence of the colonies was believed to be at stake; and New York "underwent the imputation of rebellion."

The difficulties that beset Shelburne were increased by the condition of parties in Great Britain. The old whig aristocracy was passing out of power with so ill a grace that they preferred the immediate gratification of their passions to every consideration of wisdom and expediency. America was the theme in all companies, yet was discussed according to its bearings on personal ambition. Men struggled for a momentary victory more than for any system of government; and the liberties of two millions of their countrymen, the interests of a continent, the unity of the British empire, were swayed by the accidents of a parliamentary skirmish.

Merchants of New York had sent a very temperate petition, setting forth some of the useless grievances of the acts of trade, and praying for the free exportation of their lumber and an easier exchange of products with the West Indies. Grenville and his friends perversely appealed to the reasonable request as fresh evidence that nothing would give satisfaction to the colonists but a repeal of all restrictions on trade, and freedom from all subordination and dependence; and Chatham had cause to denounce Townshend thrice as "incurable." Nothing but Chatham's presence could restore activity to the administration, and the gout had returned upon him at Marlborough, on his way to London.

Business would not wait. On the eighteenth of February, there appeared in the account of the extraordinaries a large and unusual American expenditure. Grenville advised to lessen it, and charge upon the colonies the whole of what should remain. There was a general agreement that America ought to alleviate the burdens of England. Every speaker of the opposition inveighed against Chatham, whom no one rose to defend. Rigby reproached the ministers with being but the servile instruments of their absent chief, incapable of acting but on orders from his lips. To prove his independence, Townshend explained his own system for America, and combated that of Chatham of the year before. "I would govern the Americans," said he, "as subjects of Great Britain. I would restrain their trade and their manufactures as subordinate to the mother country. These, our children, must not make themselves our allies in time of war and our rivals in peace." And he adopted the suggestions for retrenchment and an American duty. The mosaic opposition watched every opportunity to push the ministry upon extreme measures.

By this time, the friends of Grenville, of Bedford, and of Rockingham—men the most imbittered against each other by former contests, and the most opposite in character and tendencies—were ready to combine against the existing ministry, whatever might be the consequence of its destruction. During the war, and ever since, the land-tax had been at the nominal rate of four shillings in the pound, in reality at but about ninepence in the pound. On the twenty-seventh of February, Dowdeswell, the leader of the Rockingham party, regardless of his own policy when in the treasury and his knowledge of the public wants, proposed a reduction in the land-tax, nominally of a shilling, but really of only about nine farthings in the pound. Grenville supported the proposal, which would bring in its train a tax on the colonies. The question was debated between the Americans and the landed interest of England, and the chancellor of the exchequer was reminded of his pledge to derive this year some revenue from America. On the division, Edmund Burke, "too fond of the right" to vote against his conscience, and not enough fond of it to vote against his party, stayed away; the united factions of the aristocracy mustered two hundred and six against one hundred and eighty-eight for the ministry. But not one of those who planned this impolitic act derived from it any advantage. The good sense of the country condemned it; the city dreaded the wound given to public credit; Grenville, who joyfully accepted the congratulations of the country gentlemen, deceived himself in expecting a junction with Rockingham, and did not moderate the enmity of the king. The ancient whig connection compromised its principles by creating an apparent excuse for American taxes, and, for a momentary parliamentary triumph, doomed itself more surely to a fruitless opposition; and for so small a benefit as a reduction of nine farthings in the pound on but one year's rental, the oligarchy of landlords risked a continent.

This was the first overthrow, on an important question, which the government had sustained for a quarter of a century. On hearing the news, Chatham rose from his bed, and, ill as he was, hastened to London. Charles Townshend "was warm in the sunshine of majesty;" but, as Chatham wished to dismiss him, the king readily assented, and Lord North was invited to become chancellor of the exchequer. Townshend knew well what was passing, and, with easy defiance, said openly: "I expect to be dismissed for it." But Lord North would not venture to supersede him. Whom will Chatham next recommend? asked the king, through Grafton; and no other could be named. Here was a new humiliation. Chatham saw the shaft which his enfeebled hand hurled at a defenceless adversary fall harmless at his own feet. He could endure no more. "We cannot remain in office together," said he of Townshend, and, on the eleventh of March, he bade the duke of Grafton call the next council at his own house. Accumulated grief destroyed what little health remained to him; he withdrew from business, and became invisible even to Camden and to Grafton. Here, in fact, his administration was at an end. With every question of domestic, foreign, and colonial policy unsettled, the British Agamemnon retired to his tent, leaving subordinate chiefs to quarrel for the direction.

## CHAPTER XIX.

PARLIAMENT WILL HAVE AN AMERICAN ARMY AND AN AMERICAN REVENUE. ADMINISTRATION OF GRAFTON.

### MARCH–JULY 1767.

The eclipse of Chatham left Charles Townshend the lord of the ascendant. He was a man of wonderful endowments, dashed with follies and indiscretion. Impatient of waiting, his ruling passion was present success. He was ever carried away by the immediate object of his desires. In the house of commons, his brilliant oratory took its inspiration from the prevailing opinion, and, careless of consistency, heedless whom he deserted or whom he joined, he followed the floating indications of the loudest cheers. Applause was the temptation which he had no power to resist. Gay, volatile, and fickle, he lived for the hour and shone for the hour, without the thought of founding an enduring name. Finding Chatham not likely to reappear, his uncontrolled imagination was devising schemes to forward his own ambition, and he turned to pay the greatest court wherever political appearances were most inviting.

In the cabinet meeting, held on the twelfth of March 1767, at the house of Grafton, Townshend assumed to dictate to the ministry its colonial policy, and threatened an appeal from its disapproval to the house. A letter from Shelburne urged Chatham to remove him; but Chatham was too ill to do so, or to give advice. Shelburne continued to protect American liberty as well as he could, but was powerless to control events, for Grafton and even Camden yielded to Townshend's impetuosity.

The disappearance of Chatham reanimated the dissatisfied factions of the aristocracy; Rockingham gave assurances that his friends, without whom, he persuaded himself, nothing could be carried by the Bedfords, would not join in anything severe against America; but he was all the while contributing to the success of the policy which he most abhorred. Since the last winter, America had lost friends both in and out of parliament. Conway, who kept his old ground, was only laughed at. "He is below low-water mark," said Townshend to Grenville.

On the thirtieth of March, two days after news had arrived that in one of their messages the representatives of Massachusetts had given a formal defiance to parliament, as well as encouraged the resistance of New York to the billeting act, the American papers which Bedford had demanded were taken into consideration by the house of lords. Camden, accepting the right of parliament to tax America as established by its own declaratory statute, presented New York as delinquent. Grafton said well that "the present question was too serious for faction," and promised that the ministers would bring forward a suitable measure. But the lords wearied themselves all that day and all the next in scolding all the colonies with indiscriminate bitterness. They were called "undutiful, ungracious, and unthankful;" "rebels," "traitors," were epithets liberally bestowed. Some wished to make of New York an example that might terrify all the others; it was more generally proposed by act of parliament to remodel the government of them all. America had not yet finished the statues which it was raising to Chatham, when Mauduit maliciously sent over word that the plan for reducing America would be sanctioned by his name.

On the tenth of April, Massachusetts was selected for censure; and Bedford came to the house of lords to move an address that the king in council would declare the Massachusetts act of amnesty null and void. The ministry contended truly that the motion was needless, as the act would be rejected in the usual course of business. "Perhaps we had best look into the Massachusetts charter before we come to a decision," said one of the administration. "No!" cried Lord Townshend; "let us deliberate no longer; let us act with vigor now, while we can call the colonies ours. If you do not, they will very soon be lost forever."

Lord Mansfield descanted "upon the folly and wickedness of the American incendiaries," and drew an animated picture of the fatal effects which the "deplorable event of their disjunction must produce to England and to the colonies. His words carried conviction to the house of lords, and hastened the event which he deprecated.

In the six hours' debate the resistance of New York and Massachusetts had been so highly colored, that Choiseul began to think the time for the great American insurrection was come. He resolved, therefore, to send an emissary across the Atlantic, and selected for that purpose the brave and upright John Kalb. A Protestant and a German, son of a peasant who dwelt in the old land of the Franks, not far from Erlangen, he had gained in the service of France an honorable name and the brevet rank of lieutenant-colonel. His written instructions, dated on the twenty-second of April, enjoined him, after preliminary inquiries at Amsterdam, to go to the English colonies; to ascertain their wants, in respect of engineers and artillery officers, munitions of war and provisions; the strength of their purpose to withdraw from the British government; their resources in troops, citadels, and intrenched posts; their project of revolt, and their chiefs. "The commission which I give you," said Choiseul, "is difficult, and demands intelligence. Ask of me the means which you think necessary for its execution; I will furnish you with them all." Kalb brought to his work close observation and cautious judgment, but not the sagacity which could measure the movement of a revolution.

From this time Choiseul sought in every quarter accurate accounts of the progress of opinion in America, alike in the writings of Franklin, in the judgment of the best-informed merchants, and in New England sermons, from which curious extracts are to this day preserved among the state papers of France. His judgment on events was more impartial and clear than that of any British minister who succeeded Shelburne.

It still seemed easy to postpone revolution; as yet, the points in issue were trifling. The late deliberation of the peers was but a frivolous cavilling on the form of a royal veto.

The people of Massachusetts, seeing a disposition to mar

its charter and use military power in its government, needed more than ever an agent in England. Bernard insisted that no one should receive that appointment without his approval, and repeatedly negatived the dismissal of the last incumbent. But Shelburne held that the right of nomination belonged essentially to the representatives, so that this dispute could not become serious while he remained in the ministry.

The lieutenant-governor, in spite of his want of an election, had taken a seat in the council, pleading the charter as his warrant for doing so; but the attorney-general in England, to whom the case was referred, was of opinion that "the right could not be claimed by virtue of anything contained in the charter or the constitution of the province."

Bernard gave out that, by the use of his veto, he would always keep places open in the council for Hutchinson and Oliver. The menace was a violation of the spirit of the constitution; its only effect was to preserve two perpetual vacancies in the council.

Bernard advised to alter the council itself from an elective body to one of royal nomination. The change would have been a causeless breach of faith; of no colony had the council more uniformly shown loyalty than that of Massachusetts. Hutchinson at heart disapproved the proposal which from personal motives he promoted. The perfidious advice would be harmless if England would only respect the charter which nearly a century's possession had confirmed.

There remained no grounds of imminent variance except the navigation acts, the billeting act, the acts restraining industry, and the slave-trade.

To the slave-trade Virginia led the opposition. Towns at the North, especially Worcester, in Massachusetts, protested against it; but opinion through the country was divided; and complaints of the grievance had not been made in concert.

The restraints on manufactures, especially of wool and iron, were flagrant violations of natural rights; but they were not of recent date, and, as they related to products which it was still the interest of the people to import, were in a great degree inoperative and unobserved.

By the billeting act, Great Britain exposed its dignity to

the discretion or the petulance of provincial assemblies. There was no bound to the impropriety of parliament's enacting what those legislatures should enact, and accompanying the statute by a requisition from the throne. Is the measure compulsory and final? Then it should not be addressed to assemblies which are not executive officers. Does it not compel obedience? Then the assemblies have a right to deliberate, to accept in whole or in part, or to reject. And, indeed, the demand of quarters and provisions, without limitation of time or of the number of troops, was a reasonable subject for deliberation. Such was the opinion of the very few in England who considered the question on its merits, and not as a test of authority. Besides, no province had refused to comply with the spirit of the act. A slight modification, leaving some option to the colonies, would have remedied the disagreement.

The navigation acts were a source of just and ever-increasing discontent. But no public body in America had denied their validity; the relaxations which America most desired were very moderate, relating chiefly to intercourse with the West Indies, and the free export of such of its products as Great Britain would not receive. The illicit trade was partly owing to useless laws, but more to the prevailing corruption among the servants of the crown. No practical question existed, except that which Otis had raised, on the legality of the writs of assistance; and the attorney- and solicitor-general of England confirmed his opinion that they were not warranted by law.

"In America," said Andrew Eliot, of Boston, "the people glory in the name, and only desire to enjoy the liberties of Englishmen. Nothing could influence us to desire independence but such attempts on our liberties as I hope Great Britain will be just enough never to make. Oppression makes wise men mad."

To tranquillize America, no more was wanting than a respect for its rights, and some accommodation to its confirmed habits and opinions. The colonies had, each of them, a direction of its own and a character of its own, which required to be harmoniously reconciled with the motion impressed upon it by the imperial legislature. But this demanded study, self-possession, and candor. The parliament of that day, recognising no reciprocity of obligations, thought nothing so wrong as thwarting its will. A good system would have been a consummate work of deliberative wisdom; the principle of despotic government acted with more speed and uniformity, having passion for its interpreter, and a statesman like Townshend to execute its impulses.

The committee of American merchants and friends to the colonies, with Trecothick at its head, interposed with Townshend; but he answered: "I do not in the least doubt the right of parliament to tax the colonies internally; I know no difference between internal or external taxes; yet, since the Americans are pleased to make that distinction, I am willing to indulge them, and for that reason choose to confine myself to regulations of trade, by which a sufficient revenue may be raised." "Perhaps the army," rejoined Trecothick, "may with safety be withdrawn from America, in which case the expense will cease, and then there will be no further occasion for a revenue." "I will hear nothing on that subject," such was Townshend's peremptory declaration; "the moment a resolution shall be taken to withdraw the army, I will resign my office and have no more to do in public affairs. I insist it is absolutely necessary to keep up a large army there and here. An American army and consequently an American revenue are essential; but I am willing to have both in the manner most easy to the people."

On the thirteenth of May, Townshend came to the house of commons, in the consciousness of his supremacy. When the resolutions for the stamp act were voted, parliament was unenlightened. Now it had had the experience of taxing America, and of repealing the tax through fear of civil war. What is done now cannot easily be revoked. A secret consciousness prevailed that a great wrong was about to be inflicted. The liberty and interests of America were at issue; and yet the doors of the house of commons were, by special order, shut against every agent of the colonies, and even against every American merchant.

Townshend opened the debate with professions of candor and the air of a man of business. Exculpating alike Pennsyl vania and Connecticut, he named, as delinquent colonies, Massachusetts, which had invaded the king's prerogative by a general amnesty, and in a message to its governor had used expressions in derogation of the authority of parliament; Rhode Island, which had postponed but not refused an indemnity to the sufferers by the stamp act; and New Jersey, which had evaded the billeting act, but had yet furnished the king's troops with every essential thing to their perfect satisfaction. Against these colonies it was not necessary to institute severe proceedings. But New York, in the month of June last, beside appointing its own commissary, had limited its supplies to two regiments, and to those articles only which were provided in the rest of the king's dominions; and, in December, had refused to do more. Here was such clear evidence of a direct denial of the authority of parliament, and such overt acts of disobedience to one of its laws, that an immediate interposition was most strongly called for, as well to secure the just dependence of the province as to maintain the majesty and authority of government.

It became parliament not to engage in controversy with its colonies, but to assert its sovereignty, without uniting them in a common cause. For this end, he proposed to proceed against New York, and against New York alone. To levy a local tax would be to accept a penalty in lieu of obedience. He should therefore move that New York, having disobeyed parliament, should be restrained from any legislative act of its own till it should comply.

He then brought forward the establishment of a board of commissioners of the customs, to be stationed in America.

"Our right of taxation," he continued, "is indubitable; yet, to prevent mischief, I was myself in favor of repealing the stamp act. But there can be no objections to port duties on wine, oil, and fruits, if allowed to be carried to America directly from Spain and Portugal; on glass, paper, lead, and colors; and especially on tea. Owing to the high charges in England, America has supplied itself with tea by smuggling it from the Dutch possessions; to remedy this, duties hitherto levied upon it in England are to be given up, and a specific duty collected in America itself. A duty on china can be obtained by repealing the drawback On salt it was at first intended to lay an impost; but this is abandoned, from the difficulty of adjusting the drawback to be allowed on exports of cured fish and provisions, and on salt for the fisheries."

The American revenue, it was further explained, was to be placed at the disposal of the king for the payment of his civil officers. To each governor, an annual salary was to be assigned of two thousand pounds sterling; to each chief justice, of five hundred pounds.

The minister was to have the irresponsible power of establishing by sign manual a general civil list in every American province, and at his pleasure to grant salaries and pensions, limited only by the amount of the American revenue; the national exchequer was to receive no more than the crumbs that fell from the table. The proposition bore on its face the mark of owing its parentage to the holders and patrons of American offices; and yet it was received in the house with general favor. Richard Jackson was not regarded when he spoke against the duties themselves, and foretold the mischiefs that would ensue.

Grenville heard with malignant joy one of the repealers of his stamp act propose a revenue from port duties. "You are deceived," said he; "the Americans will laugh at you for your distinctions." He spoke against legalizing a direct trade between Portugal and America. As to taxes, he demanded more; all that were promised were trifles. "I," said he, "will tell the honorable gentleman of a revenue that will produce something valuable in America: issue paper bearing interest upon loan there, and apply the interest as you think proper." Townshend, perceiving that the suggestion pleased the house, stood up again, and said that that was a proposition of his own; the bill for it was already prepared.

The debate would not have continued long if there had not been a division of opinion as to the mode of coercing New York. Edmund Burke, approving a local tax on importations into that province, opposed the general system. "You will never see a single shilling from America," said he, prophetically; "it is not by votes and angry resolutions of this house, but by a slow and steady conduct, that the Americans are to be reconciled to us." Dowdeswell described the new plan as worse than to have softened and enforced the stamp-tax. "Do like the best of physicians," said Beckford, who alone seemed to understand the subject, and whom nobody minded; "heal the disease by doing nothing."

Others thought there should be an amendment to the billeting act itself, directing the civil magistrates to quarter upon private houses, where the assemblies of America did not fulfil the present requirements. Grenville advised to invest the governor and council of each colony with power to draw on the colonial treasurer, who, in case of refusal to answer such bills out of the first aids in his hands, howsoever appropriated, should be judged guilty of a capital crime, and be tried and punished in England. And, since the colonies persisted in the denial of the parliamentary right of taxation, he offered for consideration that every American, before entering into office, should subscribe a political test nearly in the words of the declaratory act, acknowledging the unlimited sovereignty of Great Britain.

These several points were discussed till one in the morning, when a question was so framed by Grenville that the Rockinghams could join him in the division; but their united voices were no more than ninety-eight against one hundred and eighty.

"The new measures for the colonies," observed Choiseul, "meet with opposition in both houses of parliament; but their execution will encounter still more considerable resistance in America."

On the fifteenth, Townshend reported his resolutions to the house, when a strenuous effort was made to have them recommitted; the friends of Rockingham pretending to wish a more lenient measure, yet joining with Grenville, who spoke for one more severe, effective, and general. But Townshend, by surpassing eloquence, brought the house back to his first resolutions, which were adopted without a division.

Grenville then moved that many of the colonies denied and oppugned the sovereignty of Great Britain; in other words, were in a state of open rebellion; and wished that they might be reduced to submission by force; but a large majority was against him. In the midst of one of his speeches he stopped short, and, looking up to the gallery, said: "I hope there are no American agents present; I must hold such language as I would not have them hear." "I have expressly ordered the sergeant to admit none," said the speaker, "and you may be assured there are none present." Yet Johnson, of Connecticut, had braved the danger of an arrest, and sat in the gallery to record the incidents of the evening for the warning of his countrymen. Grenville next moved his test for America; but the house dreaded to reproduce a union of the colonies. "At least, then," renewed Grenville, "take some notice of those in America who have suffered for their loyal support of your sovereignty;" and, naming Ingersoll, Hutchinson, Oliver, Howard, and others, he moved an address in their favor; and this, being seconded by Lord North, passed without dissent.

After ordering the bill to disfranchise New York, as well as sanctioning the new system of colonial revenue and administration, the house rose, unconscious that it had taken steps which pride would not allow to be recalled, and which, if not retracted, would unite the colonies for independence.

The bitterness against America grew with its indulgence. On the twenty-first, news came that Georgia had refused compliance with the billeting act; and this, from a colony that had been established at the public expense, was held to be "unexampled insolence." The secretary at war, therefore, as if to insure confusion, introduced a bill, extending the obnoxious law a year beyond the time when it would have expired by its own limitation.

The moment was inviting to the opposition. Raising some trivial questions on the form in which the amnesty act of Massachusetts had been disallowed, the united factions of Rockingham, Bedford, and Temple on one division left the ministry a majority of but six, and on another of but three.

On both these occasions the king made two of his brothers vote with the ministry. He wished to enforce the absolute authority of parliament in America, and to consummate his victory over the aristocracy in England. For the one, he needed to dismiss Shelburne; for the other, to employ the name of Chatham. Grafton readily adopted a plan to lead the aristocracy into disputes among themselves; and then, separating the Bedfords from the rest, to introduce a part of them to power. Keen observers predicted a "mosaic" ministry.

To proceed securely, Grafton required some understanding with Chatham; but Chatham refused to see him, pleading his disability. The king himself, in a letter framed with cool adroitness, but which seemed an effusion of confidence and affection, charged the earl, who had given in the house of lords defiance to the whole nobility, by his "duty, affection, and honor," not to "truckle" now, when the "hydra" was at the height of its power; for success, nothing was wanted but that he should have "five minutes' conversation" with Grafton.

Chatham yielded to such persuasion, though suffering from a universal tremor, which application to business visibly increased. Grafton was filled with grief at "the sight of his great mind bowed down and thus weakened by disorder;" but he obtained from him the declaration that "he would not retire except by his majesty's command."

At a second interview in June, Grafton, at the wish of the king, urged that Shelburne "could not be allowed to continue in his office." Chatham summoned spirit to vindicate his friend, and to advise the dismission of Townshend. He was with great difficulty led to believe that a junction was necessary with either the Bedfords or the Rockinghams; but, of the two, Grafton thought him inclined to prefer the former. After an interview of two full hours, the ministers parted with the most cordial professions of mutual attachment.

Grafton was left in the position of prime minister; but, from this time, the king controlled his ministers and directed affairs in hostility to public freedom, even where protected by usage and law. Liberty, nevertheless, continued to grow in strength. "Men are opening their eyes," said Voltaire, "from one end of Europe to the other. Fanaticism, which feels its humiliation and implores the arm of authority, makes the involuntary confession of its defeat. This happy revolution which has taken place in the minds of men of probity within fifteen or twenty years has exceeded my hopes."

That a greater change hung over America could not escape Jonathan Trumbull, the deputy governor of Connecticut. He was a model of a rural magistrate, never weary of business, profoundly religious, grave in manner, discriminating in judgment, fixed in his principles, steadfast in purpose, and, by his ability and patriotism, enchaining respect and confidence. His opinion was formed, that, if "methods tending to violence should be taken to maintain the dependence of the colonies, it would hasten a separation;" that the connection with England could be preserved by "gentle and insensible methods," rather than "by power or force." But not so reasoned Townshend, who, after the Whitsuntide holidays, "stole" his bill through both houses. The stamp act had called an American revenue "just and necessary," and had been repealed as impolitic. Townshend's preamble to his bill granting duties in America on glass, red and white lead, painters' colors and paper, and threepence a pound on tea, declared a "certain and adequate" American revenue "expedient." By another act, a board of customs was established at Boston; and general writs of assistance were legalized. For New York, an act of parliament suspended the functions of its representatives till they should render obedience to the imperial legislature.

On such an alternative, it was thought that that province would submit without delay; and that the Americans, as their tea would now come to them at a less price than to the consumers in England, would pay the impost in their own ports with only seeming reluctance.

But the new measures were even more subversive of right than those of Grenville, who left the civil officers dependent on the local legislators, and preserved the proceeds of the American tax in the exchequer. Townshend's revenue was to be disposed of under the sign manual at the king's pleasure, and could be burdened at will by pensions to Englishmen. In so far as it provided an independent support for the crown officers, it did away with the necessity of colonial legislatures. Governors would have little inducement to call them, and an angry minister might dissolve them without inconvenience. Henceforward, "no native" of America could hope to receive any lucrative commission under the crown unless he were one of the martyrs to the stamp act. Places would be filled by "some Briton-born," who should have exhibited proof of a readiness to govern the Americans, on the principle of bringing them to the most exact obedience to the instructions of the king.

The man who, at this moment of Chatham's illness, seized on the administration of the colonies, saw nothing but what at the moment lay near him. England had excelled all other states in founding colonies, because she sent out her sons with free institutions like her own; and now her minister of an hour, blind alike to her interest and her glory, was undoing her noblest work. Less than two centuries before, the English was heard nowhere but among the inhabitants of the larger part of one island and a few emigrants among the Celts of another. It had now seated itself on a continent beyond the Atlantic; and a comely and industrious race, as it climbed the eastern slope of the Alleghanies, carried with it the English speech and laws and letters and love of liberty. With superior wisdom and foresight, Hume contemplated the ever-expanding settlements of those who spoke the same tongue with himself, wished for them the freest and happiest development, and invited Gibbon, his great compeer, to observe that at least " the solid and increasing establishments in America promised superior stability and duration to the English language."

## CHAPTER XX.

### COALITION OF THE KING AND THE ARISTOCRACY.

#### JULY–NOVEMBER 1767.

THE anarchy in the ministry enabled the king to govern as well as to reign. Grafton made no tedious speeches in the closet, and approved the late American regulations; persuading himself that the choice of tea as the subject of taxation was his own; that the law suspending the legislative functions of New York was marked by moderation and dignity; and that abrogating the charters of the American colonies would be their emancipation from "fetters."

The king, who had looked into Conway's heart to learn how to wind and govern him, attached him by the semblance of perfect confidence, showing him all Chatham's letters, and giving him leave to treat with his own old associates.

But Rockingham, who never opened his eyes to the light that was springing from the increased intelligence of the masses, and left out of view that his glory as a statesman had come from his opposition to Grenville and Bedford, governed himself exclusively by the ancient principle of his party "to fight up against the king and against the people," and set about cementing the shattered fragments of the old whig aristocracy. He began with Bedford. "Bedford and Grenville are one," said Rigby, by authority; "and neither of them will ever depart from the ground taken, to assert and establish the entire sovereignty of Great Britain over her colonies." But Rockingham satisfied himself by declaring for a "wide and comprehensive" system, and, after a week's negotiation, with no plan but to support privilege against prerogative, he announced to Grafton his readiness to form a new administration.

The king, whom Rockingham had now to encounter, was greatly his superior in sagacity and consistency. Implacable toward Grenville, he surveyed calmly the condition of the checkered factions; and, seeing that his own consent to their union would set them at variance among themselves, he gave Rockingham leave to revive, if he could, the exclusive rule of the great whig families. He was master of the field, and he knew it. "The king may make a page first minister," said Lord Holland. But the people demanded more and more to know what was passing in parliament; and, with the ready support of the press, prepared to intervene through the force of public opinion. "Power," thought a French observer, "has passed into the hands of the populace and the merchants. The country is exceedingly jealous of its liberty."

On the twentieth of July 1767, the leaders of the two branches of the oligarchy met at the house of the duke of Newcastle. Rockingham explained the purpose of the meeting. Bedford, on behalf of Temple and Grenville, declared their readiness to support a comprehensive administration, provided it adopted the capital measure of asserting and establishing the sovereignty of Great Britain over its colonies. At this, Rockingham flew into a violent passion. Bedford insisted with firmness on the declaration. Sandwich interposed to reconcile the difference by substituting words which might be interpreted either way. The difficulty recurred on discussing the division of employments. Rockingham was inflexible against Grenville as the leader of the house of commons, and Bedford equally determined against Conway. So the meeting broke up without any result. The next day, at a second meeting, the difficulty about America could not be got over, "and we broke up," says Bedford, "with our all declaring ourselves free from all engagements to one another."

The king admitted Rockingham to an audience, to make his confession that the country required a strong, united, and permanent administration, and that he could not form one of any kind. The king was in the best humor. He bowed very graciously, and Rockingham bowed, and so they parted. "What did the king say to you?" asked Grafton and Conway, eagerly, as Rockingham came out; and the answer was: "Nothing."

Once more Rockingham was urged to join with the friends of Chatham, but he was impracticable. A leader of a party had never done more to diminish its influence; his intellect bore no analogy to his virtues, nor his conduct to his good intentions. Without ability to plan a system suited to his times, he left the field open to those who wished ill to liberty in America and in England. The king was never in better spirits.

Grafton won the credit of moderation by his readiness to retire; and, after the failure of all his offers to Rockingham, people saw him at the head of the treasury with less dissatisfaction. He retained the expectation of an alliance with Bedford, who could not keep his party together without official patronage; but, for the moment, he depended on Townshend.

So Charles Townshend remained in the cabinet, treating everything in jest, scattering ridicule with full hands, and careless on whom it fell. Grafton was apparently the chief; but the king held the helm, and, as the dissolution of parliament drew near, was the more happy in a dependent ministry. The patronage of the crown amounted to an annual disbursement of six millions sterling; and the secret service money was employed to cover the expenses of elections, at a time when less than ten thousand voters chose a majority of the house of commons. As merchants and adventurers, rich with the profits of trade or the spoils of India, competed for boroughs, the price of votes within twenty years had increased threefold. Edmund Burke grumbled because the moneyed men of his party did not engage more of "the venal boroughs."

"May the anarchy in the British government last for ages," wrote Choiseul. "Your prayer will be heard," answered Durand, then minister in London. "The opposition during this reign will always be strong, for the cabinet will always be divided; but the genius of the nation, concentrating itself on commerce and colonies, compensates the inferiority of the men in power, and makes great advances without their guidance." "My position," observed Choiseul, as he contemplated, alike in Asia and in America, the undisputed ascendency of the nation which he called his "enemy," "is the most vexatious possible; I see the ill; I do not see the remedy." Anxious to send accurate accounts, Durand made many inquiries of Franklin, and asked for all his political writings. "That intriguing nation," said Franklin, "would like very well to blow up the coals between Britain and her colonies; but I hope we shall give them no opportunity."

"In England," Durand reported, "there is no one who does not own that its American colonies will one day form a separate state. The Americans are jealous of their liberty, and will always wish to extend it. The taste for independence must prevail among them; yet the fears of England will retard its coming, for she will shun whatever can unite them." "Let her but attempt to establish taxes in them," rejoined Choiseul, "and those countries, greater than England in extent, and perhaps becoming more populous, having fisheries, forests, shipping, corn, iron, and the like, will easily and fearlessly separate themselves from the mother country." "Do not calculate," replied Durand, "on a near revolution in the American colonies. They aspire not to independence, but to equality of rights with the mother country. A plan of union will always be a means in reserve by which England may shun the greater evil. The loss of the colonies of France and of Spain will be the consequence of the revolution in the colonies of England."

The idea of emancipating the whole colonial world was alluring to Choiseul; and he judged correctly of the nearness of the conflict. "The Rubicon is passed," said men in Boston, on hearing the revenue act had been carried through. "We will form one universal combination, to eat nothing, drink nothing, and wear nothing imported from Great Britain." The fourteenth of August was commemorated as the anniversary of the first resistance to the stamp act. Of the intention of using the new revenue to make the crown officers independent of the people, the patriots said: "Such counsels will deprive the prince who now sways the British sceptre of millions of free subjects." And, when it was considered that Mansfield and the ministry declared some of the grants in colonial charters to be nugatory on the ground of their extent, the press of Boston and New York, following the precedent of Molineux for Ireland, reasoned the matter through to its logical conclusion.

"Liberty," said the writer, "is the inherent right of all mankind. Ireland has its own parliament, and makes laws;

and English statutes do not bind them, says Lord Coke, because they send no knights to parliament. The same reason holds good as to America. Consent only gives human laws their force. Therefore, the parliament of England cannot extend their jurisdiction beyond their constituents. Advancing the powers of the parliament of England, by breaking the rights of the parliaments of America, may in time have its effects."

The dangerous example of suspending the legislative functions of New York inflamed the discontent; "our strength," said the patriots of Boston, "consists in union. Let us, above all, be of one heart and one mind. Call on our sister colonies to join with us." An intimate correspondence grew up between New York and Boston. They would nullify Townshend's revenue act by consuming nothing on which he had laid a duty, and avenge themselves on England by importing no more of its goods.

In September of this year, Franklin was at Paris. His examination before the house of commons had given him a wide European reputation. He was presented to various members of the French academy, as the American who would one day disembarrass France of these English. Malesherbes recognised "his extraordinary talents for politics;" and was led to extol "the American governments, because they permitted the human mind to direct its efforts toward those important objects which promote the prosperity and happiness of the people."

Just then Charles Townshend was seized with fever; and, after a short illness, during which he met danger with the levity that had marked his conduct of the most serious affairs, he died, at the age of forty-one, famed alike for talents and instability. Where were now his gibes; his flashes of merriment, that set the table in a roar; his eloquence, which made him the wonder of parliament? If his indiscretion forbade esteem, his good humor dissipated hate. He had been courted by all parties, but never possessed the confidence of any of them. He followed no guide, and he had no plan of his own. No one wished him as an adversary; no one trusted him as an associate. He sometimes spoke with boldness; but at heart he was as timid as he was versatile. He had clear conceptions, depth of understanding, great knowledge of every branch of administration, and indefatigable assiduity in business. He had obtained the lord-lieutenancy of Ireland for his brother, and a peerage for his wife, to descend to his children; and with power, fortune, affection, and honors gathering around him, he fell in the bloom of manhood, the most celebrated statesman who has left nothing but errors to account for his fame.

The choice of his successor would decide on the continuance of the ministry, of which his death seemed to presage the overthrow. Choiseul esteemed Grenville by far the ablest financier in England, and greatly feared his return to office. Dreading nothing so much as to be ruled, the king directed that the vacant place should be offered to Lord North.

At that time, Lord North was thirty-five years old, having seen the light in the same year with Washington. While the great Virginian employed himself as a careful planter, and musing on the destinies of his country resolved to preserve its liberty, Lord North entered the cabinet, in which he was to remain for fifteen most eventful years. He was a minister after the king's own heart; not brilliant, but of varied knowledge; good humored and able; opposed to republicanism, to reform, and to every popular measure. He had voted for the stamp act, and against its repeal; and had been foremost in the pursuit of Wilkes. Though choleric, he was of an easy temperament; a friend to peace, yet not fearing war; of great passive courage; rarely violent; never enterprising; and of such moderation in his demands that he seemed comparatively disinterested. His judgment was clear and his perceptions quick; but his will was feeble, a weakness which endeared him to his royal master. He took a leading part in the conduct of affairs, just as the people of America were discussing the new revenue act, which remained as the fatal bequest of Charles Townshend.

Never was a community more divided by fear and hope than the town of Boston, to which the continent was looking for an example. "Should we be told to perceive our inability to oppose the mother country," wrote the youthful Quincy, "we answer that, in defence of our civil and religious rights, with the God of armies on our side, we fear not the hour of trial." As the lawyers of England decided that American taxation by parliament was legal and constitutional, the press of Boston sought support in "the law of nature, which," said they, "is the law of God, irreversible itself and superseding all human law." Men called to mind the words of Locke, that, when the constitution is broken by the obstinacy of the prince, "the people must appeal to heaven." A petition to the governor to convene the legislature having been rejected with "contempt," the inhabitants of Boston, assembling on the twenty-eighth of October in town meeting, voted to forbear the importation and use of a great number of articles of British produce and manufacture, appointed a committee for obtaining a general subscription to such an agreement, and ordered their resolves to be sent to the several towns in the province, and to all the other colonies.

Otis, heretofore so fervid, on this occasion warned against giving offence to Great Britain. The twentieth of November, on which day the tax act was to go into effect, passed away in quiet. Images and placards were exhibited, but were removed by the friends of the people. In a town meeting convened to discountenance riot, Otis went so far as to assert the king's right to appoint officers of the customs in what manner and by what denominations he pleased, and he advised the town to make no opposition to the new duties.

But province called to province. "A revolution must inevitably ensue," said a great student of Scripture prophecies, in a village of Connecticut. "We have discouraging tidings from a mother country," thought Trumbull. "The Americans have been firmly attached to Great Britain; nothing but severity will dissolve the union."

On the banks of the Delaware, John Dickinson, the illustrious Farmer, who had been taught from his infancy to love humanity and liberty, came before the continent to plead for American rights. He accepted the undefined relations of the parliament to the colonies as a perpetual compromise, which neither party was to disturb by pursuing an abstract theory to its ultimate conclusions.

"If once we are separated from the mother country," he asked in the sincerity of sorrow, "what new form of government shall we adopt? Torn from the body to which we were united by religion, liberty, laws, affections, relation, language, and commerce, we must bleed at every vein." Examining the statutes relating to America from its first settlement, he admitted that parliament possessed a legal authority to regulate the trade of every part of the empire; he found every one of them rested on that principle till the administration of Grenville. Never before this did the British commons think of imposing duties in the colonies for the purpose of raising a revenue. Grenville first asserted, in the preamble of one act, that it was "just and necessary" for them to give and grant such duties; and, in the preamble of another, that it was "just and necessary" to raise a further revenue in the same way; while the preamble of the last act, granting duties upon paper, glass, colors, and tea, disregarding ancient precedents under cover of these modern ones, declared that it was, moreover, "expedient" that a revenue should be so raised. "This," said the Farmer, "is an INNOVATION, and a most dangerous innovation. Great Britain claims and exercises the right to prohibit manufactures in America. Once admit that she may lay duties upon her exportations to us, for the purpose of levying money on us only, she then will have nothing to do but to lay those duties on the articles which she prohibits us to manufacture, and the tragedy of American liberty is finished. We are in the situation of a besieged city, surrounded in every part but one. If that is closed up, no step can be taken but to surrender at discretion.

"I would persuade the people of these colonies—immediately, vigorously, and unanimously—to exert themselves in the most firm but the most peaceable manner for obtaining relief. If an inveterate resolution is formed to annihilate the liberties of the governed, English history affords examples of resistance by force."

The Farmer's Letters carried conviction through all the thirteen colonies.

## CHAPTER XXI.

MASSACHUSETTS CONSULTS HER SISTER COLONIES. ADMINISTRATION OF GRAFTON. HILLSBOROUGH SECRETARY FOR THE COLONIES.

NOVEMBER 1767–APRIL 1768.

ON the twenty-fourth of November, the twelfth parliament came together for the last time previous to its dissolution. Its members were too busy in preparing for the coming elections to interfere with America, about which the king's speech was silent, and, when Grenville descanted on two or three papers in the "Boston Gazette," as infamous libels on parliament, the house showed weariness. Bedford objected to Grenville's test for America, and "preferred making an example of some one seditious fellow." The king kept the ministry from breaking, and proved himself the most efficient man among them. "He makes each of them," said Mansfield, "believe that he is in love with him, and fools them all. They will stand their ground," he added, "unless that mad man, Lord Chatham, should come and throw a fireball in the midst of them." But Chatham's long illness had for the time overthrown his powers. When his health began to give out, it was his passion to appear possessed of the unbounded confidence of the king. A morbid restlessness led him to vie in expense with his equals in the peerage, who were the inheritors of vast estates. He would drive out with ten outriders, and with two carriages, each drawn by six horses. His vain magnificence deceived no one. "He is allowed to retain office as a livelihood," observed Bedford. The king complained of him as "a charlatan, who in difficult times affected ill-health to render himself the more sought after," and, saying that politics was a vile trade, more fit for a hack than for a gentleman, he proceeded to construct a ministry that would be disunited and docile.

On the fifth of December, Bedford, just before the removal of cataracts from his eyes, renounced his connection with Grenville, saying by way of excuse, that his age, his infirmities, and his tastes disinclined him to war on the court, which was willing to enter into a treaty with him, and each member of the opposition would do well to exercise a like freedom. "He chooses to give bread to his kinsmen and friends," said those whom he deserted. Grenville could not conceal his despair. To his junction with Bedford he had sacrificed the favor of the king. Rejected by the ally for whom he had been a martyr, the famed financier saw "the nothingness of the calculations of party," and the little that remained to him of life became steeped in bitterness. At the time when the public indignation was roused by the news of the general agreement which the town of Boston was promoting, the ministry was revolutionized, but without benefit to Grenville. The colonies were taken from Shelburne and consigned to a separate department of state, with Lord Hillsborough as its secretary. Conway made room for Lord Weymouth, a vehement but not forcible speaker, yet a man of ability. Gower became president of the council; the post-office was assigned to Sandwich, the ablest of them all, as well as the most malignant against America; while Rigby was made vice-treasurer of Ireland, till he could get the pay-office. All five were friends of the duke of Bedford, and united in opinion respecting America. Jenkinson, whose noiseless industry at the treasury board exercised a prevailing influence over the negligence of Grafton and the ease of Lord North, formed the bond between the treasury and the office-holders in Boston.

To maintain the authority of parliament over America was the principle on which the friends of Bedford entered the ministry. Their partisans professed to think it desirable that "the colonies should forget themselves still further." "Five or six frigates," they clamored, "acting at sea, and three regiments on land, will soon bring them to submission." "The waves," replied Franklin, "never rise but when the winds blow," and, addressing the British public, he showed that the new system of politics tended to dissolve the bonds of union between the two countries. "What does England gain by conquests in America," wrote the French minister, "but the danger of losing her own colonies? Things cannot remain as they are; the two nations will become more and more imbittered, and their mutual griefs increase. In four years the Americans will have nothing to fear from England, and will be prepared for resistance." He thought of Holland as a precedent; yet "America," he observed, "has no recognised chieftain, and, without the qualities united in the house of Orange. Holland would never have thrown off the yoke of Spain."

In January 1768, on Hillsborough's taking possession of his newly created office, Johnson, the faithful agent of Connecticut, a churchman, and one who from his heart wished to avoid a rupture between the colonies and England, waited upon him to offer congratulations on his advancement. "Connecticut," declared Hillsborough, "may always depend upon my friendship and affection."

"Connecticut," said Johnson, "is a loyal colony." "You are a very free colony," rejoined Hillsborough; "generally you have used your very extraordinary powers with moderation; but you are very deficient in your correspondence, so that we have too little connection with you." "That," answered the agent, "is owing to the good order and tranquillity which have so generally prevailed in a quiet colony, where the government is wisely administered and the people easy and happy. Add to this: from the nature of our constitution, fewer occasions arise of troubling the king's ministers with our affairs than in the governments immediately under the crown."

"A request for a copy of your colony laws," said Hillsborough, "has been repeatedly made; but I cannot find that any obedience has been paid to the requisition." "The colony," replied Johnson, "has several times sent over copies of the printed law book; there is one or more at the plantation office." "It is the duty of the government," resumed Hillsborough, "to transmit, from time to time, not only the laws that pass, but all the minutes of the proceedings of the council and assembly, that we may know what you are about, and rectify whatever may be amiss." "If your lordship," rejoined the agent, "wants a copy of our laws for private perusal, for the information of your clerks, or for reference, the colony will send you one of their law books; and you will find it as good a code of laws, almost, as could be devised for such an infant country. But, if your lordship means to have the laws transmitted for approbation or disapprobation by his majesty in council, it is what the colony has never done, and, I am persuaded, will never submit to. By the charter which King Charles II. granted, the colony was invested with a power of legislation, not subject to revision. In point of fact, your lordship well knows that those laws have never been re-examined here; that the colony has for more than a century been in the full exercise of those powers, without the least check or interruption, except in a single instance, in such times and under such circumstances as I believe you will not mention but with detestation, much less consider as a precedent."

"I have read your charter," said Hillsborough; "it is very full and expressive, and I know what powers you have exercised under it. But there are such things as extravagant grants, which are therefore void. You will admit there are many things which the king cannot grant, as the inseparable incidents of the crown. Some things which King Charles pretended to grant may be of that nature, particularly the power of absolute legislation, which tends to the absurdity of creating an independent state."

"Nobody," replied Johnson, "has ever reckoned the power of legislation among the inseparable incidents of the crown. All lawyers are agreed that it is an undisputed prerogative of the crown to create corporations, and the power of law-making is, in some degree at least, incident to every corporation; depending not merely on the words of the grant, but founded in the reason of things, and coextensive with the purposes for which the body is created. Every corporation in England enjoys it as really, though not as extensively, as the colony of Connecticut. Since, therefore, no question can be made of the right of the crown to create such bodies and grant such powers in degree, it would be very difficult to limit the bounty of the prince. The law has not done it, and who can draw the line? Surely not the ministers of the prince. The colony charters are of a higher nature, and founded on a better title, than those of the corporations of England. These are mere acts of grace and favor, whereas those in America were granted in consideration of very valuable services done or to be performed. The services having been abundantly executed at an immense expense by the grantees in the peopling and cultivation of a fine country, the vast extension of his majesty's dominion, and the prodigious increase of the trade and revenues of the empire, the charters must now be considered as grants upon valuable considerations, sacred and most inviolable. And even if there might have been a question made upon the validity of such a grant as that to Connecticut in the day of it, yet parliament as well as the crown having, for more than a century, acquiesced in the exercise of the power claimed by it, the colony has now a parliamentary sanction, as well as a title by prescription added to the royal grant, by all which it must be effectually secured in the full possession of its charter rights."

"These are matters of nice and curious disquisition," said Hillsborough, evasively; "but at least your laws ought to be regularly transmitted for the inspection of the privy council and for disapprobation, if found repugnant to the laws of England."

"An extra-judicial opinion of the king's minister," answered Johnson, "or even of the king's privy council, cannot determine whether any particular act is within that proviso or not; this must be decided by a court of law having jurisdiction of the matter, about which the law in question is conversant. If the general assembly of Connecticut should make a law flatly contradictory to the statute of Great Britain, it may be void; but a declaration of the king in council would still make it neither more nor less so, but be as void as the law itself, for other words in the charter clearly and expressly exclude them from deciding about it."

"I have not seen these things," replied Hillsborough, "in the light in which you endeavor to place them. You are in danger of being too much a separate, independent state, and of having too little subordination to this country." And then he spoke of the equal affection the king bore his American subjects, and of the great regard of the ministers for them as Britons, whose rights were not to be injured.

"Upon the repeal of the stamp act," said Johnson, "we had hoped these were the principles adopted, but the new duties imposed last winter, and other essential regulations in America, have damped those expectations and given alarm to the colonies."

"Let neither side," said Hillsborough, "stick at small matters. As to taxes, you are infinitely better off than any of your fellow-subjects in Europe. You are less burdened than even the Irish."

"I hope that England will not add to our burdens," said Johnson; "you would certainly find it redound to your own prejudice."

Thus, for two hours together, they reasoned on the rights of Connecticut, whose charter Hillsborough wished to annul; not on the pretence that it had been violated or misused, but because by the enjoyment of it the people were too free.

Connecticut so united caution with patriotism that successive British ministers were compelled to delay abrogating its charter, for want of a plausible excuse. The apologists of the new secretary called him honest and well meaning; he was passionate and ignorant and full of self-conceit; alert in conducting business; wrong-headed in forming his opinions, and pompously stiff in adhering to them. He proposed, as his rule of conduct, to join inflexibility of policy with professions of tenderness; and, in a man of his moderate faculties, this attempt to unite firmness with suavity became a mixture of obstinacy and deceit.

His first action respecting Massachusetts betrayed his character. Hutchinson, through Jenkinson, obtained an annual grant of two hundred pounds sterling; Hillsborough gave to the grant the form of a secret warrant under the king's sign manual on the commissioners of the customs at Boston. That a chief justice, holding office during pleasure and constantly employing his power for political purposes, should receive money secretly from the king, was fatal to the independence of the bench.

The reflecting people in Boston dreaded the corrupt employment of the new revenue. "We shall be obliged," said they, "to maintain in luxury sycophants, court parasites, and hungry dependants, who will be sent over to watch and oppress those who support them. If large salaries are given, needy poor lawyers from England and Scotland, or some tools of power of our own, will be placed on the bench. The governors will be men rewarded for despicable services, hackneyed in deceit and avarice; or some noble scoundrel, who has spent his fortune in every kind of debauchery.

"Unreasonable impositions tend to alienate the hearts of the colonists. Our growth is so great, in a few years Britain will not be able to compel our submission. Who thought that the four little provinces of Holland would have been able to throw off the yoke of that powerful kingdom of Spain? Yet they accomplished it by their desperate perseverance." "Liberty is too precious a jewel to be resigned."

The attempt at concerting an agreement not to import had thus far failed; and, unless the assembly of Massachusetts should devise methods of resistance, the oppressive law would gradually go into effect. Of the country members, Hawley, than whom no one was abler or more determined, lived far in the interior; and his excitable nature, now vehement, now desponding, unfitted him to guide. The irritability of Otis had so increased that he indulged himself in "rhapsodies" and "flashes" of eloquence, but could not frame deliberate plans of conduct. Besides, his mind had early embraced the idea "of a general union of the British empire, in which every part of its wide dominions should be represented under one equal and uniform direction and system of laws;" and though the congress of New York drew from him a tardy concession that an American representation was impossible, yet his heart still turned to his original opinion; and, in his prevailing mood, he shrunk from the thought of independence. The ruling passion of Samuel Adams, on the contrary, was the preservation of the distinctive institutions of New England. He understood the tendency of the measures adopted by parliament; approved of making the appeal to heaven, if freedom could not otherwise be preserved; and valued the liberties of his country more than its temporal prosperity, more than his own life, more than the lives of all. His theory, on which the colonies were to rest their defence of their separate rights till the dawn of better days, as a small but gallant army waits for aid within well-chosen lines, he embodied in the form of a letter from the assembly of the province to their agent. On the sixth of January, and for the evening and morning of many succeeding days, the paper was under severe examination in the house. Seven times it was revised; every word was weighed; every sentence considered; and each seemingly harsh expression tempered and refined. At last, on the twelfth of January 1768, the letter was adopted, to be sent to the agent, communicated to the British ministry, and published to the world.

Disclaiming the most distant thought of independence of the mother country, provided they could have the free enjoyment of their rights, the house affirmed that "the British constitution hath its foundation in the law of God and nature; that, in every free state, the supreme legislature derives its power from the constitution," and is bounded and circumscribed "by its fundamental rules."

That the right to property exists by a law of nature, they upheld, on the one side, against "Utopian schemes of a community of goods;" on the other, against all acts of the British parliament taxing the colonists.

"In the time of James II.," they continued, "the crown and its ministers, without the intervention of parliament, demolished charters and levied taxes in the colonies at pleasure. Our case is more deplorable and remediless. Our ancestors found relief by the interposition of parliament; but by the intervention of that very power we are taxed, and can appeal from their decision to no power on earth."

They further set forth the original contract between the king and the first planters, as the royal promise in behalf of the English nation; their title by the common law and by statute law to all the liberties and privileges of natural-born subjects of the realm; and the want of equity in taxing colonies whose manufactures were prohibited and whose trade was restrained.

Still more, they objected to the appropriation of the revenues from the new duties to the support of American civil officers and an American army, as introducing an absolute government. The judges in the colonies held their commissions at the pleasure of the crown; if their salaries were to be independent, a corrupt governor might employ men who would "deprive a bench of justice of its glory, and the people of their security." Nor need the money be applied by parliament to protect the colonists; they were never backward in defending themselves, and, when treated as free subjects, they always granted aids of their own accord, to the extent of their ability, and even beyond it. Nor could a standing army among them secure their dependence; they had toward the mother country an English affection, which would forever keep them connected with her, unless it should be erased by repeated unkind usage.

They objected to the establishment of commissioners of the customs, as an expense needless in itself, and dangerous to their liberties from the increase of crown officers. Still more, they expressed alarm at the act conditionally suspending the powers of the assembly of New York.

"King James and his successors," thus they proceeded, "broke the copartnership of the supreme legislative with the supreme executive, and the latter could not exist without the former. In these remote dominions there should be a free legislative; otherwise, strange effects are to be apprehended, for the laws of God and nature are invariable."

To Shelburne, Chatham, Rockingham, Conway, Camden, the treasury board, at which sat Grafton, Lord North, and Jenkinson, the house of representatives next addressed letters which enforced the impracticability of an American representation in the British parliament. But no memorial was sent to the lords; no petition to the house of commons. The colonial legislature joined issue with the British parliament, and, adopting the draft of Samuel Adams, approached the king with their petition.

To him, in beautifully simple language, they recounted the story of the colonization of Massachusetts; the forfeiture of their first charter; and the confirmation to them, on the revolution, of their most essential rights and liberties; the principal of which was that most sacred right of being taxed only by representatives of their own free election. They complained that the acts of parliament, "imposing taxes in America, with the express purpose of raising a revenue, left them only the name of free subjects."

Relief by an American representation in parliament they declare to be "utterly impracticable;" and they referred the consideration of their present circumstances to the wisdom and clemency of the king.

In the several papers which, after a fortnight's anxious deliberation, were adopted by the assembly, not one line betrays haste or hesitation. It remained for the house "to inform the other governments with its proceedings against the late acts, that, if they thought fit, they might join therein." But this, it was said in a house of eighty-two members, would be considered, in England, as appointing a second congress; and the negative prevailed by a vote of two to one.

At this appearance of indecision, Bernard conceived "great hopes;" but the hesitancy in the assembly had proceeded not from timidity, but caution. The members spoke with one another in private, till they more clearly perceived the imminence and extent of the public danger. On the fourth day of February, a motion was made to reconsider the vote against writing to the other colonies. The house was counted; eighty-two were again found to be present; the question was carried by a large majority, and the former vote erased from the journals.

On the same day, the house, after debate, appointed a committee to inform each house of representatives or burgesses on the continent of the measure which it had taken; and on the eleventh they accepted, almost unanimously, a masterly circular letter which Samuel Adams had drafted.

Expressing a firm confidence that the united supplications of the distressed Americans would meet with the favorable acceptance of the king, they set forth the importance that proper constitutional measures respecting the acts of parliament imposing taxes on the colonies should be adopted; and that the representatives of the several assemblies upon so delicate a point should harmonize with each other. They made known their "disposition freely to communicate their mind to a sister colony, upon a common concern."

They then embodied the substance of all their representations to the ministry: that the legislative power of parliament is circumscribed by the constitution, and is self-destroyed whenever it overleaps its bounds; that allegiance, as well as sovereignty, is limited; that the right to property is an essential, unalterable one, engrafted into the British system, and to be asserted, exclusive of any consideration of charters; that taxation of the colonies by the British parliament, in which they are not represented, is an infringement of their natural and constitutional rights; that an equal representation of the American people in parliament is forever impracticable; that their partial representation would be worse even than taxation without their consent. They further enumerated as grievous the independent civil list for crown officers; the billeting act; and the large powers of the resident commissioners of the customs.

"Your assembly," they continued, "is too generous and liberal in sentiment to believe that this letter proceeds from an ambition of taking the lead, or dictating to the other assemblies. They freely submit their opinions to the judgment of others, and shall take it kind in you to point out to them anything further that may be thought necessary."

A fair copy of this circular was transmitted to England, to be produced in proof of its true spirit and design; they drew their system of conduct from reason itself, and despised concealment.

The day after the circular was adopted, the board of commissioners of the revenue at Boston, co-operating with Bernard, addressed to their superiors in England a secret memorial. Expressing apprehensions for their own safety, they complained of the American press, especially of the seeming moderation, parade of learning, and most mischievous tendency of the Farmer's Letters; of New England town meetings, "in which," they said, "the lowest mechanics discussed the most important points of government with the utmost freedom;" of Rhode Island, as if it had even proposed to stop the revenue money; of Massachusetts, for having invited every province to discountenance the consumption of British manufactures. "We have every reason," they added, "to expect that we shall find it impracticable to enforce the execution of the revenue laws until the hand of government is properly strengthened. At present, there is not a ship-of-war in the province, nor a company of soldiers nearer than New York."

The alternative was thus presented to the ministry and the king. On the one side, Massachusetts asked relief from taxation without representation, and invited the several colonies to unite in the petition; the crown officers, on the other, sent their memorial for a fleet and regiments.

But what could an armed force find to do? The opposition was passive. The house left no doubt of its purpose not to arrest the execution of any law; on the twenty-sixth of February, by a vote of eighty-one to the one vote of Timothy Ruggles, it discouraged the use of superfluities; and gave a preference to American manufactures in resolves which, said Bernard, "were so decently and cautiously worded that at another time they would scarcely have given offence." Could an army compel a colonist to buy a new coat, or to drink tea, or to purchase what he was resolved to do without? Grafton, North, even Hillsborough, disapproved of Townshend's revenue act. Why will they not quiet America by its revocation? Sending regiments into Boston will be a summons to America to make the last appeal.

Grenville and his friends insisted on declaring meetings and associations like those of Boston illegal and punishable, and advised some immediate chastisement. "I wish," said he, "every American in the world could hear me. I gave the Americans bounties on their whale fishery, thinking they would obey the acts of parliament;" and he now spoke for a prohibition of their fisheries. Some of the ministry were ready to proceed at once against Massachusetts. When America was mentioned, nothing could be heard but bitterest invectives. That it must submit, no one questioned.

While Hillsborough was writing encomiums on Bernard, praising his own "justice and lenity," and lauding the king as the tender father of all his subjects, Choiseul discerned the importance of the rising controversy; and, that he might unbosom his thoughts with freedom, he appointed to the place of ambassador in England his own most confidential friend, the Count du Châtelet, son of the celebrated woman with whom Voltaire had been connected. The new diplomatist was a person of quick perceptions, courage, and knowledge of the world, and was deeply imbued with the philosophy of his age.

The difficulty respecting taxation was heightened by personal contentions, which exasperated members of the legislature of Massachusetts. The house discovered that their leaving the crown officers out of the council had been misrepresented by Bernard to Shelburne; and, in the most temperate language, they wisely suggested the recall of the governor, of whose accusatory letters they asked for copies. A paper in the "Boston Gazette," written by Warren, exposed "the obstinate malice, diabolical thirst for mischief, effrontery, guileful treachery, and wickedness" of Bernard. The council censured the publication. The governor called on the house to order a prosecution of the printers. The house on the fourth of March answered: "The liberty of the press is the great bulwark of freedom." On proroguing the legislature, Bernard chid in public its leading members. "There are men," said he, "to whose importance everlasting contention is necessary. Time will soon pull the masks off those false patriots who are sacrificing their country to the gratification of their own passions. I shall defend this injured country from the machinations of a few, very few, discontented men." "The flagitious libel," he wrote home, "blasphemes kingly government itself;" but it was only a coarse sketch of his own bad qualities. "I told the grand jury," said Hutchinson, "almost in plain words, that they might depend on being damned if they did not find against the paper, as containing high treason." The jury refused. "Oaths and the laws have lost their force," wrote Hutchinson; while "the honest and independent grand jurors" became the favorite toast of the Sons of Liberty.

On the day on which the general court was prorogued, merchants of Boston began a subscription to renounce commerce with England, and invited the merchants of the continent to a universal passive resistance.

Kalb, who was astonished at the prosperity of the colonies

and the immense number of merchant vessels in all the waters from the Chesapeake to Boston, thought for a moment that, if the provinces could jointly discuss their interests by deputies, an independent state would soon be formed. The people were brave, and their militia not inferior to regular troops. And yet, after studying the spirit of New England, he was persuaded that all classes sincerely loved their mother country, and would never accept foreign aid. "It is my fixed opinion," said he, "that the firebrands will be worsted, and that the colonies will, in the end, obtain all the satisfaction which they demand. Sooner or later, the government must recognise its being in the wrong."

The crown officers in Boston persevered in their intrigues. "The annual election of councillors," wrote Bernard, "is the canker-worm of the constitution of this government, whose weight cannot be put in the scale against that of the people." "To keep the balance even," argued Hutchinson, "there is need of aid from the other side of the water."

How to induce the British government to change the charter and send over troops was the constant theme of discussion; and it was concerted that the eighteenth of March, the anniversary of the repeal of the stamp act, should be made to further the design. Reports were industriously spread of an intended insurrection on that day; of danger to the commissioners of the customs. The Sons of Liberty, on their part, were anxious to preserve order. At daybreak, the effigy of Paxton and that of another revenue officer were found hanging on Liberty Tree; they were instantly taken down by the friends of the people. The governor endeavored to magnify "the atrociousness of the insult," and to express fears of violence; the council justly insisted there was no danger of disturbance. The day was celebrated by a temperate festival, at which toasts were drunk to the freedom of the press; to Paoli and the Corsicans; to the joint freedom of America and Ireland; to the immortal memory of Brutus, Cassius, Hampden, and Sidney. Those who dined together broke up early. There was no bonfire lighted; and "in the evening," wrote Hutchinson within the week of the event, "we had only such a mob as we have long been used to on the fifth of November, and other holidays." Gage, who afterward made careful inquiry in Boston, declared the disturbance to have been "trifling." But Bernard reported a "great disposition to the utmost disorder," hundreds "parading the streets with yells and outcries; a very terrible night to those who thought themselves objects of the popular fury." "I can afford no protection to the commissioners," he continues. "I have not the shadow of authority or power. I am obnoxious to the madness of the people, yet left exposed to their resentment, without any possible resort of protection;" thus hinting the need of "troops, as well to support the king's government as to protect the persons of his officers."

To insure the arrival of an armed force, the commissioners of the customs applied directly to the naval commander at Halifax, and sent a second memorial to the lords of the treasury. They said that a design had certainly been formed to bring them, on the eighteenth of March, to Liberty Tree, and oblige them to renounce their commissions. "The governor and magistracy," they add, "have not the least authority or power in this place. We depend on the favor of the mob for our protection. We cannot answer for our security for a day, much less will it be in our power to carry the revenue laws into effect."

These letters went from Boston to the ministry in March. The tales of riots were false. The people were opposed to the revenue system of the British parliament, and hoped for redress; if the ministry should refuse it, they were resolved to avoid every act of violence, to escape paying the taxes, and to induce their repeal by never buying the goods on which they were imposed. England had on her side the general affection of the people, the certainty that the country could not as yet manufacture for itself, and the consequent certainty that schemes of non-importation would fail. Would she but substitute a frank and upright man for Bernard, the wants of the colonists might weary them of their self-denial.

But the administration of public affairs had degenerated into a system of patronage which had money for its object; and was supported by the king, from the love of authority. The government of England had more and more ceased to represent the noble spirit of England. The twelfth parliament, which had taxed America and was now near its dissolution, exceeded all former ones in profligacy. Direct gifts of money were grown less frequent, as public opinion increased in power; but there never was a parliament so shameless in its corruption as this twelfth parliament, which virtually severed America from England. It had its votes ready for the minister of any party. It gave an almost unanimous support to Pitt, when, for the last time in seventy years, the foreign politics of England were on the side of liberty. It had a majority for Newcastle after he had ejected Pitt; for Bute, when he dismissed Newcastle; for Grenville, so long as he was the friend of Bute; for Grenville, when he became Bute's implacable foe; and for the inexperienced Rockingham. When Charles Townshend, rebelling in the cabinet, seemed likely to become minister, he commanded its applause. When Townshend died, North easily restored subordination.

Nor was it more scrupulous as to any measure which the minister of the hour might propose. It promoted the alliance with the king of Prussia, and deserted him; it protected the issue of general warrants, and utterly condemned them; it passed the stamp act, and repealed the stamp act; it began to treat America with tenderness, then veered about, imposed new taxes, changed American constitutions, and trifled with the freedom of the American legislative. It was corrupt, and knew itself to be corrupt, and made a jest of its corruption; and when it was gone, and had no more chances at prostitution, men wrote its epitaph as of the most scandalously abandoned body that England had ever known.

Up to a recent time, the colonists had looked to parliament as the bulwark of their liberties; henceforward, they knew it to be their most dangerous enemy. They avowed that they would not pay taxes which it assumed to impose. Some still allowed it a right to restrain colonial trade, but the advanced opinion among the patriots was that each provincial legislature must be perfectly free; that laws were not valid unless sanctioned by the consent of America herself. Without disputing what the past had established, they were resolved to oppose any minister that should attempt to "innovate" a single iota in their privileges. "Almighty God himself," wrote Dickinson, "will look down upon your righteous contest with approbation. You will be a band of brothers, strengthened with inconceivable supplies of force and constancy by that sympathetic ardor which animates good men, confederated in a good cause. You are assigned by Divine Providence, in the appointed order of things, the protector of unborn ages, whose fate depends upon your virtue."

The men of Boston, whose fathers came to the wilderness for freedom to say their prayers, would not fear to take up arms against a preamble which implied their servitude. At a town-meeting, in March 1768, Malcom moved their thanks to the ingenious author of the Farmer's Letters; and Hancock, Samuel Adams, and Warren were of the committee to greet him in the name of the town as "the friend of Americans and the benefactor of mankind."

"They may with equal reason make one step more," wrote Hutchinson to the duke of Grafton: "they may deny the regal as well as the parliamentary authority, although no man as yet has that in his thoughts."

Du Châtelet, in England, having made his inquiries into the resources of America, was persuaded that, even if the detailed statements before him were one half too large, England could not reduce her colonies, should they raise the standard of rebellion. "Their population is so great," said he to Choiseul, "that a breath would scatter the troops sent to enforce obedience. The ever-existing attractions of an entire independence and of a free commerce cannot fail to keep their minds continually in a state of disgust at the national subjection. The English government may take some false step, which will in a single day set all these springs in activity. A great number of chances can hasten the revolution which all the world foresees without daring to assign its epoch. I please myself with the thought that it is not so far off as some imagine, and that we should spare neither pains nor expense to co-operate with it. We must nourish his Catholic majesty's disposition to avenge his wrongs. The ties that bind America to England are three fourths broken. It must soon throw off the yoke. To make themselves independent, the inhabitants want nothing but arms, courage, and a chief. If they had among them a genius equal to Cromwell, this republic would be more easy to establish than the one of which that usurper was the head. Perhaps this man exists; perhaps nothing is wanting but happy circumstances to place him upon an exalted theatre."

At Mount Vernon, conversation with Arthur Lee fell on the dangers that overhung the country. "Whenever my country calls upon me," said Washington, "I am ready to take my musket on my shoulder."

"Courage, Americans!" So, in April 1768, said William Livingston, one of the famed New York "triumvirate" of antiprelatic lawyers, through the press. "Liberty, religion, and sciences are on the wing to these shores. The finger of God points out a mighty empire to your sons. The land we possess is the gift of heaven to our fathers, and Divine Providence seems to have decreed it to our latest posterity. The day dawns in which the foundation of this mighty empire is to be laid, by the establishment of a regular American constitution. All that has hitherto been done seems to be little beside the collection of materials for this glorious fabric. 'Tis time to put them together. The transfer of the European part of the family is so vast, and our growth so swift, that, BEFORE SEVEN YEARS ROLL OVER OUR HEADS, the first stone must be laid."

## CHAPTER XXII.

WILL MASSACHUSETTS RESCIND? ADMINISTRATION OF GRAFTON: HILLSBOROUGH SECRETARY FOR THE COLONIES.

### April–July 1768.

"SEND over an army and a fleet to reduce them to reason," was the cry at court and the public offices in England, on every rumor of the discontents of the Americans. On the fifteenth of April 1768, the circular letter of Massachusetts reached the ministers, and their choleric haste dictated most impolitic measures. A letter was sent by Hillsborough to the governors of each of the twelve other colonies, with a copy of the circular, which was described as "of a most dangerous and factious tendency," calculated "to inflame the minds" of the people, "to promote an unwarrantable combination, and to excite open opposition to the authority of parliament." "You will therefore," said he, "exert your utmost influence to prevail upon the assembly of your province to take no notice of it, which will be treating it with the contempt it deserves. If they give any countenance to this seditious paper, it will be your duty to prevent any proceedings upon it by an immediate prorogation or dissolution." This order he sent even to the governor of Pennsylvania, who, by its charter, had no power to prorogue or dissolve an assembly. Massachusetts was told that the king considered "their resolutions contrary to the sense of the assembly, and procured by surprise. You will therefore," such was the command to Bernard, "require of the house of representatives, in his majesty's name, to rescind the resolution which gave birth to the circular letter from the speaker, and to declare their disapprobation of that rash and hasty proceeding."

"If the new assembly should refuse to comply, it is the king's pleasure that you should immediately dissolve them."

The petition of the assembly of Massachusetts to the king was received by Hillsborough for perusal, but was never officially presented. To the agent of Massachusetts the secretary said: "I had settled the repeal of these acts with Lord North; but the opposition of the colonies renders it absolutely necessary to support the authority of parliament."

The commander-in-chief in America was ordered to maintain the public tranquillity. But it was characteristic of Massachusetts that the peace had not been broken; the power of parliament was denied, but not resisted.

On the second of April, the assembly of Virginia read the circular letter from Massachusetts, and referred it to a committee of the whole house. The petitions of freeholders of the counties of Chesterfield, Henrico, Dinwiddie, and Amelia pointed to the act of parliament suspending the legislative power of New York, as of a tendency fatal to the liberties of a free people. The county of Westmoreland dwelt on the new revenue act, as well as on the billeting act. The freeholders of Prince Williams enumerated all three, which, like the stamp act, would shackle North America with slavery. On the seventh, Bland reported resolutions reaffirming the exclusive right of the American assemblies to tax the American colonies, and they were unanimously adopted. A committee of twelve, including Bland and Archibald Cary, prepared a petition to the king, a memorial to the house of lords, and a remonstrance to the house of commons, which, after being carefully considered and amended, were unanimously adopted. On the fifteenth, Bland invited a conference with the council, and the council, with Blair, the acting president after Fauquier's death, agreed to the papers which the house had prepared, and which were penned in a still bolder style than those from Massachusetts.

After this, the burgesses of Virginia, to fulfil all their duty, not only applauded Massachusetts for its attention to American liberty, but directed their speaker to make known their proceedings to the speaker of every assembly on the continent, and to intimate how necessary they thought it that the colonies should unite in a firm but decent opposition to every measure which might affect their rights and liberties.

In the midst of these proceedings of a representative body, which truly reflected the sentiments of a people, the thirteenth British parliament, the last which ever legislated for America, was returned. Of the old house, one hundred and seventy failed to be rechosen. Boroughs were sold openly, and votes purchased at advanced prices. The market value of a seat in parliament was four thousand pounds. Contested elections cost the candidates twenty to thirty thousand pounds apiece, and it was affirmed that in Cumberland one person lavished a hundred thousand pounds. The election was the most expensive ever known. The number of disputed seats exceeded all precedent, as did the riots on election days.

Wilkes was returned for Westminster. "The expulsion of Wilkes must be effected," wrote the king to Lord North, who stood ready to obey the unconstitutional mandate.

At the opening, in May, the question was raised, if strangers should be excluded from the debates. "I ever wished," said Grenville, "to have what is done here well known." The people no longer acquiesced in the secrecy of the proceedings of their professed representatives; this is the last parliament of which the debates are not reported.

Out of doors, America was not without those who listened to her complaints. The aged Oglethorpe, founder of the colony of Georgia, busied himself with distributing pamphlets in her behalf among the most considerable public men. Franklin, in London, collected and printed the Farmer's Letters. "They are very wild," said Hillsborough of them; many called them treasonable and seditious; yet Edmund Burke approved their principle. Translated into French, they were much read in Parisian saloons; their author was compared with Cicero; Voltaire joined the praise of "the farmers of Pennsylvania" to that of the Russians who aspired to liberate Greece.

"In America, the Farmer is adored," said the governor of Georgia; "and no mark of honor and respect is thought equal to his merit." At that time Georgia was the most flourishing colony on the continent. Lands there were cheap, and labor dear; it had no manufactures; though, of the poorer families, one in a hundred, perhaps, might make its own coarse clothing of a mixture of cotton and wool. Out of twenty-five members of the newly elected legislature, at least eighteen were "Sons of Liberty," "enthusiasts" for the American cause, zealous for "maintaining their natural rights." They unanimously made choice of Benjamin Franklin as their agent, and nothing but their prorogation prevented their sending words of sympathy to Massachusetts. New Jersey expressed its desire to correspond and unite with the other colonies. The Connecticut assembly, in May, after a solemn debate, concluded to petition the king only; "because," said they, "to petition the parliament would be a tacit confession of its right to lay impositions upon us, which right and authority we publicly disavow." Nor would the court issue writs of assistance, although it was claimed that they were authorized by Townshend's revenue act. Some grew alarmed for consequences, but others "were carried above fear."

At New York, the merchants held a meeting to join with the inhabitants of Boston in the agreement not to import from Great Britain; and, against the opinion of the governor, the royal council decided that the meetings were legal; that the people did but establish among themselves certain rules of economy, and had a right to dispose of their own fortune as they pleased.

While Massachusetts received encouragement from its sister colonies, its crown officers continued and extended their solicitations in England for large and fixed salaries, as the only way to keep the Americans in their dependence. Grenville's influence was the special resource of Hutchinson and Oliver, who had supported his stamp act and suffered as his martyrs; and they relied on Whately to secure for them his attention and favor, which they valued the more, as it seemed to them probable that he would one day supersede Grafton.

Bernard, on his part, addressed his importunities to Hillsborough, and asked leave to become an informer, but under an assurance that no exposure should be made of his letters. Yet how could public measures be properly founded on secret communications, known only to the minister and the king? Should the right of the humblest individual to confront witnesses against him be held sacred? and should rising nations be exposed to the loss of chartered privileges and natural rights on concealed accusations? With truer loyalty toward the mother country, Samuel Adams, through the agent, advised the repeal of the revenue acts, and the removal of a governor in whom the colonies could never repose confidence.

But Bernard went on, persuading Hillsborough that America had grown refractory in consequence of the feeble administration of the colonies during the time of Conway and Shelburne; that it required "his lordship's distinguished abilities" to accomplish the "arduous task of reducing them into good order." "It only needs," said Hutchinson, "one steady plan, pursued a little while." At that moment the people of Massachusetts, confidently awaiting a favorable result of their appeal to the king, revived their ancient spirit of loyalty. At the opening of the political year, on the last Wednesday in May, the new house of representatives came together, with a kindlier disposition toward England than had existed for several years. The two parties were nearer an equality. On the day of election, after hearing a sermon in which Shute, of Hingham, denied the supreme authority of parliament and justified resistance to laws not based on equity, the legislature seemed willing to restore Hutchinson to the council; and, on the first ballot, he had sixty-eight votes where he needed but seventy-one.

As the convention were preparing to ballot a second time, Samuel Adams rose to ask whether the lieutenant-governor was a pensioner; on which Otis, the other "chief head of the faction," stood up and declared that Hutchinson had received a warrant from the lords of the treasury for two hundred pounds a year out of the proceeds of the new duties; and, distributing votes for Artemus Ward, he cried out: "Pensioner or no pensioner, surely the house will not think a pensioner of the crown a fit person to sit in council." "But for the warrant," confessed Hutchinson, "I should have been elected." "And that," added Bernard, "would have put quite a new face upon public affairs." "The government," repeated Bernard, "should insist upon it that the lieutenant-governor and secretary should have seats and votes at the council-board without an election." "This annual election of the council spoils the constitution," wrote Hutchinson. "They will not come to a right temper until they find that, at all events, the parliament will maintain its authority." These representations were made in concert by the two for no end but to promote their own petty interests, with equal disregard of the honor and welfare of Britain and the rights of the province. Deceived by their seeming zeal in his service, Hillsborough resolved to reward Bernard's zeal with the lucrative post of lieutenant-governor of Virginia, and to leave the government of Massachusetts in the hands of Hutchinson.

In June, the ministry in England received the letters of March from the commissioners of the customs and from Bernard; and, totally misconceiving the state of things, Hillsborough, on the eighth of June, ordered Gage to send a regiment to Boston, for the assistance of the civil magistrates and the officers of the revenue. The admiralty was directed to send one frigate, two sloops, and two cutters to remain in Boston harbor; and the castle of William and Mary was to be occupied and repaired.

This first preparation for the use of arms by Great Britain was adopted at a time when America thought of nothing more than peaceable petitioning and a non-importation agreement, which the adverse interests of the merchants had as yet rendered void.

The Romney, a ship of fifty guns, sent from Halifax at their request, had, for about a month, lain at anchor in the harbor of Boston, and impressed New England men returning from sea. The request to accept a substitute for another the captain rejected with a storm of abuse; and he continued impressments, in violation, as the lawyers and the people believed, of an explicit statute. On Friday, the tenth of June, one man who had been impressed was rescued. On the same day, the sloop Liberty, belonging to John Hancock, was seized, as it seems justly, by the officers of the customs. The collector thought she might remain at the wharf; but, according to previous concert, boats from the man-of-war cut her moorings and towed her away to the Romney, near sunset, just as the laborers had broken off work.

A crowd "of boys and negroes" gathered at the heels of the custom-house officers, and threw about stones, bricks, and dirt, alarming but not hurting them. A mob broke windows in the house of the comptroller and of an inspector, burned a boat of the collector's on Boston common, and, at near one o'clock, dispersed. The next day nothing indicated a recurrence of riots; and the council appointed a committee to ascertain the facts attending the seizure.

The commissioners had not been approached nor menaced, but they chose to consider the incident of the last evening an insurrection, and four of the five went on board the Romney; perhaps a little from panic, but more to insure the interposition of the British government. Temple, one of their number, who in later days inherited two baronetcies, a devoted client of Grenville and the family of Lord Temple, one who thoroughly understood the duplicity and feebleness of mind and character of Bernard, and the hypocrisy as well as the ability of Hutchinson, refused to take part in the artifice.

On Sunday, while all the people were at church, the fugitive officers, pretending that "the honor of the crown would be hazarded by their return to Boston," informed Bernard by letter that they could not, "consistent with the honor of their commission, act in any business of the revenue under such an influence as prevailed" in Boston, and declared their wish to withdraw to the castle. "They have abdicated," said the people of Boston, and "may they never return." Everybody knew they were in no danger. The council found that the riot of Friday had been only "a small disturbance." "Dangerous disturbances," reported Gage, whose information came from royalists, "are not to be apprehended."

On the fourteenth, the attendance was so great at a legal town-meeting that they adjourned from Faneuil Hall to the Old South meeting-house, where Otis, with rapturous applause, was elected moderator.

An address to the governor was unanimously agreed upon, which twenty-one men were appointed to deliver. On adjourning to the next afternoon, Otis, the moderator, strongly recommended peace and good order; and did not despair that their grievances might, in time, be removed. "If not," said he, "and we are called on to defend our liberties and privileges, I hope and believe we shall, one and all, resist even unto blood; but I pray God Almighty that this may never so happen."

The committee moved in a procession of eleven chaises to the house of the governor in the country, to present the address, in which the town claimed for the province the sole right of taxing itself, expressed a hope that the board of customs would never reassume the exercise of their office, commented on impressment, and demanded the removal of the Romney from the harbor. In words which Otis approved and probably assisted to write, they said: "To contend with our parent state is the most dreadful extremity, but tamely to relinquish the only security we and our posterity retain for the enjoyment of our lives and properties, without one struggle, is so humiliating and base that we cannot support the reflection. It is at your option to prevent this distressed and justly incensed people from effecting too much, and from the shame and reproach of attempting too little."

Bernard received this address with obsequious courtesy, and the next day gave them a written answer, clearing himself of the measures complained of, promising to stop impressments, and desiring nothing so much as to be an instrument of conciliation between them and the parent state.

No sooner had he sent this message than he and the lieutenant-governor and other officers of the crown conspired to get regiments ordered to Boston. The commissioners of the customs besought protection of Gage and Hood, the chiefs of the British army and navy in North America.

"If there is not a revolt," wrote Bernard to Hillsborough, "the leaders of the Sons of Liberty must falsify their words and change their purposes." Hutchinson sounded the alarm to various correspondents, and, through Whately, to Grenville. To interpret and enforce the correspondence, Hallowell, the comptroller, was despatched to London.

The town divined the purpose of its enemies; and, at its legal meeting on the seventeenth, instructed its representatives in these words prepared by John Adams: "After the repeal of the last American stamp act, we were happy in the pleasing prospect of a restoration of tranquillity and harmony. But the principle on which that detestable act was founded continues in full force, and a revenue is still demanded from America, and appropriated to the maintenance of swarms of officers and pensioners in idleness and luxury. It is our fixed resolution to maintain our loyalty and due subordination to the British parliament, as the supreme legislative in all cases of necessity for the preservation of the whole empire. At the same time, it is our unalterable resolution to assert and vindicate our dear and invaluable rights and liberties, at the utmost hazard of our lives and fortunes; and we have a full and rational confidence that no designs formed against them will ever prosper.

"Every person who shall solicit or promote the importation of troops at this time is an enemy to this town and province, and a disturber of the peace and good order of both."

The next morning, the general court, which was in session, appointed a joint committee to inquire "if measures had been taken, or were taking, for the execution of the late revenue acts of parliament by a naval or military force." In the midst of these scenes arrived Hillsborough's letter, directing Massachusetts to rescind and disapprove its resolution which gave birth to their circular letter of the preceding session; and, on the twenty-first, after timid consultations between Bernard, Hutchinson, and Oliver, it was communicated to the house.

The assembly were aware that they were deliberating upon more important subjects than had ever engaged the attention of an American legislature. They were consoled by the sympathy of Connecticut and New Jersey. But the letter from Virginia gave courage more than all the rest. "This is a glorious day," said Samuel Adams on receiving it, using words which, seven years later, he was to repeat. The merchants of Boston renewed the agreement not to import from England.

The house, employing the pen of Samuel Adams, without altering one word in his draft, reported a letter to Lord Hillsborough, in which they showed that their circular letter was, indeed, the declared sense of a large majority of the body by which it was issued; and they relied on the clemency of the king, that to petition him would not be deemed inconsistent with respect for the British constitution, nor to acquaint their fellow-subjects of their having done so be discountenanced as an inflammatory proceeding.

Then came the great question, taken in the fullest house ever remembered. The votes were given by word of mouth; and, against seventeen that were willing to yield, ninety-two refused to rescind. They finished their work by a message to the governor, thoroughly affirming the doings from which they had been ordered to dissent. On this, Bernard prorogued, and then dissolved them.

The people of Massachusetts had no intention but to defend their liberties, which had the sanction of natural right and of historic tradition; and yet from July they were left without a legislature. "The Americans," observed the clear-sighted Du Châtelet, "see in the projects of their metropolis measures of tyranny and oppression." "I apprehend a breach between the two countries," owned Franklin, who could not understand what the Boston people meant by the "due subordination" of their assembly to parliament, and had reached the conclusion that the colonies and Great Britain were separate states, with the same king, but different legislatures.

"The whole body of the people of New Hampshire were resolved to stand or fall with the Massachusetts." "It is best," counselled John Langdon, of Portsmouth, "for the Americans to let the king know the danger of a violent rending of the colonies from the mother country." "No assembly on the continent," said Roger Sherman, of Connecticut, "will ever concede that parliament has a right to tax the colonies." "We cannot believe," wrote William Williams, of Lebanon, in the same province, "that they will draw the sword on their own children; but, if they do, our blood is more at their service than our liberties."

In New York, the merchants still held those meetings which Hillsborough condemned. "The circumstances of the colonies demand a firmer union," said men of Pennsylvania. The assembly of Maryland treated Lord Hillsborough's letter with the contempt he had ordered them to show for the circular of Massachusetts, and they sent their thanks to "their sister colony, in whose opinion they exactly coincided." As for South Carolina, they could not enough praise the glorious ninety-two who would not rescind, toasting them at banquets, and marching by night through the streets of Charleston, in processions to their honor, by the blaze of two-and-ninety torches.

English statesmen were blind to the character of events which were leading to the renovation of the world. Not so the Americans. Village theologians studied the Book of Revelation to see which seal was next to be broken, which angel was next to sound his trumpet. "Is not God preparing the way in his providence," thus New England ministers communed together, "for some remarkable revolutions in Christendom, both in polity and religion?"

Who will deny that humanity has a life and progress of its own, swaying its complex mind by the guiding truths which it develops as it advances? While New England was drawing from the Bible truth of the nearness of the overthrow of tyranny, Turgot, at Paris, explained to David Hume the perfectibility and onward movement of the race. "The British government," said he, "is very far from being an enlightened one. As yet none is thoroughly so. But tyranny, combined with superstition, vainly strives to stifle light and liberty by methods alike atrocious and useless; the world will be conducted through transient disorders to a happier condition."

In that progress, the emancipation of America was to form a glorious part, and was the great object of the French minister for foreign affairs. "We must put aside scheming and attend to facts," wrote Choiseul to Du Châtelet in July, after a conversation of six hours with a person intimately acquainted with America. "My idea, which perhaps is but a reverie, is to examine the possibility of a treaty of commerce, both of importation and exportation, of which the obvious advantages might attract the Americans. According to the prognostications of sensible men, who have had opportunity to study their character and to measure their progress from day to day in the spirit of independence, the separation of the American colonies from the metropolis, sooner or later, must come. The plan I propose hastens its epoch. It is the true interest of the colonies to secure forever their entire liberty, and establish their direct commerce with France and with the world. We have every reason to hope that the government on this side will conduct itself in a manner to increase the breach, not to close it up. Such is its way. True, some sagacious observers think it not only possible, but easy, to reconcile the interests of the colonies and the mother country; but the course pursued thus far by the British government seems to me completely opposite to what it ought to be to effect this conciliation."

While time and humanity, the principles of English liberty, the impulse of European philosophy, and the policy of France were all assisting to emancipate America, the British colonial administration, which was to stop the force of moral causes in their influence on the affairs of men, vibrated in its choice of measures between terror and artifice. American affairs were left by the other ministers very much to the management of Hillsborough, and he took his opinions from Bernard. That favorite governor was promising the council of Massachusetts, if they would omit to discuss the question of the power of parliament, he would support their petition for relief. The council followed the advice, and Bernard, as a fulfilling of his engagement, wrote a letter which he showed to several of them, recommending that part of the petition praying relief against such acts as were made "for the purpose of drawing a revenue from the colonies." Then, in a secret despatch of the same date, he sent an elaborate argument against the repeal or any mitigation of the late revenue act, quieting his conscience for the fraud by saying that "drawing a revenue from the colonies" meant carrying a revenue out of them, and that he wished to see the revenue from the port duties expended on the resident officers of the crown.

Great Britain at that time had a colonial secretary who encouraged this duplicity, and wrote an answer to be shown the council, keeping up the deception, and even using the name of the king, as a partner in the falsehood. Hillsborough greedily drank in the flattery offered him, and affected distress at showing the king the expressions of the partiality of Bernard. In undertaking the "very arduous task of reducing America into good order," he congratulated himself on "the aid of a governor so zealous, able, and active," who, having educated Hutchinson for his successor, was now promised the rank of a baronet and the administration of Virginia.

## CHAPTER XXIII.

UNION OF BEDFORD AND THE KING. THE REGULATORS OF NORTH CAROLINA. HILLSBOROUGH SECRETARY FOR THE COLONIES.

JULY–SEPTEMBER 1768.

THE people of Boston had gone out of favor with almost everybody in England. Even Rockingham said, the Americans were determined to leave their friends on his side the water, without the power of advancing in their behalf a shadow of excuse. This was the state of public feeling when, on the nineteenth of July 1768, Hallowell arrived in London, with letters giving an exaggerated account of what had happened in Boston on the tenth of June. London, Liverpool, and Bristol grew anxious; stocks fell. There arose rumors of a suspension of commerce, and America owed the merchants and manufacturers of England four millions sterling.

Nearly all the ministers united in denouncing "vengeance against that insolent town" of Boston. "If the government," said they, "now gives way, as it did about the stamp act, it will be all over with its authority in America." As Grafton was in the country, Hallowell was examined at the treasury chambers before Lord North and Jenkinson. He represented that the determination to break the revenue laws was not universal; that the revenue officers who remained there were not insulted; that the spirit displayed in Boston did not extend beyond its limits; that Salem and Marblehead made no opposition to the payment of the duties; that the people in the country would not join, if Boston were actually to resist government; but that the four commissioners at the castle could not return to town till measures were taken for their protection.

The memorial of the commissioners to the lords of the treasury announced that "there had been a long concerted and extensive plan of resistance to the authority of Great Britain; that the people of Boston had hastened to acts of violence sooner than was intended; that nothing but the immediate exertion of military power could prevent an open revolt of the town, which would probably spread throughout the provinces." The counter memorial in behalf of Boston, proving that the riot had been caused by the imprudent and violent proceedings of the officers of the Romney, met little notice. At the same time letters arrived from Virginia, with petitions and memorial, which, in the calmest language of "modesty and beautiful submission," uttered a protest against the right of parliament to tax America for a revenue.

Bedford and his party spoke openly of the necessity of employing force to subdue the inhabitants of Boston, and to make a striking example of the most seditious, in order to inspire the other colonies with terror. This policy, said Weymouth, will be adopted.

Shelburne, on the contrary, observed that people very much exaggerated the difficulty; that it was understood in its origin, its principles, and its consequences; that it would be absurd to wish to send to America a single additional soldier or vessel of war to reduce colonies which would return to the mother country of themselves from affection and from interest, when once the form of their contributions should be agreed upon. But his opinions had no effect, except that the king became "daily" more importunate with Grafton that Shelburne should be dismissed.

Moreover, the cabinet were "much vexed" at Shelburne's reluctance to engage in secret intrigues with Corsica, which resisted its cession by Genoa to France. The subject was therefore taken out of his hands, and the act of bad faith conducted by his colleagues. Unsolicited by Paoli, the general of the insurgents, they sent to him Dunant, a Genevese, as a British emissary, with written as well as verbal instructions.

Paoli was found destitute of everything; but he gave assurances of the purpose of the Corsican people to defend their liberty, and persuaded the British ministry that, if provided with what he needed, he could hold out for eighteen months. "A moment was not lost in supplying most of the articles requested by the Corsicans," "in the manner that would least risk a breach with France;" "and many thousand stands of arms were furnished from the stock in the Tower, yet so as to give no indication that they were sent from government."[*] While British ministers were enjoying the thought of success in their intrigues, they had the vexation to find Paoli himself obliged to retire by way of Leghorn to England. But their notorious interference was remembered in France as a precedent.

When, on the twenty-seventh of July, the cabinet definitively agreed on the measures to be pursued toward America, it sought to unite all England by resting its policy on Rockingham's declaratory act, and to divide America by proceeding only against Boston.

For Virginia, it was resolved that the office of its governor should no longer remain a sinecure, as it had been for three quarters of a century; and Amherst, who would not go out to reside there, was displaced. In selecting a new governor, the choice fell on Lord Botetourt; and it was a wise one, not merely because he had a pleasing address and was attentive to business, but because he was sure to write truly respecting Virginia, and sure never to ask the secretary to conceal his reports. He was to be conducted to his government in a seventy-four, and to take with him a coach of state. He was to call a new legislature, to closet its members as well as those of the council, and to humor them in almost anything except the explicit denial of the authority of parliament. It would have been ill for American independence if a man like him had been sent to Massachusetts.

But "with Massachusetts," said Camden, "it will not be very difficult to deal, if that is the only disobedient province." For Boston, even his voice did not entreat mercy. The cry was, it must be made to repent of its insolence, and its town-meetings no longer be suffered to threaten and defy the government of Great Britain. Two additional regiments, of five hundred men each, and a frigate, were at once to be sent there;

---

[*] The duke of Grafton's autobiographical narrative MS.

the ship of the line, which was to take Botetourt to Virginia, might remain in those seas. A change in the charter of Massachusetts was resolved on by Hillsborough, and he sent orders to inquire "if any persons had committed acts which, under the statute of Henry VIII. against treason committed abroad, might justify their being brought to England to be tried in the king's bench." Salem, a town whose representatives—contrary, however, to the judgment of their constituents—voted in favor of rescinding, was indicated as the future capital of the province.

At this time, Bernard received from Gage an offer of troops; but the council, after a just analysis of the late events, gave their opinion that it was not for his majesty's service or the peace of the province that any should be required. Bernard dared not avow his own opinion; but, in his spite, he wrote to Hillsborough for "positive orders" not to call "a new assembly until the people should get truer notions of their rights and interests."

The advice of the council was inspired by loyalty. All attempts at a concert to cease importations had hitherto failed; the menace of the arrival of troops revived the design, and, early in August, most of the merchants of the town of Boston subscribed an agreement that they would not send for any kind of merchandise from Great Britain, some few articles of necessity excepted, during the year following the first day of January 1769; and that they would not import any tea, paper, glass, paints, or colors, until the act imposing duties upon them should be repealed.

The inhabitants of Boston promised themselves that all ages would applaud their courage; and, on the anniversary of the fourteenth of August, its streets resounded with lines by Dickinson:

> Come, join hand in hand, brave Americans all,
> By uniting we stand, by dividing we fall;
> To die we can bear, but to serve we disdain;
> For shame is to freedom more dreadful than pain.
> In freedom we're born, in freedom we'll live;
> Our purses are ready; steady, boys, steady;
> Not as slaves, but as freemen, our money we'll give.

The British administration was blind to its dangers, and believed American union impossible. "You will learn what transpires in America infinitely better in the city than at court," wrote Choiseul to the French minister in England. "Never mind what Lord Hillsborough says; the private accounts of American merchants to their correspondents in London are more trustworthy."

The obedient official sought information in every direction, especially of Franklin. "He has for years been predicting to the ministers the necessary consequences of their American measures," said the French envoy; "he is a man of rare intelligence and well-disposed to England; but, fortunately, is very little consulted." While the British government neglected the opportunities of becoming well informed respecting America, Choiseul continued to collect newspapers, documents, resolves, instructions of towns, and sermons of the Puritan clergy, and proceeded to construct his theory.

"The forces of the English in America are scarcely ten thousand men, and they have no cavalry:" thus reasoned the dispassionate statesmen of France; "but the militia of the colonies numbers four hundred thousand men, and among them several regiments of cavalry. The people are enthusiastic for liberty, and have inherited a republican spirit, which the consciousness of strength and circumstances may push to extremities. They will not be intimidated by the presence of troops, too insignificant to cause alarm." It was therefore inferred that it would be hazardous for England to attempt reducing the colonies by force.

"But why," asked Choiseul, "are not deputies from each colony admitted into parliament as members?" And it was answered that "the Americans objected to such a solution, because they could not obtain a representation proportioned to their population, because their distance made regular attendance in parliament impossible, and because they knew its venality and corruption. They had no other representatives than agents at London, who kept them so well informed that no project to their disadvantage could come upon them by surprise." By this reasoning Choiseul was satisfied that an American representation in parliament was not practicable; that "no other method of conciliation" would prove less difficult, and that unanimity in America would compel the British government to risk the most violent measures, or to yield.

When, on the nineteenth of August, England heard that Massachusetts had, by a vast majority of its representatives, refused to rescind the resolutions of the preceding winter, Lord Mansfield was of the opinion that all the members of the late legislative assembly at Boston should be sent for to give an account of their conduct, and that the rigors of the law should be exercised against those who should persist in refusing to submit to parliament. "Where rebellion begins," said he, "the laws cease, and they can invoke none in their favor." *

To the ambassador of Spain he expressed in September the opinion that the affair of the colonies was the gravest and most momentous that England had had since 1688, and he saw in America the beginning of a long and even infinite series of revolutions. "The Americans," he insisted, "must first be compelled to submit to the authority of parliament; it is only after having reduced them to the most entire obedience that an inquiry can be made into their real or pretended grievances." The subject was watched in Madrid, and was the general theme of conversation in Paris, where Fuentes, the Spanish minister, expressed the hope that "the English might master their colonies, lest the Spanish colonies should catch the flame."

"I dread the event," said Camden, "because the colonies are more sober, and, consequently, more determined in their present opposition, than they were upon the stamp act." "What is to be done?" asked Grafton; and Camden answered: "Indeed, my dear lord, I do not know. The parliament cannot repeal the act in question, because that would admit the American principle to be right, and their own doctrine erroneous. Therefore it must execute the law. How to execute it, I am at a loss. Boston is the ringleading province; and, if any country is to be chastised, the punishment ought to be levelled there."

But the system which made government subordinate to the gains of patronage was everywhere producing its natural re-

* Francès to Choiseul, 16 and 29 Sept. 1768.

sults. In South Carolina, the profits of the place of provost-marshal were enjoyed under a patent as a sinecure by a resident in England, whose deputy had the monopoly of serving processes throughout the province, and yet was bound to attend courts nowhere but at Charleston. As a consequence, the herdsmen near the frontier adjudicated their own disputes and REGULATED their own police, even at the risk of a civil war.

The blood of "rebels" against oppression was first shed among the settlers on the branches of the Cape Fear river. The emigrants to the rich upland of North Carolina had little coin or currency; yet, as the revenue of the province was raised by a poll-tax, the poorest laborer among them must contribute as much as the richest merchant. The sheriffs were grown insolent and arbitrary, often distraining property even quadruple the value of the tax, and avoiding the owner, till it was too late for its redemption. All this was the more hateful, as a part of the amount was expended by the governor in building himself a palace; and a part was notoriously embezzled. The collecting officers and all others, encouraged by the imperious example of Fanning, continued their extortions, sure of support from the hierarchy of men in place. Juries were packed; the grand jury was almost the agent of the extortioners. The cost of suits at law, under any circumstances exorbitant, was enhanced by unprecedented appeals from the county court to the remote superior court, where a farmer of small means would be ruined by the expense of attendance with his witnesses. "We tell you in the anguish of our souls," said they to the governor, "we cannot, dare not go to law with our powerful antagonists; that step, whenever taken, will terminate in the ruin of ourselves and families." Besides, the chief justice was Martin Howard, a profligate time-server, raised to the bench as a convenient reward for having suffered in the time of the stamp act, and ever ready to use his place as a screen for the dishonest profits of men in office, and as the instrument of political power. Never yet had the tribunal of justice been so mocked.

Goaded by oppression and an intuitive jealousy of frauds, men associated as "regulators," binding themselves to avoid, if possible, all payment of taxes, except such as were levied and were to be applied according to law; and "to pay no more fees than the law allows, unless under compulsion, and then to bear open testimony against it." They proposed to hold a general meeting quarterly; but they rested their hopes of redress on the independent use of their elective franchise. "An officer," said the inhabitants of the west side of Haw river, "is a servant to the public; and we are determined to have the officers of this country under a better and honester regulation."

It was easy to foresee that the rashness of ignorant though well-meaning husbandmen, maddened by oppression, would expose them to the inexorable vengeance of their adversaries. As one of the regulators rode to Hillsborough, his horse was, in mere wantonness, seized for his levy, but was soon rescued by a party, armed with clubs and eleven muskets. Some one at Fanning's door showed pistols, and threatened to fire among them, upon which four or five unruly persons in the crowd discharged their guns into the roof of the house, making two or three holes, and breaking two panes of glass without further damage. At Fanning's instance, a warrant was issued by the chief justice to arrest three of the rioters, and bring them all the way to Halifax.

Raising a clamor against the odiousness of rebellion, Fanning himself, as military commander in Orange, called out seven companies of militia; but not above one hundred and twenty men appeared with arms, and, of these, all but a few stood neutral, or declared in favor of the regulators. In Anson county, on the twenty-first of April, a mob interrupted the inferior court; and, moreover, bound themselves by oath to pay no taxes, and to protect each other against warrants of distress or imprisonment.

In Orange county, the discontented did not harbor a thought of violence, and were only preparing a petition to the governor and council. "They call themselves regulators," said Fanning, "but by lawyers they must be termed rebels and traitors;" and he calumniated them as plotting to take his life, and lay Hillsborough in ashes. Meantime, Tryon, who, as the king's representative, should have joined impartiality with lenity, while he advised the people to petition the provincial legislature, empowered Fanning to call out the militia of eight counties besides Orange, and suppress insurrections by force.

The people of Orange, and equally of Anson, Rowan, and Mecklenburg, were unanimous in their resolution to claim relief of the governor. Fanning drafted for them a petition which rather invoked pardon than demanded redress, and his agent wrote to Herman Husbands, "one couched in any other terms cannot go down with the governor." But he vainly sought to terrify the rustic patriot by threats of confiscation of property, perpetual imprisonment, and even the penalties for high treason.

On the last day of April, the regulators of Orange county, peacefully assembled on Rocky river, appointed twelve men, on their behalf, "to settle the several matters of which they complained," instructed "the settlers" to procure a table of the taxables, taxes, and legal fees of public officers, and framed a petition to the general assembly for a fair hearing and redress.

Fanning, on his side, advertised their union as a daring insurrection, and bade them expect "no mitigation of punishment for their crimes;" at the same time, twenty-seven armed men of his procuring, chiefly sheriffs and their dependants and officers, were suddenly despatched on secret service, and, after travelling all night, arrived near break of day, on Monday the second of May, at Sandy creek, where they made prisoners of Herman Husbands and William Butler.

Against Husbands there was no just charge whatever. He had never so much as joined "the regulation," had never been concerned in any tumult, and was seized at home on his own land. The "astonishing news" of his captivity set the county in a ferment. Regulators and their opponents, judging that none were safe, prepared alike to go down to his rescue, but were turned back by "the glad tidings" that the governor himself had promised to receive their complaints.

Hurried to jail, insulted, tied with cords, and threatened with the gallows, Husbands succeeded, by partial concessions, the use of money, and by giving bonds, to obtain his liberty. But it seemed to him that "he was left alone;" and how could an unlettered farmer contend against so many? In his despair, he "took the woods;" but, hearing that the governor had promised that the extortioners might be brought to trial, he resolved to impeach Fanning.

The regulators prepared their petition, which was signed by about five hundred men, fortified it with a precise specification of acts of extortion, confirmed in each instance by oath, and presented it to the governor, with their plain and simple narrative, in the hope that "naked truth," though offered by the ignorant, might weigh as much as the artful representations of their "powerful adversary." Their language was that of loyalty to the king, and, with a rankling sense of their wrongs, breathed affection to the British government, "as the wholesomest constitution in being." It is Tryon himself who relates that, "in their commotions, no mischief had been done," and that "the disturbances in Anson and Orange had subsided." The regulators awaited the result of the suits at law. But Tryon would not wait; and, repairing to Hillsborough, demanded of them unconditional and immediate submission, and that twelve of them should give bonds, in a thousand pounds each, for the peaceful conduct of them all. An alarm went abroad, the first of the kind, that Indians, as well as men from the lower counties, were to be raised to cut off the inhabitants of Orange county as "rebels." About fifteen hundred men were actually in arms; and yet when, in September, the causes came on for trial in the presence of Tryon and with such a display of troops, Husbands was acquitted on every charge; and Fanning, who had been a volunteer witness against him, was convicted on six several indictments. A verdict was given against three regulators. The court punished Fanning by a fine of one penny on each of his convictions; the regulators were sentenced to pay fifty pounds each, and be imprisoned for six months.

Tryon would have sent troops to reduce the regulators by fire and sword, but was overruled. At the next election North Carolina changed thirty of its delegates; yet its people desponded, and saw no way for their extrication.

## CHAPTER XXIV.

THE TOWNS OF MASSACHUSETTS MEET IN CONVENTION. A FRENCH COMMONWEALTH IN LOUISIANA. HILLSBOROUGH SECRETARY FOR THE COLONIES.

SEPTEMBER–OCTOBER 1768.

THE approach of military rule convinced Samuel Adams of the necessity of American independence. He gave himself to his work as devotedly as though he had in his keeping the liberties of mankind. "He was," said Bernard, "one of the principal and most desperate of the chiefs of the faction;" "the all in all," wrote Hutchinson, who wished him "taken off," and who has left on record that his purity was always above all price. To promote the independence of his country, he was ready to serve, and never claim the reward of service. From a town of merchants and mechanics, Boston grew with him to be the hope of the world; and the sons of toil, as they perilled fortune and life for the liberties they inherited, rose to be, and to feel themselves to be, the champions of human freedom.

With the people of Boston, in the street, at public meetings, at the ship-yards, wherever he met them, he reasoned that it would be just to destroy every soldier whose foot should touch the shore. "The king," he would say, "has no right to send troops here to invade the country; if they come, they will come as foreign enemies." "We will not submit to any tax," he spoke out, "nor become slaves. We will take up arms, and spend our last drop of blood before the king and parliament shall impose on us, or settle crown officers, independent of the colonial legislature, to dragoon us." Not reverence for kings, he would say, brought the ancestors of New

England to America. They fled from kings and bishops, and looked up to the King of kings. "We are free, therefore," he concluded, "and want no king." "The times were never better in Rome than when they had no king, and were a free state." He saw that the vast empire which was forming in America must fashion its own institutions, and reform those of England.

Bernard had hinted that instructions might be given to reduce the province to submission by the indefinite suspension of its legislature. Was there no remedy? The men of Boston and the villages round about it were ready to spring to arms. But of what use were "unconnected" movements?

On the fifth of September 1768, there appeared in the "Boston Gazette" a paper in the form of queries, directing attention to the original charter of the colony, which left to the people the choice of their governor and legislature, and reserved to the crown no negative on their laws.

On the seventh, the Senegal left the port. The next day, the Duke of Cumberland sailed for Nova Scotia, and Bernard let it be known that both vessels of war were gone to fetch three regiments. Sullen discontent appeared on almost every brow. On the ninth, a petition was signed for a town-meeting "to consider of the most wise, constitutional, loyal, and salutary measures" in reference to the expected arrival of troops.

Union was the heart's desire of Boston; union first with all the towns of the province, and next with the sister colonies; and the confidence which must precede union could be established only by self-control. On Saturday, Otis, Samuel Adams, and Warren met at the house of Warren, and drew up the plan for the town-meeting, the resolves, and the order of the debates. Otis had long before pointed out the proper mode of redress in the contingency which had now occurred.

On Monday, the twelfth, the inhabitants of Boston gathered in a town-meeting at Faneuil Hall, where the arms belonging to the town, to the number of four hundred muskets, lay in boxes on the floor. After a fervid prayer from Cooper, minister of the congregation in Brattle street, and the election of Otis as moderator, a committee inquired of the governor the grounds of his apprehensions that regiments of his majesty's troops were daily to be expected; and requested him to issue precepts for a general assembly.

On the next morning, at ten o'clock, report was made to the town that Bernard refused an assembly, and that troops were expected. Rashness of the people of Boston would have forfeited the confidence of their own province, and the sympathies of the rest, while feebleness would have overwhelmed their cause with ridicule. It was necessary for them to halt, but to find a position where it was safe to do so; and they began their defences with the declaration that "it is the first principle in civil society, founded in nature and reason, that no law of the society can be binding on any individual, without his consent, given by himself in person, or by his representative of his own free election." They appealed to the precedents of the revolution of 1688; to the conditions on which the house of Hanover received the throne; to the bill of rights of William and Mary; and to their own charter; and then they proceeded to resolve, "That the inhabitants of the town of Boston will, at the utmost peril of their lives and fortunes, maintain and defend their rights, liberties, privileges, and immunities." To remove uncertainty respecting these rights, they voted "that money could not be levied, nor a standing army be kept up in the province, but by their own free consent."

This report was divers times distinctly read and considered, and it was unanimously voted that it be accepted and recorded. The record remains to the honor of Boston among all posterity.

"There are the arms," said Otis, pointing to the chests in which they lay. "When an attempt is made against your liberties, they will be delivered." One man cried out impatiently that they wanted a head; another, an old man, was ready to rise and resume all power; a third reasoned that liberty, like life, may be defended against the aggressor. But every excessive opinion was overruled or restrained; and the town, following the precedent of 1688, proposed a convention in Faneuil Hall. To this body they elected Cushing, Otis, Samuel Adams, and Hancock a committee to represent them; and directed their selectmen to inform the several towns of the province of their design. It was voted by a very great majority that every one of the inhabitants should provide himself with fire-arms and ammunition. A cordial letter was read from the merchants of New York, communicating their agreement to cease importing British goods.

It was unanimously voted that the selectmen wait on the several ministers of the gospel within the town, to desire that the next Tuesday might be set apart as a day of fasting and prayer; and it was so kept by all the Congregational churches.

On the fourteenth, just after a vessel had arrived in forty days from Falmouth, bringing news how angry people in England were with the Americans, that three regiments were coming over, that fifty state prisoners were to be sent home, the selectmen issued a circular, repeating the history of their grievances, and inviting every town in the province to send a committee to the convention, to give "sound and wholesome advice" and "prevent any sudden and unconnected measures." The city of London had never done the like in the great rebellion.

The proceedings of the meeting in Boston tended more toward revolution than any previous measures in any of the colonies. Bernard professed his belief that, but for the Romney, a rebellion would have broken out; he reported a design against the castle, and "that his government was subdued." The offer of a baronetcy and the vice-government of Virginia coming to hand, he accepted them "most thankfully," and hoped to embark for England in a fortnight. He had hardly indulged in this day-dream for twenty-four hours when his expectations were dashed by the account of Botetourt's appointment, and he began to fear that he should lose Massachusetts. Of a sudden he was become the most anxious and unhappy man in Boston.

On the nineteenth, Bernard announced to the council that two regiments were expected from Ireland, two others from Halifax, and desired that for one of them quarters might be prepared within the town. The council, after an adjournment of three days, during which "the militia were under arms, exercising and firing," spoke out plainly, that, as the barracks at Castle William were sufficient to accommodate both regiments ordered from Halifax, the act of parliament required that they should be quartered there. Upon this, Bernard produced the letter of General Gage, by which it appeared that one only of the coming regiments was ordered for the present to Castle William, and one to the town of Boston. "It is no disrespect to the general," answered the council, "to say that no order whatsoever, coming from a general or a secretary of war, or any less authority than his majesty and parliament, can supersede an act of parliament;" and they insisted that General Gage could not have intended otherwise, for the act provided "that, if any military officer should take upon himself to quarter soldiers in any of his majesty's dominions in America otherwise than was limited and allowed by the act, he should be *ipso facto* cashiered, and disabled to hold any military employment in his majesty's service."

The council, who were conducted in their opposition by James Bowdoin, rightly interpreted the law; but Bernard only drew from their conduct a new reason for urging the forfeiture of the colony's charter.

On the twenty-second of September, the anniversary of the king's coronation, about seventy persons, from sixty-six towns, came together in Faneuil Hall in convention; and their number increased, till ninety-six towns and eight districts, nearly every settlement in the colony, were represented. By the mere act of assembling, they showed that, if the policy of suppressing the legislature should be persisted in, legislative government could still be instituted; and they elected the speaker and clerk of the late house of representatives to the same offices in the convention.

"They have committed treason," shouted all the crown officers in America. "At least the selectmen, in issuing the circular for a convention, have done so;" and pains were taken to get at some of their original letters with their signatures. "Boston," said Gage, "is mutinous," "its resolves treasonable and desperate. Mad people procured them; mad people govern the town and influence the province."

The convention requested the governor to summon the constitutional assembly of the province, in order to consider of measures for preventing an unconstitutional encroachment of military power on the civil establishment. The governor refused to receive this petition; and he admonished "the gentlemen assembled at Faneuil Hall, under the name of a convention," to break up instantly and separate themselves, or they should be made to "repent of their rashness." The message was received with derision.

The council, adhering to their purpose of conforming strictly to the billeting act, reduced to writing the reasons for their decision to provide no quarters in town till the barracks at the castle should be full; and, on the twenty-sixth, communicated the paper to Bernard, published it in the "Boston Gazette," and sent a copy to Lord Hillsborough. It proved a disregard for an act of parliament by the very men who assumed to enforce parliamentary authority. On the side of the province, no law was violated; only men would not buy tea, glass, colors, or paper: on the side of Hillsborough, Bernard, and Gage, requisitions were made contrary to the words and the indisputable intent of the statute. In the very beginning of coercive measures, Boston gained a moral victory: it placed itself on the side of law, and proved its enemies to be lawbreakers. The immediate effect of the publication was, says Bernard, "the greatest blow that had been given to the king's government." "Nine tenths of the people considered the declaration of the council just."

The convention, which remained but six days in session, repeated the protest of Massachusetts against taxation of the colonies by the British parliament; against a standing army; against the danger to "the liberties of America from a united body of pensioners and soldiers." They renewed their petition to the king. They resolved to preserve good order, by the aid of the civil magistrate alone. Then, "relying on Him who ruleth according to his pleasure, with unerring wisdom and irresistible influence, in the hearts of the children of men," they dissolved themselves, leaving the care for the public to the council.

This was the first example in America of the restoration of affairs by delay. Indiscreet men murmured; but the intelligent perceived the greatness of the result. When the attorney- and solicitor-general of England were called upon to find traces of high treason in what had been done, De Grey as well as

Dunning, the attorney- and solicitor-general, joined in the opinion that the statute of the thirty-fifth of Henry VIII. was the only one by which criminals could be tried in England for offences committed in America; that its provisions extended only to treasons; and that there was no sufficient ground to fix the charge of high treason upon any persons named in the papers laid before them. "Look into the papers," said De Grey in the house of commons, "and see how well these Americans are versed in the crown law; I doubt whether they have been guilty of an overt act of treason, but I am sure they have come within a hair's breadth of it."

At noon of the twenty-eighth of September, just after the convention broke up, the squadron from Halifax anchored in Nantasket bay. It brought not two regiments only, but artillery, which Bernard, by a verbal message, had specially requested. Dalrymple, their commander, "expressed infinite surprise that no quarters had been prepared." On the twenty-ninth, the council, at which Smith, the commanding officer of the fleet, and Dalrymple, were present, after much altercation, adhered to the law; and the governor declared his want of power to act alone. "Since that resolution was taken to rise in arms in open rebellion," wrote Gage, "I don't see any cause to be scrupulous." On the following day, the squadron anchored off Castle William to intimidate the council, but without success. At that moment, Montresor, the engineer, arrived, with an order from General Gage to land both the regiments within the settled part of Boston.

On the first of October, the day for executing the order, the governor stole away into the country, leaving Dalrymple to despise "his want of spirit," and "to take the whole upon himself." As if they were come to an enemy's country, eight ships-of-war, with loaded cannon and springs on their cables, were anchored in the harbor so as to command the town, after which the fourteenth and twenty-ninth regiments, and a part of the fifty-ninth, with a train of artillery and two pieces of cannon, effected their landing on the Long Wharf. Each soldier having received sixteen rounds of shot, they marched, with drums beating, fifes playing, and colors flying, through the streets, and by four in the afternoon they paraded on Boston common.

"All their bravadoes ended as may be imagined," said an officer. "Men are not easily brought to fight," wrote Hutchinson, "when they know death by the sword or the halter will be the consequence." "Great Britain," remarked a wiser observer, "will repent her mistaken policy."

Dalrymple encamped the twenty-ninth regiment, which had field equipage; for the rest, he demanded quarters of the selectmen. They knew the law too well to comply; but, as the night was cold, the Sons of Liberty, from compassion, allowed them to sleep in Faneuil Hall.

On the third, Bernard laid before the council Dalrymple's requisition for the enumerated allowances to troops in barracks. "We," answered the council, "are ready, on our part, to comply with the act of parliament, if the colonel will on his."

"Tyranny begins," said Samuel Adams, "if the law is transgressed to another's harm. We must not give up the law and the constitution, which is fixed and stable, and is the collected and long digested sentiment of the whole, and substitute in its room the opinion of individuals, than which nothing can be more uncertain."

While Hood meditated embarking for Boston to winter there, Gage came from New York to demand, in person, quarters for the regiments in the town. The council would grant none till the barracks at the castle were filled.

The governor and the sheriff attempted to get possession of a ruinous building, belonging to the province; but its occupants had taken the best legal advice, and kept them at bay.

Bernard next summoned the acting justices to meet him, and renewed the general's demand for quarters. "Not till the barracks are filled," they answered, conforming to the law. "The clause," wrote Gage, "is by no means calculated for this country, where every man studies law." "I am at the end of my tether," said Bernard to his council; and he asked them to join him in naming a commissary. "To join in such appointment," answered the council, "would be an admission that the province ought to be charged with the expense." The officers could not put the troops into quarters; for they would, under the act, be cashiered, on being convicted of the fact before two justices of the peace. "Before two justices," exclaimed Gage, "the best of them the keeper of a paltry tavern."

At last, the weather growing so severe that the troops could not remain in tents, "the commanding officer was obliged to hire houses at very dear rates," as well as procure, at the expense of the crown, all the articles required by act of parliament of the colony. The main guard was established opposite the state-house, so that cannon were pointed toward the rooms in which the legislature was accustomed to sit. But, as the town gave an example of respect for law, there was nothing for the troops to do. Two regiments were there as idle lookers-on, and two more were coming to share the same inactivity. Every one knew that they could not be employed except on a requisition from a civil officer; and there was not a magistrate in the colony that saw any reason for calling in their aid, nor a person in town disposed to act in a way to warrant it.

The commissioners of the customs, having received orders to return to Boston, wished to get from the council some excuse for their departure, as well as for their return. "They had no just reason for absconding from their duty," said Bowdoin; and the council left them to return of themselves; but, in an address to Gage, adopted by a vote of fifteen out of nineteen, they explained how trivial had been the disorders on which the request for troops had been grounded. Gage became convinced by his inquiries that the disturbance in March was trifling; that on the tenth of June the commissioners were neither attacked nor menaced; that more obstructions had arisen to the service from the servants of government than from any other cause. And yet he advised barracks and a fort on Fort Hill to command the town, while Bernard owned that "troops would not restore the authority of government," and urged anew a forfeiture of the charter.

A troublesome anxiety took possession of Bernard, who began to fear his recall, and intercede to be spared. "These red coats make a formidable appearance," said Hutchinson, buoyant with the prospect of rising one step higher. The soldiers liked the country they were come to, and, sure that none would betray them, deserted in numbers. The commissioners, more haughty than before, gratified their malignity by arresting Hancock and Malcolm on charges confidently made, but never established.

Yielding to the "daily" importunities of the king, Grafton prepared to dismiss Shelburne. Camden encouraged Grafton to slight their benefactor, as "brooding over his own suspicions and discontent." "I will never retire upon a scanty income," he added, "unless I should be forced by something more compelling than the earl of Shelburne's removal. You are my pole-star, Chatham being eclipsed."

Grafton repaired to Hayes to gain Chatham's acquiescence in the proposed change. "My lord's health," answered the countess, "is too weak to admit of any communication of business; but I am able to tell your grace, from my lord himself, that Lord Shelburne's removal will never have his consent." The king awaited anxiously the result of the interview; and, notwithstanding the warning, Shelburne was removed. To Camden's surprise, the resignation of Chatham instantly followed. Grafton and the king interposed with solicitations, but he remained inflexible.* Camden remained in office, and even advised a public declaration from the king, that Townshend's revenue act should be executed, and "Boston," "the ringleading province," be "chastised."

"Depend upon it," said Hillsborough to the agent of Connecticut, who had presented him the petition of that colony, "parliament will not suffer their authority to be trampled upon. We wish to avoid severities toward you; but, if you refuse obedience to our laws, the whole fleet and army of England shall enforce it."

The inhabitants of Boston resolved more than ever not to pay money without their own consent, and to use no article from Britain till the obnoxious acts should be repealed and the troops removed.

At that time Shelburne was planning a joint intervention with France to prevent the downfall of Poland.† His removal opened the cabinet to the ignorant and incapable earl of Rochford, who owed his selection to his submissive mediocrity. He needed money, and once told Choiseul, with tears in his eyes,

* Grafton MS.
† Rayneval's report of his interview with Shelburne, September 1782.

that, if he lost the embassy which he then filled, he should be without resources. He had a passion to play a part, and would boast of his intention to rival not Chatham, he would say, but Pitt; though he could not even for a day adhere steadily to one idea. "His meddlesome disposition," said Choiseul, "makes him a worse man to deal with than one of greater ability." After his accession, the administration was the weakest and the worst which England had known since the revolution. It had no sanction in public opinion, and the subservient parliament was losing the reverence of the nation.

In October 1768, the reform of parliament was advocated by Grenville. "The number of electors," such was his publicly declared opinion, "is become too small in proportion to the whole people, and the colonies ought to be allowed to send members to parliament." "What other reason than an attempt to raise discontent," replied Edmund Burke, as the organ of the Rockingham whigs, "can he have for suggesting that we are not happy enough to enjoy a sufficient number of voters in England? Our fault is on the other side." And he mocked at an American representation as the vision of a lunatic.

On the banks of the Mississippi, uncontrolled impulses unfurled the flag of a republic. The treaty of Paris left two European powers sole sovereigns of the continent of North America. Spain accepted Louisiana with reluctance, for she lost France as her bulwark, and, to keep the territory from England, assumed new expenses and dangers. Its inhabitants loved the land of their ancestry; by every law of nature and human freedom, they had the right to protest against the transfer of their allegiance. No sooner did they hear of the cession of their country to the Catholic king than, in October 1768, an assembly sprang into being, representing every parish in the colony; and, at the instance of Lafrénière, they unanimously resolved to entreat the king of France to be touched with their affliction and their loyalty, and not to sever them from his dominions.

At Paris, their envoy, John Milhet, the wealthiest merchant of New Orleans, met with a friend in Bienville, the time-honored founder of New Orleans; and, assisted by the tears and the well-remembered early services of the venerable octogenarian, he appealed to the heart of Choiseul. "It may not be," answered Choiseul; "France cannot bear the charge of supporting the colony's precarious existence."

On the tenth of July 1765, the austere and unamiable Antonio De Ulloa, by a letter from Havana, announced to the superior council at New Orleans his orders to take possession of that city for the Catholic king; but the flag of France was left flying, and continued to attract Acadian exiles. On the fifth of March 1766, during a violent thunder-gust and rain, Ulloa landed, with civil officers, three capuchin monks, and eighty soldiers. His reception was cold and gloomy. He brought no orders to redeem the seven million livres of French paper money, which weighed down a colony of less than six thousand white men. The French garrison of three hundred refused to enter the Spanish service, the people to give up their nationality, and Ulloa was obliged to administer the government under the French flag by the old French officers, at the cost of Spain.

In May of the same year, the Spanish restrictive system was applied to Louisiana; in September, an ordinance compelled French vessels having special permits to accept the paper currency in pay for their cargoes, at an arbitrary tariff of prices. "The extension and freedom of trade," remonstrated the merchants, "far from injuring states and colonies, are their strength and support." The ordinance was suspended, but not till the alarm had destroyed all commerce. Ulloa retired from New Orleans to the Balise. Only there, and opposite Natchez, and at the river Iberville, was Spanish jurisdiction directly exercised.

This state of things continued for a little more than two years. But the arbitrary and passionate conduct of Ulloa, the depreciation of the currency with the prospect of its becoming an almost total loss, the disputes respecting the expenses incurred since the session of 1762, the interruption of commerce, a captious ordinance which made a private monopoly of the traffic with the Indians, uncertainty of jurisdiction and allegiance, agitated the colony from one end to the other. It was proposed to make of New Orleans a republic, like Amsterdam or Venice, with a legislative body of forty men, and a single executive. The people of the country parishes crowded in a mass into the city, joined those of New Orleans, and formed a numerous assembly, in which Lafrénière, John Milhet, Joseph Milhet, and the lawyer Doucet were conspicuous. "Why," said they, "should the two sovereigns form agreements which can have no result but our misery, without advantage to either?" On the twenty-fifth of October 1768, they adopted an address to the superior council, written by Lafrénière and Caresse, rehearsing their griefs; and, in their petition of rights, they claimed freedom of commerce with the ports of France and America, and the expulsion of Ulloa from the colony. The address, signed by five or six hundred persons, was adopted the next day by the council, in spite of the protest of Aubry; when the French flag was displayed on the public square, children and women ran up to kiss its folds, and it was raised by nine hundred men, amid shouts of "Long live the king of France! we will have no king but him." Ulloa retreated to Havana, and sent his representations to Spain. The inhabitants elected their own treasurer and syndics, sent envoys to Paris with supplicatory letters to the duke of Orleans and the prince of Conti, and memorialized the French monarch to stand as intercessor between them and the Catholic king, offering no alternative but to be a colony of France or a free commonwealth.

In February of the next year, Du Châtelet wrote to Choiseul: "The success of the people of New Orleans in driving away the Spaniards is a good example for the English colonies; may they set about following it."

## CHAPTER XXV.

THE KING AND PARLIAMENT AGAINST THE TOWN OF BOSTON. HILLSBOROUGH SECRETARY FOR THE COLONIES.

OCTOBER 1768–FEBRUARY 1769.

AGAINST the advice of Shelburne, and to the great joy of Spain, every post between Mobile and Fort Chartres was abandoned. The occupation of the country between the Alleghanies and the Mississippi was opposed by the British government. John Finley, a backwoodsman of North Carolina, who, in 1768, passed through Kentucky, found not one white man's cabin in all the enchanting wilderness. Gage even advised the retirement from Fort Chartres and Pittsburg. But this policy encountered difficulties from the existence of French settlements in Illinois and on the Wabash, the roving disposition of the Americans, and the avarice of British officers who coveted profit from concessions of lands.

The Spanish town of St. Louis was fast rising into importance, as the centre of the fur-trade with the Indian nations on the Missouri; but the population of Illinois had declined, and scarcely amounted to more than one thousand three hundred and fifty-eight, of whom rather more than three hundred were Africans. Kaskaskia counted six hundred white persons, and three hundred and three negroes. At Kahokia, there were about three hundred persons; at Prairie du Rocher, one hundred and twenty-five; at St. Philip, fifteen, and not more at Fort Chartres. To Hillsborough's great alarm, the adult men had been formed into military companies. Vincennes, the only settlement in Indiana, had rapidly and surprisingly increased. Its own population, consisting of two hundred and thirty-two white persons, ten negro and seventeen Indian slaves, was recruited by one hundred and sixty-eight "strangers." Detroit had now about six hundred souls. The western villages abounded in wheat, Indian corn, and swine; of beeves, there was more than one to each human being, and more than one horse to every two, counting slaves and children.

The course of the rivers inclined the French in the West to send their furs to New Orleans, or across the river by night to St. Louis, where they could be exchanged for French goods. All English merchandise came burdened with the cost of land carriage from Philadelphia to Fort Pitt. In November 1768, Wilkins, the new commandant in Illinois, following suggestions from Gage, appointed seven civil judges to decide local controversies, yet without abdicating his own overruling authority. He was chiefly intent on enriching some Philadelphia fur-traders, who were notorious for their willingness to bribe, and, in less than a year after his arrival, executed, at their request, inchoate grants of large tracts of land, of which one sixth part was reserved for himself. The procedure contravened the orders of Hillsborough, who renewed imperatively the instruction to extend an unbroken line of Indian frontier from Georgia to Canada, as an impassable barrier to emigration.

This purpose was strenuously opposed by Virginia. From its second charter, the discoveries of its people, the authorized grants of its governors since 1746, the encouragement of its legislature to settlers in 1752 and 1753, the promise of lands as bounties to officers and soldiers who served in the French war, and the continued emigration of its inhabitants, the Ancient Dominion derived its title to occupy the great West. Carolina stopped at the line of thirty-six and a half degrees; on the north, New York could at most extend to Lake Erie; Maryland and Pennsylvania were each limited by definitive boundaries. Virginia alone claimed the Ohio lands, south of the line of Connecticut. But, in spite of her objections, Stuart was ordered to complete the demarcation with the Indians, and to accept no new territory from the Cherokees.

Faithful to his superior, the agent, without regarding the discontent of Virginia, which declined co-operating with him, met the chiefs of the upper and lower Cherokees in council, at Hard Labor in Western South Carolina; and, on the fourteenth of October 1768, concluded a treaty by which the Cherokees, who had no right to lands in Kentucky, were made to establish as the western boundary of Virginia a straight line drawn from Chiswell's mine, on the eastern bank of the Great Kanawha, in a northerly course to the confluence of that river with the Ohio.

To thwart the negotiation of Stuart, Virginia had appointed Thomas Walker its commissioner to the congress held at Fort Stanwix with the Six Nations. Sir William Johnson, the Indian agent for the northern district, was thoroughly versed in the methods of making profit by his office. William Franklin, of New Jersey, readily assisted in obtaining the largest cessions of lands. The number of Indians who appeared was but little short of three thousand. Unusual largesses won over the chiefs of the Six Nations; the line that was established on the fifth of November began at the north, where Canada creek joins Wood creek; on leaving New York, it passed from the nearest fork of the West Branch of the Susquehannah to Kittaning on the Alleghany, whence it followed that river and the Ohio. Had it stopped at the mouth of the Kanawha, the Indian frontier would have been marked all the way from northern New York to Florida. But, instead of following his instructions, Sir William Johnson, assuming groundlessly a right of the Six Nations to the largest part of Kentucky, continued the line down the Ohio to the Tennessee river, which was thus constituted the western boundary of Virginia.

While the congress was in session, Botetourt, the new governor of Virginia, arrived on the James river, in the delicious season of the fall of the leaf. He was charmed with the scenes on which he entered; his house seemed admirable; the grounds around it well planted and watered by beautiful rills. Everything was just as he could have wished. Coming up without state to an unprovided residence, he was asked abroad every day; and, as a guest, gave pleasure and was pleased. He thought nothing could be better than the disposition of the colony, and augured well of everything that was to happen. Received with frankness, he dealt frankly with the people to whom he was deputed. He wrote to Hillsborough that they would never willingly submit to being taxed by the mother country; but he justified them by their universal avowal of a most ardent desire to assist upon every occasion, if they might do it as formerly only on requisition. The duties complained of were collected in every part of the colony, without a shadow of resistance. He was persuaded that the new assembly would come together in good humor, which he was resolved not wantonly to disturb.

The western boundary invited immediate attention. Botetourt entered heartily into the wishes of Virginia, and put in pledge his life and fortune to carry its jurisdiction to the Tennessee river where it strikes the parallel of thirty-six and a half degrees. "This boundary," it was said, "will give some room to extend our settlements for ten or twelve years."

England, at this time, began to think reconciliation with Massachusetts hopeless, when news arrived that the troops had landed at Boston without opposition, that the convention had dissolved, and that all thoughts of resistance were at an end. "They act with highest wisdom and spirit," said Thomas Hollis; "they will extricate themselves with firmness and magnanimity." But most men expressed contempt for them, as having made a vain bluster. No one doubted that, on the arrival of the additional regiments from Ireland, Otis and Cushing and sixteen other members of the late political assemblies would be arrested.* Hillsborough hastened to send Bernard's despatches to the attorney- and solicitor-general, asking what crimes had been committed, and if the guilty were to be impeached by parliament.

The king, on his opening parliament in November, railed at "the spirit of faction breaking out afresh in some of the colonies." "Boston," said he, "appears to be in a state of disobedience to all law and government, with circumstances that might manifest a disposition to throw off its dependence on Great Britain."

In the house of commons, Lord Henly, moving the address, signalized the people of Boston for their "defiance of all legal authority." "I gave my vote to the revenue act of Charles Townshend," thus he was seconded by Hans Stanley, "that we might test the obedience of the Americans to the declaratory

* Francès to Choiseul, 4 November 1768.

law of 1766. Men so unsusceptible of all middle terms of accommodation call loudly for our correction. The difficulties in governing Massachusetts are insurmountable, unless its charter and laws shall be so changed as to give to the king the appointment of the council, and to the sheriffs the sole power of returning juries." Samuel Adams, at Boston, weighed well the meaning of these words, uttered by an organ of the ministry; but England hardly noticed the menace of the subversion of chartered rights and of the independence of juries.

Edmund Burke poured out a torrent of invective against Camden for the inconsistency of his former opposition to the declaratory act with his present support of the ministry. "My astonishment at the folly of his opinions," he said, "is lost in indignation at the baseness of his conduct." Grenville agreed with him that the order, requiring the Massachusetts assembly to rescind a vote under a penalty, was illegal and unconstitutional. "I wish the stamp act had never been passed," said Barrington; "but the Americans are traitors against the legislature. The troops are to bring rioters to justice." Wedderburn, who at that moment belonged to himself, and spoke in opposition to enhance his price, declaimed against governing by files of musketeers; and condemned the ministerial mandate as illegal. "Though it were considered wiser," said Rigby, "to alter the American tax than to continue it, I would not alter it so long as the colony of the Massachusetts bay continues in its present state." "Let the nation return to its old good nature and its old good humor," were the words of Alderman Beckford, whom nobody minded, and who spoke more wisely than they all; "it were best to repeal the late act, and conciliate the colonies by moderation and kindness."

Lord North made reply: "America must fear you before she can love you. If America is to be the judge, you may tax in no instance, you may regulate in no instance. We shall go through our plan, now that we have brought it so near success. I am against repealing the last act of parliament, securing to us a revenue out of America; I will never think of repealing it until we see America prostrate at our feet." The irrevocable words spoke the feeling of parliament. The address was carried in the commons without a division; the peers seemed unanimous; and scarcely more than five or six in both houses defended the Americans from principle. Everybody expected "the chastisement of Boston."

But the employment of soldiery failed from the beginning. There were, on the tenth of November, more than four regiments in Boston; what could be given them to do? They had been sent over to bring "to justice" those whom Barrington called "rioters," whom the king described as "turbulent and mischievous persons." But the statesmen who guided Boston through its difficulties acted with a prudence equal to their vigor. No breach of the law could be charged against them; and, besides, the pusillanimity of the governor of Massachusetts was so remarkable that it was his fixed rule not to assume the responsibility of giving the word to any military officer; and without such authority everybody knew that the regiments for which he had asked could not be employed. The troops found no rebellion at Boston; could they make one?

Each American assembly, as it came together, denied the right of parliament to impose taxes on America, and embodied its denial in petitions to the king. The king, instead of hearing the petitions, disapproved and rejected them; Virginia was soothingly reprimanded; Pennsylvania, Rhode Island, Connecticut, Maryland, received, as their answer, copies of the addresses of parliament, and assurances that "wicked men," who questioned the supreme authority of that body, would not be listened to.

The governor of South Carolina invited its assembly to treat the letters of Massachusetts and Virginia "with the contempt they deserved;" a committee, composed of Parsons, Gadsden, Pinkney, Lloyd, Lynch, Laurens, Rutledge, Elliott, and Dart, reported them to be "founded upon undeniable, constitutional principles;" and the house, sitting with its doors locked, unanimously directed its speaker to signify to both provinces its entire approbation. The governor, that same evening, dissolved the assembly by beat of drum; but the general toast at Charleston remained, "The UNANIMOUS TWENTY-SIX, who would not rescind the Massachusetts circular." The assembly of New York was in session, fully resolved to go beyond the common example; and Hillsborough had only opened the way to a complaint from the colonies, that the king would not even receive their petitions.

The refusal of America to draw supplies from England was an invitation to other powers to devise the means of sharing her commerce; the three secretaries of state were therefore called upon to issue orders to the ministers, consuls, and agents of the British government in the ports of Europe, Madeira, and the Azores, to watch the coming in of an American ship or the sailing of any ship for the continent of America.

"Can the ministry reduce the colonies?" asked Du Châtelet. "Of what avail is an army in so vast a country? The Americans have made these reflections, and they will not give way." "To the menace of rigor," replied Choiseul, "they will never give way, except in appearance and for a time. The fire will be but imperfectly extinguished unless other means than those of force conciliate the interests of the metropolis and its colonies. The Americans will not lose out of view their rights and privileges; and, next to fanaticism for religion, the fanaticism for liberty is the most daring in its measures and the most dangerous in its consequences."

The simplest mode of taking part with the colonists was by a commerce of the French and Spanish colonies with the British colonies on the continent of North America; and on this subject Choiseul sent to Du Châtelet an elaborate digest of all the materials he had collected. But the simple-hearted king of Spain, though he enjoyed the perplexity of "the natural enemy" of the two crowns, showed no disposition to interfere.

"What a pity," resumed Du Châtelet to Choiseul, "that neither Spain nor France is in a condition to take advantage of so critical a conjuncture! Precipitate measures on our part might reconcile the colonies to the metropolis; but if the quarrel goes on, a thousand opportunities cannot fail to offer, of which decisive advantage may be taken. The objects presented to you, to the king, and to his council, demand the most profound combinations, the most inviolable secrecy. A plan which shall be applicable to every circumstance of change should be concerted in advance with Spain."

At the same time, Du Châtelet studied intercolonial commerce; and continued to seek information from the American agents, particularly from Franklin, whom he more and more extolled as "upright and enlightened, one of the wisest and most sagacious men that could be found in any country."

The agents had separately waited on Lord Hillsborough. On the sixth of December, he communicated to them in a body the result of a cabinet council: "Administration will enforce the authority of the legislature of Great Britain over the colonies in the most effectual manner, but with moderation and lenity. All the petitions we have received are very offensive, for they contain a denial of the authority of parliament. We have no fondness for the acts complained of; particularly, the late duty act is so anti-commercial that I wish it had never existed; and it would certainly have been repealed had the colonies said nothing about it, or petitioned against it only on the ground of expediency: but the principle you proceed upon extends to all laws; and we cannot therefore think of repealing it, at least this session of parliament, or until the colonies shall have dropped the point of right. Nor can the conduct of the people of Boston pass without a severe censure." A very long discussion ensued; but he was inflexible.

The attention of parliament was to be confined to the colony of the Massachusetts bay; Beckford and Trecothick, as friends to America, demanded rather such general inquiry as might lead to measures of relief. "The question of taxation is not before us," interposed Lord North; "but the question is, whether we are to lay a tax one year when America is at peace, and take it off the next when America is in arms against us. The repeal of the act would spread an alarm, as if we did it from fear. The encouragement it would give our enemies and the discouragement it would give our friends bind us not to take that question into consideration again. The expression of the united opinion of Great Britain must awe Boston into obedience."

"The Americans believe," rejoined Beckford, "that there is a settled design in this country to rule them with a military force." "I never wish for dominion, unless accompanied by the affection of the people governed," said Lord John Cavendish. "Want of knowledge, as well as want of temper," said Lord Beauchamp, "has gradually led us to the brink of a precipice, on which we look down with horror." Phipps, a captain in the army, added: "My heart will bleed for every drop of American blood that shall be shed, while their grievances are unredressed. I wish to see the Americans in our arms as friends, not to meet them as enemies." "Dare you not trust yourselves with a general inquiry?" asked Grenville. "How do we know, parliamentarily, that Boston is the most guilty of the colonies?" "I would have the Americans obey the laws of the country, whether they like them or not," said Lord Barrington.

Out of two hundred who were present, one hundred and twenty-seven divided with the government to confine the inquiry. The king set himself, his ministry, parliament, and all Great Britain to subdue to his will one stubborn town on the sterile coast of the Massachusetts bay. The odds against it were fearful; but it showed a life inextinguishable, and had been chosen to keep guard over the liberties of mankind.

The Old World had not its parallel. It counted about sixteen thousand inhabitants of European origin, all of whom learned to read and write. Good public schools were the foundation of its political system; and Benjamin Franklin, one of their pupils, in his youth apprenticed to the art which makes knowledge the common property of mankind, had gone forth from them to stand before the nations as the representative of the modern industrial class.

As its schools were for all its children, so the great body of its male inhabitants of twenty-one years of age, when assembled in a hall which Faneuil, of Huguenot ancestry, had built for them, was the source of all municipal authority. In the meeting of the town, its taxes were voted, its affairs discussed and settled, its agents and public servants annually elected by ballot, and abstract political principles freely debated. A property qualification was attached to the right of voting, but it was so small that it did not change the character of the suffrage. There had never existed a considerable municipality, approaching so nearly to a pure democracy; and, for so populous a place, it was undoubtedly the most orderly and best governed in the world.

Its ecclesiastical polity was in like manner republican. The great mass were Congregationalists, of whom each church formed an assembly by voluntary agreement, self-constituted, self-supported, and independent. They were clear that no person or church had power over another church. There was not a Roman Catholic altar in the place; the usages of "papists" were looked upon as worn-out superstitions, fit only for the ignorant. But the people were not merely the fiercest enemies of "popery and slavery," they were Protestants even against Protestantism; and, though the English church was tolerated, Boston kept up the fight against prelacy. Its ministers were still its prophets and its guides; its pulpit, in which now that Mayhew was no more Cooper was admired above all others for eloquence and patriotism, inflamed by its weekly appeals alike the fervor of piety and of liberty. In the "Boston Gazette" it enjoyed a free press, which gave currency to its conclusions on the natural right of man to self-government.

Its citizens were inquisitive, seeking the causes of existing institutions in the laws of nature. Yet they controlled their speculative turn by practical judgment, exhibiting the seeming contradiction of susceptibility to enthusiasm and calculating shrewdness. They were adventurous, penetrating, and keen in the pursuit of gain; yet their avidity was tempered by a well-considered and continuing liberality. Nearly every man was struggling to make his own way in the world and his own fortune; and yet, individually and as a body, they were public-spirited. In the seventeenth century, the community had been distracted by those who were thought to pursue the great truth of justification by faith to Antinomian absurdities; the philosophy of the eighteenth century had influenced theological opinion; and, though the larger number still acknowledged the fixedness of the divine decrees and the resistless certainty from all eternity of election and of reprobation, some, even among the clergy, framed, from the self-direction of the active powers of man, a protest against predestination and election. Still more were they boldly speculative on questions respecting their constitution. Every house was a school of politics; every man discussed the affairs of the world, studied more or less the laws of his own land, and was sure of his ability to ascertain and to make good his rights. The ministers, whose prayers, being from no book, caught the hue of the times; the merchants, cramped in their enterprise by legal restrictions; the mechanics, who by their skill in ship-building bore away the palm from all other nations, and by their numbers ruled the town—all alike, clergy and laity, in the pulpit or closet, on the wharf or in the counting-room, at their ship-yards or in their social gatherings, reasoned upon government. As the descendants of the Puritans of England, they had no more superstitious veneration for monarchy than for priestcraft. They unconsciously developed the theory of an independent representative commonwealth; and such was their instinctive capacity for organization, that they had actually seen a convention of the people of the province start into life at their bidding. While the earth was still wrapt in gloom, they welcomed the daybreak of popular freedom, and looked undazzled into the beams of the morning.

The opinion of parliament was hardly pronounced when Du Châtelet again pressed America on the attention of Choiseul. "Without exaggerating the projects or the union of the colonies," said he, "the time of their independence is very near. Their prudent men believe the moment not yet come; but, if the English government undertakes vigorous measures, who can tell how far the fanaticism for liberty may carry an immense people, dwelling for the most part in the interior of a continent, remote from imminent danger? And, if the metropolis should persevere, can the union, which is now their strength, be maintained without succor from abroad? Even if the rupture should be premature, can France and Spain neglect the opportunity which they may never find again?

"Three years ago the separation of the English colonies was looked upon as an object of attention for the next generation; the germs were observed, but no one could foresee that they would be so speedily developed. This new order of things, which will necessarily have the greatest influence on the political system of Europe, will probably be brought about within a very few years."

"Your views," replied Choiseul, "are as acute as they are comprehensive and well considered. The king is perfectly aware of their sagacity and solidity; and I will communicate them to the court of Madrid."

The statesmen of France had their best allies in the British ministry. "The matter is now brought to a point," said Hillsborough, in the house of lords. "Parliament must give up its authority over the colonies, or bring them to effectual submission. Not the amount of the duties, which will not be more than ten thousand pounds per annum in all North America, but the principle upon which the laws are founded, is complained of. Legislation and taxation will stand or fall together. The notion of the Americans is a polytheism in politics, absurd, fatal to the constitution, and never to be admitted. The North Americans are a very good set of people, misled by a few wicked, factious, and designing men. I will, therefore, for the present only propose several resolutions which may show the sense of the legislature. If this is not sufficient, the whole force of the country must be exerted to bring the colonies into subjection." The resolutions condemned the assembly of Massachusetts, its council, and still more its convention; approved of sending a military force to Boston; and foreshadowed the abrogation of the municipal liberties of that town, and a change in the charter of the province.

Hillsborough was seconded by Bedford, who further proposed an address to the king, to bring to "condign punishment the chief authors and instigators of the late disorders;" and, if sufficient ground should be seen, to put them on trial for "treason" before a special commission in England, "pursuant to the statute of Henry VIII." The resolutions and address were adopted, with no opposition except from Richmond and Shelburne.

"The semblance of vigor," said Choiseul, "covers pusillanimity and fear. If those who are threatened with a trial for high treason are not alarmed, the terror and discouragement will affect nobody but the British ministers; the main question of taxing the colonies is as far from a solution as ever."

Samuel Adams, whom it was especially desired to "take off" for treason, was "unawed by the menaces of arbitrary power." "I must," said he, "tell the men, who on both sides of the Atlantic charge America with rebellion, that military power will never prevail on an American to surrender his liberty;" and, through the press, he taught that a standing army, kept up in the colonies in time of peace without their consent, was as flagrant a violation of the constitution as the tax on paper, glass, painters' colors, and tea. He called upon the magistrates of Boston to govern, restrain, and punish " soldiers of all ranks," according to the laws of the land. The justices of the peace for Suffolk at their quarter sessions, and the grand jury, over which the crown had no control, found indictments against soldiers and officers for their frequent transgressions of the law; and the convicted escaped punishment only through the favoritism of a higher court.

Georgia approved the correspondence of Massachusetts and Virginia. New York unanimously asserted its legislative rights with unsurpassed distinctness, and appointed an intercolonial committee of correspondence.

At this time, Choiseul, incensed at the public subscription in England in aid of the Corsicans, was threatening the British minister that he would requite the grievance by opening subscriptions in France for the inhabitants of New York. The new year brought a dissolution of the assembly of that province; and, in the following elections, the government party employed every art to create confusion. It excused the violence of recent disputes. It sought to gratify the cravings of every interest. It connived at importations from St. Eustatius and Holland, and supported an increase of the paper currency. It encouraged the tenantry in their wish to vote by ballot; and in New York city, for the old cry of "No Presbyterian," it raised that of "No Lawyer." The Delanceys, who had long seemingly led the opposition in the province, were secretly won over to the side of authority. Add to this, that all parties still hoped for an escape from strife by some plan of union to which Grafton was believed to be well disposed; that the population was not homogeneous in religion, language, customs, or origin; that the government and the churchmen acted together; that the city was a corporation in which the mayor was appointed by the king—and the reasons appear why, at the hotly contested election, which was the last ever held in New York under the crown, the coalition gained success over John Morin Scott and the Sons of Liberty.

In Massachusetts, Bernard kept up the ferment. He knew

it to be a part of Lord Hillsborough's system that there never should be another election of councillors; and he and Hutchinson most secretly furnished lists of persons whose appointment they advised. They both importuned the ministry to remove Temple, who would not conceal his opinion that the affection of the colonists for the mother country was wasting away through the incapacity and "avarice" of his associates. The wily Hutchinson opposed the repeal of the revenue act; recommended to remove the main objection to parliamentary authority by the offer to the colonists of such "a plan of representation" in the British parliament as he knew they must reject; informed against the free constitutions of Massachusetts, Connecticut, and Rhode Island, as tending to produce another congress; and advised and solicited and importuned for such an extension of the laws of treason as would have rendered every considerable man in Boston liable to its penalties. In letters communicated to Grenville, Lord Temple, and others, he declared that "measures which he could not think of without pain were necessary for the peace and good of the colony," that "there must be an abridgment of what are called English liberties." He avowed his desire to see some further restraint, lest otherwise the connection with Great Britain should be broken; and he consoled himself for his advice by declaring it impossible for so distant a colony to "enjoy all the liberty of the parent state." He had put many suggestions on paper, but behind all he had further "thoughts, which he dared not trust to pen and ink."

"Poison will continue to be instilled into the minds of the people," wrote Oliver, "if there be no way found to take off the original incendiaries." The Bedford address for shipping American traitors to England having come to hand, a way was open for "taking them off." Bernard and Oliver and Hutchinson, with the attorney-general, collected evidence against Samuel Adams; and affidavits, sworn to before Hutchinson, were sent to England, to prove him fit to be transported under the act of Henry VIII. Edes and Gill, "the trumpeters of sedition," and through them "all the chiefs of the faction, all the authors of numberless treasonable and seditious writings," were to be called to account.

While Hutchinson was taking depositions, so that "the principal actors might be compelled to answer" for "proceedings amounting to treason," those whom he sought to arraign as traitors, aware of his designs, reproached him for his baseness in performing "the office of an informer" while he held the post of chief justice, and avowed their opinions more boldly than ever. "Parliament will offer you a share in the representative body," said the royalists; and the suggestion was spurned, since a true representation was impossible. "Boston may be deprived of its trade," thus they foreshadowed the policy adopted five years later. "What then?" it was asked. "Will the decline of British credit be remedied by turning our seaports into villages?" "Governor Bernard has been spoken of with great respect," reported the official journal. "And so has Otis," rejoined the "Boston Gazette;" "and has been compared to the Pyms, the Hampdens, the Shippens of Britain." "The opposition to government is faction," said the friends to government. "As well," answered Samuel Adams, "might the general uneasiness that introduced the revolution by William III., or that settled the succession in the house of Hanover, be called a faction." Since Britain persisted in enforcing her revenue act, he knew no remedy for America but independence.

Lord North, though he feared to strike, wished to intimidate. He would not allow a petition from the council of Massachusetts for the repeal of Townshend's act to be referred with the other American papers; nor would he receive a petition which denied that the act of Henry VIII. extended to the colonies; and on the twenty-sixth of January, after a delay of many weeks, he asked the house of commons to agree with the resolves and address of the house of lords. "No lawyer," said Dowdeswell, "will justify them; none but the house of lords, who think only of their dignity, could have originated them." "Suppose," said Edmund Burke, "you do call over two or three of these unfortunate men; what will become of the rest? *Let me have the heads of the principal leaders*, exclaimed the duke of Alva; these heads proved hydra's heads. Suppose a man brought over for high treason; if his witnesses do not appear, he cannot have a fair trial. God and nature oppose you."

Grenville scoffed at the whole plan, as no more than "angry words," and "the wisdom fools put on." Lord North, assuming the responsibility of the measure, refused "ever to give up an iota of the authority of Great Britain," and promised good results in America from the refusal to repeal the revenue act.

"It is not a question of one refractory colony," cried Barré; "the whole country is ripe for revolt. Let us come to the point. Are the Americans proper objects of taxation? I think they are not. I solemnly declare, I think they will not submit to any law imposed upon them for revenue.

"On a former occasion, the noble lord told us that he would listen to no proposition for repeal until he saw America prostrate at his feet. But does any friend of his country really wish to see America thus humbled? In such a situation, she would serve only as a monument of your vengeance and your folly. For my part, the America I wish to see is America increasing and prosperous, raising her head in graceful dignity, with freedom and firmness asserting her rights at your bar, vindicating her liberties, pleading her services, and conscious of her merit. This is the America that will have spirit to fight your battles, to sustain you when hard pushed by some prevailing foe, and by her industry will be able to consume your manufactures, support your trade, and pour wealth and splendor into your towns and cities. If we do not change our conduct toward her, America will be torn from our side. I repeat it: unless you repeal this law, you run the risk of losing America."

His reasoning was just; his action animated; warmed by the nobleness of his subject, he charmed all that heard him; yet the resolutions and address were adopted by a large majority.

"An attempt to seize the defenders of American liberties," wrote the watchful French ambassador to Choiseul, "would precipitate the revolution. How great will be the indignation of the Americans when they learn that Britain, without receiving their representations, without hearing their agents, treats them as slaves and condemns them as rebels! They never will recognise the right claimed by parliament; their hearts will own no other country than the wilderness which their industry has made productive. The bonds of their dependence will be severed on the first opportunity. Spain and France, even at the risk of transient inconveniences, should depart from the ancient prohibitory laws of commerce. The two courts must consider whether it is for their interest to second the revolution which menaces England, at the risk of the consequences which may a little later result from it for the totality of the New World, and whether the weakening of a common enemy can compensate the risk of such an example to their own colonies.

"If this question is answered in the affirmative, no precautions must be omitted to profit by the favorable circumstances, which imprudence alone could have created, and which human wisdom could hardly have foreseen. The inflammatory remedies applied by the parliament of England, the spirit of revolt, and still more the spirit of contempt shown by a factious people for a vacillating and humiliated administration, the disunion and indecision which reign in the British cabinet, the acknowledged weakness and instability of the principles of the king's government—all presage coming calamities to England; the only man whose genius might still be feared is removed from affairs and enfeebled by gout, and his state of mind is a problem. Of the others, whom birth, credit, wealth, or eloquence may destine to high places, not one appears likely to become a formidable enemy."

This letter from Du Châtelet to Choiseul was inspired by the philosophy of the eighteenth century, the ripened wisdom of the ages from Descartes to Turgot, uttering its oracles and its counsels in the palaces of absolute monarchs. It excited the most attentive curiosity of Louis XV. and of every one of his council. An extract of it was sent to Madrid, to ascertain the sentiments of the Catholic king; the minister of the marine and the minister of finance were directed to consult the chambers of commerce of the kingdom; while Choiseul, aware of the novelty of a system founded on the principal of a free trade, looked about him on every side for prevailing arguments against hereditary prepossessions.

On the eighth of February the Bourbon kings were still deliberating, the state of America was again the theme of conversation in the house of commons, and strenuous efforts were once more made to prove the illegality and cruelty of fetching Americans across the Atlantic for trial.

"They may save themselves," said Rose Fuller, "by going still further, and bringing the question to the point of arms." "You have no right to tax the colonies," repeated Beckford; "the system has not produced a single shilling to the exchequer; the money is all eaten up by the officers who collect it." "Your measures," cried Phipps, after an admirable statement, "are more calculated to raise than to quell a rebellion. It is our duty to stand between the victim and the altar." "The statute of the thirty-fifth year of Henry VIII.," observed Frederic Montagu, "was passed in the worst times of the worst reign, when the taste of blood had inflamed the savage disposition of Henry." "The act," declared Sir William Meredith, "does not extend to America; and, were I an American, I would not submit to it." Yet the British parliament, by a great majority, requested the king to make inquisition at Boston for treason; and "ample information" was promptly sent by Hutchinson and others, so that the principal Sons of Liberty might be arraigned in Westminster Hall and hanged at Tyburn.

The press gave to the world an elaborate reply to the Farmer's Letters, by Knox, to whom the board of trade furnished materials, and Grenville the constitutional argument. "I am tempted," owned Knox, "to deny that there is any such thing as representation at all in the British constitution; until this notion of representation is overthrown, it will be very difficult to convince either the colonies or the people of England that wrong is not done the colonies."

While England was enforcing its restrictive commercial system, Du Châtelet continued his intercession with Choiseul, to employ free trade as the great liberator of colonies. "The question," he pleaded, "cannot be submitted to the decision of the chambers of commerce. They regard everything in colonial commerce which does not turn exclusively to the benefit of the kingdom as contrary to the end for which colonies were established, and as a theft from the state. To practice on these maxims is impossible. The wants of trade are stronger than the laws of trade. The north of America can alone furnish supplies to its south. This is the only point of view under which the cession of Canada can be regarded as a loss for France; but that cession will one day be amply compensated, if it shall cause in the English colonies the rebellion and independence, which become every day more probable and more near." The Parisian world was alive with admiration for the Americans and their advocates.

But Spain had been the parent of the protective system, and remained the supporter of that restrictive policy by which, in the midst of every resource of wealth, she had been impoverished. From the first proposal of throwing colonial commerce open, she feared the contraband exportation of gold and silver. "Besides," thus Grimaldi, the Spanish minister, gave his definitive answer, "the position and strength of the countries occupied by the Americans excite a just alarm for the rich Spanish possessions on their borders. Their interlopers have already introduced their grain and rice into our colonies. If this should be legalized and extended to other objects, it would increase the prosperity of a neighbor already too formidable. Moreover, this neighbor, if it should separate from its metropolis, would assume the republican form of government; and a republic is a government dangerous from the wisdom, the consistency, and the solidity of the measures which it would adopt for executing such projects of conquests as it would naturally form."

The opinion of Spain was deliberately pronounced and sternly adhered to. She divided the continent of North America with England, and loved to see "her enemy" embarrassed by war with its colonies; but she already feared America more than she feared England, and, for a neighbor, preferred a dependent colony to an independent republic.

## CHAPTER XXVI.

VIRGINIA COMES TO THE AID OF MASSACHUSETTS. GRAFTON'S ADMINISTRATION. HILLSBOROUGH COLONIAL MINISTER.

MARCH–AUGUST 1769.

THE decision of the king of Spain had been hastened by tidings of the rebellion in New Orleans. The cabinet, with but one dissentient, agreed that Louisiana must be retained, as a granary for Havana and Porto Rico, a precaution against the contraband trade of France, and a barrier to keep off English encroachments by the indisputable line of a great river.

"Still more," said the duke of Alva, "the world, and especially America, must see that the king can and will crush even an intention of disrespect." "If France should recover Louisiana," said Masones de Lima, "she would annex it to the English colonies, or would establish its independence." "A republic in Louisiana," such was Aranda's carefully prepared opinion, "would be independent of the European powers, who would all cultivate her friendship and support her existence. She would increase her population, enlarge her limits, and grow into a rich, flourishing, and free state, contrasting with our exhausted provinces. From the example before them, the inhabitants of our vast Mexican domain would be led to consider their total want of commerce, the extortions of their governors, the little esteem in which they themselves are held, the few offices which they are permitted to fill; they would hate still more the Spanish rule, and would think to brave it with security. If, by improving the government of the Mexican provinces and the condition of their inhabitants, *we should avoid the fatal revolution*, Louisiana would still trade with the harbors on our coast, and by land with Texas and New Mexico, and through them with Old Mexico. Between Louisiana and Mexico there are no established limits; the rebels, if they remain as they are, will have a pretext for claiming an arbitrary extension of territory." He therefore advised to subdue the colony, but to keep New Orleans in such insignificance as to tempt no attack.

The king accepted the decision of his cabinet, adding his fear lest the example of Louisiana should influence the colonies "of other powers," in which he already discerned the "spirit of sedition and independence."

Choiseul watched the rising spirit of colonial independence with joy; and the paper which he sent for the consideration of the French ambassdor at London reasoned as follows: "Here is the happy opportunity of dividing the British empire, by placing before its colonies the interesting spectacle of two potentates who pardon, who protect, and who deign in concert to utter the powerful word of liberty. War between France and England would bind these countries more firmly to their metropolis. The example of happiness will allure them to the independence toward which they tend. By leading them to confide in France and Spain, they will dare more and dare sooner. Nothing can better persuade to this confidence than to establish liberty in Louisiana, and to open the port of New Orleans to men of all nations and all religions.

"The passion for extended dominion must not hide from Spain that a discontented and ill-guarded colony cannot arrest the march of the English, and will prove an unprofitable expense. Were we to take back Louisiana, our best efforts could effect less than the charm of liberty. Without the magic of liberty, the territory will never become more than a simple line of demarcation. Severity would throw it into despair and into the arms of the English. To give voluntarily what the British parliament haughtily refuses, to assimilate New Orleans in its form to the freest of the British colonies, to adopt for it from each of them whatever is the dearest to them, to do more—to enfranchise it and maintain invariably privileges capable of intoxicating the English and the Americans—this is to arm English America against England."

The idea and the reasoning in its support pleased Du

Châtelet infinitely. "Spain," said he, "can never derive benefit from Louisiana. She neither will nor can take effective measures for its colonization and culture. She has not inhabitants enough to furnish emigrants; and the religious and political principles of her government will always keep away foreigners, and even Frenchmen. Under Spanish dominion, the vast extent of territory ceded by France to Spain on the banks of the Mississippi will soon become a desert.

"The expense of colonies is requited only by commerce; and the commerce of Louisiana, under the rigor of the Spanish prohibitive laws, will every day become more and more a nullity. Spain then will make an excellent bargain, if she accords liberty to the inhabitants of Louisiana, and permits them to form themselves into a republic. Nothing can so surely keep them from falling under English rule as making them cherish the protection of Spain and the sweetness of independence. The example of a free and happy nation, under the guardianship of two powerful monarchs, without restraint on its commerce, without any taxes but those which the wants of the state and of the common defence would require, without any dependence on Europe but for necessary protection, would be a tempting spectacle for the English colonies; and, exhibited at their very gates, would hasten the epoch of their revolution."

But, while the statesmen of France indulged the thought of founding at New Orleans a commercial republic like Venice or Amsterdam, as a place of refuge for the discontented of every creed and tongue, Spain took counsel only of her pride. "The world must see that I," said the Catholic king, "unaided, can crush the audacity of sedition." Aware of the wishes of the French ministers, he concealed his purpose by making no military preparations at Cadiz, and despatched Alexander O'Reilly in all haste for Cuba, with orders to extirpate the sentiment of independence at New Orleans.

England had proved herself superior in war to the combined power of Spain and France. Could not she crush the insolent town of Boston, suppress its free schools, shut up its town-hall, sequester its liberties, drag its patriots to the gallows, and, for the life, restless enterprise, fervid charities, and liberal spirit of that moral and industrious town, substitute the monotony of obsequious obedience? England could not do what a feebler despotism might have undertaken without misgivings. She stood self-restrained. A part of the ministry wished the charter of Massachusetts abrogated; and the lawyers declared that nothing had been done to forfeit it. They clamored for judicial victims; the lawyers said that treason had not been committed. Few and fluctuating as was the opposition in parliament, they uttered the language of the British constitution when they spoke for freedom; and they divided the ministry, when they counselled moderation. England was a land of liberty and law; and the question between her and her colonies must be argued at the bar of reason. Spain could send an army and a special tribunal to sequester estates and execute patriots. England must arraign its accused before a jury; and the necessity of hunting up an enactment of Henry VIII. discovered the supremacy of law, of which the petulant ministry must respect the bounds.

The patriots of Boston were confident of recovering their rights either with the consent of England or by independence. John Adams, though anxious for advancement, scorned the service of the king; and his associates at the bar rendered "themselves unfit for the favor of government" by "abetting" "the popular party." The people of Lexington came into a resolution to drink no more tea till the unconstitutional revenue act should be repealed. On the anniversary of the repeal of the stamp act, Samuel Adams held up to public view the grievances inflicted on Americans, by combining taxation with a commercial monopoly, and enforcing both by fleets, armies, commissioners, guarda-costas, judges of the admiralty, and a host of insolent and rapacious petty officers. He pointed out, on the one hand, the weakness of Great Britain, arising from its corruption, its debt, its intestine divisions, its insufficient supply of food, its want of alliances; and, on the other, the state of the American colonies, their various climates, soils, produce, rapid increase of population, and the virtue of their inhabitants, and drew the inference that the conduct of Old England was "permitted and ordained by the unsearchable wisdom of the Almighty for hastening" American independence.

The intrepid patriot knew the end at which he aimed; the British ministry of the moment had no system; but Thomas Pownall wrote to Cooper of Boston, describing the opinion of all parties: "We have but one word, and that is our sovereignty, and it is like some word to a madman, which, whenever mentioned, throws him into his ravings and brings on a paroxysm. The representation of New York, though carefully written, was rejected by the house of commons, because it questioned the right of parliamnet to tax America. But this sovereignty being asserted, the ministry of Grafton, terrified by the recovery of Chatham and by the diminution of exports, wished the controversy with the colonies well over. Hillsborough's plan for altering the charter of Massachusetts was laid aside; discretionary orders were transmitted to Gage to "send back to Halifax the two regiments, which were brought from that station, and to send two others to Ireland." Bernard was to be superseded by Hutchinson, a town-born citizen of Boston. New York was to be soothed by a confirmation of its jurisdiction over Vermont, and the permission to issue paper money; Virginia, by a more extended boundary at the West.

At the same time, England professed to seek a good understanding with France. But Choiseul remembered too well the events of 1755, when, during peaceful negotiations and without a declaration of war, she sent out a squadron to attack French ships on their way to America. He witnessed the effort of England to counterbalance the influence of France by a northern alliance. It was Rochford's fixed desire that the empress of Russia should derive advantage from the war against the Turks, should be able to dispose of the whole North by main strength or by predominant influence, and should then enter into an alliance with the court of London.

"The English secretary," reasoned Choiseul, "does not look at these objects from the higher point of view, which should engage the attention of a great minister. Nothing can be more dangerous for the repose of humanity, nor more to be feared for the principal powers of Europe, than the success of the ambitious projects of Russia. Far from seeking, on such a supposition, the alliance of the empress, it would become their most essential interest to unite to destroy her preponderance. If the pretended balance of power can be annihilated, it will be by the prodigious increase of the material and moral strength of Russia. She is now laboring to enslave the North; she will next encroach on the liberty of the South, unless an effective check is seasonably put to her inordinate passion of despotism. Instead of contributing to the aggrandizement of Russia, the principal courts ought jointly to restrain her cupidity, which may in some respects realize the chimerical idea, once attributed to France, of aiming at universal monarchy."

The rivalry of England and France met at every point; yet how changed were their relations! The cabinet of France desired to loosen the bonds that shackled trade; that of England, to hold them close. France desired the independence of all colonial possessions; England, to retain her own in complete dependence. Both needed peace; but Choiseul, fearing a rupture at any moment, "never lost out of sight that, to preserve peace, it was necessary to be in a condition to sustain a war;" while England more and more forgot that her greatness sprung from her liberty.

The publication of American letters, which had been laid before parliament and copied for Beckford, unmasked Bernard's duplicity. The town of Boston repelled the allegation that they were held to their allegiance only by "terror and force of arms." In their representation to the king, which Barré presented, they entreated the removal of the troops, a communication of the charges against them, and an opportunity to make their defence. The council calmly and unanimously proved their own undeviating respect for law: they set in a strong light Bernard's duplicity and petty malice; his notoriously false assertions; his perpetual conspiracy for "the destruction of their constitution."

While the people of Massachusetts were filled with grief and indignation at the conspiracy against their charter, which was dearer to them than fortune and life, they and all the colonies, one after another, matured agreements for passive resistance to parliamentary taxation. On the tenth of April, the general assembly of New York, at the motion of Philip Livingston, thanked the merchants of the city and colony for suspending trade with Great Britain. He would next have renewed the resolves, which had occasioned the dissolution of the last assembly; but he was himself ousted from the present one, for want of a residence within the manor for which he had been returned. Yet the system of non-importation was rigorously carried out. The merchants of Philadelphia unanimously adopted the agreement, which a few months before they had declined.

At Mount Vernon, Washington tempered yet animated his neighbors. "Our lordly masters in Great Britain," said he, "will be satisfied with nothing less than the deprivation of American freedom. Something should be done to maintain the liberty which we have derived from our ancestors. No man should hesitate a moment to use arms in defence of so valuable a blessing. Yet arms should be the last resource. We have proved the inefficacy of addresses to the throne and remonstrances to parliament; how far their attention to our rights and privileges is to be awakened by starving their trade and manufactures, remains to be tried." And, counselling with his friend George Mason, he prepared a scheme to be offered at the coming session of the Virginia house of burgesses.

While the British ministry was palsied by indecision, Thomas Pownall urged "parliament at once, in advance of new difficulties, to repeal the act, end the controversy, and give peace to the two countries." Trecothick seconded the motion, dwelling on commercial reasons. "We will not consent," replied Lord North, "to go into the question, on account of the combinations in America. To do so would be to furnish a fresh instance of haste, impatience, levity, and fickleness. I see nothing uncommercial in making the Americans pay a duty upon tea."

The Rockingham party were willing that the act should remain to embarrass the ministers. Conway proposed, as a middle course, to defer its consideration to the next session. "I approve the middle course," said Beckford. "The duty upon tea, with a great army to collect it, has produced in the southern part of America only two hundred and ninety-four pounds, fourteen shillings; in the northern part, it has produced nothing." "For the sake of a paltry revenue," cried Lord Beauchamp, "we lose the affection of two millions of people."

"We have trusted to terror too long," observed Jackson. "Washing my hands of the charge of severity," answered Lord North, "I will not vote for holding out hopes that may not be realized." "If you are ready to repeal this act," retorted Grenville, "why keep it in force for a single hour? You ought not to do so from anger or ill-humor. Why dally and delay in a business of such infinite importance? Why pretend that this is not the time, when the difficulty is every day increasing? If the act is wrong, or you cannot maintain it, give it up like men. If you do not mean to bind the colonies by your laws in cases of taxation, tell the Americans so fairly, and conciliate their affections." "The British administration will come to no decision," such was Du Châtelet's report to Choiseul, "till the Americans consolidate their union, and form a general plan of resistance."

America was not alone in asserting the right of representation. In England, the freeholders of Middlesex elected Wilkes to represent their shire in parliament. The king wished him expelled; and the house of commons expelled him. The city of London made him one of its magistrates; by the unanimous vote of Middlesex, he was again returned. The house of commons voted the return to be null and void. "Supporters of the bill of rights" united to pay his debts and his election expenses. The third time his intended competitor proved too much of a craven to appear, and he was returned unanimously. Once more his election was annulled. At a fourth trial, he was opposed by Luttrell, but polled nearly three fourths of all the votes. The house of commons this time treated him as a person incapacitated to be a candidate, and admitted Luttrell. In disfranchising Wilkes by their own resolution, without authority of law, they violated the vital principle of representative government; by admitting Luttrell, they sequestered and usurped the elective franchise of Middlesex. In this way the administration of Grafton set against itself the more liberal part of parliament. It was further imperilled by the widely extending passive resistance of the Americans. Besides, Chatham might reappear; and Grafton and Camden, in their constant dread of his rebuke, insisted that some attempt should be made to conciliate the colonies.

On the first day of May, just on the eve of the prorogation of parliament, the cabinet discussed the policy which it should definitively adopt. All agreed that the duties on the British manufactures of glass, paper, and painters' colors, were contrary to the true principles of commerce, and should be repealed: there remained of Charles Townshend's revenue act nothing but the duty on tea; and this, evaded by smuggling or by abstinence from its use, yielded in all America not fifteen hundred dollars, not three hundred pounds a year. Why should it be retained, at the cost of the affections of thirteen provinces and two millions of people? Grafton, the head of the treasury board, spoke first and earnestly for its repeal; Camden seconded him with equal vigor; Granby and Conway gave their voice and their vote on the same side; and Sir Edward Hawke, whom illness detained from the meeting, was of their opinion. Had not Grafton and Camden consented to remove Shelburne, the measure would have been carried, and American independence indefinitely postponed. But Rochford, with Gower and Weymouth, adhered to Hillsborough. The responsibility of deciding fell to Lord North. He was known to be at heart for the repeal of the tax on tea; yet his ambition and consequent desire of the favor of the king swayed him to give his deciding vote in the cabinet against the repeal.

Neither the Bedford party nor the king meant to give up the right to tax; and they clung to the duty on tea as an evidence of lordly superiority. "We can grant nothing to the Americans," said Hillsborough, "except what they may ask with a halter round their necks."* "They are a race of convicts," said the famous Samuel Johnson, "and ought to be thankful for anything we allow them short of hanging." A circular was sent forthwith to all the colonies, promising, on the part of the ministry, to lay no more taxes on America for revenue, and to repeal those on paper, glass, and colors. It was pitiful in Camden to blame the paper as not couched in terms so conciliatory as those in the minute of the cabinet, for the substance of the decision was truly given. More honeyed words would have been useless hypocrisy. When Camden

* Du Châtelet to Choiseul, 12 May 1769.

acquiesced in the removal of Shelburne, he prepared his own humiliation.

On the day of the prorogation of parliament the legislature of Virginia assembled at Williamsburg. Great men were there; some who were among the greatest—Washington, Patrick Henry, and, for the first time, Jefferson. Botetourt, who opened the session in state, was in perfect harmony with the council, received from the house of burgesses a most dutiful address, and entertained fifty-two guests at his table on the first day, and as many more on the second. He took care to make " a judicious use " of the permission which he had received to negotiate an extended boundary with the Cherokees. Presiding in the highest court in Virginia, he concurred with the council in deciding that the grant of a writ of assistance to custom-house officers was not warranted by act of parliament. But the assembly did not forget its duty, and devised a measure which became the example for the continent.

It claimed the sole right of imposing taxes on the inhabitants of Virginia. With equal unanimity, it asserted the lawfulness and expediency of a concert of the colonies in defence of the violated rights of America. It laid bare the flagrant tyranny of applying to America the obsolete statute of Henry VIII.; and it warned the king of "the dangers that would ensue" if any person in any part of America should be seized and carried beyond sea for trial. It consummated its work by communicating its resolutions to every legislature in America, and asking their concurrence. The resolves were concise, simple, and effective; so calm in manner and so perfect in substance that time finds no omission to regret, no improvement to suggest. The menace of arresting patriots lost its terrors; and Virginia's declaration and action consolidated union.

Is it asked who was the adviser of the measure? None can tell. Great things were done, and were done tranquilly and modestly, without a thought of the glory that was their due. Had the Ancient Dominion been silent, I will not say that Massachusetts might have faltered; but mutual trust would have been wanting. The assembly had but one mind, and their resolves were the act of Virginia. Had they been framed by the men of Massachusetts, " they could not have been better adapted to vindicate their past proceedings, and encourage them to perseverance."

The next morning, the assembly had just time to adopt an address to the king, when the governor summoned them, and said: "I have heard of your resolves, and augur ill of their effects; you have made it my duty to dissolve you, and you are dissolved accordingly."

Upon this, the burgesses met together as patriots and friends, with their speaker as moderator. They adopted the resolves which Washington had brought with him from Mount Vernon, and which formed a well-digested, stringent, and practicable scheme of non-importation, until all the "unconstitutional" revenue acts should be repealed. Such, too, was their zeal against the slave-trade that they made a special covenant with one another not to import any slaves, nor purchase any imported. These associations were signed by Peyton Randolph, Richard Bland, Archibald Cary, Robert Carter Nicholas, Richard Henry Lee, Washington, Carter Braxton, Henry, Jefferson, Nelson, and all the burgesses of Virginia there assembled; and were then sent throughout the country for the signature of every man in the colony.

The voice of the Old Dominion roused the merchants of Pennsylvania to approve what had been done. The assembly of Delaware adopted the Virginia resolves word for word; and every colony south of Virginia followed the example.

For more than ten months, Massachusetts remained without an assembly. Of five hundred and eight votes that were cast in Boston at the ensuing choice of its representatives, Otis, Cushing, Samuel Adams, and Hancock, the old members, received more than five hundred. They were instructed to insist on the departure of the army from the town and province, and not to pay anything toward its support. Of the ninety-two representatives in the former assembly who voted not to rescind, eighty-one, probably all who were candidates, were re-elected; of the seventeen rescinders, only five. Especially Salem condemned the conduct of its former representatives, and substituted two Sons of Liberty. Cambridge charged Thomas Gardner, its representative, "to use his best endeavors that all their rights might be transmitted inviolable to the latest posterity." Nor let history omit the praise of a husbandman like him; for he was rich in the virtues of daily life, of calm and modest courage, trustworthy and unassuming, and, when sent from cultivating his fields to take part in legislation, he carried to his larger task a discerning mind, a guileless heart, and fidelity even to death. The town of Roxbury recommended a correspondence between the house of representatives in Massachusetts and the assemblies of other provinces.

Meantime, Bernard received his letters of recall. The blow came on him unexpectedly, as he was engaging settlers for his lands, and promising himself a long enjoyment of office under military protection. True to his character, he remained, to get, if he could, an appropriation for his own salary for a year, and to bequeath confusion to his successor. The legislature, before even electing a clerk or a speaker, complained to him of the presence of "the armament by sea and land, in the port and the gates of the city, during the session of the assembly." On the election of councillors, he disapproved of no less than eleven; among them, of Brattle and Bowdoin, who had been chosen by a unanimous vote. The house then considered the presence among them of troops, over whom the governor avowed that the civil power in the province did not extend. In a message to him, they represented that the employment of the military to enforce the laws was inconsistent with the spirit of a free constitution; that a standing army, in so far as it was uncontrollable by the civil government of the province, was an absolute power. Gage had at that time discretionary authority to withdraw all the forces from Boston; he had ordered two regiments to Halifax, and was disposed to send away the rest; but Bernard, after consultation with the crown officers, gave his written opinion that it would be ruinous to remove them.

To worry the house into voting him, on the eve of his departure, a full year's salary, he adjourned the legislature to Cambridge; the house, by a unanimous vote, one hundred and nine members being present, petitioned the king to remove him forever from the government. Another week passes. Bernard threatened to give his assent to no act which the grant of his salary did not precede. The house, disdainfully rejecting his renewed demand, adopted, nearly word for word, the three resolutions of Virginia on taxation, intercolonial correspondence, and trial by a jury of the vicinage.

For the troops thus quartered in Boston against the will of the province, Bernard vainly demanded the appropriations which the billeting act required. "Be explicit and distinct," said he, in a second message, "that there may be no mistake." After grave deliberation in a most unusually numerous house of one hundred and seven, they made answer: "As representatives, by the royal charter and the nature of our trust, we are only empowered to grant such aids as are reasonable, of which we are free and independent judges, at liberty to follow the dictates of our own understanding, without regard to the mandates of another. As we cannot, consistently with our honor or interest, and much less with the duty we owe our constituents, so we shall NEVER make provision for the purposes mentioned in your messages."

"To his majesty," rejoined Bernard in his last words, "and, if he pleases, to his parliament, must be referred your invasion of the rights of the imperial sovereignty. By your own acts you will be judged." And he prorogued the general court.

Newport, Rhode Island, witnessed bolder resistance. A vessel with a cargo of prohibited goods was rescued from the revenue officers, whose ship, named Liberty, was destroyed.

Just as this was heard of at Boston, Hillsborough's circular, promising relief from all "real" grievances and a repeal of the duties on glass, paper, and colors, as contrary to the true principles of commerce, was made public by Bernard. The merchants, assembling on the twenty-seventh of July, unanimously voted this partial repeal insufficient, since the duty reserved on tea was to save "the right" of taxing, and they resolved to send for no more goods from Great Britain, a few specified articles excepted, unless the revenue acts should be repealed. The inhabitants were to purchase nothing from violators of this engagement; the names of recusant importers were to be published, and a committee was appointed to state the embarrassments to commerce, growing out of the late regulations.

On the last evening of July, Bernard, having completed

his pecuniary arrangements with Hutchinson, who was to be his successor, left Boston. "He was to have sent home whom he pleased," said the Bostonians; "but, the die being thrown, poor Sir Francis Bernard was the rogue to go first."

Trained as a wrangling proctor in an ecclesiastical court, he had been as governor a quarrelsome disputant. His parsimony went to the extreme of meanness; his avarice was restless and insatiable. So long as he connived at smuggling, he reaped a harvest in that way; when Grenville's sternness inspired alarm, his greed was for forfeitures and penalties. Assuming to respect the charter, he was unwearied in zeal for its subversion; professing to the colony opposition to taxation by parliament, he most assiduously urged the measure on the ministry; asserting solemnly that he had never asked for troops, he persistently importuned for ships-of-war and an armed force. His reports were often false, partly with design, partly from the credulity of panic. He placed everything in the most unfavorable light, and was at all times ready to magnify trivial incidents into acts of treason. The officers of the army and the navy openly despised him for his cowardly duplicity. "He has essentially served us," said the clergyman Cooper; "had he been wise, our liberties might have been lost."

As he departed, the bells were rung and cannon fired from the wharfs, Liberty Tree was gay with flags, and at night a great bonfire was kindled upon Fort Hill. When he reached England, he found that the ministry had promised the London merchants never again to employ him in America.

## CHAPTER XXVII.

GROWTH OF REPUBLICANISM IN LOUISIANA, KENTUCKY, AND MASSACHUSETTS. LORD NORTH FORMS AN ADMINISTRATION.

MAY 1769–JANUARY 1770.

WHILE Boston was driven toward republicanism, the enthusiasm which had made the revolution at New Orleans could not shape for that colony a tranquil existence. A new petition to France expressed the resolve of the inhabitants to preserve the dear and inviolable name of French citizens, at the peril of their lives and fortunes. They applied to the English; but the governor at Pensacola abstained from offending powers with which his sovereign was at peace. The dread of Spain inspired the design of founding a republic, with an elective council of forty and a protector. When, near the end of July, O'Reilly arrived at the Balise with an overwhelming force, despair prevailed for a moment; and white cockades were distributed by the republicans. "O'Reilly is not come to ruin the colony," said Aubry, who had received instructions to feign ingenuous candor. "If you submit," he repeated publicly and by authority, "the general will treat you with kindness, and you may have full confidence in the clemency of his Catholic majesty." These promises won faith; and, with Aubry's concurrence, a committee of three, Lafrénière for the council, Marquis for the colonists, and Milhet for the merchants, waited on O'Reilly at the Balise, to recognise his authority and implore his mercy.

O'Reilly welcomed the deputies with the fairest promises, detained them to dine, and dismissed them confident of a perfect amnesty. Villeré, who had escaped, returned to the city.

On the morning of the eighth of August, the Spanish

squadron of four-and-twenty vessels, bearing three thousand chosen troops, anchored in front of New Orleans; before the day was over, possession was taken in behalf of the Catholic king, and the Spanish flag was raised at every post. On the twentieth, Aubry made a full report of the events of the revolution, and named its chiefs in the enterprise. "It was not easy to arrest them," wrote O'Reilly; "but I contrived to cheat their vigilance." On the twenty-first, he received at his home the principal inhabitants; and he invited the people's syndics, one by one, to pass into his private apartment. Each one accepted the invitation as a special honor, till, finding themselves assembled and alone, they showed signs of anxiety. "For me," says O'Reilly, "I now had none for the success of my plan." Entering his cabinet with Aubry and three Spanish civil officers, he spoke to those who were thus caught in his toils: "Gentlemen, the Spanish nation is venerated throughout the globe. Louisiana is the only country in the universe where it fails to meet with the respect which is its due. His Catholic majesty is greatly provoked at the violence to his governor, and at the publications outraging his government and the Spanish nation. You are charged with being the chiefs of this revolt; I arrest you in his name." The accused were conducted with ostentation to separate places of confinement; Villeré, to the frigate that lay at the levee. It is the tradition that his wife vainly entreated admission to him; that Villeré, hearing her voice, demanded to see her; became frantic with love, anger, and grief, struggled with his guard, and fell dead from passion or from their bayonets. The official report sets forth that he did not survive the first day of bondage.

The unexpected blow spread consternation. An amnesty for the people reserved the right of making further arrests. On the twenty-sixth and the following days, the inhabitants of New Orleans and its vicinity took the oath of allegiance to the Catholic king.

Nearly two months passed in collecting evidence against the devoted victims. They denied the jurisdiction of the Spanish tribunal over actions done under the flag of France during the prevalence of French laws. But the estates of the twelve, who were the richest and most considerable men in the province, were confiscated in whole or in part for the benefit of the officers employed in the trial; six were sentenced to imprisonment for six or ten years, or for life; the memory of Villeré was declared infamous; the remaining five, Lafrénière, his young son-in-law Noyau, Caresse, Marquis, and Joseph Milhet, were condemned to be hanged.

The citizens of New Orleans entreated time for a petition to Charles III.; the wives, daughters, and sisters of those who had not shared in the revolution appealed to O'Reilly for mercy, but without effect. Tradition will have it that the young and gallant Noyau, newly married, might have escaped; but he refused to fly from his associates. On the twenty-fifth of October, the five martyrs to their love of France and liberty were brought forth pinioned, and, in presence of the troops and the people, were shot. "At length," said O'Reilly, "the insult done to the king's dignity and authority in this province is repaired. The example now given can never be effaced." Spaniards, as well as men of other nations, censured the sanguinary revenge. In the parishes of Louisiana, O'Reilly was received with silent submission. The king of Spain approved his acts. By the intervention of France, the six prisoners were set free.

The census of the city of New Orleans showed a population of eighteen hundred and one white persons, thirty-one free blacks, sixty-eight free persons of mixed blood, sixty domiciliated Indians, and twelve hundred and twenty-five slaves: in all, three thousand one hundred and ninety souls. The population in the valley of the Mississippi, then subject to the Spanish sway, is estimated at thirteen thousand five hundred. The privileges granted by France were abolished, and the colony was organized like other possessions of Spain. But Spain willingly kept New Orleans depressed, that it might not attract the cupidity of England.

The settlement of the wilderness was promoted by native pioneers. Jonathan Carver, of Connecticut, had in three former years explored the borders of Lake Superior, and the country of the Sioux beyond it; had obtained more accurate accounts of the Great River, which bore, as he reported, the name of Oregon and flowed into the Pacific; and he returned to celebrate the richness of the copper mines of the North-west; to recommend English settlements on the western extremity of the continent; and to propose opening, by aid of lakes and rivers, a passage to the Pacific, as the best route for communicating with China and the East Indies.

Illinois invited emigrants more than ever, for its aboriginal inhabitants were fast disappearing. In April 1769, Pontiac had been assassinated by an Illinois Indian, in time of peace; the Indians of the North-west sent belts to all the nations to avenge the murder. In vain did five or six hundred of the Illinois crowd for protection round the walls of Fort Chartres; the ruthless spirit of reciprocal slaughter was not appeased till the Illinois tribes were nearly all exterminated.

Connecticut, which at this time was exercising a disputed jurisdiction in the valley of Wyoming, did not forget that by its charter its possessions extended indefinitely to the west; and a company of "military adventurers," headed by one of its most intelligent sons, was soliciting leave from England to found a colony on the Mississippi.

In his peaceful habitation on the banks of the Yadkin, in North Carolina, Daniel Boone had heard Finley, the memorable pioneer trader, describe a tract of land west of Virginia as the richest in North America, or in the world. In May 1769, having Finley as his pilot, and four others as companions, the young man, then about three-and-twenty, leaving his wife and offspring, wandered forth "in quest of the country of Kentucky," midway between the subjects of the Five Nations and the Cherokees, known to the savages as "the Dark and Bloody Ground." After a fatiguing journey through mountain ranges, the party found themselves in June on the Red river, a tributary of the Kentucky, and from the top of an eminence they surveyed with delight the beautiful plain that stretched to the north-west. Here they built their shelter, and began to reconnoitre the country and to hunt. All the kinds of wild beasts that were natural to America—the stately elk, the timid deer, the antlered stag, the wild-cat, the bear, the panther, and the wolf—couched among the canes, or roamed over the rich grasses which sprung luxuriantly even beneath the thickest shade. The buffaloes cropped fearlessly the herbage, or browsed on the leaves of the reed; sometimes there were hundreds in a drove, and round the salt licks their numbers were amazing.

The summer, in which for the first time a party of white men remained near the Elkhorn, passed away in explorations and the chase. But Boone's companions dropped off, till he was left alone with John Stewart. These two found unceasing delight in the wonders of the forest, till one evening, near Kentucky river, they were taken prisoners by a band of Indians, wanderers like themselves. They escaped, and were joined by Boone's brother; so that, when Stewart was soon after killed by savages, the first among the hecatombs of white men slain by them in their desperate battling for the lovely hunting-ground, Boone still had his brother to share with him the building and occupying of the first cottage in Kentucky.

In the spring of 1770, that brother returned to the settlements for horses and supplies of ammunition, leaving the renowned hunter "by himself, without bread, or salt, or sugar, or even a horse, or a dog." "The idea of a beloved wife," anxious for his safety, tinged his thoughts with sadness; but otherwise the cheerful, meditative man, careless of wealth, knowing the use of the rifle, though not the plough, of a strong, robust frame, in the vigorous health of early manhood, ignorant of books, but versed in forest life, ever fond of tracking the deer on foot, away from men, yet in his disposition humane, generous, and gentle, was happy in the uninterrupted succession "of sylvan pleasures."

He held unconscious intercourse with beauty
Old as creation.

One calm summer's evening, as he climbed a commanding ridge, and looked out upon remote "venerable mountains," the nearer ample plains, and the distant Ohio, his heart overflowed with gladness for the beautiful land which he had found. "All things were still." Not a breeze so much as shook a leaf. Kindling a fire near a fountain of sweet water, he feasted on the loin of a buck. He was no more alone than a bee among flowers, but communed familiarly with the whole universe of life. Nature was his intimate; and, as the contemplative woodsman leaned trustingly on her bosom, she responded to his love. For him, the rocks and the crystal springs, the leaf and the blade of grass, had life; the cooling air, laden with the wild perfume, came to him as a friend; the dewy morning wrapped him in its embrace; the trees stood up gloriously round about him, as so many myriads of companions. How could he be afraid? Triumphing over danger, he knew no fear. The nightly howling of the wolves, near his cottage or his bivouac in the brake, was his diversion; and by day he had joy in surveying the various species of animals that neighbored him. He loved the solitude better than the thrifty hamlet or rivalry with men. Near the end of July 1770, his faithful brother came back to him at the old camp; and they proceeded together to Cumberland river, giving names to the different waters. He then returned to his wife and children, fixed in his purpose, at the risk of life and fortune, to move them as soon as possible to Kentucky, which he held to be a second paradise.

Unlike this guileless rover were the plotters against Boston. "The lieutenant-governor well understands my system," wrote Bernard to Hillsborough, as he transferred his government. Hutchinson was descended from one of the earliest settlers of Massachusetts, and loved the land of his birth. A native of Boston, he was its representative for ten years, during three of which he was speaker of the assembly; for more than ten other years he was a member of the council, as well as judge of probate; since June 1758, he had been lieutenant-governor, and since September 1760, chief justice also; and twice he had been chosen colonial agent. No man was so experienced in the affairs of the colony, or so familiar with its history, usages, and laws. In the legislature, he had assisted to raise the credit of Massachusetts by substituting hard money for a paper currency. As a judge, though he decided political questions with the subserviency of a courtier, yet, in approving wills, he was considerate toward the orphan and the widow, and he heard private suits with unblemished integrity. In adjusting points of difference with a neighboring jurisdiction, he was faithful to the province by which he was employed. His advancement to administrative power was fatal to Britain and to himself; for the love of money, which was his ruling passion in youth, had grown with his years.

A nervous timidity, which was a part of his nature, had

been increased by age as well as by the riots on account of the stamp act, and at times made him false to his employers. While he cringed to the minister, he trembled before the people. At Boston, he professed zeal for the interests and liberties of the province; had at one time courted its favor by denying the right of parliament to tax America either internally or externally; and had argued with conclusive ability against the expediency and the equity of such a measure. He now redoubled his attempts to deceive; wrote patriotic letters which he never sent, but read to those about him as evidence of his good-will; and professed even to have braved hostility in England for his attachment to colonial liberties while he secretly gave in his adhesion to the absoluteness of metropolitan authority, and suggested a system of coercive measures, which England gradually and reluctantly adopted.

Wherever the colony had a friend, he would set before him such hints as might incline him to harsh judgments. Even to Franklin he vouched for the tales of Bernard as "most just and candid." He paid court to the enemies of American liberty by stimulating them to the full indulgence of their malignity. He sought out great men, and those who stood at the door of great men, the underlings of Grenville or Hillsborough or Jenkinson or the king, and urged incessantly the bringing on of the crisis by the immediate intervention of parliament. He advised the change of the charter of the province, as well as of those of Rhode Island and Connecticut; the dismemberment of Massachusetts; the diminution of the liberties of New England towns; the establishment of a citadel within the town of Boston; the stationing of a fleet in its harbor; the experiment of martial law; the transportation of "incendiaries" to England; the prohibition of the New England fisheries; with other measures, like closing the port of Boston, which he dared not trust to paper, and recommended only by insinuations and verbal messages. At the same time, he entreated the concealment of his solicitations. "Keep secret everything I write," said he to Whately, his channel for communicating with Grenville. "I have never yet seen any rational plan for a partial subjection," he writes to Jenkinson's influential friend, Mauduit, whom he retained as his own agent; "my sentiments upon these points should be concealed." Though he kept back many of his thoughts, he begged Bernard to burn his letters. "It will be happy if, in the next session, parliament make thorough work," he would write to the secretary of the board of trade; and then "caution" him to "suffer no parts of his letters to transpire." "I humbly entreat your lordship that my letters may not be made public," was his ever renewed prayer to successive secretaries of state, so that he conducted the government like one engaged in a conspiracy. But some of his letters could hardly fail to be discovered; and then it would be disclosed that he had laid snares for the life of patriots, and had urged the "thorough" overthrow of English liberty in America.

In New York, where the agreement of non-importation originated, every one, without so much as a single dissentient, approved it as wise and legal; men in high stations declared against the revenue acts; and the governor wished their repeal. His acquiescence in the associations for coercing that repeal led the moderate men among the patriots of New York to plan a union of the colonies in an American parliament, preserving the governments of the several colonies, and having the members of the general parliament chosen by their respective legislatures. Their confidence of immediate success assisted to make them alike disinclined to independence, and confident of bringing England to reason by suspending trade.

The people of Boston, stimulated by the scrupulous fidelity of New York, were impatient that a son of Bernard, two sons of Hutchinson, and about five others, would not accede to the agreement. At a meeting of merchants in Faneuil Hall, Hancock proposed to send for Hutchinson's two sons, hinting what was true, that their father was a partner with them in their late importations of tea. As the best means of coercion, it was voted not to purchase anything of the recusants; subscription papers to that effect were carried round from house to house, and everybody signed them.

The anniversary of the fourteenth of August was commemorated with unusual solemnity. Three or four hundred dined together in the open field at Dorchester; and, since the ministry had threatened the leading patriots with death for treason, the last of their forty-five toasts was: "Strong halters, firm blocks, and sharp axes, to such as deserve them." The famous liberty song was sung, and all the company with one heart joined in the chorus. At five in the afternoon they returned in a procession a mile and a half long, entered the town before dark, marched round the state-house, and quietly retired each to his own home.

Incensed at having been aspersed by the public officers in Boston in letters which had been laid before parliament, Otis, who was become almost irresponsible from his nearness to insanity, provoked an affray, in which he, being alone, was set upon by one of the commissioners of the customs, aided by bystanders, and was grievously injured by a blow on the head.

Early in October, a vessel, laden with goods shipped by English houses themselves, arrived at Boston. The military officers stood ready to protect the factors; but Hutchinson permitted the merchants to reduce the consignees to submission, and even directed his two sons to give up eighteen chests of tea, and enter fully into the agreement. Only four merchants held out; and their names, with those of the two sons of Hutchinson, whose sincerity was questioned, remain inscribed as infamous in the journals of the town of Boston. On the fifteenth, another ship arrived; again the troops looked on as bystanders, and witnessed the victory of the people.

New York next invited Boston to extend the agreement against importing until every act imposing duties should be repealed; and on the seventeenth, by the great influence of Molineux, Otis, Samuel Adams, and William Cooper, this new form was adopted.

On the eighteenth, the town, summoned together by lawful authority, made their "Appeal to the World." They refuted and covered with ridicule "the false and malicious aspersions" of Bernard, Gage, Hood, and the revenue officers; and adopted the language and intrepidity of Samuel Adams as their own. "A legal meeting of the town of Boston," these were their words, "is an assembly where a noble freedom of speech is ever expected and maintained; where men think as they please and speak as they think. Such an assembly has ever been the dread, often the scourge of tyrants. We should yet be glad that the ancient and happy union between Great Britain and this country might be restored. The taking off the duties on paper, glass, and painters' colors, upon commercial principles only, will not give satisfaction. Discontent runs through the continent upon much higher principles. Our rights are invaded by the revenue acts; therefore, until they are ALL repealed," "and the troops recalled," "the cause of our just complaints cannot be removed."

To meet this fearless and candid declaration, Hutchinson, through secret channels, sent word to Grenville, to Jenkinson and Hillsborough, that all would be set right if parliament, within the first week of its session, would change the municipal government of Boston, incapacitate its patriots to hold any public office, and restore the vigor of authority by decisive action. But, foreseeing the inaction of parliament, he wrote orders for a new and large supply of teas for his sons' shop; and instructed his correspondent how to send them to market, so as to elude the vigilance of the Boston committees.

On the twenty-eighth, a great multitude of people laid hold of an informer, besmeared him with tar and feathers, and, with the troops under arms as spectators, carted him through the town, which was illuminated for the occasion. Dalrymple and the two British regiments could not interfere unless Hutchinson should give the word. Terrified by the commotions, the only importers who had continued to stand out capitulated.

The local magistrates put the soldiers on trial for every transgression of the provincial laws. "If they touch you, run them through the bodies," said a captain in the twenty-ninth regiment to his soldiers, and he was indicted for the speech. In November, a true bill was found by the grand jury against Thomas Gage, as well as many others, "for slandering the town of Boston." "A military force," Hutchinson owned, "was of no sort of use," and was "perfectly despised." "Troops," said Samuel Adams, "which have heretofore been the terror of the enemies to liberty, parade the streets to become the objects of the contempt even of women and children." The menace that he and his friends should be arrested and shipped to England was no more heeded than idle words.

But a different turn was given to public thought when

Botetourt communicated to the assembly of Virginia the ministerial promises of a partial repeal of Townshend's taxes, and with the most solemn asseverations abdicated in the king's name all further intentions of taxing America, adding "that his majesty would rather forfeit his crown than keep it by deceit." The council, in its reply, advised the entire repeal of the existing taxes; the burgesses expressed their gratitude for "information sanctified by the royal word," and considered the king's influence to be pledged "toward perfecting the happiness of all his people." Botetourt was so pleased with their address that he praised their loyalty, and wished them freedom and happiness "till time should be no more."

The flowing and positive assurances of Botetourt encouraged the expectation that the unproductive tax on tea would be given up; such was his wish; and such the advice of Eden, the new lieutenant-governor of Maryland. To the legislature of New York, Colden, who, on the death of Moore, administered the government, announced "the greatest probability that the late duties imposed by the authority of parliament, so much to the dissatisfaction of the colonies, would be taken off in the ensuing session." The confident promise confirmed the loyalty of the house, though, by way of caution, they adopted and put upon their journals the resolves of Virginia.

In the seeming tendency to conciliation, the merchants of Boston, seeing that those of Philadelphia confined their agreement for non-importation to the repeal of Townshend's act, gave up their more extensive covenant, and, for the sake of union, reverted to their first stipulations. In the billeting act, the legislature of New York, gratified at the leave to issue bills of credit, sanctioned a compromise by a majority of one.

So all America confined its issue with Great Britain to the repeal of the act imposing a duty on tea. "Will not a repeal of all other duties satisfy the colonists?" asked one of the ministerial party, of Franklin, in London. And he answered: "I think not; it is not the sum paid in the duty on tea that is complained of as a burden, but the principle of the act, expressed in the preamble."

The question was not a narrow colonial one respecting threepence a pound duty on tea; it involved the reality of representative government. As the cause of the people was everywhere the same, South Carolina in December remitted to London ten thousand five hundred pounds currency to the society for supporting the bill of rights, that the liberties of Great Britain and America might alike be protected.

In Ireland, Bushe, the friend of Grattan, in imitation of Molineux, published "The Case of Great Britain and America," with a vehement invective against Grenville. "Hate him," said he to Grattan; "I hope you hate him." It was Grenville's speeches and Grenville's doctrine "that roused Grattan to enter on his great career in Ireland." In the history of the English people, this year marks the establishment of public meetings, under the lead of Yorkshire. The principle of representation, trampled upon by a venal parliament, was to be renovated by the influence of voluntary assemblies. "Can you conceive," wrote the anonymous Junius to the king, "that the people of this country will long submit to be governed by so flexible a house of commons? The oppressed people of Ireland give you every day fresh marks of their resentment. The colonists who left their native land for freedom and found it in a desert are looking forward to independence."

The meeting of parliament in January 1770 would decide whether the British empire was to escape dismemberment. Chatham recommended to the more liberal aristocracy the junction with the people, which, after sixty years, achieved the reform of the British constitution; but in that day it was opposed by the passions of Burke and the reluctance of the highborn.

The debate on the ninth turned on the rights of the people, and involved the complaints of America and of Ireland, not less than the disfranchisement of Wilkes. "It is vain and idle to found the authority of this house upon the popular voice," said Jenkinson. "The discontents that are held up as spectres," said Thomas de Grey, brother of the attorney-general, "are the senseless clamors of the thoughtless and the ignorant, the lowest of the rabble. The Westminster petition was obtained by a few despicable mechanics headed by baseborn people." "The privileges of the people of this country," interposed Sergeant Glynn, "do not depend upon birth and fortune; they hold their rights as Englishmen, and cannot be divested of them but by the subversion of the constitution." "Were it not for petition hunters and incendiaries," said Rigby, "the farmers of Yorkshire could not possibly take an interest in the Middlesex election of representatives in parliament. The majority, even of the freeholders, is no better than an ignorant multitude."

Up rose the representative of Yorkshire, "the spotless" Sir George Saville. "The greatest evil," said he, "that can befall this nation is the invasion of the people's rights by the authority of this house. I do not say that the majority have sold the rights of their constituents; but I do say, I have said, and I shall always say, that they have betrayed them. The people understand their own rights and know their own interests as well as we do; for a large paternal estate, a pension, and support in the treasury are greater recommendations to a seat in this assembly than either the honesty of the heart or the clearness of the head."

Gilmour invited censure on such unprecedented expressions; Conway excused them as uttered in heat. "I am not conscious," resumed Saville, "that I have spoken in heat; if I did, I have had time to cool, and I again say, as I said before, that this house has betrayed the rights of its constituents." "In times of less licentiousness," rejoined Gilmour, "members have been sent to the Tower for words of less offence." "The mean consideration of my own safety," answered Saville, "shall never be put in the balance against my duty to my constituents. I will own no superior but the laws, nor bend the knee to any but to Him who made me."

The accusation which Saville brought against the house of commons was the gravest that could be presented; if false, was an outrage, in comparison with which that of Wilkes was a trifle. But Lord North bore the reproach meekly, and soothed the majority into quietude. The debate proceeded, and presently Barré spoke: "The people of England know, the people of Ireland know, and the American people feel, that the iron hand of ministerial despotism is lifted up against them; but it is not less formidable against the prince than against the people." "The trumpeters of sedition have produced the disaffection," replied Lord North, speaking at great length. "The drunken ragamuffins of a vociferous mob are exalted into equal importance with men of judgment, morals, and property. I can never acquiesce in the absurd opinion that all men are equal. The contest in America, which at first might easily have been ended, is now for no less than sovereignty on one side, and independence on the other." The ministry, though vanquished in the argument, carried the house by a very large majority.

In the house of lords, Chatham, whose voice had not been heard for three years, proposed to consider the causes of the discontent which prevailed in so many parts of the British dominions. "I have not," said he, "altered my ideas with regard to the principles upon which America should be governed. I own I have a natural leaning toward that country; I cherish liberty wherever it is planted. America was settled upon ideas of liberty, and the vine has taken deep root and spread throughout the land. Long may it flourish. Call the combinations of the Americans dangerous, yet not unwarrantable. The discontent of two millions of people should be treated candidly; and its foundation removed. Let us save this constitution, dangerously invaded at home, and extend its benefits to the remotest corners of the empire. Let slavery exist nowhere among us; for whether it be in America, or in Ireland, or here at home, you will find it a disease which spreads by contact, and soon reaches from the extremity to the heart." Camden, whom Chatham's presence awed more than office attracted, awoke to his old friendship for America, and by implication accused his colleagues of conspiring against the liberties of the country.

Lord Mansfield, whose reply to Chatham "was a masterpiece of art and address," declined giving an opinion on the legality of the proceedings of the house of commons in reference to the Middlesex election, but contended that, whether they were right or wrong, the jurisdiction in the case belonged to them, and from their decision there was no appeal. "I distrust," rejoined Chatham, "the refinements of learning, which fall to the share of so small a number of men. Providence has taken better care of our happiness, and given us, in the simplicity of common sense, a rule for our direction by which we shall never be misled." The words were revolutionary. Scotland, in unconscious harmony with Kant and the ablest minds in Germany, was renovating philosophy by the aid of common sense and reason; Chatham transplanted the theory, so favorable to democracy, into the halls of legislation. "Power without right," he continued, aiming his invective at the venal house of commons, "is a thing hateful in itself, and ever inclining to its fall. Tyranny is detestable in every shape; but in none so formidable as when it is assumed and exercised by a number of tyrants." Though the house of lords opposed him by a vote of more than two to one, the ministry was shattered; and Chatham, feeble and emaciated as he was, sprang forward with the party of Rockingham, to beat down the tottering system, and raise on its ruins a government more friendly to liberty.

But the king was the best politician of them all. Dismissing Camden, he sent an offer of the chancellor's place to Charles Yorke, who was of the Rockingham connection. Yorke had long coveted the high dignity beyond anything on earth. Now that it was within his reach, he vacillated, wished delay, and put the temptation aside. "If you will not comply," said the king, "it must make an eternal breach between us." Yorke gave way, was reproached by Hardwicke his brother, and by Rockingham; begged his brother's forgiveness, kissed him, and parted friends; and then, with a fatal sensibility to fame, went home to die by his own hand. His appalling fate dismayed the ministry.

On the twenty-second, Rockingham, overcoming his nervous weakness, summoned resolution to make a long speech in the house of lords in favor of restraining the royal prerogative by privilege. While the leader of the great whig party cherished no hope of improvement from any change in the forms of the constitution, Chatham, once more the man of the people, rose to do service to succeeding generations. "Whoever," said he, "understands the theory of the English constitution, and will compare it with the fact, must see at once how widely they differ. We must reconcile them to each other, if we wish to save the liberties of this country. The constitution intended that there should be a permanent relation between the constituent and representative body of the people. As the house of commons is now formed, that relation is destroyed;" and he proceeded to open, as the mature result of long reflection, a most cautious beginning of parliamentary reform. The reform of the English parliament! How much must take place before that event can come about!

Shrinking from the storm, Grafton threw up his office. The king affected regret, but was prepared for it. He would not hear of trying Rockingham and his friends; and "as for Chatham," said he, "I will abdicate the crown sooner than consent to his requirements." Before the world knew of the impending change, he sent Weymouth and Gower, of the Bedford party, "to press Lord North in the most earnest manner to accept the office of first lord commissioner of the treasury," preceding their visit by a friendly autograph note of his own. Lord North did not hesitate; and the king exerted all his ability and his ten years' experience to establish his choice.

On the last day of January, the new prime minister, amid great excitement and the sanguine hopes of the opposition, appeared in the house of commons. "The ship of state," said Barré, "tossed on a stormy sea, is scudding under a jury-mast, and hangs out signals for pilots from the other side." "The pilots on board are very capable of conducting her into port," answered North; and he prevailed by a majority of forty. "A very handsome majority," said the king; "a very favorable auspice on your taking the lead in administration. A little spirit will soon restore order in my service." From that night the new tory party ruled the cabinet. Its opponents were divided between those who looked back to privilege as their harbor of refuge, and those who looked forward to an increase of popular power.

## CHAPTER XXVIII.

THE BOSTON "MASSACRE." LORD NORTH'S ADMINISTRATION.

### JANUARY–MARCH 1770.

"THE troops must move to the castle," said Samuel Adams; "it must be the first business of the general court to move them out of town." Otis went about declaiming that "the governor had power to do it by the constitution." "We consider this metropolis, and indeed the whole province, under duress," wrote Cooper, the minister. "The troops greatly corrupt our morals, and are in every sense an oppression;" and his New Year's prayer to heaven asked deliverance from their presence.

The Massachusetts assembly was to meet on the tenth of January, and distant members were on their journey, when Hutchinson suddenly prorogued it to the middle of March. The delay prevented any support of its petition against Bernard. The reason assigned for the prorogation was neither the good of the colony nor the judgment of the lieutenant-governor, but a pretended instruction from Hillsborough; and of such an instruction, if it had existed, Samuel Adams denied the validity.

The spirit of non-importation had not abated; yet, as tea had advanced one hundred per cent, Hutchinson, who was himself a very large importer of it, could no longer restrain his covetousness. His two eldest sons, therefore, who were his agents, violating their engagement, broke open the lock, of which they had given the key to the committee of merchants, and secretly made sales. "Do they imagine," asked Samuel Adams, "they can still weary the patience of an injured country with impunity?" and avowing that, in the present case, the will of society was not declared in its laws, he called not on the merchants only, but on every individual of every class in city and country, to compel the strictest adherence to the agreement. "This," said Bernard's friends, "is as good a time as any to call out the troops;" for they thought it best to bring matters "to extremities," and Dalrymple ordered his men to equip themselves with twelve rounds for an attack.

The merchants, in pursuance of a vote at a very full meeting, went in a body to the house of the Hutchinsons. Allowing none of them to enter, the lieutenant-governor himself threw up a window, and pretended to charge them with a tumultuous and menacing application to him as chief magistrate. "We come," they answered, "to treat with your sons, who have violated their own contract, to which they had pledged their honor." "A contract," answered Hutchinson, from the window, "without a valuable consideration is not valid in law;" but he remained in great perplexity, fearing loss of property by riot. Early the next morning, he sent for the upright William Phillips, the moderator of the meeting, and engaged for his sons to deposit the price of the tea that had been sold, and to return the rest. The capitulation was reported to the meeting, and accepted.

"He has now thrown down the reins into the hands of the people," cried the customs' commissioners, "and he can never recover them." "I am a ruined man," said he, despondingly, to Phillips. "I humbly hope," thus he wrote to those who dealt out offices in London, "that a single error in judgment will not cancel more than thirty years' laborious and disinterested services in support of government." He looked to his council; and they would take no part in breaking up the system of non-importation. He called in all the justices who lived within fifteen miles; and they thought it not incumbent on them to interrupt the proceedings. He sent the sheriff into the adjourned meeting of the merchants with a letter to the moderator, requiring them in his majesty's name to disperse; and the meeting, of which justices of peace, selectmen, representatives, constables, and other officers made a part, sent him an answer that their assembly was warranted by law. He saw that the answer was in Hancock's handwriting; and he treasured up the autograph, to be produced should Hancock one day be put on trial.

"It is hard," said Trumbull, governor of Connecticut, "to break connections with our mother country; but, when she strives to enslave us, the strictest union must be dissolved. The accomplishment of some notable prophecies is at hand."

The liberty pole raised by the people of New York in the Park stood safely for nearly three years. The soldiery, in February, resolved to cut it down, and, after three repulses, succeeded. The people, assembling in the fields to the number of three thousand, and, without planning retaliation, expressed abhorrence of the soldiers, as enemies to the constitution and to the peace of the city. The soldiers replied by an insulting placard; and, on two successive days, engaged in an affray with the citizens, in which the latter had the advantage. The newspapers loudly celebrated the victory; and the Sons of Liberty, purchasing a piece of land near the junction of Broadway and the high road to Boston, erected a pole, strongly guarded by iron bands and bars, and inscribed "Liberty and Property." At the same time, Macdougall, son of a Presbyterian of the Scottish isle of Ila, having publicly censured the act of the assembly in voting supplies to the troops, was indicted for a libel; and, refusing to give bail, this "first Son of Liberty in bonds for the glorious cause" was visited by such throngs in his prison that he was obliged to appoint hours for their reception.

The men of Boston emulously applauded the spirit of the "Yorkers." Hatred of the parliament's taxes spread into every social circle. One week three hundred wives of Boston, the next a hundred and ten more, with one hundred and twenty-six of the young and unmarried of their sex, renounced the use of tea till the revenue acts should be repealed. How could the troops interfere? Everybody knew that it was against the law for them to fire without the authority of a civil magistrate; and the more they paraded with their muskets and twelve rounds of ball, the more they were despised, as men who desired to terrify and had no power to harm. Hutchinson was taunted with wishing to destroy town-meetings, through which he himself had risen; and the press, calling to mind his days of shopkeeping, jeered him as in former days a notorious smuggler.

Theophilus Lillie, who had begun to sell contrary to the agreement, found a post planted before his door, with a hand pointed toward his house in derision. Richardson, an informer, asked a countryman to break the post down by driving the wheel of his cart against it. A crowd of boys chased Richardson to his own house and threw stones. Provoked but not endangered, he fired among them, and killed a boy of eleven years old, the son of a poor German. At his funeral, five hundred children walked in front of the bier; six of his schoolfellows held the pall; and men of all ranks moved in procession from Liberty Tree to the town-house, and thence to the "burying-place." Soldiers and officers looked on with wounded pride. Dalrymple was impatient to be set to work in Boston, or to be ordered elsewhere. The common soldiers of the twenty-ninth regiment were notoriously bad fellows, licentious and overbearing. "I never will miss an opportunity of firing upon the inhabitants," said one of them, Kilroi by name. It was a common feeling in the regiment. A year and a half's training had perfected the people in their part. It was no breach of the law for them to express contempt for the soldiery; they were ready enough to confront them, but they were taught never to do it, except to repel an attack. If any of the soldiers broke the law, which they often did, complaints were still made to the local magistrates, who were ever ready to afford redress. On the other hand, the officers screened their men from legal punishment, and sometimes even rescued them from the constables.

On Friday, the second day of March, a soldier of the twenty-ninth asked to be employed at Gray's rope-walk, and was repulsed in the coarsest words. He then defied the ropemakers to a boxing match; and, one of them accepting his challenge, he was beaten off. Returning with several of his companions, they too were driven away. A larger number came down to renew the fight with clubs and cutlasses, and in their turn encountered defeat. By this time, Gray and others interposed, and for that day prevented further disturbance.

At the barracks, the soldiers inflamed each other's passions, as if the honor of the regiment were tarnished. On Saturday, they prepared bludgeons, and, being resolved to brave the citizens on Monday night, they forewarned their particular acquaintances not to be abroad. Without duly restraining his men, Carr, the lieutenant-colonel of the twenty-ninth, made complaint to the lieutenant-governor of the insult they had received. The council, deliberating on Monday, seemed of opinion that the town would never be safe from quarrels between the people and the soldiers, as long as soldiers should be quartered among them. In the present case, the owner of the ropewalk gave satisfaction by dismissing the workman complained of. The officers should, on their part, have kept their men within the barracks after nightfall; instead of it, they left them to roam the streets. Hutchinson should have insisted on measures of precaution; but he too much wished the favor of all who had influence at Westminster.

The evening of the fifth came on. The young moon was shining in a cloudless winter sky, and its light was increased by a new-fallen snow. Parties of soldiers were driving about the streets, making a parade of valor, challenging resistance, and striking the inhabitants indiscriminately with sticks or sheathed cutlasses.

A band, which poured out from Murray's barracks in Brattle street, armed with clubs, cutlasses, and bayonets, provoked resistance, and a fray ensued. Ensign Maul, at the gate of the barrack yard, cried to the soldiers: "Turn out, and I will stand by you; kill them; stick them; knock them down; run your bayonets through them." One soldier after another levelled a firelock, and threatened to "make a lane" through the crowd. Just before nine, as an officer crossed King street, now State street, a barber's lad cried after him: "There goes a mean fellow who hath not paid my master for dressing his hair;" on which the sentinel, stationed at the westerly end of the custom house, on the corner of King street and Exchange lane, left his post, and with his musket gave the boy a stroke on the head that made him stagger and cry for pain.

The street soon became clear, and nobody troubled the sentry, when a party of soldiers issued violently from the main guard, their arms glittering in the moonlight, and passed on, hallooing: "Where are they? where are they? Let them come." Presently twelve or fifteen more, uttering the same cries, rushed from the south into King street, and so by way of Cornhill, toward Murray's barracks. "Pray, soldiers, spare my life," cried a boy of twelve, whom they met. "No, no, I'll kill you all," answered one of them, and with his cutlass knocked him down. They abused and insulted several persons at their doors and others in the street, "running about like madmen in a fury," crying, "Fire!" which seemed their watchword, and "Where are they? knock them down." Their outrageous behavior occasioned the ringing of the bell at the head of King street.

The citizens, whom the alarm set in motion, came out with canes and clubs, and, partly by the courage of Crispus Attucks, a mulatto of nearly fifty years old, and some others, partly by the interference of well-disposed officers, the fray at the barracks was soon over. Of the citizens, the prudent shouted, "Home! home!" others, it was said, called out, "Huzza for the main guard! there is the nest;" but the main guard was not molested the whole evening.

A body of soldiers came up Royal Exchange lane, crying, "Where are the cowards?" and, brandishing their arms, passed through King street. From ten to twenty boys came after them, asking, "Where are they? where are they?" "There is the soldier who knocked me down," said the barber's boy, and they began pushing one another toward the sentinel. He loaded and primed his musket. "The lobster is going to fire," cried a boy. Waving his piece about, the sentinel pulled the trigger. "If you fire, you must die for it," said Henry Knox, who was passing by. "I don't care," replied the sentry; "if they touch me, I'll fire." "Fire!" shouted the boys, for they were persuaded he could not do it without leave from a civil officer, and a young fellow spoke out, "We will knock him down for snapping," while they whistled through their fingers and huzzaed. "Stand off!" said the sentry, and shouted aloud, "Turn out, main guard!" "They are killing the sentinel," reported a servant from the custom-house, running to the main guard. "Turn out! why don't you turn out?" cried Preston, who was captain of the day, to the guard. "He appeared in a great flutter of spirits," and "spoke to them roughly." A party of six, two of whom, Kilroi and Montgomery, had been worsted at the rope-walk, formed with a corporal in front and Preston following. With bayonets fixed, they "rushed through the people" upon the trot, cursing them, and pushing them as they went along. They found about ten persons round the sentry, while about fifty or sixty came down with them. "For God's sake," said Knox, holding Preston by the coat, "take your men back again; if they fire, your life must answer for the consequences." "I know what I am about," said he hastily, and much agitated. None pressed on them or provoked them, till they began loading, when a party of about twelve in number, with sticks in their hands, moved from the middle of the street where they had been standing, gave three cheers, and passed along the front of the soldiers, whose muskets some of them struck as they went by. "You are cowardly rascals," they said, "for bringing arms against naked men." "Lay aside your guns, and we are ready for you." "Are the soldiers loaded?" inquired Palmes of Preston. "Yes," he answered, "with powder and ball." "Are they going to fire upon the inhabitants?" asked Theodore Bliss. "They cannot, without my orders," replied Preston; while "the town-born" called out, "Come on, you rascals, you bloody backs, you lobster scoundrels, fire, if you dare. We know you dare not." Just then Montgomery received a blow from a stick which had hit his musket, and the word "Fire!" being given by Preston, he stepped a little on one side, and shot Attucks, who at the time was quietly leaning on a long stick. The people immediately began to move off. "Don't fire!" said Langford, the watchman, to Kilroi, looking him full in the face; but yet he did so, and Samuel Gray, who was standing next Langford, with his hands in his bosom, fell lifeless. The rest fired slowly and in succession on the people, who were dispersing. One aimed deliberately at a boy, who was running in a zigzag line for safety. Montgomery then pushed at Palmes to stab him; on which the latter knocked his gun out of his hand, and, levelling a blow at him, hit Preston. Three persons were killed, among them Attucks the mulatto; eight were wounded, two of them mortally.

Of the eleven, not more than one had had any share in the disturbance.

When the men returned to take up the dead, the infuriated soldiers prepared to fire again, but were checked by Preston, while the twenty-ninth regiment appeared under arms in King street. "This is our time," cried soldiers of the fourteenth, and dogs were never seen more greedy for their prey.

The bells rung in all the churches; the town drums beat. "To arms! to arms!" was the cry. All the sons of Boston came forth, nearly distracted by the sight of the dead bodies, and of the blood, which ran plentifully in the street, and was imprinted in all directions by foot-tracks on the snow. "Our hearts," says Warren, "beat to arms, almost resolved by one stroke to avenge the death of our slaughtered brethren;" but, self-possessed, they demanded justice according to the law. "Did you not know that you should not have fired without the order of a civil magistrate?" asked Hutchinson, on meeting Preston. "I did it," answered Preston, "to save my men."

The people would not be pacified or retire till the regiment was confined to the guard-room and the barracks, and Hutchinson himself gave assurances that instant inquiries should be made by the county magistrates. One hundred persons remained to keep watch on the examination, which lasted till three hours after midnight. A warrant was issued against Preston, who surrendered himself to the sheriff, and the soldiers of his party were delivered up and committed to prison.

The next morning, the selectmen of the town and the justices of the county spoke with Hutchinson at the council chamber. "The inhabitants," said the former, "will presently meet, and cannot be appeased while the troops are among them." Quincy, of Braintree, on behalf of the justices, pointed out the danger of "the most terrible consequences." "I have no power to remove the troops," said Hutchinson, "nor to direct where they shall be placed;" but Dalrymple and Carr, the commanding officers, attended on his invitation in council, and the subject was "largely discussed."

At eleven, the town-meeting was opened in Faneuil Hall with prayer by Cooper; then Samuel Adams and fourteen others, among them Hancock and Molineux, were chosen to proceed to the council chamber, where in the name of the town they delivered this message: "The inhabitants and soldiery can no longer live together in safety; nothing can restore peace and prevent further carnage but the immediate removal of the troops."

Hutchinson desired to parley with them. "The people," they answered, "not only in this town, but in all the neighboring towns, are determined that the troops shall be removed." "An attack on the king's troops," replied Hutchinson, "would be high treason, and every man concerned would forfeit his life and estate." The committee, unmoved, recalled his attention to their peremptory demand, and withdrew.

My readers will remember that the instructions from the king, which placed the army above the civil power in America, contained a clause that, where there was no officer of the rank of brigadier, the governor of the colony or province might give the word. Dalrymple accordingly offered to obey the lieutenant-governor, who, on his part, neither dared to bid the troops remain nor order their withdrawal. So the opinion which had been expressed by Bernard during the last summer and at the time had been approved by Dalrymple, was called to mind as the rule for the occasion. The lieutenant-governor acquainted the town's committee that the twenty-ninth regiment, which was particularly concerned in the late differences, should without delay be placed at the castle, and the fourteenth only be retained in town under efficient restraint. Saying this, he adjourned the council to the afternoon.

As Faneuil Hall could not hold the throng from the surrounding country, the town had adjourned to the Old South meeting-house. The street between the state-house and that church was filled with people. "Make way for the committee!" was the shout of the multitude, as Samuel Adams came out from the council chamber, and, baring his head, which was already becoming gray, moved through their ranks, inspiring confidence.

To the people, who crowded even the gallery and isles of the spacious meeting-house, he made his report, and pronounced the answer insufficient. On ordinary occasions he seemed like ordinary men; but, in moments of crisis, he rose naturally and unaffectedly to the highest dignity, and spoke as if the hopes of humanity hung on his words. The town, after deliberation, raised a new and smaller committee, composed of Samuel Adams, Hancock, Molineux, William Phillips, Warren, Henshaw, and Pemberton, to bear their final message. They found the lieutenant-governor surrounded by the council and by the highest officers of the British army and navy on the station.

Hutchinson had done all he could to get Samuel Adams shipped to England as a traitor; at this most important moment in their lives, the patriot and the courtier stood face to face. "It is the unanimous opinion of the meeting," said Samuel Adams to him, "that the reply made to the vote of the inhabitants in the morning is unsatisfactory; nothing less will satisfy than a total and immediate removal of all the troops." "The troops are not subject to my authority," repeated Hutchinson; "I have no power to remove them." Stretching forth his arm, which slightly shook, as if "his frame trembled at the energy of his soul," in tones not loud, but clear and distinctly audible, Adams rejoined: "If you have power to remove one regiment, you have power to remove both. It is at your peril if you do not. The meeting is composed of three thousand people. They are become very impatient. A thousand men are already arrived from the neighborhood, and the country is in general motion. Night is approaching; an immediate answer is expected." As he spoke he gazed intently on his irresolute adversary. "Then," said Adams, who not long afterward described the scene, "at the appearance of the determined citizens, peremptorily demanding the redress of grievances, I observed his knees to tremble; I saw his face grow pale; and I enjoyed the sight." As the committee left the council chamber, Hutchinson was going back in his reverie to the days of the revolution of 1688. He saw, in his mind, Andros seized and imprisoned, and the people instituting a new government; he reflected that the citizens of Boston and the country about it were become four times as numerous as in those days, and their "spirit full as high." He fancied them insurgent, and himself their captive; and he turned to the council for advice. "It is not such people as formerly pulled down your house who conduct the present measures," said Tyler; "but they are people of the best characters among us, men of estates, and men of religion. It is impossible for the troops to remain in town; there will be ten thousand men to effect their removal, be the consequence what it may."

Russell of Charlestown, and Dexter of Dedham, a man of superior ability, confirmed what was said. They spoke truly; men were ready to come from the hills of Worcester county and from the vale of the Connecticut. The council unanimously advised sending the troops to the castle forthwith. "It is impossible for me," said Dalrymple again and again, weakening the force of what he said by frequently repeating it, "to go any further lengths in this matter. The information given of the intended rebellion is a sufficient reason against the removal of his majesty's forces."

"You have asked the advice of the council," said Gray to the lieutenant-governor; "they have given it unanimously; you are bound to conform to it." "If mischief should come, by means of your not joining with us," pursued Irving, "the whole blame must fall upon you; but if you join with us, and the commanding officer after that should refuse to remove the troops, the blame will then be at his door." Hutchinson finally agreed with the council, and Dalrymple assured him of his obedience. The town's committee, being informed of this decision, left the state-house to make their welcome report to the meeting. The inhabitants listened with the highest satisfaction; but, ever vigilant, they provided measures for keeping up a strong military watch of their own, until the regiments should leave the town.

It was a humiliation to the officers and soldiers to witness the public funeral of the victims of the fifth of March; but they complained most of the watch set over them. The colonel of the town militia had, however, taken good legal advice, and showed the old province law under which he acted; and the justices of the peace in their turns attended every night during its continuance. The British officers gnashed their teeth at the contempt into which they had been brought. The troops came to overawe the people and maintain the laws; and they were sent as law-breakers to a prison rather than to a garrison. "There," said Edmund Burke, "was an end of the spirited way we took, when the question was whether Great Britain should or should not govern America."

## CHAPTER XXIX.

THE KING VIOLATES THE CHARTER OF MASSACHUSETTS.

March–October 1770.

The removal of the troops from Boston smoothed the way for conciliation. The town was resolved on bringing to trial the officer who had given the command to fire without the sanction of the civil authority and the men who had obeyed the order, that the supremacy of the civil authority might be vindicated; at the same time, it wished to the prisoners every opportunity of defence.

The instructions which the town of Boston, adopting the language of the younger Quincy, in May 1770, addressed to the representatives of its choice, made a plain reference to the Bedford protest, which appeared in the journals of the house of lords as evidence of "a desperate plan of imperial despotism," which was to be resisted, if necessary, "even unto the uttermost;" and therefore martial virtues and the lasting union of the colonies were recommended.

Of this document, Hutchinson made an effective use; and its reception contributed to that new set of measures, which hastened American independence by seeking to crush its spirit. England assumed a design for a general revolt, when there only existed a desire to guard against "innovations."

Hutchinson called the first legislature, elected since he became governor, to meet at Cambridge. "Not the least shadow of necessity," said the house in its remonstrance, "exists for it. Prerogative is a discretionary power vested in the king only for the good of the subject." Hutchinson had overacted his part, and found himself embarrassed by his own arbitrary act, for which he dared not assign the true reason, and could not assign a good one. The house censured his conduct by a vote of ninety-six against six, and refused to proceed to any other business than that of organizing the government.

In July, Hutchinson once more summoned the legislature to Cambridge, for which he continued to offer no other excuse than his instructions. The highest advocate for regal power had never gone so far as to claim that it might be used at caprice, to inflict wanton injury. There was no precedent for the measure but during the worst of times in England, or in France, where a parliament had sometimes been worried into submission by exile. Moreover, the plea was false, for Hillsborough had left him discretionary power; and he acted on the advice of Bernard, whom he feared to disregard.

The assembly asserted in the strongest terms the superiority of the legislative body to royal instructions; and, in answer to the old question of what is to be done upon the abusive exercise of the prerogative, they went back to the principles of the revolution and the words of Locke: "In this as in all other cases, where they have no judge on earth, the people have no remedy but to appeal to heaven." They drew a distinction between the king and his servants; and attributed to "wicked ministers" the encroachments on their liberty, as well as "the impudent mandate" to one assembly "to rescind an excellent resolution of a former one."

On the third of August, Hutchinson communicated to the house that the instruction to rescind, which they had called an impudent mandate, was an order from the king himself, whose "immediate attention," he assured them, they would not be able "to escape." In this manner the royal dignity and character were placed on trial before a colonial assembly, and monarchy itself was exposed to contempt.

It was for England to remove the cause of the strife. In the house of lords, Chatham, affirming, as he had done four years before, the subordination of the colonies and the right of parliament to bind their trade and industry, disclaimed the American policy adopted by his colleagues when he was nominally the minister. "The idea of drawing money from the Americans by taxes was ill-judged; trade is your object with them. Those millions are the industrious hive who keep you employed;" and he invited the entire repeal of the revenue act of Charles Townshend.

On the evening of the fifth of March, in the house of commons, Lord North founded a motion for a partial relief; not on the petitions of America, because they were marked by a denial of the right, but on one from merchants and traders of London. "The subject," said he, "is of the highest importance. The combinations and associations of the Americans for the temporary interruption of trade have already been called unwarrantable in an address of this house; I will call them insolent and illegal. The duties upon paper, glass, and painters' colors bear upon the manufacturers of this country, and ought to be taken off. It was my intention to have extended the proposal to the removal of the other duties; but the Americans have not deserved indulgence. The preamble to the act and the duty on tea must be retained, as a mark of the supremacy of parliament and the efficient declaration of its right to govern the colonies.

"I saw nothing unjust, uncommercial, or unreasonable in the stamp act; nothing but what Great Britain might fairly demand of her colonies; America took flame and united against it. If there had been a permanence of ministers, if there had been a union of Englishmen in the cause of England, that act would at this moment have been subsisting. I was much inclined to yield to the many, who desire that the duty upon tea should be repealed. But tea is, of all commodities, the properest for taxation. The duty is an external tax, such as the Americans have admitted the right of parliament to impose. It is one of the best of all the port duties. When well established, it will go a great way toward giving additional support to our government and judicatures in America. If we are to run after America in search of reconciliation, I do not know a single act of parliament that will remain. Are we to make concessions to these people, because they have the hardihood to set us at defiance? No authority was ever confirmed by the concession of any point of honor or of right. Shall I give up my right? No, not in the first step. New York has kept strictly to its agreements; but the infractions of them by the people of Boston show that they will soon come to nothing.

The necessities of the colonies and their want of union will open trade. If they should attempt manufacturing and be likely to succeed, it is in our power to make laws, and so to check the manufactures in America for many years to come. This method I will try before I will give up my right."

Thomas Pownall moved the repeal of the duty on tea. The house of commons, like Lord North in his heart, was disposed to do the work of conciliation thoroughly. It was known that Grenville would not give an adverse vote. "It is the sober opinion of the Americans," said Mackay, fresh from the military command in Boston, "that you have no right to tax them. When beaten out of every argument, they adduce the authority of the first man of the law, and the first man of the state." Grenville assumed fully the responsibility of the stamp act; but he revealed to the house that taxing America had been the wish of the king. On the present occasion, had the king's friends remained neutral, the duty on tea would have been repealed; with all their exertions, in a full house, the majority for retaining it was but sixty-two. Lord North seemed hardly satisfied with his success; and reserved to himself liberty to accede to the repeal, on some agreement with the East India company.

The decision came from the king, who was the soul of the ministry, busying himself even with the details of affairs. He had many qualities that become a sovereign: temperance, regularity, and industry; decorous manners and unaffected piety; frugality in his personal expenses, so that his pleasures laid no burden on his people; a moderation which made him averse to wars of conquest; courage, which dared to assume responsibility, and could even contemplate death serenely; a fortitude that rose with adversity.

But he was bigoted, morbidly impatient of being ruled, and incapable of reconciling the need of reform with the establishments of the past. He was the great founder and head of the new tory or conservative party, which had become dominant through his support. In zeal for authority, hatred of reform, and antipathy to philosophical freedom and to popular power, he was inflexibly obstinate and undisguised; nor could he be justly censured for dissimulation, except for that disingenuous ness which studies the secret characters of men, in order to use them as its instruments. No one could tell whether the king really liked him. He could flatter, cajole, and humor, or frown and threaten; he could conceal the sense of injuries and forget good service; bribe the corrupt by favors, or terrify deserters by punishment. In bestowing rewards, it was his rule to make none but revocable grants; and he required of his friends an implicit obedience. He was willing to govern through parliament, yet was ready to stand by his ministers, even in a minority; and he was sure that one day the government must disregard majorities.

With a strong physical frame, he had a nervous susceptibility which made him rapid in his utterance; and so impatient of contradiction that he never could bear the presence of a minister who resolutely differed from him, and was easily thrown into a state of excitement bordering upon madness. Anger, which changed Chatham into a seer, pouring floods of light upon his mind and quickening his discernment, served only to cloud the mind of George III., so that he could not hide his thoughts from those about him, and, if using the pen, could neither spell correctly nor write coherently. Hence the proud, unbending Grenville was his aversion; and his years with the compliant Lord North, though full of public disasters, were the happiest of his life. Conscious of his devotion to the cause of legitimate authority, and viewing with complacency his own correctness of morals, he identified himself with the cause which he venerated. The crown was to him the emblem of all rightful power. He had that worst quality of evil, that he, as it were, adored himself; and regarded opposition to his designs as an offence against integrity and patriotism. He thought no exertions too great to crush the spirit of revolution, and no punishment too cruel or too severe for rebels.

The chaotic state of parties in England, at this period of transition from their ancient forms, favored the king's purposes. The liberal branch of the aristocracy had accomplished the duty it had undertaken, and had not yet discovered the service on which humanity would employ it next. The old whig party, which was fast becoming the party of the past, could hold office only by making an alliance with the party of the future. For eighty years they had fought strenuously alike against the prerogative and against the people; but time, which is the greatest of all innovators, was changing their political relations. The present king found the whig aristocracy divided; and he readily formed a coalition with that part of it which respected the established forms more than the spirit of the revolution. No combination could succeed against this organized conservatism of England, but one which should insist on a nearer harmony between the liberal principles which inspired the revolution and the aristocratic form to which it confined the British constitution. As yet, Rockingham and his adherents avowed the same political creed with Bedford, and were less friendly to reform than Grenville. When Burke and Wedderburn acted together, the opposition wore the aspect of a selfish struggle of the discontented for place; and the old whig aristocracy, continuing its war against the people as well as against the king, fell more and more into disrepute. A few commoners, Chatham and Shelburne and Stanhope among the peers, cried out for parliamentary reform; they were opposed by the members of the great whig connection, who may have had a good will to public liberty, but were too haughty to learn of men of humble birth. The king, therefore, had nothing to fear from an opposition. The changing politicians were eager to join his standard; and, while the great seal was for a time put in commission, Thurlow superseded the liberal Dunning.

The new solicitor-general, whose "majestic sense" and capacity were greatly overrated, had a coarse nature and a bad heart; was strangely profane in language, and reckless of morals and of decorum in domestic life. He enjoyed the credit of being fearless of the aristocracy, because his manners were rough; but no man was more subservient to their interests. Lord North governed himself on questions of law by his advice; and Thurlow proved the evil genius of that minister and of England. Toward America no man was more unrelenting.

Plans were revived for admitting representatives from the American colonies into the British house of commons; but they attracted little attention. On the ninth of April, one more attempt was made to conciliate America; and Trecothick, supported by Beckford and Lord Beauchamp, by Dowdeswell, Conway, Dunning, and Sir George Saville, proposed the repeal of the duty on tea. The king was indignant at this "debate in the teeth of a standing order," on a proposal which had already been voted down. "I wish to conciliate the Americans, and to restore harmony to the two countries," said Lord North; "but I will never be intimidated by the threats nor compelled by the combinations of the colonies to make unreasonable or impolitic concessions." So the next order of the day was called for by a vote of eighty to fifty-two.

A few days later, the news of the Boston "massacre," as it was named in Boston, reached England. "God forbid," said Grenville, in the house of commons, on the twenty-sixth of April, "we should send soldiers to act without civil authority." "Let us have no more angry votes against the people of America," cried Lord Beauchamp. "The officers agreed in sending the soldiers to Castle William; what minister," asked Barré, "will dare to send them back to Boston?" "The very idea of a military establishment in America," said William Burke, "is wrong." In a different spirit, Lord Barrington proposed to change the too democratical charter of Massachusetts.

The American question became more and more complicated with the history and the hopes of freedom in England. The country was suffering from the excess of aristocracy; Edmund Burke prescribed more aristocracy as the cure. Chatham, unable to obtain from Rockingham the acceptance of his own far-reaching views, stepped forward, almost alone, as the champion of the people. "I pledge myself to their cause," said he in the house of lords, on the first of May, "for it is the cause of truth and justice." Stanhope gave the same pledge. "I trust the people of this country," said Camden, "will renew their claims to true and free and equal representation, as their inherent and unalienable right." Shelburne insisted that Lord North, for his agency with regard to the Middlesex elections, deserved impeachment.

In the commons, Burke, arraigning the new minister, spoke merely as a partisan. The chief supporter of Burke was Wedderburn, who said: "Lord Hillsborough is unfit for his office;

the nation suffers by his continuance; the people have a right to say they will not be under the authority of the sword. At the close of the last reign, you had the continent of America in one compact country. Not quite ten years have passed over, and, by domestic mismanagement, all America, the fruit of so many years' settlement, is lost to the crown of Great Britain in the reign of George III." Lord North questioned the veracity of Wedderburn, and exposed the ill-cemented coalition as having no plan beyond the removal of the present ministers. "God forgive the noble lord for the idea of there being a plan to remove him," retorted Wedderburn; "I know no man of honor and respectability who would undertake to do the duties of the situation." Burke's resolutions, which were only censures of the past, were defeated by a vote of more than two to one. When like resolutions were brought forward in the house of lords, Chatham would not attend the debate, but placed himself before the nation as the guide to "a more full and equal representation."

Meantime, in America, the difficulty of binding a continent by separate associations for preventing importations was becoming uncontrollable. Carolina and Georgia, and even Maryland and Virginia, had increased their importations; New England and Pennsylvania had imported nearly one half as much as usual; New York alone had been true to its engagement, and its imports had fallen off more than five parts in six. It was impatient of a system of renunciation which was so unequally kept. Merchants of New York, therefore, consulted those of Philadelphia on a general importation of all articles except tea; the Philadelphians favored the proposition, till a letter arrived from Franklin, urging them to persevere on their original plan. Sears and Macdougall in New York resisted concession; but men went from ward to ward to take the opinions of the people, and it was found that eleven hundred and eighty against three hundred were disposed to confine the restriction to tea alone. An appeal was again taken to the people; and, as the majority favored resuming importations, the July packet, which had been detained for a few days, sailed before the middle of the month with orders for all other merchandise. "Send us your old liberty pole, as you can have no further use for it," said the Philadelphians. The students at Princeton, one of whom was James Madison, appeared in their black gowns, and, with the bell tolling, burned the New York merchants' letter in the college yard. Boston tore it into pieces and threw it to the winds. South Carolina, whose patriots had just raised a statue to Chatham, read it with disdainful anger. At a meeting of the planters, merchants, and mechanics of Charleston, Thomas Lynch, a man of sense and inflexible firmness, strove to keep alive the spirit of resistance, and even shed tears for the expiring liberty of his country. He was seconded by Gadsden, and by John Mackenzie, whose English education at Cambridge had increased his ability to defend the rights of the colonies. But South Carolina alone could neither continue non-importation nor devise a new system. There was no help; so far, Lord North had reasoned correctly; the non-importation agreement had been enforced by New York alone, and now trade between America and Britain was open in everything but TEA.

The ministry and the king, when they carried the repeal of every measure offensive to the Americans except the tax on tea and its preamble, gained a most commanding position. If the Americans should be able to forego the use of, tea, the British exchequer would be in no worse condition than before. It might prove impossible for a people so widely dispersed to act in concert; and opportunities for conciliation and concession would arise with the return of commerce and tranquillity. Never was there a moment when prudence demanded of the supreme power to do nothing but watch and wait. The cardinal policy of New York was the security and development of colonial liberty through an American constitution, resting upon a union of the colonies in one general congress, without dissolving the connection with Great Britain, the very system which is now established for the British colonies to the north of the United States. "They are jealous of the scheme in England," said William Smith; "yet they will find the spirit of democracy so persevering that they will be under the necessity of coming into it." Under the pretext of framing common regulations of trade with the Indians, the assembly of New York, with the concurrence of its lieutenant-governor, had, in the previous December, invited each province to elect representatives to a body which should exercise legislative power for them all. This was a great step toward the American union, which could have amicably fixed the quotas of the several colonies for the common charges of America. Virginia, when she heard of the proposal, which was designed to regulate and preserve the connection with England, directed Patrick Henry and Richard Bland to appear as her representatives. But the British ministry, who saw in union the forerunner of independence, defeated the scheme.

The measures against the charter of Massachusetts had been rejected by the administration of Grafton, and nothing had happened to invite a revival of them; but, early in July, a most elaborate paper on the disorders in America was laid before the British council. Long and earnest deliberations ensued. Hillsborough pressed impetuously for the abrogation of the charter of Massachusetts as the only means of arresting the progress of America toward independence. But the charter of Massachusetts was the well-considered creation of the British revolution of 1688. It was made after the most careful consultation of the great lawyers of the day; it had the sanction of King William. To destroy it was to condemn the English revolution itself; the king in council gave an order for making a beginning of martial law within the province of Massachusetts Bay, and preparing the way for closing the port of Boston; to abridge or alter it by the prerogative alone had no precedent, but in the times of the Stuarts, and was inconsistent with the British law and the British constitution, as established by the revolution; and yet, on the sixth of July, the king, without previous authority from parliament, transcending the limits of his prerogative, proceeded, by his own order in council, to infringe the charter granted to Massachusetts by William and Mary.

The session of the legislature of Massachusetts had passed without the transaction of any business, when, near the evening of the eighth of September, Hutchinson received the order which had been adopted in July by the king in council. The harbor of Boston was made "the rendezvous of all ships stationed in North America," and the fortress which commanded it was to be delivered up to such officer as Gage should appoint, to be garrisoned by regular troops, and put into a respectable state of defence. But the charter of Massachusetts reserved to its governor the command of its militia and of its forts; the castle had been built and repaired and garrisoned by the colony, at its own expense; to take the command from the civil governor, and bestow it on the commander-in-chief, was a violation of the charter, as well as of immemorial usage. For a day, Hutchinson hesitated; but, on second thoughts, he resolved to obey the order. Enjoining secrecy on the members of the council upon their oaths, he divulged to them his instructions. The council was struck with amazement, for the town was very quiet, and the measure seemed a wanton provocation. "Does not the charter," they demanded of him, "place the command of the castle in the governor?" After a secret discussion, which lasted for two hours, he entered his carriage which was waiting at the door, hurried to the Neck, stole into a barge, and was rowed to the castle. The officers and garrison were discharged without a moment's warning; he then delivered up the keys to Dalrymple, and in the twilight retired to his country house at Milton. But he was in dread of being waylaid; and the next day fled for safety to the castle, as he and Bernard had done five years before, and remained there every night for the rest of the week. The breach of the Massachusetts charter by the delivery of the castle was a commencement of civil war; yet the last appeal was not to be made without some prospect of success.

"As a citizen of the world," wrote Turgot to Josiah Tucker, the English apostle of free trade, "I see with joy the approach of an event which, more than all the books of the philosophers, will dissipate the puerile and sanguinary phantom of a pretended exclusive commerce. I speak of the separation of the British colonies from their metropolis, which will soon be followed by that of all America from Europe. Then, and not till then, will the discovery of that part of the world become for us truly useful. Then it will multiply our enjoyments far more abundantly than when we bought them by torrents of blood."

To prevent that separation, Hillsborough thought it necessary, without loss of time, to change "the constitution of the Massachusetts Bay." Conspiring against the liberties of his native country, Hutchinson, in October, advised not a mere change of the mode of electing the council, but "a bill for the vacating or disannulling the charter in all its parts, and leaving it to the king to settle the government by a royal commission." As Hillsborough and the king seemed content with obtaining the appointment of the council, Hutchinson forwarded lists from which the royal councillors were to be named. "If the kingdom," said he, "is united and resolved, I have but very little doubt we shall be as tame as lambs;" and he presented distinctly the option, either to lay aside taxation as inexpedient, or to deal with the inhabitants as being "in a state of revolt." After that should be decided, he proposed to starve the colony into obedience by narrowing its commerce and excluding it from the fisheries. If this should fail, the military might be authorized to act by their own authority, free from the restraints of civil government. Boston, he thought, should be insulated from the rest of the colony, and specially dealt with; and he recommended the example of Rome, which, on one occasion, seized the leading men in rebellious colonies, and detained them in the metropolis as hostages. An act of parliament curtailing Massachusetts of all the land east of the Penobscot was a supplementary proposition.

Less occasion never existed for martial rule than at Boston. At the ensuing trial of Preston, every indulgence was shown him by the citizens. Auchmuty, his counsel, had the assistance of John Adams and Josiah Quincy the foremost patriot lawyers of the town. The prosecution was conducted with languor and inefficiency; important witnesses were sent out of the way; the judges held office at the will of the king, and selected talesmen were put upon the jury. The defence was left to John Adams and Quincy, and was conducted with consummate ability. As the firing upon the citizens took place at night, it was not difficult to raise a doubt whether Preston or some other person had cried to the soldiers to fire; and on that doubt a verdict of acquittal was obtained. The public acquiesced, but was offended at the manifest want of uprightness in the court. "The firmness of the judges" was vaunted, to obtain for them all much larger salaries, to be paid directly by the crown. The chief justice, who was a manufacturer, wanted money in the shape of pay for some refuse products of his workshop.

The trial of the eight soldiers who were with Preston followed a few weeks after. Two of them were proved to have fired, and were found guilty of manslaughter. As seven guns only were fired, the jury acquitted the other six; choosing that five guilty should escape rather than one innocent be convicted.

In selecting an agent to lay their complaints before the king, Samuel Adams and about one third of the house, following the advice of Joseph Reed, of Philadelphia, gave their suffrages for Arthur Lee; but, by the better influence of Bowdoin and of the minister Cooper, Benjamin Franklin, greatest of the sons of Boston, was elected. Arthur Lee was then chosen as his substitute. Franklin held under the crown the office of deputy postmaster-general for America, and his son was a royal governor; but his mind reasoned on politics with the same freedom from prejudice which marked his investigations into the laws of nature. At the time when he was thus called by the people of Massachusetts to be their mediator with the mother country, he was sixty-four years of age. Experience had ripened his judgment, and he still retained the vigor of mind, the benignity of manner, genial humor, and comprehensive observation, which made him everywhere welcome. The difficult service demanded of him by the colony of his nativity was attended by embarrassments of all kinds. Hutchinson negatived all appropriations for his salary, and reminded Hillsborough not to recognise him as an agent.

## CHAPTER XXX.

### THE ORIGIN OF TENNESSEE.

#### October 1770–June 1771.

No one had more vividly discerned the capacity of the Mississippi valley, not only to sustain commonwealths, but to connect them with the world by commerce, than Franklin; and when the ministers would have rejected the Fort Stanwix treaty, which conveyed from the Six Nations an inchoate title to an immense territory south-west of the Ohio, his influence secured its ratification, by organizing a powerful company to plant a province in that part of the country which lay between the Alleghanies and a line drawn from the Cumberland gap to the mouth of the Scioto.

Virginia resisted the proposed limitation of her jurisdiction, as fatal to her interests, entreating an extension of her borders westward to the Tennessee river. It would be tedious to rehearse the pleas of the colony; the hesitations of Hillsborough; the solicitations of Botetourt; the adverse representations of the board of trade; the meetings of agents with the beloved men of the Cherokees. On the seventeenth of October, two days after the death of Botetourt, a treaty, conforming to the decision of the British cabinet, was made at Lochaber, confining the Ancient Dominion on the north-west to the mouth of the Kanawha, while on the south it extended only to within six miles of the Holston river. When in the following year the line was run by Donelson for Virginia, the Cherokee chief consented that it should cross from the Holston to the Louisa, or Kentucky river, and follow it to the Ohio. But the change was disapproved in England; so that the West, little encumbered by valid titles, was reserved for the self-directed emigrant.

The people of Virginia and others were exploring and marking the richest lands, not only on the Redstone and other waters of the Monongahela, but along the Ohio, as low as the Little Kanawha; and with each year went farther and farther down the river. When Washington, in 1770, having established for the soldiers and officers who had served with him in the French war their right to two hundred thousand acres in the western valley, undertook to select for them suitable tracts, he was obliged to descend to the Great Kanawha. As he floated in a canoe down the Ohio, whose banks he found enlivened by innumerable wild turkeys and other fowl, with deer browsing on the plains, or stepping down to the water's edge to drink, no good land escaped his eye. Where the soil and growth of timber were most inviting, he would walk through the woods, and set his mark on a maple or elm, a hoop-wood or ash, as the corner of a soldier's survey; for he watched over the interests of his old associates in arms as sacredly as if he had been their trustee; and by his exertions, and "by these alone," he had secured to each one of them, or, if they were dead, to their heirs, the full bounty that had been promised. His journey to the wilderness was not without its pleasures; he amused himself with the sports of the forest, or observing new kinds of water-fowl, or taking the girth of the largest trees. His fame had gone before him; the red men received him in council with public honors. Nor did he turn homeward without inquiring of Nicholson, an Indian interpreter, and of Connolly, an intelligent forester, the character of the country farther west. From these eye-witnesses he received glowing accounts of the climate, soil, good streams, and plentiful game of the Cumberland valley, and there he was persuaded a new and most desirable government might be established.

Daniel Boone was then exploring the land of promise. Of forty adventurers who from the Clinch river plunged into the West under the lead of James Knox, and became renowned as "the Long Hunters," some found their way down the Cumberland to the limestone bluff where Nashville stands, and where the gently undulating fields, covered with groves of beech and walnut, were in the possession of countless buffaloes, whose bellowings resounded from hill and forest.

Sometimes trappers and restless emigrants, boldest of their class, took the risk of crossing the country from Carolina to the Mississippi; but of those who perished, no tradition preserves the names. Others, following the natural highways of the West, descended from Pittsburg, and from Red Stone to Fort Natchez. The pilot who conducted the party, of which Samuel Wells and John MacIntire were the chiefs, was so attracted by the lands round the fort that he promised to remove there in the spring with his wife and family, and believed a hundred families from North Carolina would follow.

This year, James Robertson, from the home of the regulators in North Carolina, an unlettered forester, of humble birth, but of inborn nobleness of soul, cultivated maize on the Watauga, and trod the soil as its lord. Intrepid, loving virtue for its own sake, and emulous of honorable fame, he had self-possession, quickness of discernment, and a sound judgment. Wherever he was thrown, he knew how to apply all the means within his reach, whether small or great, to their proper end, seeing at a glance the latent capacities of the country, and devising the simplest way to bring them forth; and so he became the greatest benefactor of the early settlers of Tennessee.

He was followed to the West by men from North Carolina, where the courts of law offered no redress against extortion. At the inferior courts, the justices, who themselves were implicated in the pilfering of public money, named the juries. The sheriff and receivers of taxes were in arrears for near seventy thousand pounds, which they had extorted from the people, and of which more than two thirds had been irretrievably embezzled. In the northern part of the colony, where the ownership of the soil had been reserved to one of the old proprietaries, there was no land-office; so that the people who were attracted by the excellence of the land could not obtain freeholds. Every art was employed to increase the expenses of suits at law; and, as some of the people wreaked their vengeance in acts of folly and madness, they were misrepresented as enemies to the constitution; and the oppressor acquired the protection which was due to the oppressed. In March 1770, one of the associate justices reported that they could not enforce the payment of taxes. At the court in September, the regulators appeared in numbers. "We are come down," they said, "with the design to have justice done;" they would have business proceed, but with no attorney except the king's; and, finding that it had been resolved not to try their causes, some of them pursued Fanning and another lawyer, and beat them with cowskin whips.

The assembly, which convened in December, at Newbern, was chosen under a state of alarm and vague apprehension. Tryon had secured Fanning a seat, by chartering the town of Hillsborough as a borough; but the county of Orange, with great unanimity, selected Herman Husbands as its representative. The rustic patriot possessed a good reputation and a considerable estate, and was charged with no illegal act whatever; yet he was voted a disturber of the public peace; on the twentieth of December, was expelled the house; and, against the opinion of the council, and without evidence that he had been even an accessory to the riots at Hillsborough, Tryon seized him under a warrant concerted with the chief justice, and kept him in prison without bail.

To conciliate the Presbyterian party, which was the strongest in the house, a law was passed for endowing Queen's college in the town of Charlotte, Mecklenburg county; a deceitful act of tolerance, for it was sure to be annulled by the king in council. But the great object of Tryon was the riot act, by which it was declared a felony for more than ten men to remain assembled after being required to disperse. For a riot committed before or after the publication of the act, persons might be tried in any superior court, no matter how distant from their homes; and if within sixty days they did not make their appearance, whether with or without notice, they were to be proclaimed outlaws, and to forfeit their lives with all their property. The governor sent letters into the neighboring counties, to ascertain how many would volunteer to serve in a military expedition against "the rebels;" but the assembly, by withholding grants of money, set itself against civil war.

Tryon had won at the colonial office the reputation of being the ablest governor in the thirteen colonies; the death of

Botetourt opened the way for his transfer to New York; the earl of Dunmore, a needy Scottish peer of the house of Murray, passionate, narrow, and unscrupulous in his rapacity, being promoted to the more desirable one of Virginia.

Dunmore came over to amass a fortune, and, in his passion for sudden gain, cared as little for the policy of the ministers or his instructions from the crown, as for the rights of property, the respective limits of jurisdiction of the colonies, or their civil and political privileges. To get money for himself was his whole system. He did not remain in New York long enough to weary the legislature into a spirited resistance. Its members were steadfast in their purpose to connect loyalty with their regard for American liberty; and, adopting the nomination made by Schuyler a year before, they unanimously elected Edmund Burke their agent in England, allowing "for his services at the rate of five hundred pounds per annum."

In foreign relations, Lord North was most fortunate. England, following the impulse given by Lord Egmont during the administration of Grenville, had taken possession of the Falkland islands as the key to the Pacific, and had been ejected from them by Spain. Weymouth would have retaken them at all hazards; Lord North gained honor by consenting to abandon Port Egmont, on its temporary restitution and a disavowal of its seizure by the Spanish government. The terms would have been rejected with disdain had not Choiseul, who would not have feared war for a great cause like the emancipation of the colonial world, checked the rashness of Spain. The opposition to the English ministry raised a vehement clamor against the wise settlement of the question. Sir Robert Walpole had yielded to a similar clamor, and had yet lost his place; Lord North resisted it, and, suffering Weymouth to retire, gained strength by securing peace without a compromise of the public dignity. The administration needed for its defence no more than the exposition of the madness of modern wars in the brilliant and forcible language of Samuel Johnson; it obtained the applause of Adam Smith and the approval of the country.

Moreover, by the death of George Grenville in November 1770, a way was opened to the ministry to induce Lord Suffolk, "a young man of thirty-two, unpracticed in business, pompous, ignorant and of no parts," and Wedderburn who owed his seat in parliament to a friend of Grenville, to desert the Grenville connection. Suffolk became secretary of state instead of Weymouth, and took for his under-secretary Thomas Whately, the secretary of the treasury when Grenville was its first lord. Thurlow being promoted, Wedderburn, whose "credit for veracity" Lord North so lately impeached, and who, in his turn, had denied to that minister "honor and respectability," refused to continue upon a forlorn hope, and accepted the office of solicitor-general. "The part of Wedderburn," said Chatham, "is deplorable; of Suffolk pitiable;" and Lord Temple seems to have received the news with equal indignation and contempt.*

By these arrangements Lord North obtained twelve new votes; and still further good luck was in store for him. On the twenty-fourth of December, just as he had rendered to his country the benefit of averting a war without a national object, Choiseul, the ablest French minister of the century, was dismissed from office and exiled to Chanteloupe, not because he was impassioned for war, as his enemies pretended, but because he was the friend of philosophy, freedom of industry, and colonial independence. Thoroughly a Frenchman, as Chatham was thoroughly an Englishman, he longed to renovate France that she might revenge the wounds inflicted on her glory. For this end, he had sought to improve her finances, restore her marine, reform her army, and surround her by allies. Marie Antoinette, the wife of the dauphin, was a pledge for the friendship of Austria; Prussia was conciliated; and, as the family compact was in force at Naples and in the Spanish peninsula, he left France with friends, and friends only, from the Bosphorus to Cadiz. Crowds paid their homage to the retiring statesman; he was dear to the parliaments he had defended, to men of letters he had encouraged, and to Frenchmen whose hearts beat for the honor of their land in its rivalry with England. His policy was so identified with the passions, the sympathies, and the culture of his country, was so thoroughly national and so liberal, that it was sure to return in

---

* William James Smith's Grenville Papers, III lviii, IV. 530.

spite of the royalist party and the court. But for the time dynastic monarchy carried the day; and, had America then risen, she would have found no friends to cheer her on.

This was the happiest period in the career of Lord North. His government acquired stability, and was sure of majorities. No danger hung over him but from his own love of ease. "Seated on the treasury bench, between his attorney- and solicitor-general," his equals in ability, but most unlike him in character, he indulged in slumber when America required all his wakefulness. As he failed in vigilance at the helm, he was soon thrown upon a lee shore by the selfishness and vainglory of American governors. Hutchinson was lapping himself in the promise of being paid a secure and bountiful salary out of the tax on tea; and Tryon, just before leaving his province, was trampling out all trust in the uprightness of the servants of the crown.

In February 1771, the regulators of North Carolina gathered together in the woods, on hearing that their representative had been expelled and arbitrarily imprisoned and they themselves menaced with exile or death as outlaws. They had toiled honestly for their own support; not living on the spoils of other men's labors, nor snatching the bread out of other men's hands. They accepted the maxim, that laws, statutes, and customs, which are against God's law or nature, are all null; and that civil officers who exacted illegal taxes and fees from the industrious poor were guilty of a worse crime than open robbery. They asked no more than that extortioners might be brought to fair trials, and "the collectors of the public money called to proper settlements of their accounts." Honor and good faith prompted them to join for the rescue of Husbands.

Without some sanction of law, Tryon dared no longer detain in custody the sturdy freeholder, who had come down under the safeguard of his unquestioned election to the legislature; he therefore conspired with the chief justice to get Husbands indicted for a pretended libel. But the grand jury refused to do the work assigned them; and the prisoner was set free.

The liberation of Husbands having stopped the march of

the regulators, it occurred to some of them on their return to visit Salisbury superior court. On the sixth of March, about four or five hundred of them encamped in the woods near the ferry, west of the Yadkin river. "The lawyers are everything," they complained. "There should be none in the province." "We shall be forced to kill them all." "There never was such an act as the riot act in the laws of England." This last was true; the counsel to the board of trade, making his official report upon that law, declared its clause of outlawry "altogether unfit for any part of the British empire." "We come," said the chiefs in the regulators' camp to an officer from Salisbury, "with no intention to obstruct the court, or to injure the person or property of any one, but only to petition for a redress of grievances against officers taking exorbitant fees." "Why, then," it was asked, "are some of you armed?" "Our arms," said they, "are only to defend ourselves." They were told that no court would be held on account of the disturbances; but the very persons of whom they complained, finding them "peaceably disposed beyond expectation," agreed with them that all differences with the officers of the county of Rowan should be settled by arbitration on the third Tuesday in May. The umpires being named, the regulators marched through Salisbury, gave three cheers, and quietly returned to their homes.

But Tryon and Fanning were bent on revenge. The governor, by a new commission, had called another court for the eleventh of March at Newbern; and by the strictest orders to the sheriffs many of whom were defaulters, and by the indefatigable exertions of his own private secretary, he took care to obtain jurors and witnesses suited to his purpose. On the appointed day, the court opened. With willing witnesses and a unanimous grand jury, sixty-one indictments were found for felonies or riots against the leading regulators in Orange county, who lived two hundred miles off, and many of whom had been at home during the riots of which they were accused. By law, criminal jurisdiction belonged in the first instance to the district within which offences were charged to have been committed; every one of the indictments was illegal; and yet those charged with felony must appear within sixty days, or a merciless governor will declare them outlaws.

Tryon next received the grand jury at the palace, and volunteered to them to lead troops into the western counties. The obsequious body, passing beyond their functions, applauded his purpose; and the council acquiesced. To obtain the necessary funds, which the legislature had refused to provide, Tryon created a paper currency by drafts on the treasury.

The northern treasurer declined to sanction the illegal drafts, and, in consequence, the eastern counties took no part in the scenes that followed; but the southern treasurer complied. From Wilmington, a body of militia, under the command of Waddel, was sent to Salisbury, while Tryon himself, having written a harsh rebuke of the agreement in Rowan county for arbitration, marched into Orange county. His progress was marked by the destruction of wheat-fields and orchards, the burning of every house which was found empty; the seizure of cattle, poultry, and all the produce of the plantations. The terrified people ran together like sheep chased by a wolf. Tryon crossed the Eno and the Haw; and the men who had been indicted at Newbern for felonies were already advertised as outlaws, when, on the evening of the fourteenth, he reached the Great Alamance.

His army was composed of one thousand and eighteen foot soldiers and thirty light-horse, besides the officers. The regulators, who had been drawn together not as insurgents, but from alarm—many, perhaps most of them, without guns—may have numbered rather more, and were encamped about five miles to the west of the stream. They gathered round James Hunter as their "general;" and his capacity and courage won from the unorganized host implicit obedience. They were almost in despair, lest the governor "would not lend a kind ear to the just complaints of the people." Still, on the evening of the fifteenth, they entreated that harmony might yet be restored, that "the presaged tragedy of warlike marching to meet each other might be prevented;" that the governor would give them leave to present "their petition," and treat for peace.

The next day, Tryon crossed Alamance river, and marched

out to meet the regulators. As he approached, James Hunter, and Benjamin Merrill, a captain of militia, "a man in general esteem for his honesty, integrity, piety, and moral good life," received from him this answer: "I require you to lay down your arms, surrender up the outlawed ringleaders, submit yourselves to the laws, and rest on the lenity of the government. By accepting these terms in one hour, you will prevent an effusion of blood, as you are at this time in a state of war and rebellion."

The demands were unjustifiable. No one of the regulators had been legally outlawed, or even legally indicted. The governor acted against law as against right. Yet the regulators reluctantly accepted the appeal to arms; for they had nothing to hope from victory itself.

The action began before noon, by firing a field-piece into the midst of the people. Many of the regulators, perhaps the larger number, retired; but those who remained disputed the field for two hours, fighting first in the open ground and then from behind trees, till, having nearly expended their ammunition, Hunter and his men were compelled to retreat. Nine of the king's troops were killed and sixty-one wounded. Of the regulators, above twenty fell in battle, besides the wounded. Some prisoners were taken in the pursuit. Before sunset, Tryon returned in triumph to his camp.

The next day, James Few, one of the prisoners, was, by the governor's order, hanged on a tree as an outlaw; and his parents were ruined by the destruction of their estate. Then followed one proclamation after another, excepting outlaws and prisoners from mercy, and promising it to none but those who should take an oath of allegiance, pay taxes, submit to the laws, and deliver up their arms

After this, Tryon proceeded to the Yadkin to join Waddel, who had incurred some danger of being cut off. Waddel then moved through the south-western counties, unmolested, except that in Mecklenburg his ammunition was blown up; while Tryon turned back, living at free quarters on the regulators, burning the houses and laying waste the plantations of every one whom he chose to call an outlaw.

On the ninth of June, he arrived at Hillsborough, where

the court awaited him. His first work was a proclamation inviting "every person" to shoot Herman Husbands, or James Hunter, or Redknap Howell, or William Butler; and offering a hundred pounds and a thousand acres of land as a reward for the delivery of either of them alive or dead. Then twelve men, taken in battle, were tried and brought in guilty of treason; and, on the nineteenth of June, six of them were hanged under the eye of the governor, who himself marked the spot for the execution, gave directions for clearing the field, and sketched in general orders the line of march of the army, with the station of each company round the gallows. The victims died bravely. It is yet kept in memory how heroically Benjamin Merrill met his fate, sustained by the affection of his children, and declaring that he died at peace with his Maker, in the cause of his country.

The next day, Tryon, taking care to make the most of the confiscated lands, which were among the best on the continent, left Hillsborough; and, on the thirtieth, sailed to New York, leaving the burden of an illegally contracted debt of more than forty thousand pounds. His successor dared not trust the people with the immediate election of a new assembly, though terror and despair had brought six thousand of the regulators to submission.

The governors of South Carolina and of Virginia were requested not to harbor the fugitives. But the wilderness offered shelter beyond the mountains. Without concert, instinctively impelled by discontent and the wearisomeness of life exposed to bondage, men crossed the Alleghanies, and, descending into the basin of the Tennessee, made their homes in the valley of the Watauga. There no lawyer followed them with writs; there no king's governor came to be their lord; there the flag of England never waved. By degrees, they extended their settlements to the broader Nolichucky, whose sparkling waters spring out of the tallest mountains in the range. The health-giving westerly wind prevailed at all seasons; in spring, the wild crab-apple filled the air with the sweetest of perfumes. A fertile soil gave to industry good crops of maize; the clear streams flowed pleasantly without tearing floods; where the closest thickets of spruce and rhododendron flung the cooling shade farthest over the river, trout abounded. The elk and the red deer were not wanting in the natural parks of oak and hickory, of maple, elm, black ash, and buckeye. Of quails and turkeys and pigeons, there was no end. The golden eagle built its nest on the topmost ledge of the mountain, wheeling in wide circles high above the pines, or dropping like a meteor upon its prey. The black bear, whose flesh was held to be the most delicate of meats, grew so fat upon the abundant acorns and chestnuts that he could be run down in a race of three hundred yards; and sometimes the hunters gave chase to the coward panther, strong enough to beat off twenty dogs, yet flying from one. To acquire a peaceful title to their lands, the settlers despatched James Robertson to the council of the Cherokees, from whom he obtained promises of confidence and friendship, and a lease of territory. For government, its members, in 1772, came together as brothers in convention and founded a republic by a written association; appointed their own magistrates, Robertson among the first; framed laws for their present occasions; and "set to the people of America the example of erecting themselves into a state, independent of the authority" of the British king.

Fanning followed Tryon to the North with obsequious adulation. To Lord Hillsborough Tryon boasted that his western expedition tended to establish the royal authority on the frontiers of every colony in British America. The extortionate officers, whom the regulators had vainly sued for redress in the courts, taunted their victims, saying: "Alamance is your court of record." Yet the record was not closed. In the memories of the inhabitants of Orange and Mecklenburg counties in North Carolina and of the troop of mountaineers who planted the commonwealth of Tennessee, a tyrannical governor, hiding his own rapacity under pretended zeal for the crown, had treasured up wrath for the day of wrath.

## CHAPTER XXXI.

GREAT BRITAIN CENTRES IN ITSELF POWER OVER ITS COLONIES. HILLSBOROUGH'S RETIREMENT.

JUNE 1771–AUGUST 1772.

"THE glorious spirit of liberty is vanquished, and left without hope but in a miracle," was the language of desponding patriots in Boston. "I confess," said Samuel Adams, "we have, as Wolfe expressed it, a choice of difficulties. Too many flatter themselves that their pusillanimity is true prudence; but, in perilous times like these, I cannot conceive of prudence without fortitude." John Adams retired from "the service of the people," and, devoting himself to his profession, for a time ceased even to employ his pen in their defence. Otis, disordered in mind and jealous of his declining influence, did but impede the public cause. In Hancock, vanity so mingled with patriotism that the government hoped to win him over.

The assembly, which for the third year was convened at Cambridge, adopted a protest in which Samuel Adams drew the distinction between a prerogative and its abuse; and inquired what would follow in England if a British king should call a parliament in Cornwall and keep it there seven years. Nor did he omit to expose the rapid consolidation of power in the hands of the executive, by the double process of making all civil officers dependent for support solely on the king, and giving to arbitrary instructions an authority paramount to the charter and the laws.

The protest had hardly been adopted when, in July 1771, the application of its doctrines became necessary. The commissioners of the customs had, through Hutchinson, applied for an exemption of their salaries from the colonial income tax; and

Hillsborough, disregarding a usage of more than fifty years, commanded the compliance of the legislature. The engrossed tax bill for the year was of the same tenor with the annual acts from time immemorial. The assessors had, moreover, rated the commissioners with extreme moderation. Persons who had less income were taxed as much as they, so that it did not even appear that any regard was had to their salaries. Paxton's provincial tax, for his personal estate and income, was for the last year less than three pounds sterling; and what he paid to the town and county not much more.* To prevent the levy of this inconsiderable, customary, and most moderate tax, Hutchinson, on the fourth of July, greatly against his own judgment, negatived the tax bill, and declared his obligation under his instructions to negative any other drawn in the same usual terms.

The stopping of supplies by a veto of the crown was unknown in England; an order from the king to exempt special individuals from their share of taxation was unconstitutional; the exemption, if submitted to by the assembly, would have been an acquiescence in an unwarrantable instruction. On the next day the house replied in the words of Samuel Adams: "We know of no commissioners of his majesty's customs, nor of any revenue his majesty has a right to establish in North America; we know and feel a tribute levied and extorted from those who, if they have property, have a right to the absolute disposal of it. To withhold your assent to this bill, merely by force of instruction, is effectually vacating the charter, and giving instructions the force of laws, within this province. If such a doctrine shall be established, the representatives of a free people would be reduced to this fatal alternative: either to have no taxes levied and raised at all, or to have them raised and levied in such a way, and upon" such persons only as "his majesty pleases." At the first meeting of the assembly, loyalty had prevailed; in his rejoinder Hutchinson again kept the ministers out of sight, and brought the king and the colony into direct conflict. "I know," he said, "that your messages and resolves of the last year were very displeasing to the king; I shall transmit my messages, and this your extraordinary answer, to be laid before him."

* Hutchinson's Letters of 17 and 19 July 1771—in Letter Book. MS.

Wise men saw the event that was approaching, but not that it was so near. Franklin foretold a bloody struggle, in which "America's growing strength and magnitude" would give her the victory. The letter of the house to its agent, claiming that colonial legislation was independent of parliament and of royal instructions, was drawn by Samuel Adams, who had long before said, in town-meeting: "Independent we are, and independent we will be." "I doubt," wrote Hutchinson, "whether there is a greater incendiary than he in the king's dominions." His language became more explicit as danger drew nearer.

In August, Boston saw in its harbor twelve vessels of war, carrying more than two hundred and sixty guns, commanded by Montagu, the brother of Lord Sandwich. Yet Eden from Maryland could congratulate Hillsborough on the return of confidence and harmony. "The people," so wrote Johnson, the agent of Connecticut, after his return home, "appear to be weary of their altercations with the mother country; a little discreet conduct on both sides would perfectly re-establish that warm affection and respect toward Great Britain for which this country was once so remarkable." Hutchinson, too, in October, reported "a disposition in all the colonies to let the controversy with the kingdom subside." The king sent word to tempt Hancock by marks of favor. "Hancock and most of the party," said the governor, "are quiet; and all of them, except Adams, abate of their virulence."

While America generally was so tranquil, Samuel Adams continued musing, till the thought of correspondence and union among the friends of liberty ripened in his mind. "It would be an arduous task," he said, meditating a project which required a year's reflection for its maturity, "to awaken a sufficient number in the colonies to so grand an undertaking. Nothing, however, should be despaired of." Through the press, in October, he continued: "We have nothing to rely upon but the interposition of our friends in Britain, of which I have no expectation, or the LAST APPEAL. The tragedy of American freedom is nearly completed. A tyranny seems to be at the very door. They who lie under oppression deserve what they suffer; let them perish with their oppressors. Could millions be enslaved, if all possessed the independent spirit of Brutus, who, to his immortal honor, expelled the tyrant of Rome and his royal and rebellious race? The liberties of our country are worth defending at all hazards. If we should suffer them to be wrested from us, millions yet unborn may be the miserable sharers in the event. Every step has been taken but one; and the last appeal would require prudence, unanimity, and fortitude. America must herself, under God, work out her own salvation."

In the annual proclamation which appointed the November festival of thanksgiving, and which was always read from every pulpit, Hutchinson sought to ensnare the clergy by enumerating as a cause for gratitude "that civil and religious liberties were continued," and "trade enlarged." He was caught in his own toils. All the Boston ministers except one refused to read the paper; when Pemberton, of whose church the governor was a member, began confusedly to do so, the patriots of his congregation, turning their backs on him, walked out of the meeting; and nearly all the ministers agreed on the Thanksgiving day "to implore of Almighty God the restoration of lost liberties."

Nowise disheartened, Hutchinson waited "to hear how the extravagance of the assembly in their last session would be resented by the king;" now striving to set Hancock against Adams; now seeking to lull the people into security; now boasting of his band of writers on the side of government, Church, a professed patriot, being of the number; now triumphing at the spectacle of Otis who was carried into the country, bound hand and foot as a maniac; now speculating on the sale of cheap teas at high prices; now urging the government in England to remodel all the New England provinces, even while he pretended that they were quiet and submissive. His only fears were lest his advice should become known in America.

Confirmed by the seeming tranquillity in America, and by the almost unprecedented strength of the ministry in parliament, Hillsborough gave free scope to his conceit, wrongheadedness, obstinacy, and passion, and perplexed affairs by the senseless exercise of authority. He still required the legislature of Massachusetts to exempt the commissioners from taxation, or the tax bill should be negatived; and Gage was enjoined to attend to the security of the fortress in Boston harbor.

In Georgia, Noble Wimberley Jones, a man of exemplary life and character, had been elected speaker. Wright, who reported him to be "a very strong Liberty Boy," would not consent to the choice; and the house voted the interference a breach of their privileges. To crush this claim of the house, Hillsborough directed the governor "to put his negative upon any person whom they should next elect for speaker, and to dissolve the assembly in case they should question the right of such negative."

The affections of South Carolina were still more thoroughly alienated. Its public men were ruled by their sense of honor, and felt a stain upon it as a wound. From the day when Lyttelton had abruptly dismissed a Carolinian from the king's council, it became the pride of native Carolinians not to accept a seat in that body. The members of the assembly "disdained to take any pay for their attendance." Since March 1771, no legislative act had been perfected, because the governor refused to pass any appropriations which should cover the grant of the assembly to the society for the bill of rights; but patriot planters by their private credit and purses met the wants of colonial agents and committees. To extend the benefit of courts of justice into the interior, the province, at an expense of five thousand pounds, bought the monopoly of Richard Cumberland as provost by patent for the whole; and offered to establish salaries for the judges, if the commissions of those judges were but made permanent as in England. At last, in 1769, trusting to the honor of the crown, they voted perpetual grants of salaries. When this was done, Rawlins Lowndes and others, their own judges, taken from among themselves, were dismissed; and, in 1772, an Irishman, a Scotchman, and a Welshman were sent over by Hillsborough to take their places. "The honors of the state," said the planters, "are all given away to worthless sycophants." The governor, Lord Charles Greville Montagu, had no palace at Charleston; he uttered a threat to convene the South Carolina assembly at Port Royal, unless they would vote him a house to his mind. This is the culminating point of administrative insolence.

The system of concentrating all colonial power in England was resisted at the West. In Illinois, the corruption and favoritism of the military commander compelled the people to a remonstrance. The removal of them all to places within the limits of some established colony was the mode of pacification which Hillsborough approved, but the Spanish jurisdiction across the river offered so near a sanctuary that such a policy was impracticable. An establishment of government by the crown upon the lowest plan of expense, and without any intermixture of popular power, was thought of. "A regular constitutional government for them," said Gage, "cannot be suggested. They don't deserve so much attention." "I agree with you," replied Hillsborough; "a regular government for that district would be highly improper." The people of Illinois, weary of the shameless despotism which aimed only at forestalling tracts of land, the monopoly of the Indian trade, or the ruin of the French villages, took their cause into their own hands; they demanded institutions like those of Connecticut, and set themselves against any proposal for a government which should be irresponsible to themselves. In 1771, they assembled in a general meeting, and fixed upon their scheme, from which they never departed, "expecting to appoint their own governor and all civil magistrates." Toward the people at Vincennes, Hillsborough was less relenting; for they were at his mercy, with no Spanish shore to which they could fly. In April 1772, they were, by formal proclamation, peremptorily commanded to retire within the jurisdiction of some one of the colonies. But the men of Indiana were as unwilling to abandon their homes in a settlement which they claimed to be already seventy years old, as those of Illinois to give up the hope of freedom. And what allegiance would men of French origin bear to a British king who proposed to take away their estates and deny them liberty?

The people of Virginia were overruled on a subject of vital importance to them and their posterity. Their halls of legislation had resounded with eloquence directed against the terrible plague of negro slavery. The struggle for their own liberty made them more thoughtful of the sorrows of the humble who were oppressed by themselves. An act of 1748 had imposed unequal taxes on the wives and female children of free people of color; in November 1769, the grievance was redressed, because, says the statute-book, "it is found very burdensome to such negroes, mulattoes, and Indians, and is, moreover, derogatory of the rights of free-born subjects." To Jefferson, it did not seem enough to guard the rights of the free-born subjects of African descent; in this same session he brought in a bill for permitting the unrestricted emancipation of slaves. But the abrogation of the slave-trade was regarded by the legislature as the necessary preliminary to successful efforts at getting rid of slavery itself. Again and again they had passed laws restraining the importations of negroes from Africa; but their laws were disallowed. How to prevent them from protecting themselves against the increase of the overwhelming evil was debated by the king in council; and, on the tenth of December 1770, he issued an instruction, under his own hand, commanding the governor, " upon pain of the highest displeasure, to assent to no law by which the importation of slaves should be in any respect prohibited or obstructed." In April 1772, this rigorous order was solemnly debated in the assembly of Virginia. The negro slaves in the low country were double the number of the white people, and gained every year from importations and from births, so as to alarm not only Virginia, but all America. "The people of this colony," it was said, "must fall upon means not only of preventing their increase, but of lessening their number; and the interest of the country would manifestly require the total expulsion of them. Supposing it possible, by rigor and exemplary punishment, to prevent any insurrection, yet, in case of a war, the people, with great reason, tremble at the facility that an enemy would find in procuring such a body of men, attached by no tie to their masters or their country, ready to join the first that would encourage them to revenge themselves, by which means a conquest of this country would inevitably be effected in a very short time." The abhorred instruction, which maintained the nefarious trade in men, sprung directly from the throne; Virginia, therefore, resolved to address the king himself. They entreated of him leave to defend themselves against the crimes of commercial avarice, and these were their words:

"The importation of slaves into the colonies from the coast of Africa hath long been considered as a trade of great inhumanity; and, under its present encouragement, we have too much reason to fear, will endanger the very existence of your majesty's American dominions. We are sensible that some of your majesty's subjects in Great Britain may reap emoluments from this sort of traffic; but, when we consider that it greatly retards the settlement of the colonies with more useful inhabitants, and may in time have the most destructive influence, we presume to hope that the interest of a few will be disregarded, when placed in competition with the security and happiness of such numbers of your majesty's dutiful and loyal subjects.

"Deeply impressed with these sentiments, we most humbly beseech your majesty to remove all those restraints on your majesty's governors of this colony which inhibit their assenting to such laws as might check so very pernicious a commerce."

Thousands in Maryland and in New Jersey were ready to adopt a similar petition; so were the legislatures of North Carolina, of Pennsylvania, of New York. Massachusetts, in its towns and in its legislature, had reprobated the condition of slavery, as well as the sale of slaves. There was no jealousy of one another in the strife against the crying evil; Virginia represented the moral sentiment and policy of them all. How strong were her convictions, how earnest and united the efforts of her statesmen, appears from this, that Dunmore himself, giving utterance to a seemingly unanimous desire, was constrained to plead with the ministry in behalf of the petitioners for leave to prohibit the slave-trade by law.

When the prayer reached England, a slave had just refused to serve his master during his stay in England; whereupon, by his master's orders, he was put on board a ship by force, to be carried out of the kingdom and sold. "So high an act of dominion," said Lord Mansfield in June, 1772, pronouncing the opinion of all the judges present, "must derive its authority, if any such it has, from the law of the kingdom where executed. The state of slavery is of such a nature that it is incapable of being introduced by courts of justice upon mere reasoning, or inferences from any principles natural or political; it must take its rise from positive law, and, in a case so odious as the condition of slaves, must be taken strictly. No master was ever allowed here to take a slave by force to be sold abroad for any reason whatever. We cannot say the cause set forth by this return is allowed or approved of by the laws of this kingdom, therefore the man must be discharged." But the king of England, though avoiding to reject in form the appeal of Virginia to himself, stood forth as the stubborn protector of the African slave-trade.

"Pharisaical Britain!" said Franklin, through the press; "to pride thyself in setting free a single slave that happened to land on thy coasts, while thy merchants in all thy ports are encouraged by thy laws to continue a commerce whereby so many hundreds of thousands are dragged into a slavery that can scarce be said to end with their lives, since it is entailed on their posterity." Yet the decision of the king's bench was momentous; for it settled the question that slavery, in any part of the British dominions of those days, rested only on local laws.

The great men of Virginia already looked forward to a thorough social change. In January 1773, Patrick Henry, writing to a member of the society of Friends, chid those of them who were "lukewarm in the abolition of slavery." "Is it not amazing," so he expressed himself, "that, at a time when the rights of humanity are defined and understood with precision, in a country above all others fond of liberty, in such an age, we find men professing a religion the most humane, mild, meek, gentle, and generous, adopting a principle as repugnant to humanity as it is inconsistent with the Bible and destructive to liberty? Every thinking honest man rejects it in speculation; but how few in practice, from conscientious motives! Believe me, I shall honor the Quakers for their noble efforts to abolish slavery; they are equally calculated to promote moral and political good. Would any one believe that I am master of slaves of my own purchase? I am drawn along by the general inconvenience of living without them. I will not, I cannot, justify it; however culpable my conduct, I will so far pay my *devoir* to virtue as to own the excellence and rectitude of her precepts, and to lament my want of conformity to them. I believe a time will come when an opportunity will be offered to abolish this lamentable evil; everything we can do is to improve it, if it happens in our day; if not, let us transmit to our descendants, together with our slaves, a pity for their unhappy lot and an abhorrence of slavery. We owe to the purity of our religion to show that it is at variance with that law which warrants slavery. I exhort you to persevere. I could say many things on this subject, a serious view of which gives a gloomy prospect to future times."

But the voice of Virginia gained its clearest utterance through one of her sons, who was of a deeper, sadder, and more earnest nature than Henry or Jefferson. Early in 1773, George Mason addressed to its legislature these prophetic words:

"Mean and sordid, but extremely short-sighted and foolish, is that self-interest which, in political questions, opposeth itself to the public good: a wise man can no other way so effectually consult the permanent welfare of his own family and posterity as by securing the just rights and privileges of that society to which they belong.

"Perhaps the constitution may by degrees work itself clear by its own innate strength, the virtue and resolution of the community; as hath often been the case in our mother country. This last is the natural remedy, if not counteracted by that slow poison which is daily contaminating the minds and morals of our people. Every gentleman here is born a petty tyrant. Practiced in arts of despotism and cruelty, we become callous to the dictates of humanity, and all the finer feelings of the soul. Taught to regard a part of our own species in the most abject and contemptible degree below us, we lose that idea of the dignity of a man which the hand of nature hath planted in us for great and useful purposes. Habituated from our infancy to trample upon the rights of human nature, every generous, every liberal sentiment, if not extinguished, is enfeebled in our minds; and in such an infernal school are to be educated our future legislators and rulers. The laws of impartial Providence may, even by such means as these, avenge upon our posterity the injury done to a set of wretches whom our injustice hath debased to a level with the brute creation. These remarks were extorted by a kind of irresistible, perhaps an enthusiastic impulse; and the author of them, conscious of his own good intentions, cares not whom they please or offend."

Rhode Island at that day, especially in Newport, had many slaves; in April 1773, Samuel Hopkins unfolded to Ezra Stiles his design of educating negroes to be ministers of the gospel, and sending them on a mission to Guinea; and, in August 1773, they issued a circular in behalf of sending two emancipated slaves as missionaries to Africa. The appeal was renewed in April 1776.

Inhabitants of Providence, in Rhode Island, had, in March 1772, complained to the deputy governor of Lieutenant Dudingston, commander of the Gaspee. Hopkins, the chief justice, on being consulted, gave the opinion "that any person who should come into the colony and exercise any authority by force of arms, without showing his commission to the governor, and, if a custom-house officer, without being sworn into his office, was guilty of a trespass, if not piracy." The governor, therefore, sent a sheriff on board the Gaspee, to ascertain by what orders the lieutenant acted Dudingston referred the subject to the admiral, who answered from Boston: "The lieutenant, sir, has done his duty. I shall give the king's officers directions that they send every man taken in molesting them to me. As sure as the people of Newport attempt to rescue any vessel, and any of them are taken, I will hang them as pirates." Dudingston seconded the insolence of his superior officer, insulted the inhabitants, plundered the islands of sheep and hogs, cut down trees, fired at market-boats, detained vessels without a colorable pretext, and made illegal seizures of goods of which the recovery cost more than they were worth.

In the afternoon of the ninth of June, the Providence packet was returning to Providence, and, proud of its speed, went gayly on, heedless of the Gaspee. Dudingston gave chase. The tide being but two hours on ebb, the packet ventured near shore; the Gaspee, confidently following, ran aground on Namquit, a little below Pawtuxet, without a chance of moving before the return of high tide. Informed of the accident, John Brown of Providence instantly raised a party of shipmasters, Whipple, Hopkins, and others, skillful oarsmen, Mawney a physician, Bowen, with other young companions. Embarking after nightfall in six or seven boats, they boarded the stranded schooner, after a scuffle in which Dudingston was wounded took and landed its crew and their personal property, and then set it on fire. The whole was conducted on a sudden impulse; yet Lord Sandwich, who was at the head of the British admiralty, resolved never to leave pursuing the colony of Rhode Island until its charter should be taken away. "A few punished at Execution dock would be the only effectual preventive of any further attempt," wrote Hutchinson, who wished to see a beginning of punishing American offenders in England. There now existed a statute authorizing such a procedure. Two months before, the king had assented to an act for the better securing dock-yards, ships, and stores, which made death the penalty for destroying even the oar of a cutter's boat or the head of an empty cask belonging to the fleet, and subjected the accused to a trial in any county in Great Britain; and this act extended to the colonies.

For the last five years, there had been no contested election in Boston. Deceived by the apparent tranquillity, the friends of government in 1772 attempted to defeat the choice of Samuel Adams as representative; but he received more than twice and a half as many votes as his opponent.

The legislature was for the fourth year convened at Cambridge; but the governor had grown weary of the strife, and, against his declared purpose, adjourned the session to the accustomed house in Boston. There the assembly gave attention to the gradual change in the constitution of the colony effected by the payment of the king's civil officers through warrants under his sign manual, drawn on a perennial fund raised by an act of parliament. By their charter, which they respected as "a most solemn compact" between them and Great Britain, they maintained that over their governor and judges the power of the king was protected by the right of nomination, the power of the colony by the exclusive right of providing support. These views were embodied by Hawley in a report to the assembly, and, on the tenth of July 1772, adopted by a vote of eighty-five to nineteen. It followed, and was so resolved, that a governor who, like Hutchinson, was not dependent on the people for support, was not such a governor as the people had consented to, at the granting of the charter; the house most solemnly protested "that the innovation was an important change of the constitution, and exposed the province to a despotic administration of government." The inference was unavoidable. If the principle contained in the preamble to Townshend's revenue act should become the rule of administration, obedience would no longer be due to the governor, and the rightful dependence on England would be at an end.

On the seventh of August, the secretary, with eager haste, announced that the king, with the "entire concurrence of Lord North, had made provision for the support of his law servants in the province of Massachusetts Bay." This act, constituting judges, who held their offices at the king's pleasure, stipendiaries of the crown, was the crisis of revolution.

Meantime, Hillsborough was left with few supporters except the flatterers who had made his vanity subservient to their selfishness. The king was weary of him; his colleagues conspired to drive him into retirement. The occasion was at hand. Franklin had negotiated with the treasury for a grant to a company of about twenty-three millions of acres of land south of the Ohio and west of the Alleghanies; Hillsborough, from the fear that men in the backwoods would be too independent, opposed the project. Franklin persuaded Hertford, Gower, Camden, the secretaries of the treasury, and others, to become share-holders in his scheme; by their influence, the lords of council disregarded the adverse report of the board of trade, and decided in favor of planting the new province. Hillsborough was too proud to brook this public insult; and the king, soothing his fall by a patent for a British earldom, accepted his resignation; but Thurlow took care that the grant for the western province should never be sealed. The pious and amiable Lord Dartmouth, who succeeded Hillsborough as secretary for the colonies, had been taught to believe, with Lord North and the king, that it was necessary to carry out the policy of consolidation, as set forth in Townshend's preamble.

## CHAPTER XXXII.

### THE TOWNS OF MASSACHUSETTS HOLD CORRESPONDENCE.

### AUGUST 1772–JANUARY 1773.

"WE must get the colonies into order before we engage with our neighbors," were the words of the king to Lord North in August, 1772; and a cordial understanding sprung up between George III. and Louis XV., that monarchy might triumph in France over philosophy, in America over the people.

On the subject of royal authority, Louis XV. never wavered. To him Protestants were republicans; and he would not even legalize their marriages. He violated the constitutions of Languedoc and Brittany without scruple, employing military force against their states. The parliament of Paris, even more than the other companies of judges, had become an aristocratic senate, not only distributing justice, but exercising some check on legislation; he demanded their unqualified registry of his edicts. "Sire," remonstrated the upright magistrate Malesherbes, in 1771, "to mark your dissatisfaction with the parliament of Paris, the most essential rights of a free people are taken from the nation. The greatest happiness of the people is always the object and end of legitimate power. God places the crown on the heads of kings to preserve to their subjects the enjoyment of life, liberty, and property. This truth flows from the law of God and from the law of nature, and is peculiar to no constitution. In France, as in all monarchies, there exist inviolable rights, which belong to the nation. Interrogate, sire, the nation itself: the incorruptible testimony of its representatives will at least let you know if the cause which we defend to-day is that of all this people, by whom you reign and for whom you reign." "I will never change," replied Louis. Exiling Malesherbes, he overturned all the parliaments and reconstructed the courts. "The crown is rescued from the dust of the rolls," cried his flatterers. "It is the tower of Babel," said others, "or chaos come again, or the end of the world."

The king of England, in like manner, had no higher object than to confirm his authority. In September the ministers of Prussia, Austria, and Russia were signing at St. Petersburg the treaty for the first partition of Poland; he did not question its justice. Toward European affairs the British policy, like that of France, was one of inertness and peace. Poland might perish, that Louis XV. might confirm his arbitrary power, and George III. obtain leisure to reduce America.

There, in New England, the marriage vow was austerely sacred. There industry created wealth, and, at the death of the parents, divided it among all the children; and none professed that the human race lives for the few. There every man was, or expected to become, a freeholder; the owner of the land held the plough; he who held the plough held the sword; and liberty, acquired by the sacrifices and sufferings of a revered ancestry, was guarded, under the blessing of God, as a sacred trust for posterity. There Hopkins, discoursing from the pulpit to the tillers of the soil, and to merchants and mariners, founded morals on the doctrine of disinterested love, establishing it as the duty of every one to be willing to sacrifice himself for the glory of God, the freedom of his country, the well-being of his race.

The younger Quincy misunderstood his countrymen when he wrote: "The word of God has pointed the mode of relief from Moabitish oppression: prayers and tears, with the help of a dagger. The Lord of light has given us the fit message to send to a tyrant: a dagger of a cubit in his belly; and every worthy man who desires to be an Ehud, the deliverer of his country, will strive to be the messenger." Hutchinson knew the people too well to be in dread of assassination; but this wild outbreak of frenzy seems to have been brought without delay to the notice of the secretary of state and of the king.

This is a people, said Samuel Adams of his countrymen,

"who of all the people on the earth deserve most to be free." Yet, when he first proposed organizing revolution through committees of correspondence, every one of his colleagues in the delegation from Boston dissuaded from the movement. Hancock, who disapproved the measure as rash or insufficient, joined with three or four others of the selectmen of the town; and they rejected the first petition for a town-meeting.

"America may assert her rights by resolves," insinuated Cushing; "but, before enforcing them, she must wait to grow more powerful." "We are at a crisis," was the answer; "this is the moment to decide whether our posterity shall inherit liberty or slavery." A new petition, signed by one hundred and six inhabitants, explaining how the judges would be corrupted into political partisans by their complete dependence, prevailed with the selectmen; and a meeting of the town of Boston was summoned for the twenty-eighth of October. The day came "We must now strike a home blow," said the "Boston Gazette," "or sit down under the yoke of tyranny. The people in every town must instruct their representatives to send a remonstrance to the king, and assure him, unless their liberties are immediately restored whole and entire, they will form an independent commonwealth after the example of the Dutch provinces, and offer a free trade to all nations. Should any one province begin the example, the other provinces will follow; and Great Britain must comply with our demands, or sink under the united force of the French and Spaniards. This is the plan that wisdom and Providence point out to preserve our rights, and this alone."

Toward that design Adams moved with undivided purpose, conducting public measures so cautiously that no step needed to be retraced. The attendance at Faneuil Hall was not great; the town only raised a committee to inquire of the governor if the judges of the province had become the stipendiaries of the crown. "This country," said Samuel Adams, in the interval, "must shake off its intolerable burdens at all events; every day strengthens our oppressors, and weakens us; if each town would declare its sense, our enemies could not divide us;" and he urged Elbridge Gerry, of Marblehead, to convoke the citizens of that port.

As the governor refused to answer the inquiry of the town, they next asked that he would allow the general assembly to meet on the day to which it had been prorogued.

A determined spirit began to show itself in the country; yet when, on the second of November, Boston reassembled, no more persons attended than on ordinary occasions. "If in compliance with your petition," such was Hutchinson's message to them, "I should alter my determination, and meet the assembly at such time as you judge necessary, I should, in effect, yield to you the exercise of that part of the prerogative. There would," moreover, "be danger of encouraging the inhabitants of the other towns in the province to assemble from time to time, in order to consider of the necessity or expediency of a session of the general assembly, or to debate and transact other matters, which the law, that authorizes towns to assemble, does not make the business of a town-meeting."

By denying the right of the towns to discuss public questions, the governor placed himself at variance with the institution of town governments, the oldest and dearest and most characteristic of the established rights of New England, rooted in custom and twined with a thousand tendrils round the faith of the people. The meeting read over the reply several times, and voted unanimously "that its inhabitants have, ever had, and ought to have a right to petition the king or his representative for the redress or the preventing of grievances, and to communicate their sentiments to other towns."

Samuel Adams then arose, and made that motion which included the whole revolution, "that a committee of correspondence be appointed, to consist of twenty-one persons, to state the rights of the colonists, and of this province in particular, as men, as Christians, and as subjects; to communicate and publish the same to the several towns in this province and to the world, as the sense of this town, with the infringements and violations thereof that have been, or from time to time may be, made; also requesting of each town a free communication of their sentiments on this subject." The assembly was to confirm the doings of the towns, and invite the other colonies to join; and this would lead to a general confederacy against the authority of parliament.

The motion was readily adopted; but it was difficult to raise the committee. Cushing, Hancock, and Phillips, three of the four representatives of Boston, pleaded private business and refused to serve; so did Scollay and Austin, two of the selectmen. The name of James Otis, who was now but a wreck, appears first on the list, as a tribute to former services. The two most important members were Samuel Adams and Joseph Warren, the first now recognised as a "masterly statesman," and the ablest political writer in New England; the second, a rare combination of gentleness with daring courage, of respect for law with the love of liberty. The two men never failed each other; the one growing old, the other in youthful manhood; thinking one set of thoughts, having one heart for their country, joining in one career of public policy and action; differing only in this, that, while Warren still clung to the hope of conciliation, Adams foresaw and desired the conflict for independence.

On the third of November, the Boston committee of correspondence met at the representatives' chamber, and organized itself by electing the true-hearted William Cooper its clerk. They next, by a unanimous vote, gave each to the others the pledge of "honor not to divulge any part of the conversation at their meetings to any person whatsoever, excepting what the committee itself should make known." Samuel Adams was then appointed to prepare the statement of the rights of the colonists, and Joseph Warren of the several grievous violations of those rights; while a letter was addressed to the other towns. Meantime, Adams roused his friends throughout the province. No more "complaining," thus he wrote to James Warren, of Plymouth; "it is more than time to be rid of both tyrants and tyranny;" and, explaining "the leading steps" which Boston had taken, he entreated co-operation.

The flame caught. Plymouth, Marblehead, Roxbury, Cambridge, prepared to second Boston. "God grant," said Samuel Adams, "that the love of liberty, and a zeal to support it, may enkindle in every town." "Their scheme of keeping up a correspondence through the province," wrote Hutchinson, in a letter which was laid before the king, "is such a foolish one that it must necessarily make them ridiculous."

After the report of the Boston committee was prepared, Otis was appointed to present it to the town. As they chose on this last great occasion of his public appearance to name him with the honors of precedence, history may express satisfaction that he whose eloquence first awakened the thought of resistance should have been able to lend his presence and his name to the grand movement for union. He was a man of many sorrows; familiar with grief, as one who had known little else. The burden of his infirmities was greater than he could bear; his fine intellect became a ruin, which reason wandered over, but did not occupy, and by its waning light showed less the original beauty of the structure than the completeness of its overthrow. The remainder of his life was passed in seclusion; years afterward, when his country's independence had been declared, he stood one summer's day in the porch of the farm-house which was his retreat, watching a sudden shower. One flash, and only one, was seen in the sky; one bolt fell, and, harming nothing else, struck James Otis. In this wise all that was mortal of him perished.

On the twentieth of November, Boston, in a legal town-meeting, received the report of their committee. Among their natural rights, they claimed a right to life, to liberty, to property; in case of intolerable oppression, to change allegiance for their sake; to resume them, if they had ever been renounced; to rescue and preserve them, sword in hand.

The grievances of which they complained were the assumption by the British parliament of absolute power in all cases whatsoever; the exertion of that power to raise a revenue in the colonies without their consent; the appointment of officers unknown to the charter to collect the revenue; the investing these officers with unconstitutional authority; the supporting them by fleets and armies in time of peace; the establishment of a civil list out of the unconstitutional revenue even for judges whose commissions were held only during pleasure, and whose decisions affected property, liberty, and life; the oppressive use of royal instructions; the enormous extension of the power of the vice-admiralty courts; the infringement of the right derived from God and nature to make use of their skill and industry, by prohibiting or restraining the manufacture of iron, of hats, of wool; the violence of authorizing persons in the colonies to be taken up under pretence of certain offences, and carried to Great Britain for trial; the claim of a right to establish a bishop and episcopal courts without the consent of the colony; the frequent alteration of the bounds of colonies, followed by a necessity for the owners of the land to purchase fresh grants of their property from rapacious governors. "This enumeration," they said, "of some of the most open infringements of their rights will not fail to excite the attention of all who consider themselves interested in the happiness and freedom of mankind, and will by every candid person be judged sufficient to justify whatever measures have been or may be taken to obtain redress."

Having thus joined issue with the king and parliament, the inhabitants of the town of Boston voted, by means of committees of correspondence, to make an appeal to all the towns in the colony, "that the collected wisdom and fortitude of the whole people might dictate measures for the rescue of their happy and glorious constitution." "These worthy New Englanders," said Chatham, as he read the report, "ever feel as Old Englanders ought to do."

And what was England gaining by the controversy? The commissioners of the stamp office were just then settling their accounts for their expenses in America, which were found to have exceeded twelve thousand pounds, while they had received for revenue only about fifteen hundred, and this almost exclusively from Canada and the West India islands. The result of the tax on tea had been more disastrous. Even in Boston, under the eyes of the commissioners of the customs, seven eighths of the teas consumed were Dutch teas, and in the southern governments the proportion was much greater; so that the whole remittance of the last year for duties on teas and wines and other articles taxed indirectly, amounted to no more than eighty-five or eighty pounds; while ships and soldiers for the support of the collecting officers had cost some hundred thousands, and the East India company had lost the sale of goods to the amount of two and a half millions of dollars annually. England was growing weary of the fruitless strife; Lord North wished it at an end; Dartmouth desired the king to "reign in the affections of his people," and would have regarded conciliation as "the happiest event of his life."

Temple, the commissioner of customs in America, remained always in strife with his associates in the American board of customs, which Grenville had established; for he never discovered in them the least view to the real interest of the revenue. They were rather guided by an anxious desire to light up a war between the colonies and the mother country, and left no means unattempted to effect it. "I am perfectly of opinion with General Gage," so he wrote, in November 1768, to Grenville, "that the king's cause has been more hurt in this country by some of his own servants than by all the world beside, and time must turn this up to public view." In the latter part of the following year, to the great dismay of Hutchinson, he returned to England, partly to answer the charge made in form against him by his colleagues of favoring the popular party, and partly to charge them and the governor with insolence, indiscretion, and abuse of their powers. Lord Temple acted toward him the part of a real father, and in Lord Chatham, between whom and Lord Temple there had been a reconciliation, he found an able and kind adviser. The return of Temple to England dismayed Hutchinson, who was sure to find in him an implacable enemy. From another source Grenville knew well the purposes of Hutchinson, for Thomas Whately had communicated to his old patron letters which Hutchinson, and Oliver, Hutchinson's brother-in-law, had written to him to stimulate the British government in the policy of coercing the colonies into submission. These letters Grenville showed to Lord Temple, and they were seen by others.

In December 1772, after the death alike of George Grenville and of Thomas Whately, a member of parliament having discovered that every perverse "measure and every grievance complained of took their rise not from the British government, but were projected, proposed to administration, solicited, and obtained by some of the most respectable among the Americans themselves, as necessary for the welfare of that country," endeavored to convince Franklin of the well-ascertained fact. Franklin remaining skeptical, he returned in a few days with these very letters from Hutchinson and Oliver, which Grenville had shown to Lord Temple.

These, which were but moderate specimens of a most persevering and extensive correspondence of a like nature, Franklin was authorized to send to his constituents, not for publication, but to be retained for some months, and perused by the corresponding committee of the legislature, by members of the council, and by some few others to whom the chairman of that committee might think proper to show them.

Had the conspiracy, which was thus laid bare, aimed at the life of a minister, or the king, any honest man must have immediately communicated the discovery to the secretary of state; to conspire to introduce into America a military government and abridge American liberty, was a still more heinous crime, of which irrefragable evidence had come to light. Franklin, as agent of Massachusetts, made himself the public accuser of those whose conduct was now exposed; and, in an official letter, sent the proofs of their designs to the speaker of the Massachusetts house of representatives, with no concealment or reservation but such as his informer had required. "All good men," wrote Franklin, as he forwarded the letters, "wish harmony to subsist between the colonies and the mother country. My resentment against this country for its arbitrary measures in governing us has been exceedingly abated, since my conviction by these papers that those measures were projected, advised, and called for by men of character among ourselves. I think they must have the same effect with you. As to the writers, when I find them bartering away the liberties of their native country for posts, negotiating for salaries and pensions extorted from the people, and, conscious of the odium these might be attended with, calling for troops to protect and secure the enjoyment of them; when I see them exciting jealousies in the crown, and provoking it to wrath against so great a part of its most faithful subjects; creating enmities between the different countries of which the empire consists; occasioning a great expense to the old country for suppressing or preventing imaginary rebellions in the new, and to the new country for the payment of needless gratifications to useless officers and enemies—I cannot but doubt their sincerity even in the political principles they profess, and deem them mere time-servers, seeking their own private emoluments through any quantity of public mischief; betrayers of the interest not of their native country only, but of the government they pretend to serve, and of the whole English empire."

While the letters were on their way, the towns in the province were coming together under the invitation from Boston. The people of Marblehead, whose fishermen were returned from their annual excursion to the Grand Banks, at a full meeting, with but one dissentient, expressed "their unavoidable disesteem and reluctant irreverence for the British parliament;" their sense of the "great and uncommon kind of grievance" of being compelled "to carry the produce of Spain and Portugal, received for their fish, to Great Britain, and there paying duties;" how "justly they were incensed at the unconstitutional, unrighteous proceedings" of ministers; how they "detested the name of a Hillsborough;" how ready they were to "unite for the recovery of their violated rights;" and, like Roxbury and Plymouth, they appointed their committee. Warren, of Plymouth, was desponding. "The towns," said he, "are dead, and cannot be raised without a miracle." "I am very sorry to find in you the least approach toward despair," answered Adams. "*Nil desperandum* is a motto for you and me. All are not dead; and where there is a spark of patriotic fire we will rekindle it." The patriot's confidence was justified. In Plymouth itself "there were ninety to one to fight Great Britain."

In December, the people of Cambridge, in a full meeting, expressed themselves "much concerned to maintain and secure their own invaluable rights, which were not the gift of kings, but purchased with the precious blood and treasure of their ancestors;" and they "discovered a glorious spirit, like men determined to be free." Roxbury, which had moved with deliberation, found "the rights of the colonists fully supported and warranted by the laws of God and nature, the New Testament, and the charter of the province." "Our pious forefathers," said they, "died with the pleasing hope that we their children should live free; let none, as they will answer it another day, disturb their ashes by selling their birthright."

On Monday, the twenty-eighth of December, towns were in session from the Kennebec to Buzzard's bay. The people of Charlestown beheld their own welfare "and the fate of unborn millions in suspense." "It will not be long," said Rochester, "before our assembling for the cause of liberty will be determined to be riotous, and every attempt to prevent the flood of despotism from overflowing our land will be deemed open rebellion." Woolwich, "an infant people in an infant country," did not "think their answer perfect in spelling or the words placed," yet hearty good feeling got the better of their false shame. Does any one ask who had precedence in proposing a union of the colonies, and a war for independence? The thoughts were the offspring of the time, and were in every patriot's breast. It were as well to ask which tree in the forest is the earliest to feel the reviving year. The first official utterance of revolution did not spring from a congress of the colonies, or the future chiefs of the republic; from the rich who falter, or the learned who weigh and debate. The people of the little interior town of Pembroke, in Plymouth county, unpretending husbandmen, full of the glory of their descent from the pilgrims, concluded a clear statement of their grievances with the prediction that, "if the measures so justly complained of were persisted in and enforced by fleets and armies, they must, they will, in a little time issue in the total dissolution of the union between the mother country and the colonies." In a louder tone the freemen of Gloucester declared their readiness to stand for their rights and liberties, which were dearer to them than their lives, and to join with all others in an appeal to the Great Lawgiver, not doubting of success according to the justice of their cause.

Salisbury, a small town on the Merrimack, counselled an American union. Ipswich, in point of numbers the second town in the province, advised "that the colonies in general, and the inhabitants of their province in particular, should stand firm as one man, to maintain all their just rights and privileges." In the course of December, the earl of Chatham was reading several New England writings "with admiration and love;" among others, an election sermon by Tucker, in which he found "the divine Sidney rendered practical, and the philosophical Locke more demonstrative;" and, on that same day, the people of the town of Chatham, at the extremity of Cape Cod, were declaring their "civil and religious principles to be the sweetest and essential part of their lives, without which the remainder was scarcely worth preserving."

But the excitement increased when it became known that Thurlow and Wedderburn had reported the burning of the Gaspee to be a crime of a much deeper dye than piracy, and that the king, by the advice of his privy council, had ordered its authors and abettors to be delivered to Rear-Admiral Montagu, and, with the witnesses, brought for "condign punishment" to England. To send an American across the Atlantic for trial for his life was an intolerable violation of justice; Hutchinson urged what was worse, to abrogate the Rhode Island charter. In this hour of greatest peril, the men of Rhode Island, by the hands of Darius Sessions, their deputy governor, and Stephen Hopkins, their chief justice, appealed to Samuel Adams for advice. And he answered immediately that the occasion "should awaken the American colonies, and again unite them in one band; that an attack upon the liberties of one colony was an attack upon the liberties of all, and that, therefore, in this instance all should be ready to yield assistance."

Employing this event to promote a general union, the Boston committee, as the year went out, were, "by the people's thorough understanding of their civil and religious rights and liberties, encouraged to trust in God that a day was hastening when the efforts of the colonists would be crowned with success, and the present generation furnish an example of public virtue worthy the imitation of all posterity."

In a like spirit, the eventful year of 1773 was rung in by the men of Marlborough. "Death," said they, unanimously, on the first of January, "is more eligible than slavery. A free-born people are not required by the religion of Jesus Christ to submit to tyranny, but may make use of such power as God has given them to recover and support their laws and liberties." And, advising all the colonies to prepare for war, they "implored the Ruler above the skies that he would make bare his arm in defence of his church and people, and let Israel go."

"As we are in a remote wilderness corner of the earth, we know but little," said the farmers of Lenox; "but neither nature nor the God of nature requires us to crouch, Issachar-like, between the two burdens of poverty and slavery." "We prize our liberties so highly," thus spoke the men of Leicester, with the districts of Spencer and Paxton, "that we think it our duty to risk our lives and fortunes in defence thereof." "For that spirit of virtue which induced your town at so critical a day to take the lead in so good a cause," wrote the town of Petersham, "our admiration is heightened, when we consider your being exposed to the first efforts of power. The time may come when you may be driven from your goodly heritage; if that should be the case, we invite you to share with us in our small supplies of the necessaries of life; and, should we still not be able to withstand, we are determined to retire, and seek repose among the inland aboriginal natives, with whom we doubt not but to find more humanity and brotherly love than we have lately received from our mother country." "We join with the town of Petersham," was the reply of Boston, " in preferring a life among the savages to the most splendid condition of slavery; but heaven will bless the united efforts of a brave people."

"It is only some people in the Massachusetts Bay making a great clamor, in order to keep their party alive," wrote time-servers to Dartmouth, begging for further grants of salaries, and blind to the awakening of a nation. "This unhappy contest between Britain and America," wrote Samuel Adams, "will end in rivers of blood; but America may wash her hands in innocence." Informing Rhode Island of the design of "administration to get their charter vacated," he advised them to protract, without conceding any of their rights; and to address the assemblies of all the other colonies for support.

## CHAPTER XXXIII.

### VIRGINIA CONSOLIDATES UNION.

### JANUARY–JULY 1773.

ON the sixth of January 1773, the day on which the legislature of Massachusetts assembled at Boston, the affairs of America were under consideration in England. The king, who read even the semi-official letters in which Hutchinson described the Boston committee of correspondence as in part composed of "deacons" and "atheists," and "black-hearted fellows whom one would not choose to meet in the dark," "very much approved the temper and firmness" of his governor, and was concerned lest "the inhabitants of Boston should be deluded into acts of disobedience and the most atrocious criminality toward individuals;" he found "consolation" in the assurance that "the influence of the malignant spirits was daily decreasing," and "that their mischievous tenets were held in abhorrence by the generality of the people." But already eighty towns or more, including almost every one of the larger towns, had chosen their committees; and Samuel Adams was planning how to effect a union of all the colonies in congress. When the assembly met, the speaker transmitted the proceedings of the town of Boston for organizing the provincial committees of correspondence to Richard Henry Lee, of Virginia.

The governor, in his speech to the two houses, with calculating malice summoned them to admit or disprove the supremacy of parliament. The disorder in the government he attributed to the denial of that supremacy, which he undertook to establish by arguments derived from the history of the colony, its charter, and English law. "I know of no line," he said, "that can be drawn between the supreme authority of parliament and the total independence of the colonies. It is impossible there should be two independent legislatures in one and the same state." He therefore invited the legislature to adhere to his principles or convince him of his error. Elated with vanity, he thought himself sure in any event of a victory; for, if they should disown the opinions of the several towns, he would gain glory in England; if they should avow them, then, said he in a letter which was to go straight to the king, "I shall be enabled to make apparent the reasonableness and necessity of coercion, and justify it to all the world."

The speech was printed and industriously circulated in England, and for a short time its indiscretion was not perceived. In Boston, Samuel Adams prepared to "take the fowler in his own snare." No man in the province had reflected so much as he on the question of the legislative power of parliament over the colonies; no man had so early arrived at the total denial of that power. For nine years he had been seeking an opportunity of promulgating that denial as the opinion of the assembly; and caution had always stood in his way. At last the opportunity had come; and the assembly, with one consent, placed the pen in his hand.

Meantime, the towns of Massachusetts were still vibrating from the impulse given by Boston. "The swords which we whet and brightened for our enemies are not yet grown rusty," wrote the town of Gorham. "We offer our lives as a sacrifice in the glorious cause of liberty," was the response of Kittery. "We will not sit down easy," voted Shirley, "until our rights and liberties are restored." The people of Medfield would also "have a final period put to that most cruel, inhuman, and unchristian practice, the slave-trade." Acton spoke out concisely and firmly. "Prohibiting slitting-mills," said South Hadley, "is similar to the Philistines prohibiting smiths in Israel, and shews we are esteemed by our brethren as vassals." "We think ourselves obliged to emerge from our former obscurity, and speak our minds with freedom," declared Lunenburg, "or our posterity may otherwise rise up and curse us." "We of this place are unanimous," was the message from Pepperell; "our resentment riseth against those who dare invade our natural and constitutional rights." With one voice they named

Captain William Prescott to be the chief of their committee of correspondence; and no braver heart beat in Middlesex than his. Lynn called for a provincial convention; Stoneham invited the sister colonies to harmony; Danvers would have "strict union of all the provinces on the continent." "Digressions from compacts," said the men of Princeton, "lessen the connection between the mother country and the colonies."

South Carolina, too remote for immediate concert, was engaged in the same cause. Its assembly elected Rawlins Lowndes their speaker. The governor "directed the assembly to return to their house and choose another;" and, as they persisted in their first choice, he prorogued them, and did it in so illegal a manner that, as a remedy, he dissolved them by a proclamation, and immediately issued writs for choosing a new house. By the order for a new election, he himself brought the subject home to the thoughts of every voter in the province, and consolidated resistance.

This controversy was local; the answers of the legislature of Massachusetts to the challenge of Hutchinson would be of general importance. That of the council, drafted by Bowdoin, clearly traced the existing discontents to the acts of parliament, subjecting the colonies to taxes without their consent. The removal of this original cause would remove its effects. Supreme or unlimited authority can with fitness belong only to the Sovereign of the universe; from the nature and end of government, the supreme authority of every government is limited; and from the laws of England, its constitution, and the provincial charter, the limits of that authority do not include the levying of taxes within the province. The council conceded nothing, and yet avoided a conflict with the opinions of Chatham, Camden, and Shelburne.

The house in their reply, which Samuel Adams, aided by the sound legal knowledge of Hawley, had constructed with his utmost skill at sarcasm, and which, after two days' debate, was unanimously adopted and carried up by its author, chose a different mode of dealing with the governor's positions. Like the council, they traced the disturbed state of government to taxation of the colonists by parliament; but, as to the supremacy of that body, they took the governor at his word. "It is difficult, perhaps impossible," they agreed, "to draw a line of distinction between the universal authority of parliament over the colonies and no authority at all;" and, laying out all their strength to prove the only point which Hutchinson's statement required to be proved, that that authority was not universal, they opened the door to his own inference. "If there be no such line," said they, "between the supreme authority of parliament and the total independence of the colonies, then either the colonies are vassals of the parliament or they are totally independent. As it cannot be supposed to have been the intention of the parties in the compact that one of them should be reduced to a state of vassalage, the conclusion is that it was their sense that we were thus independent." "But it is impossible," the governor had insisted, "that there should be two independent legislatures in one and the same state." "Then," replied the house, "the colonies were by their charters made distinct states from the mother country." "Although there may be but one king," Hutchinson had said, "yet the two legislative bodies will make two governments as distinct as the kingdoms of England and Scotland before the union." "Very true," replied the house; "and, if they interfere not with each other, what hinders but that, being united in one head and sovereign, they may live happily in that connection, and mutually support and protect each other?"

"But is there anything," the governor had asked, "which we have more reason to dread than independence?" And the house answered: "There is more reason to dread the consequences of absolute uncontrolled power, whether of a nation or of a monarch." "To draw the line of distinction," they continue, "between the supreme authority of parliament and the total independence of the colonies would be an arduous undertaking, and of very great importance to all the other colonies; and, therefore, could we conceive of such a line, we should be unwilling to propose it without their consent in congress."

Having thus won an unsparing victory over the logic of Hutchinson by accepting all his premises and fitting to them other and apter conclusions, they rebuked the governor for having reduced them to the alternative either of appearing by silence to acquiesce in his sentiments, or of freely discussing the supreme authority of parliament.

The governor was overwhelmed with confusion. He had intended to drive them into a conflict with parliament; and they had denied its supremacy by implication from his own premises, in a manner that could bring censure on no one but himself.

During this controversy, a commission, composed of Admiral Montagu, the vice-admiralty judge at Boston, the chief justices of Massachusetts, New York, and New Jersey, and the governor of Rhode Island, met at Newport to inquire into the affair of the Gaspee. Darius Sessions, the deputy governor, and Stephen Hopkins, formerly governor, now chief justice, were the two pillars on which Rhode Island liberty depended. They notified the commissioners that there had been no neglect of duty or connivance on the part of the provincial government; from which it followed that the presence of the special court was as unnecessary as it was alarming.

The assembly having met at East Greenwich to watch the commissioners, the governor laid before it his instructions to arrest offenders and send them for trial to England. The order excited general horror and indignation. The chief justice asked directions how he should act. The assembly referred him to his discretion. "Then," said Hopkins, in the presence of both houses, "for the purpose of transportation for trial, I will neither apprehend any person by my own order, nor suffer any executive officers in the colony to do it." "The people would not have borne an actual seizure of persons." The attempt would have produced a crisis.

The commissioners elicited nothing, and in February adjourned with bitterness in their hearts. Smyth, the chief justice of New Jersey, who had just been put on the civil list, threw all blame on the popular government of Rhode Island. Horsmanden, the chief justice of New York, advised to take away the charter of that province, and of Connecticut, and consolidate the "twins in one royal government." Yet Connecticut, the land of steady habits, was at that day the most orderly and quietly governed people in the world; and the charter of Rhode Island, in spite of all its enemies, had vitality enough to outlast the unreformed house of commons.

The doctrines of Massachusetts gained strength in that colony, and extended to others. Hutchinson was embarrassed by the controversy which he had provoked, and would now willingly have ended. Meantime, the house made the usual grants to the justices of the superior court; but the governor refused his assent, because he expected warrants for their salaries from the king. The house replied: "No judge, who has a due regard to justice or even to his own character, would choose to be placed under such an undue bias as they must be under by accepting their salaries of the crown. We are more and more convinced that it has been the design of administration totally to subvert the constitution, and introduce an arbitrary government into this province; and we cannot wonder that the apprehensions of this people are thoroughly awakened." The towns of Massachusetts were all the while continuing their meetings. "The judges," said the men of Eastham, "must reject the detestable plan with abhorrence, if they would have their memories blessed." "We deny the parliamentary power of taxing us, being without the realm of England and not represented there," declared Stoughtenham. "Let the colonies stand firm as one man," voted Winchendon. "Divine Providence and the necessity of things may call upon us and all the colonies to make our last appeal," wrote the farmers who dwelt on the bleak hills of New Salem.

Yet Hutchinson seemed compelled to renew his discussion with the legislature; and in a long argument, which contained little that was new, endeavored to prove that the colony of Massachusetts was holden as feudatory of the imperial crown of England, and was therefore under the government of the king's laws and the king's court. Again Bowdoin for the council, with still greater clearness, affirms that parliamentary taxation is unconstitutional, because imposed without consent; again Samuel Adams for the house, aided briefly, in Hawley's temporary absence, by the strong natural powers of John Adams and his good knowledge of the laws, proves from the governor's own premises that parliament has no supremacy over the colony, because the feudal system admits no idea of the authority of parliament.

At the same time, both parties looked beyond the province for aid. Hutchinson sought to intimidate his antagonists by telling them "that the English nation would be roused, and could not be withstood;" that "parliament would, by some means or other, maintain its supremacy." To his correspondents in England, he sent word what measures should be chosen; advising a change in the political organization of towns, a prohibition of the commerce of Boston, and the option to the province between submission and the forfeiture of their rights. "I wish," said he, "government may be convinced that something is necessary to be done." "We want a full persuasion that parliament will maintain its supremacy at all events." "Without it, the opposition here will triumph more than ever."

The people on their part drew from their institution of committees of correspondence throughout the province the hope of a union of all the colonies. "Some future congress," said the Boston orator of the fifth of March, "will be the glorious source of the salvation of America; the Amphictyons of Greece, who formed the diet or great council of the states, exhibit an excellent model for the rising Americans."

Whether that great idea should become a reality rested on Virginia. Its legislature came together in March. Its members had authentic information of the proceedings of the town of Boston; and public rumors had reached them of the commission for inquiry into the affairs of Rhode Island. They had read and approved of the answers which the council and the house of Massachusetts had made in January to the speech of Hutchinson. They formed themselves, therefore, into a committee of the whole house on the state of the colony; and in that committee Dabney Carr, of Charlotte, a young statesman of brilliant genius as well as fervid patriotism, moved a series of resolutions for a system of intercolonial committees of correspondence. His plan included a thorough union of councils throughout the continent. If it should succeed and be adopted by the other colonies, America would stand before the world as a confederacy. The measure was supported by Richard Henry Lee, with an eloquence which never passed away from the memory of his hearers; by Patrick Henry, with commanding majesty. The assembly did what greatness of mind counselled; and they did it quietly, as if it were but natural to them to act with greatness of mind. On Friday, the twelfth, the resolutions were reported to the house and unanimously adopted. They appointed their committee, on which appear the names of Bland and Lee, of Henry and Carr and Jefferson. Their resolves were sent to every colony, with a request that each would appoint its committee to communicate from time to time with that of Virginia. In this manner Virginia laid the foundation of our union. Massachusetts organized a province; Virginia promoted a confederacy. Were the several committees to come together, the world would see an American congress.

The associates of Dabney Carr were spared for further service to humanity. He himself was cut down in his prime; but the name of him who at this moment of crisis beckoned the colonies onward to union must not perish from the memory of his countrymen.

The effect of these resolutions of the Old Dominion gladdened every heart in Massachusetts. "Virginia and South Carolina, by their steady perseverance," inspired the hope that the fire of liberty would spread through the continent. "A congress and then an assembly of states," reasoned Samuel Adams, is no longer "a mere fiction in the mind of a political enthusiast." What though "the British nation carry their liberties to market, and sell them to the highest bidder!" "America," said he, repeating the words of Arthur Lee, "shall rise full plumed and glorious from the mother's ashes."

A copy of the proceedings of Virginia was sent to every town and district in Massachusetts, that " all the friends of American independence and freedom" might welcome the intelligence; and, as one meeting after another echoed back the advice for a congress, they could hardly find words to express how their gloom had given way to light, and how "their hearts even leapt for joy." "We trust the day is not far distant," said Cambridge, by the hand of Thomas Gardner, " when our rights and liberties shall be restored unto us, or the colonies, united as one man, will make their most solemn appeal to heaven, and drive tyranny from these northern climes."

"The colonies must assert their liberties whenever the opportunity offers," wrote Dickinson from Pennsylvania. The opportunity was nearer than he thought; in England, Chatham saw plainly that "things were hastening to a crisis at Boston, and looked forward to the issue with very painful anxiety." It was the king who precipitated the conflict. He had no dread of the interposition of France, for that power, under the ministry of the day, feared lest the enfranchisement of the Anglo-American colonies should create a power dangerous to itself, and was eager to fortify the good understanding with England by a defensive treaty, or at least by a treaty of commerce. Louis XV. was resolved at all events to avoid war.

From the time, therefore, that the representatives of Massachusetts avowed their legislative independence, the king dismissed the thought of obtaining obedience "by argument and persuasion." The most thorough search was made into every colonial law that checked, or even seemed to check, the slave-trade; and an act of Virginia, which put no more obstructions upon it than had existed for a generation, was negatived. Parliamentary taxation was to be enforced.

The continued refusal of America to receive tea from England had brought distress upon the East India company, which had on hand, wanting a market, great quantities imported in the faith that that agreement could not hold. They were able to pay neither their dividends nor their debts; their stock depreciated nearly one half; and the government must lose their annual payment of four hundred thousand pounds. The bankruptcies, brought on partly by this means, gave such a shock to credit as had not been experienced since the South Sea year; and the great manufacturers were sufferers. The directors came to parliament with an ample confession of their humbled state, together with entreaties for assistance and relief; and particularly praying that leave might be given to export teas free of all duties to America and to foreign ports.

Instead of this, Lord North proposed to give to the company itself the right of exporting its teas. The existing law granted on their exportation to America a drawback of three fifths only of the duties paid on importation. Lord North now offered a drawback of the whole. Trecothick in the committee advised to take off the import duty in America of threepence the pound, as it produced no income to the revenue; but the ministry would not listen to the thought of relieving America from taxation. "Then," added Trecothick in behalf of the East India company, "as much or more may be brought into the revenue by not allowing a full exemption from the duties paid here." But Lord North insisted that no difficulty could arise, that under the new regulation America would be able to buy tea from the company at a lower price than from any other European nation, and that men will always go to the cheapest market.

The ministry was still in its halcyon days; no opposition was made even by the whigs; and the measure, which was the king's own, and was designed to put America to the test, took effect as a law from the tenth of May. It was immediately followed by a most carefully prepared answer from the king to petitions from Massachusetts, announcing that he "considered his authority to make laws in parliament of sufficient force and validity to bind his subjects in America in all cases whatsoever, as essential to the dignity of the crown, and a right appertaining to the state which it was his duty to preserve entire and inviolate;" that he, therefore, "could not but be greatly displeased with the petitions and remonstrance in which that right was drawn into question;" but that he "imputed the unwarrantable doctrines held forth in the said petitions and remonstrance to the artifices of a few." All this while Lord Dartmouth "had a true desire to see lenient measures adopted toward the colonies," not being in the least aware that he was drifting with the cabinet toward the system of coercion.

In America, men began to prepare for extreme measures. "Glorious Virginia!" cried the legislature of Rhode Island, glowing with admiration for "its patriotic and illustrious house of burgesses;" and this New England province was the first to follow the example of the Old Dominion, by electing its committees and sending its circular through the land.

In Massachusetts, so soon as the government for the year

was organized, the house, on the motion of Samuel Adams, and by a vote of one hundred and nine to four, expressed its gratitude to the burgesses of Virginia for their uniform vigilance, firmness, and wisdom, and its hearty concurrence in their judicious and spirited resolves. And then it elected its committee of correspondence, fifteen in number. New Hampshire and Connecticut did the same, so that all New England and Virginia were now one political body, with an organization inchoate, yet so perfect that on the first emergency they could convene a congress. Every other colony on the continent was sure to follow their example.

While the patriot party was cheered by the hope of union, the letters of Hutchinson and Oliver, which Franklin had sent over to the speaker of the Massachusetts assembly, were received. "Cool, thinking, deliberate villains; malicious and vindictive, as well as ambitious and avaricious," said John Adams, who this year was chosen into the council, but negatived by the governor. "Bone of our bone, flesh of our flesh, born and educated among us," cried others. Hancock, who was angry at being named in the correspondence, determined to lay bare their hypocrisy; and Cooper from the pulpit preached of "the old serpent, which deceiveth the whole world, but was cast out into the earth, and his angels with him."

The letters had circulated privately in the province for more than two months, when, on the second of June, Samuel Adams read them to the house in secret session. They showed a thorough complicity with Bernard and the commissioners of the customs, to bring military sway into the province, and to abridge colonial liberties by the interposition of parliament. The house after a debate voted, by one hundred and one against five, "that the tendency and design of the letters was to subvert the constitution of the government, and to introduce arbitrary power into the province." "I have never wrote any public or private letter that tends to subvert the constitution," was Hutchinson's message the next day.

The house, on the fourth, sent him a transcript of their proceedings, with the date of his letters that were before them, and asked for copies of these, and such others as he should think proper to communicate. "If you desire copies with a view to make them public," answered Hutchinson, after five days' reflection, "the originals are more proper for that purpose than the copies;" and he refused to communicate other letters, declaring that it had not been the design of them "to subvert the constitution of the government, but rather to preserve it entire." Then, conscious of guilt, he by the very next packet sent word to his confidential friend in London to burn such of his letters as might raise a clamor; for, said he, "I have wrote what ought not to be made public."

He had written against every part of the constitution, the elective character of the council, the annual choice of the assembly, the New England organization of the towns; had advised and solicited the total dependence of the judiciary on the crown; had hinted at making the experiment of declaring martial law, and of abrogating English liberty; had advised to the restraint of the commerce of Boston and the exclusion of the province from the fisheries; had urged the immediate suppression of the charter of Rhode Island; had for years "been begging for measures to maintain the supremacy of parliament" by making the denial of that supremacy a capital felony: and all for the sake of places for his family, and a salary and a pension for himself. To corrupt pure and good and free political institutions of a happy country and infuse into its veins the slow poison of tyranny, is the highest crime against humanity. And how terribly was he punished! For what is life without the esteem of one's fellow-men! Had he been but honest, how New England would have cherished his memory! Now his gray hairs, which should ever be kept purer than the ermine, were covered with shame; his ambition was defeated, and he suffered all the tortures of avarice trembling for the loss of place. It was Hancock who, taking advantage of the implied permission of Hutchinson, produced to the house copies of the letters, which were then published and scattered throughout New England and the continent. A series of resolves was adopted, expressing their true meaning, and was followed by a petition to the king that he would remove Hutchinson and Oliver forever from the government. The council in like manner, after a thorough analysis of the real intent of the correspondence, joined in the same prayer. So great unanimity had never been known.

Timid from nature, from age, and from an accusing conscience, Hutchinson expressed his desire to resign. "I hope," he said, "I shall not be left destitute, to be insulted and triumphed over. I fall in the cause of government; and, whenever it shall be thought proper to supersede me, I hope for some appointment;" and, calumniating Franklin as one who wished to supplant him in the government of Massachusetts, he made interest for Franklin's desirable office of deputy postmaster-general.

All the summer long, the insidious letters that had come to light circulated through the province, and were discussed by the single-minded country people during the week, as they made hay or gathered in the early harvest; on Sundays, the ministers discoursed on them, and poured out their hearts in prayer for the preservation of their precious inheritance of liberty. "We devote not only what little we have in the world," said the people of Pearsontown, "but even our lives, to vindicate rights so dearly purchased by our ancestors." The town of Abington became convinced that the boasted connection with Great Britain was "not worth a rush." The natural right of mankind to improve the form of government under which they live was inculcated from the pulpit, and some of the clergy of Boston, so Hutchinson bears witness, predicted that "in fifteen years" the people of America would mould for themselves a new constitution.

## CHAPTER XXXIV.

### THE BOSTON TEA-PARTY.

#### August–December 1773.

The East India company, who were now by act of parliament authorized to export tea to America duty free in England, were warned by Americans that their adventure would end in loss; but their scruples were overruled by Lord North, who answered peremptorily: " It is to no purpose making objections, for the king will have it so. The king means to try the question with America."

The time was short, the danger to Boston imminent, resistance at all hazards was the purpose of its committee of correspondence; violent resistance might become necessary, and to undertake it without a certainty of union would only bring ruin on the town and on the cause.

A congress, therefore, on " the plan of union proposed by Virginia," was the fixed purpose of Samuel Adams. He would have no delay, no waiting for increased strength; for, said he, " when our liberty is gone, history and experience will teach us that an increase of inhabitants will be but an increase of slaves." Through the press he appealed to the continent for a congress, in order to insist effectually upon such terms with England as would not admit for the interior government of the colonies any other authority than that of their respective legislatures. It was not possible to join issue with the king more precisely.

The first difficulty to be overcome existed in Boston itself. Cushing, the speaker, who had received a private letter from Dartmouth, and was lulled into confiding in " the noble and generous sentiments " of that minister, advised that for the time the people should bear their grievances. "Our natural increase in wealth and population," said he, "will in a course of years settle this dispute in our favor; whereas, if we persist in denying the right of parliament to legislate for us, they may think us extravagant in our demands, and there will be great danger of bringing on a rupture fatal to both countries." He thought the redress of grievances would more surely come "if these high points about the supreme authority of parliament were to fall asleep." Against this feeble advice, the Boston committee of correspondence aimed at the union of the province, and "the confederacy of the whole continent of America." They refused to waive the claim of right, which could only divide the Americans in sentiment and confuse their counsels. "What oppressions," they asked, in their circular to all the other towns, "may we not expect in another seven years, if through a weak credulity, while the most arbitrary measures are still persisted in, we should be prevailed upon to submit our rights, as the patriotic Farmer expresses it, to the tender mercies of the ministry? Watchfulness, unity, and harmony are necessary to the salvation of ourselves and posterity from bondage. We have an animating confidence in the Supreme Disposer of events, that he will never suffer a sensible, brave, and virtuous people to be enslaved."

Sure of Boston and its committee, Samuel Adams next conciliated the favoring judgment of the patriot Hawley, whose influence in the province was deservedly great, and who had shared with him the responsibility of the measures of the assembly. "I submit to you my ideas at this time, because matters seem to me to be drawing to a crisis." Such were his words on the fourth and the thirteenth of October. "The present administration, even though the very good Lord Dartmouth is one of them, are as fixed as any of their predecessors in their resolution to carry their favorite point, an acknowledgment of the right of parliament to make laws binding us in all cases whatever. Some of our politicians would have the people believe that administration are disposed or determined to have all the grievances which we complain of redressed, if we will only be quiet; but this would be a fatal delusion. If the king himself should make any concessions, or take any steps contrary to the right of parliament to tax us, he would be in danger of embroiling himself with the ministry. Under the present prejudices, even the recalling an instruction to the governor is not likely to be advised. The subject-matter of our complaint is not that a burden greater than our proportion was laid upon us by parliament—such a complaint we might have made without questioning the authority of parliament—but that the parliament has assumed and exercised the power of taxing us. His majesty, in his answer to our late petitions, implies that the parliament is the supreme legislature, and that its authority over the colonies is the constitution. All allow the minister in the American department to be a good man. The great men in England have an opinion of us as being a mightily religious people, and suppose that we shall place an entire confidence in a minister of the same character. In fact, how many were filled with the most sanguine expectations, when they heard that the good Lord Dartmouth was intrusted with a share in administration. Yet, without a greatness of mind equal, perhaps superior, to his goodness, it will be impossible for him singly to stem the torrent of corruption. This requires much more fortitude than he is possessed of. The safety of the Americans depends upon their pursuing their wise plan of union in principle and conduct."

Such were the thoughts which Samuel Adams unbosomed to his faithful fellow-laborer. The press, which he directed, continued to demand an annual "congress of American states to frame a bill of rights," or to "form an independent state, an American commonwealth." Union was the first, the last, the only hope for America. Massachusetts, where the overruling will of Samuel Adams swayed the feebler politicians, was thoroughly united. But that was not enough; "we must have a convention of all the colonies," he would say to his friends; and the measure was recognised by the royalists as "of all others the most likely to kindle a general flame." His advice was confirmed by the concurrent opinion of Franklin, to whose "greatness" he had publicly paid a tribute. His influence brought even Cushing to act as one of a select committee with himself and Heath of Roxbury; and they sent forth a secret circular, summoning all the colonies to be prepared to assert their rights, when time and circumstances should give to their claim the surest prospect of success. "And when we consider," they said, "how one great event has hurried on after another, such a time may come and such circumstances take place sooner than we are now aware of." They advised to contentment with no temporary relief. They explained that the king would certainly maintain the power of parliament to extort and to appropriate a tribute from the colonies; that the connection between Great Britain and America should be broken, unless it could be perpetuated on the terms of equal liberty; that the necessary contest must be entered upon while "the ideas of liberty" were strong in men's minds; and they closed with desiring each colony to resist the designs of the English ministry in allowing the East India company to ship its teas to America.

That company was despatching its consignments simultaneously to Charleston, to Philadelphia, to New York, and to Boston. The system gave universal offence, not only as an enforcement of the tax on tea, but as an odious monopoly of trade. Philadelphia, the largest town in the colonies, began the work of prevention. Its inhabitants met on the eighteenth of October, in great numbers, at the state-house, and in eight resolutions denied the claim of parliament to tax America; specially condemned the duty on tea; declared every one who should, directly or indirectly, countenance its imposition, an enemy to his country; and requested the agents of the East India company to resign. The movement was so general and so commanding that the agents, some cheerfully, others reluctantly, renounced their appointment. Within a few days not one remained.

South Carolina, by her spirit and perseverance, gave, as she had ever done, evidence that her patriotism would be the support of union. The province was at that time in a state of just excitement at the arbitrary act of its council in imprisoning Thomas Powell, the publisher of the "South Carolina Gazette," for an alleged contempt. Of the council, whose members were chiefly crown officers, and held their places at the king's pleasure, the power to imprison on their mere warrant was denied; the prisoner was taken before Rawlins Lowndes and another magistrate on a writ of habeas corpus, and was released. The questions involved in the case were discussed with heat; but they did not divert attention from watching the expected tea-ships.

The "ideas of liberty," on which resistance was to be founded, had taken deep root in a soil which the circular of Massachusetts did not reach. The people of Illinois were most opportunely sending their last message respecting their choice of a government directly to Dartmouth. We have seen how vainly they had reasoned with Gage and Hillsborough for some of the privileges of self-direction. Here, as on other occasions, Dartmouth adopted the policy of his predecessor. He censured "the ideas of the inhabitants of the Illinois district with regard to a civil constitution as very extravagant;" and rejected their proposition to take some part in the election of their rulers as "absurd and inadmissible." A plan of government was therefore prepared, of great simplicity, leaving all power with the executive officers of the crown; and Gage had been summoned to England to give advice on the administration of the colonies, and especially on the mode of governing the West. It was on the fourth of November that the fathers of the commonwealth of Illinois, through their agent, Daniel Blouin, forwarded their protest against the proposed form, which they rejected as "oppressive and absurd," "much worse than that of any of the French or even the Spanish colonies." "Should a government so evidently tyrannical be established," such was their language to the British minister, "it could be of no long duration;" there would exist "the necessity of its being abolished." The words were nobly uttered, and were an assurance that the villages on the Illinois would join the great American family of republics.

The issue was to be tried at Boston. The governor himself, under the name of his sons, was selected as one of those to whom the tea-ships for that port were consigned; the moment for the decision was hastening on. In the night, between the first and second of November, a knock was heard at the door of each of the consignees commissioned by the East India company, and a summons left for them to appear without fail at Liberty Tree on the following Wednesday, at noon, to resign their commission; printed notices were posted up, desiring the freemen of Boston and the neighboring towns to meet at the same time and place as witnesses.

On the appointed day, a large flag was hung out on the pole at Liberty Tree; the bells in the meeting-houses were rung from eleven till noon. Adams, Hancock, and Phillips, three of the four representatives of the town of Boston, the selectmen, and William Cooper, the town clerk, with about five hundred more, gathered round the spot. As the consignees did not make their appearance, the assembly, appointing Molineux, Warren, and others a committee, marched into State street to the warehouse of Richard Clarke, where all the consignees were assembled. Molineux presented himself for a parley.

"From whom are you a committee?" asked Clarke. "From the whole people." "Who are the committee?" "I am one," replied Molineux; and he named all the rest. "And what is your request?" Molineux read a paper, requiring the consignee to promise not to sell the teas, but to return them to London in the same bottoms in which they were shipped. "Will you comply?" "I shall have nothing to do with you," answered Clarke, roughly and peremptorily. The same question was put to the other consignees, one by one, who each and all answered: "I cannot comply with your demand." Molineux then read another paper, containing a resolve passed at Liberty Tree, that the consignees who should refuse to comply with the request of the people were enemies to their country. Descending into the street, he made his report to the people. "Out with them! out with them!" was the cry; but he dissuaded from violence.

On the fifth, Boston, in a legal town-meeting, with Hancock for moderator, adopted the Philadelphia resolves, and then sent to invite Thomas and Elisha Hutchinson to resign their appointment; but they, and all the other consignees, declined to do so, in letters addressed to Hancock, the moderator. At this, some spoke of "taking up arms," and the words were received with clapping of hands; but the meeting only voted the answers "daringly affrontive," and then dissolved itself. On the same day, the people of New York assembled at the call of their committee of vigilance. Let the tea come free or not free of duty, they were absolutely resolved it should not be landed. After a few days' reflection, the commissioners for that city, finding the discontent universal, threw up their places; yet the Sons of Liberty continued their watchfulness; a paper signed "Legion" ordered the pilots not to bring tea-ships above the Hook; and "the Mohawks" were notified to be ready in case of their arrival. The same spirit pervaded the country people. The more than octogenarian Charles Clinton, of Ulster county, with his latest breath charged his sons "to stand by the liberties of their country."

The example of New York renewed the hope that a similar expedient might succeed in Boston. Members of the council, of greatest influence, intimated that the best thing that could be done to quiet the people would be the refusal of the consignees to execute the trust; and the merchants, though they declared against mobs and violence, generally wished that the teas might not be landed.

On the seventeenth, a ship which had made a short passage from London brought an authentic account that the Boston tea-ships had sailed; the next day, there was once more a legal town-meeting to entreat the consignees to resign. Upon their repeated refusal, the town passed no vote and uttered no opinion, but immediately broke up. The silence of the dissolution struck more terror than former menaces; for the consignees saw that henceforward they were in the hands of the committee of correspondence. On the twenty-second, the committees of Dorchester, Roxbury, Brookline, and Cambridge met the Boston committee by invitation at the selectmen's chamber in Faneuil Hall. Their first question was: "Whether it be the mind of this committee to use their joint influence to prevent the landing and sale of the teas exported from the East India company?" And it passed in the affirmative unanimously.

A motion next prevailed unanimously for a letter to be sent by a joint committee of the five towns to all the other towns in the province. "Brethren," they wrote, "we are reduced to this dilemma, either to sit down quiet under this and every other burden that our enemies shall see fit to lay upon us, or to rise up and resist this and every plan laid for our destruction, as becomes wise freemen. In this extremity, we earnestly request your advice."

The governor in his alarm proposed to flee to "the castle, where he might with safety to his person more freely give his sense of the criminality of the proceedings." Dissuaded from so abject a display of pusillanimity, he yet never escaped the helpless irresolution of fear. "Nothing will satisfy the people but reshipping the tea to London," said the Boston selectmen to the consignees. "It is impracticable," they answered. "Nothing short of it," said the selectmen, "will be satisfactory. Think, too, of the dreadful consequences that must in all probability ensue on its not being done." After much discussing, they "absolutely promised that, when the tea arrived, they would immediately hand in proposals to be laid before the town;" with dishonesty of purpose negotiating only to gain time.

But the people were as vigilant as they were determined. The men of Cambridge assembled on the twenty-sixth, and, after adopting the Philadelphia resolves, "very unanimously" voted "that, as Boston was struggling for the liberties of their country, they could no longer stand idle spectators, but were ready on the shortest notice to join with it and other towns in any measure that might be thought proper, to deliver themselves and posterity from slavery." The next day, the town of Charlestown assembled, and showed such a spirit that ever after its committee was added to those who assumed the executive direction.

The combination was hardly finished when, on Sunday, the twenty-eighth of November, the ship Dartmouth appeared in Boston harbor, with one hundred and fourteen chests of the East India company's tea. To keep the sabbath strictly was the New England usage. But hours were precious; let the tea be entered, and it would be beyond the power of the consignee to send it back. The selectmen held one meeting by day, and another in the evening; but they sought in vain for the consignees, who had taken sanctuary in the castle.

The committee of correspondence was more efficient. Meeting on Sunday, they obtained from the Quaker Rotch, who owned the Dartmouth, a promise not to enter his ship till Tuesday; and they authorized Samuel Adams to invite the committees of the five surrounding towns—Dorchester, Roxbury, Brookline, Cambridge, and Charlestown, with their townsmen and those of Boston—to hold a mass meeting the next morning. Faneuil Hall could not contain the people that poured in on Monday. Adjourning to "the Old South" meeting-house, Jonathan Williams acted as moderator, and Samuel Adams, Hancock, Young, Molineux, and Warren conducted the business of the meeting. On the motion of Samuel Adams, who entered fully into the question, the assembly, composed of several thousand persons, resolved unanimously that "the tea should be sent back to the place from whence it came at all events, and that no duty should be paid on it." "The only way to get rid of it," said Young, "is to throw it overboard." The consignees asked for time to prepare their answer; and "out of great tenderness" the meeting postponed receiving it to the next morning. Meantime, the owner and master of the ship were forced to promise not to land the tea. A watch was proposed. "I," said Hancock, "will be one of it, rather than that there should be none;" and a party of twenty-five persons, under the orders of Edward Proctor as its captain, was appointed to guard the tea-ship during the night.

On the same day, the council, who had been solicited by the governor and the consignees to assume the guardianship of the tea, coupled their refusal with a reference to the declared opinion of both branches of the general court, that the tax upon it by parliament was unconstitutional. The next morning the consignees jointly gave as their answer: "It is utterly out of our power to send back the teas; but we now declare to you our readiness to store them until we shall receive further directions from our constituents;" that is, until they could notify the British government. The wrath of the meeting was kindling, when the sheriff of Suffolk entered, with a proclamation from the governor, "warning, exhorting, and requiring them, and each of them there unlawfully assembled, forthwith to disperse, and to surcease all further unlawful proceedings, at their utmost peril." The words were received with hisses, derision, and a unanimous vote not to disperse. "Will it be safe for the consignees to appear in the meeting?" asked Copley; and all with one voice responded that they might safely come and return; but they refused to appear. In the afternoon, Rotch, the owner, and Hall, the master of the Dartmouth, yielding to an irresistible impulse, engaged that the tea should return as it came, without touching land or paying a duty. A similar promise was exacted of the owners of the other tea-ships whose arrival was daily expected. In this way "it was thought the matter would have ended." "I should be willing to spend my fortune and life itself in so good a cause," said Hancock, and this sentiment was general; they all voted "to carry their resolutions into effect at the risk of their lives and property."

Every ship-owner was forbidden, on pain of being deemed an enemy to the country, to import or bring as freight any tea from Great Britain, till the unrighteous act taxing it should be repealed; and this vote was printed, and sent to every seaport in the province, and to England.

Six persons were chosen as post-riders, to give due notice to the country towns of any attempt to land the tea by force; and by the care of the committee of correspondence, as the executive organ of the meeting, a military watch was regularly kept up by volunteers armed with muskets and bayonets, who at every half hour in the night regularly passed the word, "All is well," like sentinels in a garrison. Had they been molested by night, the tolling of the bells would have been the signal for a general rising. An account of all that had been done was sent into every town in the province.

The ships, after landing the rest of their cargo, could neither be cleared in Boston with the tea on board, nor be entered in England, and, on the twentieth day from their arrival, would, by the revenue laws, be liable to seizure. "They find themselves," said Hutchinson, "involved in invincible difficulties." Meantime, in private letters he advised to separate Boston from the rest of the province, and to commence criminal prosecutions against its patriot sons.

The spirit of the people rose with the increase of danger. Two more tea-ships which arrived were directed to anchor by the side of the Dartmouth at Griffin's Wharf, that one guard might serve for all. The people of Roxbury, on the third of December, voted that they were bound by duty to themselves and posterity to join with Boston and other sister towns, to preserve inviolate the liberties handed down by their ancestors. The next day the men of Charlestown, as if foreseeing that their town was destined to be a holocaust, declared themselves ready to risk their lives and fortunes. On Sunday, the fifth, the committee of correspondence wrote to Portsmouth in New Hampshire, to Providence, Bristol, and Newport in Rhode Island, for advice and co-operation. On the sixth they entreated New York, through Macdougall and Sears, Philadelphia, through Mifflin and Clymer, to insure success by "a harmony of sentiment and concurrence in action." In Boston the consignees conspired with the revenue officers to throw on the owner and master of the Dartmouth the whole burden of landing the tea, and would neither agree to receive it, nor give up their bill of lading, nor pay the freight.

On the ninth there was a vast gathering at Newburyport of the inhabitants of that and the neighboring towns; and, none dissenting, they agreed to assist Boston, even at the hazard of their lives. "This is not a piece of parade," they say, "but, if an occasion should offer, a goodly number from among us will hasten to join you."

On Saturday, the eleventh, Rotch, the owner of the Dartmouth, is summoned before the Boston committee, with Samuel Adams in the chair; and asked why he has not kept his engagement, to take his vessel and the tea back to London within twenty days of its arrival. He pleaded that it was out of his power. "The ship must go," was the answer; "the people of Boston and the neighboring towns absolutely require and expect it;" and they bade him ask for a clearance and pass, with proper witnesses of his demand. "Were it mine," said a leading merchant, "I would certainly send it back." Hutchinson acquainted Admiral Montagu with what was passing; on which the Active and the Kingfisher, though they had been laid up for the winter, were sent to guard the passages out of the harbor. At the same time, orders were given by the governor to load guns at the castle, so that no vessel, except coasters, might go to sea without a permit. He had no thought of what was to happen: the wealth of Hancock, Phillips, Rowe, Dennie, and others, seemed to him a security against violence; and he flattered himself that he had increased the perplexities of the committee.

On the morning of Monday, the thirteenth, the committees of the five towns were at Faneuil Hall, with that of Boston. Now that danger was really at hand, the men of the little town of Malden offered their blood and their treasure; for that which they once esteemed the mother country had lost the tenderness of a parent, and become their great oppressor. "We trust in God," wrote the men of Lexington, "that, should the state of our affairs require it, we shall be ready to sacrifice our estates and everything dear in life, yea, and life itself, in support of the common cause." Whole towns in Worcester county were "on tiptoe to come down." "Go on as you have begun," wrote the committee of Leicester, on the fourteenth; "and do not suffer any of the teas already come or coming to be landed, or pay one farthing of duty. You may depend on our aid and assistance when needed."

It was intended, if possible, to get the tea carried back to London in the vessel in which it came. A meeting of the people on Tuesday afternoon directed and as it were "compelled" Rotch, the owner of the Dartmouth, to apply for a clearance. He did so, accompanied by Kent, Samuel Adams, and eight others as witnesses. The collector was at his lodgings, and declined to answer till the next morning; the assemblage, on their part, adjourned to Thursday, the sixteenth, the last of the twenty days before it would become legal for the revenue officers to take possession of the ship, and so land the teas at the castle. In the evening the Boston committee finished their preparatory meetings. After their consultation on Monday with the committee of the five towns, they had been together that day and the next, both morning and evening; but, during the long and anxious period, their journal has only this entry: "No business transacted, matter of record."

At ten o'clock on the fifteenth, Rotch was escorted by his witnesses to the custom-house, where the collector and comptroller unequivocally and finally refused his ship a clearance till it should be discharged of the teas.

Hutchinson began to clutch at victory; for, said he, the ship cannot pass the castle without a permit from me, and that I shall refuse. On that day the people of Fitchburg pledged their word " never to be wanting according to their small ability;" for "they had an ambition to be known to the world and to posterity as friends to liberty." The men of Gloucester expressed their joy at Boston's glorious opposition; cried, with one voice, that "no tea subject to a duty should be landed in their town;" and held themselves ready for the last appeal. The town of Portsmouth met on the morning of the sixteenth; and, with six only protesting, its people adopted the principles of Philadelphia, appointed their committee of correspondence, and resolved to make common cause with the colonies.

Thursday, the sixteenth of December 1773, dawned upon Boston, a day by far the most momentous in its annals. The inhabitants of the town must count the cost, and know well if they dare defy the wrath of Great Britain, and if they love exile and poverty and death rather than submission. At ten o'clock the men of Boston, with at least two thousand from the country, assembled in the Old South meeting-house. A report was made that Rotch had been denied a clearance from the collector. "Then," said they to him, "protest immediately against the custom-house, and apply to the governor for his pass, so that your vessel may this very day proceed on her voyage for London."

The governor had stolen away to his country-seat at Milton. Bidding Rotch make all haste, the meeting adjourned to three in the afternoon. At that hour Rotch had not returned. It was incidentally voted, as other towns had already done, to abstain totally from the use of tea; and every town was advised to appoint its committee of inspection, to prevent the detested tea from being brought within any of them. Then, since the governor might refuse his pass, the question recurred, "whether it be the sense and determination of this body to abide by their former resolutions with respect to the not suffering the tea to be landed." On this question Samuel Adams and Young addressed the meeting, which was become far the most numerous ever held in Boston. Among them was Josiah Quincy, a patriot of fervid feeling, passionately devoted to liberty; still young, but wasting with hectic fever. He knew that for him life was ebbing. The work of vindicating American freedom must be done soon, or he will be no party to the achievement. He rises, but it is to restrain; and, being truly brave and truly resolved, he speaks the language of moderation: "Shouts and hosannas will not terminate the trials of this day, nor popular resolves, harangues, and acclamations vanquish our foes. We must be grossly ignorant of the value of the prize for which we contend, of the power combined against us, of the inveterate malice and insatiable revenge which actuate our enemies, public and private, abroad and in our bosom, if we hope that we shall end this controversy without the sharpest conflicts. Let us consider the issue before we advance to those measures which must bring on the most trying and terrible struggle this country ever saw." "The hand is to the plough," said others, "there must be no looking back;" and the thousands who were present voted unanimously that the tea should not be landed.

It had been dark for more than an hour. A delay of a few hours would place the tea under the protection of the admiral at the castle. The church in which they met was dimly lighted by candles, when, at a quarter before six, Rotch appeared, and related that the governor would not grant him a pass, because his ship was not properly cleared. As soon as he had finished his report, loud shouts were uttered; then Samuel Adams rose and gave the word: "This meeting can do nothing more to save the country." On the instant a cry was heard at the porch; the war-whoop resounded; a body of men, forty or fifty in number, clad in blankets as Indians, each holding a hatchet, passed by the door; and encouraged by Samuel Adams, Hancock, and others, and increased on the way to near two hundred, marched two by two to Griffin's Wharf, posted guards to prevent the intrusion of spies, took possession of the three tea-ships, and, in about three hours, three hundred and forty chests of tea, being the whole quantity that had been imported, were emptied into the bay, without the least injury to other property. "All things were conducted with great order, decency, and perfect submission to government." The people who looked on were so still that the noise of breaking open the tea-chests was plainly heard. After the work was done, the town became as quiet as if it had been holy time. That very night the men from the country took home the great news to their villages.

The next morning the committee of correspondence appointed Samuel Adams and four others to draw up a declaration of what had been done. They sent Paul Revere as express with the information to New York and Philadelphia.

The joy that sparkled in the eyes and animated the countenances and the hearts of the patriots, as they met one another, is unimaginable. The governor, meantime, was consulting his books and his lawyers to make out that the resolves of the meeting were treasonable. Threats were muttered of arrests, of executions, of transporting the accused to England; while the committee of correspondence pledged themselves to support and vindicate each other and all persons who had shared in their effort. The country was united with the town, and the colonies with one another, more firmly than ever. The Philadelphians unanimously approved what Boston had done. New York, all impatient at the winds which had driven its tea-ship off the coast, was resolved on following the example.

In South Carolina, the ship, with two hundred and fifty-seven chests of tea, arrived on the second of December; the spirit of opposition ran very high; but the consignees were persuaded to resign: so that, though the collector after the twentieth day seized the dutiable article, there was no one to vend it or to pay the duty, and it perished in the cellars where it was stored.

Late on Saturday, the twenty-fifth, news reached Philadelphia that its tea-ship was at Chester. It was met four miles below the town, where it came to anchor. On Monday, at an hour's notice, men, said to number five thousand, collected in a town-meeting; at their instance, the consignee who came as passenger resigned; and the captain agreed to take his ship and cargo directly back to London, and to sail the very next day. The Quakers, though they did not appear openly, gave every private encouragement. "The ministry had chosen the most effectual measures to unite the colonies. The Boston committee were already in close correspondence with the other New England colonies, with New York and Pennsylvania. Old jealousies were removed, and perfect harmony subsisted between all." "The heart of the king was hardened like that of Pharaoh;" and none believed he would relent. Union, therefore, was the cry—a union which should reach "from Florida to the icy plains" of Canada. "No time is to be lost," said the "Boston Gazette;" "a congress or a meeting of the American states is indispensable, and what the people wills shall be effected." Samuel Adams had led his native town to offer itself cheerfully as a sacrifice for the liberties of mankind.

## CHAPTER XXXV.

**THE KING IN COUNCIL INSULTS MASSACHUSETTS AND ITS AGENT.**

December 1773–February 1774.

The just man enduring the opprobrium of crime, yet meriting the honors due to virtue, is the sublimest spectacle that can appear on earth. Against Franklin were arrayed the court, the ministry, parliament, and an all-pervading social influence; but he only assumed a firmer demeanor and a loftier tone. On delivering to Lord Dartmouth the address to the king for the removal of Hutchinson and Oliver, he gave assurances that the people of Massachusetts aimed at no novelties; that, "having lately discovered the authors of their grievances to be some of their own people, their resentment against Britain was thence much abated." The secretary expressed pleasure at receiving the petition, promised to lay it before the king, and hoped for the restoration "of the most perfect tranquillity and happiness." It was the unquestionable duty of "the agent of the house of representatives of the Massachusetts Bay" to communicate to his employers the proof that the governor and lieutenant-governor of the province were conspiring against its constitution; to bring censure on this fulfilment of duty, it was necessary to raise a belief that the evidence had been surreptitiously obtained. The newspaper press was therefore employed to spread a rumor that they had been purloined by John Temple, from the papers of Thomas Whately in the hand of his executors. The anonymous calumny which was attributed to Bernard, William Knox, and Mauduit was denied by "a member of parliament," who truly affirmed that the letters which were sent to Boston had never been in the executor's hands. But William Whately, the executor, who had been suddenly appointed a banker to the treasury, published an evasive card, in which he did not clearly relieve Temple from the implication.

A duel followed between Temple and William Whately, without witnesses; and newspaper altercations on the incidents of the meeting seemed likely to renew the quarrel. Temple, who risked offices producing a thousand pounds a year, publicly denied having "had any concern directly or indirectly in procuring or transmitting the letters which were sent to Boston." To prevent bloodshed, Franklin announced publicly: "Two gentleman have been unfortunately engaged in a duel about a transaction and its circumstances of which both of them are totally ignorant and innocent. I alone am the person who obtained and transmitted to Boston the letters in question."

On the eleventh of January 1774, Franklin for Massachusetts, and Mauduit with Wedderburn for Hutchinson and Oliver, appeared before the privy counsel. "I thought," said Franklin, "that this had been a matter of politics, and not of law, and have not brought any counsel." The hearing was therefore adjourned to the twenty-ninth. Meantime, the enraged ministry and the courtiers suggested his dismissal from office; his arrest, and imprisonment at Newgate; a search among his papers for proofs of treason. Wedderburn avowed his intention to inveigh personally against him; and he was harassed with a subpœna from the chancellor, to attend his court at the suit of William Whately, respecting the letters.

In England a greater clamor rose against the Americans than ever before. Hypocrites, traitors, rebels, and villains were the softest epithets applied to them; some menaced war, and would have given full scope to blood-thirsty rancor. On the twenty-seventh the government received official information that the people of Boston had thrown the tea overboard. In this angry state of public feeling, Franklin, on the twenty-ninth, assisted by Dunning and John Lee, came before the privy council to support the request of the great province of Massachusetts—one of the oldest of the thirteen English colonies and first of them all in the number and power of its free population—for the removal of Hutchinson and Oliver, in whose behalf appeared Israel Mauduit, the old adviser of the stamp-tax, and Wedderburn, the solicitor-general, who had so lately deserted the Grenville connection. It was a day of great expectation. Thirty-five lords of the council were present, a larger number than had ever attended a hearing; and the room was filled with a crowd, among whom were Priestley, Jeremy Bentham, and Edmund Burke.

The petition and accompanying papers having been read, Dunning asked, on the part of his client, the reason of his being ordered to attend. "No cause," said he, "is instituted; nor do we think advocates necessary; nor are they demanded on the part of the colony. The petition is not in the nature of accusation, but of advice and request. It is an address to the king's wisdom, not an application for criminal justice; when referred to the council, it is a matter for political prudence, not for judicial determination. The matter, therefore, rests wholly in your lordships' opinion of the propriety or impropriety of continuing persons in authority, who are represented by legal bodies, competent to such representation, as having (whether on sufficient or insufficient grounds) entirely forfeited the confidence of the assemblies whom they were to act with, and of the people whom they were to govern. The resolutions on which that representation is founded lie before your lordships, together with the letters from which they arose.

"If your lordships should think that these actions, which appear to the colony representative to be faulty, ought in other places to appear meritorious, the petition has not desired that the parties should be punished as criminals for these actions of supposed merit, nor even that they may not be rewarded. It only requests that these gentlemen may be removed to places where such merits are better understood, and such rewards may be more approved." He spoke well, and was seconded by Lee.

The question as presented by Dunning was already decided in favor of the petitioners; it was the universal opinion that Hutchinson ought to be superseded. Wedderburn changed the issue, as if Franklin were on trial; and, in a speech woven of falsehood and ribaldry, turned his invective against the petitioners and their messenger. Of all men, Franklin was the most important in any attempt at conciliation. He was the agent of the two great colonies, Massachusetts and Pennsylvania, and of New Jersey and Georgia; was the friend of Edmund Burke, who was agent for New York. All the troubles in British colonial policy had grown out of the neglect of his advice, and there was no one who could have mediated like him. He was now thrice venerable, from genius, fame in the world of science, and age. Him Wedderburn, turning from the real question, employed all the cunning powers of distortion and misrepresentation to abuse. With an absurdity of application which the lords of the privy council were too much prejudiced to observe, he drew a parallel between Boston and Capri, Hutchinson and Sejanus, the humble petition of the Massachusetts assembly, and a verbose and grand epistle of the Emperor Tiberius. Franklin, whose character was marked by benignity, and who, from obvious motives of thoughtfulness for the safety of others, had assumed the sole responsibility of obtaining the letters, he described as a person of the most deliberate malevolence, realizing in life what poetic fiction only had imagined in the breast of a bloody African. The speech of Hutchinson, challenging a discussion of the supremacy of parliament, had been not only condemned by public opinion in England, but disapproved by the secretary of state. Wedderburn pronounced it "a masterly one," which had "stunned the faction." Franklin for twenty years had exerted wonderful power as a conciliator, had never once employed the American press to alarm the American people, but had sought to prevent parliamentary taxation of America by private and successful representation during the time of the Pelhams; by seasonable remonstrance with Grenville against the stamp act; by honest and true answers to the inquiries of the house of commons; by the best advice to Shelburne. When sycophants sought by flattery to mislead the minister for America, he had given correct information and safe counsel to the ministry of Grafton, and had repeated it emphatically, and in writing, to the ministry of North: so that his advice, if accepted, would, like his conductor, have drawn the lightning from the cloud; but Wedderburn stigmatized this wise and hearty lover of both countries as "a true incendiary." The letters which had been written by public men in public offices on public affairs, to a member of the parliament that had been declared to possess absolute power over America, and which had been written for the purpose of producing a tyrannical exercise of that absolute power, he called private. Hutchinson had solicited the place held by Franklin, from which Franklin was to be dismissed; this fact was suppressed, and the wanton falsehood substituted that Franklin had desired the governor's office, and had basely planned "his rival's overthrow." Franklin had enclosed the letters officially to the speaker of the Massachusetts assembly, without a single injunction of secrecy in regard to the sender: Wedderburn maintained that they were sent anonymously and secretly; and, by an argument founded on a misstatement, but which he put forward as irrefragable, he pretended to convict Franklin of having obtained the letters by fraudulent and corrupt means, or of having stolen them from the person who stole them.

The lords of council, as he spoke, cheered him on by their laughter; and the cry of "Hear him! hear him!" burst repeatedly from a body which professed to be sitting in judgment as the highest court of appeal for the colonies, and yet encouraged the advocate of one of the parties to insult a public envoy, present only as the person delivering the petition of a great and royal colony. Meantime, the modern Prometheus, as Kant called Franklin, stood conspicuously erect, confronting his vilifier and the privy council; while calumny, in the service of lawless force, aimed what was meant to be a death-blow at his honor.

The reply of Dunning, who was very ill and fatigued, could scarcely be heard; and that of Lee produced no impression. There was but one place in England where fit reparation could be made; and there was but one man who had the eloquence, courage, and weight of character to effect the atonement. For the present, Franklin must rely on the approval of the monitor within his own breast. "I have never been so sensible of the power of a good conscience," said he to Priestley; "for, if I had not considered the thing for which I have been so much insulted as one of the best actions of my life and what I should certainly do again in the same circumstances, I could not have supported it." But it was not to him, it was to the people of Massachusetts, to New England, to all America, that the insult was offered.

Franklin and Wedderburn parted: the one to spread freedom among men; to make his name a cherished word in every nation of Europe; and, in the beautiful language of Washington, "to be venerated for benevolence, to be admired for talents, to be esteemed for patriotism, to be beloved for philanthropy:" the other childless, though twice wedded, unbeloved, busy only in "getting everything he could" as the wages of corruption. Franklin, when he died, had nations for his mourners, and the great and the good throughout the world as his eulogists; when Wedderburn died, no senate spoke his praise; no poet embalmed his memory; no man mourned; and his king, hearing that he was certainly gone, said only: "He has not left a greater knave behind him in my dominions." The report of the lords, which had been prepared beforehand, was immediately signed; and "they went away, almost ready to throw up their hats for joy, as if by the vehement philippic against the hoary-headed Franklin they had obtained a triumph."

And who were the lords of the council that thus thought to brand the noblest representative of free labor, who for many a year had earned his daily bread as apprentice, journeyman, or mechanic, and "knew the heart of the working man," and felt for the people of whom he remained one? If they who upon that occasion pretended to sit in judgment had never come into being, whom among them all would humanity have missed? But how would it have suffered if Franklin had not lived!

The men in power who on that day sought to rob Franklin of his good name wounded him on the next in his fortunes, by turning him out of his place in the American post-office, that institution which had yielded no revenue till he organized it, and yielded none after his dismissal.

Superior to injury, the "magnanimous" "old man," as Rockingham called Franklin, still sought for conciliation; and, seizing the moment when he was sure of all sympathies, he wrote to his constituents to begin the work, by making compensation to the East India company before any compulsive measures were thought of. But events proceed as they are ordered. The opinion in England was very general that America would submit; that government had been surprised into a repeal of the stamp act; and that all might be recovered.

The king admitted no misgivings. On the fourth of February he consulted the American commander-in-chief, who had recently returned from New York. "I am willing to go back at a day's notice," said Gage, "if coercive measures are adopted. They will be lions, while we are lambs; but, if we take the resolute part, they will undoubtedly prove very meek. Four regiments sent to Boston will be sufficient to prevent any disturbance." The king adopted these opinions. He would enforce the claim of authority at all hazards. "All men," said he, "now feel that the fatal compliance in 1766 has increased the pretensions of the Americans to absolute independence." In the letters of Hutchinson he saw nothing to which the least exception could be taken; and condemned the cautious address of Massachusetts as the production of "falsehood and malevolence."

Accordingly, on the seventh of February 1774, in the court at St. James's, the report of the privy council embodied the vile insinuations of Wedderburn; and the petition, of which every word was true, was described as formed on false allegations, and dismissed as "groundless, vexatious, and scandalous." History keeps the record of no similar petition dismissed with more insolence or avenged with more speed.

## CHAPTER XXXVI.

### THE CRISIS.

#### FEBRUARY–MAY 1774.

THE ministry, overruling the lingering scruples of Dartmouth and Lord North, decided that there existed a rebellion which required coercion. Inquiries were made, with the object of enabling the king to proceed in "England against the ringleaders," and inflict on them immediate and exemplary punishment. But, after laborious examinations before the privy council, and the close attention of Thurlow and Wedderburn, it appeared that British law and the British constitution set bounds to the anger of the government, which gave the first evidence of its weakness by acknowledging a want of power to wreak its will.

During the delay attending an appeal to parliament, the secretary of state would speak with the French minister of nothing but harmony; and he said to the representative of Spain: "Never was the union between Versailles, Madrid, and London so solid; I see nothing that can shake it." Yet the old distrust lurked under the pretended confidence.

One day in February 1774, while the government feared no formidable opposition, Charles James Fox, then of the treasury board, censured Lord North for want of decision and courage. "Greatly incensed at his presumption," the king wrote: "That young man has so thoroughly cast off every principle of common honor and honesty that he must become as contemptible as he is odious." Dismissed from office, and connected with no party, he was left free to follow his own generous impulses, and "to discover powers for regular debate, which neither his friends had hoped nor his enemies foreboded." Disinterested observers already predicted that he would one day be classed among the greatest statesmen of his country.

The cause of liberty obtained in him a friend who was independent of party allegiance and traditions, just when the passion for ruling America by the central authority was producing anarchy in the colonies. In South Carolina, whose sons esteemed themselves disfranchised on their own soil by the appointment of strangers to every office, the governor had for four years negatived every tax bill, in the hope of controlling the appropriations. In North Carolina the law establishing courts of justice had expired; in the conflict of claims of power between the governor and the legislature every new law on the subject was negatived, and there were no courts of any kind in the province. The most orderly and the best governed part of Carolina was the self-organized republic of Watauga, beyond the mountains, where the settlements were extending along the Holston, as well as south of the Nollichucky.

An intrepid population, heedless of proclamations, was pouring westward through all the gates of the Alleghanies; seating themselves on the New River and the Greenbrier, on the branches of the Monongahela, or even making their way to the Mississippi; accepting from nature their title-deeds to the unoccupied wilderness. Connecticut kept in mind that its charter bounded its territory by the Pacific; and had already taken courage to claim lands westward to the Mississippi, "seven or eight hundred miles in extent of the finest country and happiest climate on the globe. In fifty years," said they, pleasing themselves with visions of the happiness of their posterity and "the glory of this New World," "our people will be more than half over this tract, extensive as it is; in less than one century the whole may become even well cultivated. If the coming period bears due proportion to that from the first landing of poor distressed fugitives at Plymouth, nothing that we can in the utmost stretch of imagination fancy of the state of this country at an equally future period, can exceed what it will then be. A commerce will and must arise, independent of everything external, and superior to anything ever known in Europe, or of which a European can have an adequate idea." The commerce of Philadelphia and New York had outgrown the laws of trade; and the revenue officers, weary of attempts to enforce them, received what duties were paid almost as a favor.

The New England people who dwelt on each side of the Green Mountains repelled the jurisdiction which the royal government of New York would have enforced even at the risk of bloodshed, and administered their own affairs by means of permanent committees.

The people of Massachusetts knew that "they had passed the river and cut away the bridge." In March, voting the judges of the superior court ample salaries from the colonial treasury, they called upon them to refuse the corrupting donative from the crown. Four of them yielded; Oliver, the chief justice, alone refused; the house, therefore, impeached him before the council, and declared him suspended till the issue of the impeachment. They began to familiarize the public mind to the thought of armed resistance, by ordering some small purchases of powder on account of the colony to be stored in a building of its own, and by directing the purchase of twelve pieces of cannon. "Don't put off the boat till you know where you will land," advised the timid. "We must put off the boat," cried Boston patriots, "even though we do not know where we shall land." "Put off the boat; God will bring us into a safe harbor," said Hawley of Northampton. "Anarchy itself," repeated one to another, "is better than tyranny."

The proposal for a general congress was deferred to the next June; but the committees of correspondence were to prepare the way for it. A circular letter explained why Massachusetts had been under the necessity of proceeding so far of itself, and entreated for its future guidance the benefit of the councils of the whole country. Hancock, on the fifth of March, spoke to a crowded audience in Boston: "Permit me to suggest a general congress of deputies from the several houses of assembly on the continent as the most effectual method of establishing a union for the security of our rights and liberties." "Remember," he continued, "from whom you sprang. Not only pray, but act; if necessary, fight, and even die, for the prosperity of our Jerusalem;" and, as he pointed out Samuel Adams, the vast multitude seemed to promise that in all succeeding times the great patriot's name, and with him "the roll of fellow-patriots, should grace the annals of history."

Samuel Adams prepared the last instructions of Massachusetts to Franklin. "It will be in vain," such were his solemn words officially pronounced, "for any to expect that the people of this country will now be contented with a partial and temporary relief; or that they will be amused by court promises, while they see not the least relaxation of grievances. By means of a brisk correspondence among the several towns in this province they have wonderfully animated and enlightened each other. They are united in sentiments, and their opposition to unconstitutional measures of government is become systematical. Colony begins to communicate freely with colony. There is a common affection among them; and shortly the whole continent will be as united in sentiment and in their measures of opposition to tyranny as the inhabitants of this province. Their old good-will and affection for the parent country are not totally lost; if she returns to her former moderation and good humor, their affection will revive. They wish for nothing more than a permanent union with her upon the condition of equal liberty. This is all they have been contending for; and nothing short of this will or ought to satisfy them."

Such was the ultimatum of America, sent by one illustrious son of Boston for the guidance of another. But the sense of the English people was manifestly with the ministers, who were persuaded that there was no middle way, and that the American continent would not interpose to shield Boston from the necessity of submission.

On the seventh of March, Dartmouth and North, grievously lamenting their want of greater executive power, and the consequent necessity of laying their measures before parliament, presented to the two houses a message from the king. "Nothing," said Lord North, "can be done to re-establish peace without additional powers." "The question now brought to issue," said Rice, on moving the address which was to pledge parliament to the exertion of every means in its power, "is whether the colonies are or are not the colonies of

Great Britain." Nugent, now Lord Clare, entreated that there might be no divided counsels. "On the repeal of the stamp act," said Dowdeswell, " all America was quiet ; but in the following year you would go in pursuit of a pepper-corn ; you would collect from pepper-corn to pepper-corn ; you would establish taxes as tests of obedience. Unravel the whole conduct of America ; you will find out the fault is at home." " The dependence of the colonies is a part of the constitution," said Pownall, the former governor of Massachusetts. " I hope, for the sake of this country, for the sake of America, for the sake of general liberty, that this address will go with a unanimous vote."

Edmund Burke only taunted the ministry with their wavering policy. Lord George Germain derived all the American disturbance from the repeal of the stamp-tax. Conway pleaded for unanimity. " I speak," said William Burke, " as an Englishman ; we applaud ourselves for the struggle we have had for our constitution ; the colonists are our fellow-subjects ; they will not lose theirs without a struggle." Barré thought the subject had been discussed with good temper, and refused to make any opposition. "The leading question," said Wedderburn, who bore the principal part in the debate, "is the dependence or independence of America." The address was adopted without a division.

In letters which arrived the next day from America, calumny, with its hundred tongues, exaggerated the turbulence of the people, and invented wild tales of violence ; so that the king believed there was, in Boston, a regular committee for tarring and feathering ; and that they were next, to use his own words, to " pitch and feather " Hutchinson himself. The press roused the national pride, till the zeal of the English people for maintaining English supremacy became equal to the passions of the ministry. Even the merchants and manufacturers were made to believe that their command of the American market depended on the enforcement of British authority.

It was, therefore, to a parliament and people as unanimous as when in Grenville's day they sanctioned the stamp act, that Lord North, on the fourteenth of March, opened the first branch of his American plan by a measure for the instant punishment of Boston. Its port was to be closed against all commerce until it should have indemnified the East India company, and until the king should be satisfied that for the future it would obey the laws. All branches of the government, all political parties, alike those who denied and those who asserted the right to tax, members of parliament, peers, merchants, all ranks and degrees of people, were invited to proceed steadily in the one course of maintaining the authority of Great Britain. Yet it was noticed that Lord North spoke of the indispensable necessity for vigorous measures with an unusual air of languor. This appeal was successful. Of the Rockingham party, Cavendish approved the measure, which was but a corollary from their own declaratory act. "After having weighed the noble lord's proposition well," said even Barré, "I cannot help giving it my hearty and determinate affirmative. I like it, adopt and embrace it for its moderation." "There is no good plan," urged Fox, "except the repeal of the taxes forms a part of it." "The proposition does not fully answer my expectations," said John Calvert; "seize the opportunity, and take away their charter."

On the eighteenth, Lord North, by unanimous consent, presented to the house the Boston port bill. To its second reading, George Bynge was the only one who cried no. "This bill," said Rose Fuller, in the debate, on the twenty-third, "shuts up one of the ports of the greatest commerce and consequence in the English dominions in America. The North Americans will look upon it as a foolish act of oppression. You cannot carry this bill into execution but by a military force." "If a military force is necessary," replied Lord North, "I shall not hesitate a moment to enforce a due obedience to the laws of this country." Fox would have softened the bill by opening the port on the payment of indemnity to the East India company; and he took care that his motion should appear on the journal. "Obedience," replied Lord North, "not indemnification, will be the test of the Bostonians." "The offence of the Americans is flagitious," said Van. "The town of Boston ought to be knocked about their ears and destroyed. You will never meet with proper obedience to the laws of this country until you have destroyed that nest of locusts." The clause to which Fox had objected was adopted without any division, and with but one or two negatives.

The current, within doors and without, set strongly against America. It was only for the acquittal of their own honor and the discharge of their own consciences that, two days later, on the third reading, Dowdeswell and Edmund Burke, unsupported by their former friends, spoke very strongly against a bill which punished the innocent with the guilty, condemned both without an opportunity of defence, deprived the laborer and the sailor of bread, injured English creditors by destroying the trade out of which the debts due them were to be discharged, and ultimately oppressed the English manufacturer. "You will draw a foreign force upon you," said Burke; "I will not say where that will end, but think, I conjure you, of the consequences" "The resolves at Boston," said Gray Cooper, "are a direct issue against the declaratory act;" and half the Rockingham party went with him. Rose Fuller opposed the bill, unless the tax on tea were repealed. Pownall was convinced that the time was not proper for a repeal of the duty on tea. "This is the crisis," said Lord North, who had by degrees assumed a style of authority and decision. "The contest ought to be determined. To repeal the tea duty or any measure would stamp us with timidity." "The present bill," observed Johnstone, late governor of West Florida, "must produce a confederacy, and will end in a general revolt." But it passed without a division, and very unfairly went to the lords as the unanimous voice of the commons. The king sneered at "the feebleness and futility of the opposition."

In the midst of the general anger, a book was circulating in England, on the interest of Great Britain in regard to the colonies, and the only means of living in peace and harmony with them, which judged the past and estimated the future with calmness and sagacity. Its author, Josiah Tucker, dean of Gloucester, a most loyal churchman, an apostle of free trade, saw clearly that the reduction of Canada had put an end to the sovereignty of the mother country; that it is in the very nature of all colonies, and of the Americans more than others, to aspire after independence. He would not suffer things to go on as they had lately done, for that would only make the colonies more headstrong; nor attempt to persuade them to send over deputies or representatives to sit in parliament, for that scheme could only end in furnishing a justification to the mother country for making war against them; nor have recourse to arms, for the event was uncertain, and England, if successful, could still never treat America as an enslaved people, or govern them against their own inclinations. There remained but one wise solution; and it was to declare the American colonies to be a free and independent people.

"If we separate from the colonies," it was objected, "we shall lose their trade." "Why so?" answered Tucker. "The colonies will trade even with their bitterest enemies in the hottest of a war, provided they shall find it their interest so to do. The question before us will turn on this single point: Can the colonists, in a general way, trade with any other European state to greater advantage than they can with Great Britain? If they cannot, we shall retain their custom;" and he demonstrated that England was for America the best market and the best storehouse; that the prodigious increase of British trade was due, not to prohibition, but to the suppression of monopolies and exclusive companies for foreign trade; to the repeal of taxes on raw materials; to the improvements, inventions, and discoveries for the abridgment of labor; to roads, canals, and better postal arrangements. The measure would not decrease shipping and navigation, or diminish the breed of sailors.

But, "if we give up the colonies," it was pretended, "the French will take immediate possession of them." "The Americans," resumed Tucker, "cannot brook our government; will they glory in being numbered among the slaves of the grand monarch?" "Will you leave the church of England in America to suffer persecution?" asked the churchmen. "Declare North America independent," replied Tucker, "and all their fears of ecclesiastical authority will vanish away; a bishop will be no longer looked upon as a monster, but as a man; and an episcopate may then take place." No minister, he confessed, would dare, as things were then circumstanced, to do so much good to his country; neither would their opponents wish to see it done; and "yet," he added, "measures evidently right will prevail at last."

A love of liberty revealed the same truth to John Cartwright. The young enthusiast was persuaded that humanity, as well as the individual man, obtains knowledge, wisdom, and virtue progressively, so that its latter days will be more wise, peaceable, and pious than the earlier periods of its existence. He was destined to pass his life in efforts to purify the British constitution, which, as he believed, had within itself the seeds of immortality. With the fervid language of sincerity, he advocated the freedom of his American kindred, and proclaimed American independence to be England's interest and glory.

Thus spoke the forerunners of free trade and reform. But the infatuated people turned from them to indulge unsparingly in ridicule and illiberal jests on the Bostonians, whom the hand of power was extended to chastise and subdue. At the meeting of the commons on the twenty-eighth, Lord North asked leave to bring in a bill for regulating the government of the province of Massachusetts Bay. On this occasion Lord George Germain showed anxiety to take a lead. "I wish," said he, "to see the council of that country on the same footing as that of other colonies. Put an end to their town-meetings. I would not have men of a mercantile cast every day collecting themselves together and debating about political matters. I would have them follow their occupations as merchants, and not consider themselves as ministers of that country. I would wish that all corporate powers might be given to certain people in every town, in the same manner that corporations are formed here. Their juries require regulation. I would wish to bring the constitution of America as similar to our own as possible; to see the council of that country similar to a house of lords in this; to see chancery suits determined by a court of chancery. At present their assembly is a downright clog; their council thwart and oppose the security and welfare of that government. You have no government, no governor; the whole are the proceedings of a tumultuous and riotous rabble, who ought, if they had the least prudence, to follow their mercantile employment, and not trouble themselves with politics and government, which they do not understand. Some gentlemen say: 'Oh, don't break their charter; don't take away rights granted them by the predecessors of the crown.' Whoever wishes to preserve such charters, I wish him no worse than to govern such subjects. By a manly perseverance, things may be restored from anarchy and confusion to peace, quietude, and obedience."

"I thank the noble lord," said Lord North, "for every one of the propositions he has held out; they are worthy of a great mind; I see their propriety, and wish to adopt them;" and the house directed North, Thurlow, and Wedderburn to prepare and bring in a bill accordingly.

On the twenty-ninth of March the Boston port bill underwent in the house of lords a fuller and fairer discussion. Rockingham, supported by the duke of Richmond, resisted it with firmness. "Nothing can justify the ministers hereafter," said Temple, "except the town of Boston proving in an actual state of rebellion." The good Lord Dartmouth called what passed in Boston commotion, not open rebellion. Lord Mansfield, a man "in the cool decline of life," acquainted only with the occupations of peace, a civil magistrate, covered with ermine that should have no stain of blood, with eyes broad open to the consequences, rose to take the guidance of the house out of the hands of the faltering minister. "What passed in Boston," said he, "is the last overt act of high treason, proceeding from our over-lenity and want of foresight. It is, however, the luckiest event that could befall this country; for all may now be recovered. Compensation to the East India company I regard as no object of the bill. The sword is drawn, and you must throw away the scabbard. Pass this act, and you will have passed the Rubicon. The Americans will then know that we shall temporize no longer; if it passes with tolerable unanimity, Boston will submit, and all will end in victory without carnage." In vain did Camden meet the question fully; in vain did Shelburne prove the tranquil and loyal condition in which he had left the colonies on giving up their administration. There was no division in the house of lords; and its journal, like that of the commons, declares that the Boston port bill passed unanimously.

The king in person made haste to give it his approval. To bring Boston on its knees and terrify the rest of America by enforcing the act, Gage, the military commander-in-chief for all North America, received the commision of civil governor of Massachusetts as swiftly as official forms would permit; and, in April, was sent over with four regiments, which he had reported would be sufficient to enforce submission. He was ordered to shut the port of Boston; and, having as a part of his instructions the opinion of Thurlow and Wedderburn, that acts of high treason had been committed there, he was directed to bring the ringleaders to condign punishment. Foremost among these, Samuel Adams was marked out for sacrifice as the chief of the revolution. "He is the most elegant writer, the most sagacious politician, and celebrated patriot, perhaps, of any who have figured in the last ten years," is the contemporary record of John Adams. "I cannot sufficiently respect his integrity and abilities," said Clymer, of Pennsylvania; "all good Americans should erect a statue to him in their hearts." Even where his conduct had been questioned, time proved that he had been right, and many in England "esteemed him the first politician in the world." He saw that "the rigorous measures of the British administration would the sooner bring to pass" the first wish of his heart, "the entire separation and independence of the colonies, which Providence would erect into a mighty empire." Indefatigable in seeking for Massachusetts the countenance of her sister colonies, he had no anxiety for himself, no doubt of the ultimate triumph of freedom; but, as he thought of the calamities that hung over Boston, he raised the prayer "that God would prepare that people for the event by inspiring them with wisdom and fortitude."

"We have enlisted in the cause of our country," said its committee of correspondence, "and are resolved at all adventures to promote its welfare; should we succeed, our names will be held up by future generations with that unfeigned plaudit with which we recount the great deeds of our ancestors." Boston has now no option but to make good its entire independence, or to approach the throne as a penitent, and promise for the future passive "obedience" to British "laws" in all cases whatsoever. In the palace there were no misgivings. "With ten thousand regulars," said the creatures of the ministry, "we can march through the continent."

The act closing the port of Boston did not necessarily provoke a civil war. It was otherwise with the second. The opinion of Lord Mansfield had been obtained in favor of altering the charter of Massachusetts; and the king learned "with supreme satisfaction" that, on the fifteenth of April, a bill to regulate the government of the province of Massachusetts Bay had been read for the first time in the house of commons. Without any hearing or even notice to that province, parliament was to change its charter and its government. Its institution of town-meetings was the most perfect system of local self-government that the world had ever known; the king's measure abolished them, except for the choice of town officers, or on the special permission of the governor. The council had been annually chosen in a convention of the outgoing council and the house of representatives, and men had in this manner been selected more truly loyal than the councillors of any one of the royal colonies; the clause in the charter establishing this method of election was abrogated. The power of appointing and removing sheriffs was conferred on the executive; and the trial by jury was changed into a snare, by intrusting the returning of juries to dependent sheriffs. Lord North placed himself in conflict with institutions sanctioned by royal charters, rooted in custom, confirmed by possession through successive generations, endeared by the just and fondest faith, and infolded in the affections and life of the people.

Against the bill Conway spoke with firmness. The administration, he said, would take away juries from Boston; though Preston, in the midst of an exasperated town, had been acquitted. They sent the sword, but no olive branch. The bill at its different stages in the house of commons was combated by Dowdeswell, Pownall, Sir George Saville, Conway, Burke, Fox, Barré, and most elaborately by Dunning; yet it passed the commons by a vote of more than three to one. Though vehemently opposed in the house of lords, it was carried by a still greater majority, but not without an elaborate protest. The king did not dream that by that act, which, as he writes, gave him "infinite satisfaction," all power of command in Massachusetts had, from that day forth, gone out from him, and that there his word would never more be obeyed.

The immediate repeal of the tax on tea and its preamble

remained the only possible avenue to conciliation. On the nineteenth of April this repeal was moved by Rose Fuller in concert with the opposition. The subject in its connections was the gravest that could engage attention, involving the prosperity of England, the tranquillity of the British empire, the principles of colonization, and the liberties of mankind. But Cornwall, speaking for the ministers, stated the question to be simply " whether the whole of British authority over America should be taken away." On this occasion Edmund Burke pronounced an oration such as had never been heard in the British parliament. His boundless stores of knowledge came obedient at his command; and his thoughts and arguments, the facts which he cited, and his glowing appeals, fell naturally into their places; so that his long and elaborate speech was one harmonious and unbroken emanation from his mind. He first demonstrated that the repeal of the tax would be productive of unmixed good; he then surveyed comprehensively the whole series of the parliamentary proceedings with regard to America, in their causes and their consequences. After exhausting the subject, he entreated parliament to "reason not at all," but to "oppose the ancient policy and practice of the empire, as a rampart against the speculations of innovators on both sides of the question."

"Again and again," such was his entreaty, "revert to your old principles; seek peace and ensue it; leave America, if she has taxable matter, to tax herself. Be content to bind America by laws of trade; you have always done it; let this be your reason for binding their trade. Do not burden them by taxes; you were not used to do so from the beginning. Let this be your reason for not taxing. These are the arguments of states and kingdoms. Leave the rest to the schools. The several provincial legislatures ought all to be subordinate to the parliament of Great Britain. She, as from the throne of heaven, superintends and guides and controls them all. To coerce, to restrain, and to aid, her powers must be boundless."

During the long debate, the young and fiery Lord Carmarthen had repeated what so many had said before him: "The Americans are our children, and how can they revolt against their parent? If they are not free in their present state, England is not free, because Manchester and other considerable places are not represented." "So, then," retorted Burke, "because some towns in England are not represented, America is to have no representative at all. Is it because the natural resistance of things and the various mutations of time hinder our government, or any scheme of government, from being any more than a sort of approximation to the right, is it therefore that the colonies are to recede from it infinitely? When this child of ours wishes to assimilate to its parent, are we to give them our weakness for their strength, our opprobrium for their glory? and the slough of slavery which we are not able to work off, to serve them for their freedom?"

The words fell from him as burning oracles; while he spoke for the rights of America, he seemed to prepare the way for renovating the constitution of England. Yet it was not so. Though more than half a century had intervened, Burke would not be wiser than the whigs of the days of King William. It was enough for him if the aristocracy applauded. He did not believe in the dawn of a new light, in the coming on of a new order, though a new order of things was at the door, and a new light had broken. He would not turn to see, nor bend to learn, if the political system of Somers and Walpole and the Pelhams was to pass away; if it were so, he himself was determined not to know it, but "rather to be the last of that race of men." As Dante sums up the civilization of the middle age so that its departed spirit still lives in his immortal verse, Burke idealizes as he portrays the lineaments of that old whig aristocracy which in its day achieved mighty things for liberty and for England. He that will study under its best aspect the enlightened character of England in the first half of the eighteenth century, the wonderful intermixture of privilege and prerogative, of aristocratic power and popular liberty, of a free press and a secret house of commons, of an established church and a toleration of Protestant sects, of a fixed adherence to prescription and liberal tendencies in administration, must give his days and nights to the writings of Edmund Burke. But time never keeps company with the mourners; it flies from the memories of the expiring past, though clad in the brightest colors of imagination; it leaves those who stand still to their despair, and hurries onward to fresh fields of action and scenes forever new.

Resuming the debate, Fox said, earnestly: "If you persist in your right to tax the Americans, you will force them into open rebellion." On the other hand, Lord North asked that his measures might be sustained with firmness and resolution; and then, said he, "there is no doubt but peace and quietude will soon be restored." "We are now in great difficulties," said Dowdeswell, speaking for all who adhered to Lord Rockingham; "let us do justice before it is too late." But it was too late. Even Burke's motive had been "to refute the charges against that party with which he had all along acted." After his splendid eloquence, no more divided with him than forty-nine, just the number that had divided against the stamp act, while on the other side stood nearly four times as many. "The repeal of the tea-tax was never to be obtained so long as the authority of parliament was publicly rejected or opposed.

On the day on which the house of commons was voting not to repeal the duty on tea, the people of New York sent back the tea-ship which had arrived but the day before; and eighteen chests of tea, found on board of another vessel, were hoisted on deck and emptied into "the slip."

A third penal measure, which had been questioned by Dartmouth and recommended by the king, transferred the place of trial of any magistrates, revenue officers, or soldiers, indicted for murder or other capital offence in Massachusetts Bay, to Nova Scotia or Great Britain. As Lord North brought forward this wholesale bill of indemnity to the governor and soldiers, if they should trample upon the people of Boston and be charged with murder, it was noticed that he trembled and faltered at every word, showing that he was the vassal of a stronger will than his own, and vainly struggled to wrestle down the feelings which his nature refused to disavow. "If the people of America," said Van, "oppose the measures of government that are now sent, I would do as was done of old in the time of the ancient Britons: I would burn and set fire to all their woods, and leave their country open. If we are likely to lose it, I think it better lost by our own soldiers than wrested from us by our rebellious children." "The bill is meant to enslave America," said Sawbridge, with only forty to listen to him. "I execrate the present measure," cried Barré; "you have had one meeting of the colonies in congress; you may soon have another. The Americans will not abandon their principles; for, if they submit, they are slaves"

The bill passed the commons by a vote of more than four to one. But evil comes intermixed with good: the ill is evanescent, the good endures. The British government inflamed the passions of the English people against America, and courted their sympathy; as a consequence, the secrecy of the debates in parliament came to an end; and this great change in the political relation of the legislature to public opinion was the irrevocable concession of a tory government, seeking strength from popular excitement.

A fourth measure legalized the quartering of troops within the town of Boston. The fifth professed to regulate the affairs of the province of Quebec. The nation, which would not so much as legally recognise the existence of a Catholic in Ireland, from political considerations sanctioned on the St. Lawrence "the free exercise of the religion of the church of Rome, and confirmed to its clergy their accustomed dues and rights," with the tithes as fixed in 1672 by the edict of Louis XIV. But the act did not stop there. In disregard of the charters and rights of Massachusetts, Connecticut, New York, and Virginia, it extended the boundaries of the new government of Quebec to the Ohio and the Mississippi, and over the region which included, besides Canada, the area of the present states of Ohio, Michigan, Indiana, Illinois, and Wisconsin; and, moreover, it decreed for this great part of a continent an unmixed arbitrary rule. The establishment of colonies on principles of liberty is "the peculiar and appropriated glory of England," rendering her venerable throughout all time in the history of the world. The office of peopling a continent with free and happy commonwealths was renounced. The Quebec bill, which quickly passed the house of lords without an adverse petition or a protest, and was borne through the commons by the zeal of the ministry and the influence of the king, left the people who were to colonize the most fertile territory in the world without the writ of habeas corpus to protect the rights of persons, and without a share of power in any one branch of the government. "The Quebec constitution," said Thurlow, in the house of commons, "is the only proper constitution for colonies; it ought to have been given to them all, when first planted; and it is what all now ought to be reduced to."

In this manner Great Britain, allured by a phantom of absolute authority over colonies, made war on human freedom. The liberties of Poland had been sequestered, and its territory began to be parcelled out among the usurpers. The aristocratic privileges of Sweden had been swept away by treachery and usurpation. The free towns of Germany, which had preserved in that empire the example of republics, were "like so many dying sparks that go out one after another." Venice and Genoa had stifled the spirit of independence in their prodigal luxury. Holland was ruinously divided against itself. In Great Britain, the house of commons had become so venal that it might be asked whether a body so chosen and so influenced was fit to legislate even within the realm. If it shall succeed in establishing by force of arms its "boundless" authority over America, where shall humanity find an asylum? But this decay of the old forms of liberty was the forerunner of a new creation. The knell of the ages of servitude and inequality was rung; those of equality and brotherhood were to come in.

As the fleets and armies of England went forth to consolidate arbitrary power, the sound of war everywhere else on the earth died away. Kings sat still in awe, and nations turned to watch the issue.

# APPENDIX.

PREFACE prefixed to the first edition of the sixth volume of this history as published in 1854.

The present volume completes the History of the American Revolution, considered in its causes. The three last * explain the rise of the union of the United States from the body of the people, the change in the colonial policy of France, and the consequences of the persevering ambition of Great Britain to consolidate its power over America. The penal acts of 1774 dissolved the moral connection between the two countries, and began the civil war.

The importance of the subject justified comprehensive research. Of printed works my own collection is not inconsiderable; and whatever else is to be found in the largest public or private libraries, particularly in those of Harvard college, the Boston Athenæum—which is very rich in pamphlets—and the British Museum, have been within my reach.

Still greater instruction was derived from manuscripts. The records of the state paper office of Great Britain best illustrate the colonial system of that country. The opportunity of consulting them was granted me by the earl of Aberdeen, when secretary of state, and continued by Viscount Palmerston, by Earl Grey, and by the duke of Newcastle. They include the voluminous correspondence of all military and civil officers, and Indian agents employed in America; memorials of the American commissioners of customs; narratives, affidavits, informations, and answers of witnesses, illustrating the most important occurrences; the journals of the board of

* In this edition, volume ii from page 314 and the whole of volume iii.

trade; its representations to the king; its intercourse with the secretary of state; the instructions and letters sent to America, whether from the king, the secretary of state, or the board of trade; the elaborate abstracts of documents prepared for the council; opinions of the attorney- and solicitor-general; and occasionally private letters. I examined these masses of documents slowly and carefully; I had access to everything that is preserved; and of no paper, however secret it may have been in its day, or whatever its complexion, was a copy refused me.

I owe to Lord John Russell permission to extend my inquiries to the records of the treasury, of which he at the time was the head; so that all the volumes of its minutes and its letter-books, which could throw light on the subject of my inquiries, came under my inspection.

The proceedings in parliament till 1774 had something of a confidential character; from sources the most various, private letters, journals, and reports, preserved in France, or in England, or in America, I have obtained full and trustworthy accounts of the debates on the days most nearly affecting America.

Many papers, interesting to Americans, are preserved in the British Museum, where I have great reason to remember the considerate attention of Sir Henry Ellis. At the London Institution, in Albemarle street, the secretary, Mr. Barlow, obtained for me leave to make use of its great collection of American military correspondence.

It was necessary to study the character and conduct of the English ministers themselves. Of Chatham's private letters, perhaps few remain unpublished; Mr. Disney imparted to me at the Hyde two volumes of familiar notes that passed between Chatham and Hollis, full of allusions to America. The marquis of Lansdowne consented to my request for permission to go through the papers of his father, the earl of Shelburne, during the three periods of his connection with American affairs; and allowed me to keep them till by a continued examination and comparison they could be understood in all their aspects. Combined with manuscripts which I obtained in France, they give all the information that can be desired for illustrating Lord Shelburne's relations with America. My thanks are also due to the duke of Grafton for having communicated to me unreservedly the autobiography of the third duke of that name, who, besides having himself been a prime minister, held office with Rockingham, Chatham, Lord North, and Shelburne. The late earl of Dartmouth showed me parts of the journal of his grandfather, written while he occupied the highest place at the board of trade.

Of all persons in England, it was most desirable to have a just conception of the character of the king. Mr. Everett, when minister at the court of St. James, keeping up in his busiest hours the habit of doing kind offices, obtained for me, from Lady Charlotte Lindsay, copies of several hundred notes, or abstracts of notes, from George III. to her father, Lord North. Afterward I received from Lady Charlotte herself communications of great interest, and her sanction to make such use of the letters as I might desire, even to the printing of them all. Others written by the king in his boyhood to his governor, Lord Harcourt, Mr. Harcourt was so obliging as to allow me to peruse at Nuneham.

The controversy between Great Britain and her colonies attracted the attention of all Europe, till at length it became universally the subject of leading interest. To give completeness to this branch of my inquiries, in so far as Great Britain was concerned, either as a party or as an observer, the necessary documents, after the most thorough and extensive search, were selected from the correspondence with ministers, agents, and others in France, Spain, Holland, Russia, Austria, Prussia, and several of the smaller German courts, especially Hesse-Cassel and Brunswick. The volumes examined for this purpose were very numerous, and the copies for my use reach to all questions directly or indirectly affecting America; to alliances, treaties of subsidy, mediations, and war and peace.

The relations of France to America were of paramount importance. I requested of Mr. Guizot, then the minister, authority to study them in the French archives. "You shall see everything we have," was his instant answer, enhancing his consent by the manner in which it was given. The promise was most liberally interpreted and most fully redeemed by Mr. Mignet, whose good advice and friendly regard lightened my toils, and left me nothing to desire. Mr. Dumont, the assistant keeper of the archives, under whose immediate superintendence my investigations were conducted, aided them by his constant good-will. The confidence reposed in me by Mr. Guizot was continued by Mr. Lamartine, Mr. Drouin de Lhuys, and by Mr. de Tocqueville.

As the court of France was the centre of European diplomacy, the harvest from its archives was exceedingly great. There were found the reports of the several French agents sent secretly to the American colonies; there were the papers tracing the origin and progress of the French alliance, including opinions of the ministers, read in the cabinet council to the king. Many volumes illustrate the direct intercourse between France and the United States. But, besides these, I had full opportunity to examine the subject in its complication with the relations of France to England, Spain, Holland, Prussia, Russia, and other powers; and this I did so thoroughly that, when I took my leave, Mr. Dumont assured me that I had seen everything; that nothing, not the smallest memorandum, had been withheld from me.

Besides this, I acquired papers from the ministry of the marine, and from that of war. The Duke de Broglie gave me a most pleasing journal of his father when in America; Mr. Augustin Thierry favored me with exact and interesting anecdotes, derived from Lafayette; and my friend Count Circourt was never weary of furthering my inquiries.

My friend Mr. J. Romeyn Brodhead was so kind as to make for me selections of papers in Holland, and I take leave to acknowledge that Mr. J. A. de Zwaan, of the Royal Archives at the Hague, was most zealous and unremitting in his efforts to render the researches undertaken for me effective and complete.

I have obtained so much of Spanish correspondence as to have become accurately acquainted with the maxims by which the court of Spain governed its conduct toward our part of America.

Accounts of the differences between America and England are to be sought not only in the sources already referred to, but specially in the correspondence of the colony agents resident in London, with their respective constituents. I pursued the search for papers of this class till I succeeded in securing letters, official or private, from Bollan; Jasper Mauduit; Richard Jackson—the same who was Grenville's secretary at the exchequer, a distinguished member of parliament, and at one time agent for three colonies; Arthur Lee; several unpublished ones of Franklin; the copious and most interesting official and private correspondence of William Samuel Johnson, agent for Connecticut; one letter and fragments of letters of Edmund Burke, agent for New York; many and exceedingly valuable ones of Garth, a member of parliament and agent for South Carolina; and specimens of the correspondence of Knox and Franklin as agents of Georgia.

Analogous to these are the confidential communications which passed between Hutchinson and Israel Mauduit and Thomas Whately; between one of the proprietaries of Pennsylvania and Deputy-Governor Hamilton; between Cecil Calvert and Hugh Hammersley, successive secretaries of Maryland, and Lieutenant-Governor Sharpe; between ex-Governor Pownall and Dr. Cooper, of Boston; between Hollis and Mayhew and Andrew Eliot, of Boston. Of all these I have copies.

Of the letter-books and draughts of letters of men in office, I had access to those of Bernard for a single year; to those of Hutchinson for many years; to that of Dr. Johnson, the patriarch of the American Episcopal church, with Archbishop Secker; to those of Colden; to those of Lieutenant-Governor Sharpe. Many letters of their correspondents fell within my reach.

For the affairs of the colonies I have consulted their own archives, and to that end have visited in person more than half the old thirteen colonies.

Long-continued pursuit, favored by a general good-will, has brought into my possession papers, or copies of papers, from very many of the distinguished men of the country in every colony. Among those who have rendered me most valuable aid in this respect I must name, in an especial manner, the late Mr. Colden, of New York, who intrusted to me all the manuscripts of Lieutenant-Governor Colden, covering a period in New York history of nearly a quarter of a century;

the late Mr. Johnson, of Stratford, Connecticut, who put into my hands those of his father, containing excellent contributions alike to English and American history; my friend Dr. Potter, the present bishop of Pennsylvania, who furnished me numerous papers of equal interest and novelty, illustrating the history of New York and of the union; Mr. Force, of Washington city, whose success in collecting materials for American history is exceeded only by his honest love of historic truth; Mr. J. F. Eliot, of Boston; Mr. William B. Reed, Mr. Langdon Elwyn, and Mr. Edward D. Ingraham, of Philadelphia; Mr. Tefft, of Georgia, and Mr. Swain, of North Carolina, who show constant readiness to further my inquiries; the Connecticut Historical Society; the president and officers of Yale college, who sent me unique documents from the library of that institution; Mr. William C. Preston, of South Carolina, to whom I owe precious memorials of the spirit and deeds of the South.

The most valuable acquisition of all was the collection of the papers of Samuel Adams, which came to me through the late Samuel Adams Welles. They contain the manuscripts of Samuel Adams, especially draughts of his letters to his many correspondents, and draughts of public documents. They contain the complete journals of the Boston Committee of Correspondence, draughts of the letters it sent out, and the letters it received, so far as they have been preserved. The papers are very numerous; taken together, they unfold the manner in which resistance to Great Britain grew into a system, and they perfectly represent the sentiments and the reasonings of the time. They are the more to be prized, as much of the correspondence was secret, and has remained so to this day.

If I have failed in giving a lucid narrative of the events which led to the necessity of independence, it is not for want of diligence in studying the materials which I have brought together, or of laborious care in arranging them. The strictest attention has been paid to chronological sequence, which can best exhibit the simultaneous action of general causes. The abundance of my collections has enabled me, in some measure, to reproduce the very language of every one of the principal actors in the scenes which I describe, and to represent their conduct from their own point of view. I hope, at least, it will appear that I have written with candor, neither exaggerating vices of character, nor reviving national animosities, but rendering a just tribute to virtue wherever found.

NEW YORK, *13 May, 1854.*

*July, 1883*

P. S.—Among printed materials I did not fail to give the most thorough attention to the newspapers of the times treated of, so far as they were accessible to me, especially to those in the collections of the American Antiquarian Society at Worcester, Massachusetts; in the Library of Congress at Washington; of the Athenæum at Boston; of the Historical Society at New York, and of the public libraries in Philadelphia.

END OF VOLUME III.

# BIBLIOLIFE

## Old Books Deserve a New Life
www.bibliolife.com

Did you know that you can get most of our titles in our trademark **EasyScript**™ print format? **EasyScript**™ provides readers with a larger than average typeface, for a reading experience that's easier on the eyes.

Did you know that we have an ever-growing collection of books in many languages?

Order online:
www.bibliolife.com/store

Or to exclusively browse our **EasyScript**™ collection:
www.bibliogrande.com

At BiblioLife, we aim to make knowledge more accessible by making thousands of titles available to you – quickly and affordably.

Contact us:
BiblioLife
PO Box 21206
Charleston, SC 29413

CPSIA information can be obtained at www.ICGtesting.com
Printed in the USA
LVOW09*1416200116

471537LV00007B/16/P